Recent Research in Psychology

Recent Research in Psychology

Steven R. Yussen
M Cecil Smith
Editors

Reading Across the Life Span

With 13 Illustrations

Springer-Verlag
New York Berlin Heidelberg London Paris
Tokyo Hong Kong Barcelona Budapest

Steven R. Yussen, Ph.D.
School of Education
University of Iowa
Iowa City, IA 52242, USA

M Cecil Smith, Ph.D.
Assistant Professor
Department of Educational Psychology, Counseling
    and Special Education
Northern Illinois University
DeKalb, IL 60115-2854, USA

Library of Congress Cataloging-in-Publication Data
Reading across the life span / Steven R. Yussen, M Cecil Smith
    editors
        p.   cm.—(Recent research in psychology)
    Includes bibliographical references and index.
    ISBN 0-387-97978-6. — ISBN 3-540-97978-6
    1. Reading.   2. Reading, Psychology of. 3. Reading (Adult
education) 4. Literacy. I. Yussen, Steven R.   II. Smith, Cecil M.
III. Series
LB1050.R35258   1993
428'.071—dc20
DNLM/DLC   92-40972

Printed on acid-free paper.

Production managed by Christin R. Ciresi; manufacturing supervised by Jacqui Ashri.
Camera-ready copy prepared by the authors using Wordperfect.
Printed and bound by Edwards Brothers, Ann Arbor, MI.
Printed in the United States of America.

9 8 7 6 5 4 3 2 1

ISBN 0-387-97978-6 Springer-Verlag New York Berlin Heidelberg
ISBN 3-540-97978-6 Springer-Verlag Berlin Heidelberg New York

Preface

One of the liveliest areas of research in the social sciences is reading. Scholarly activity is currently proceeding along a number of different disciplinary lines, addressing a multitude of questions and issues about reading. A short list of disciplines involved in the study of reading would include linguistics, psychology, education, history, and gerontology. Among the important questions being addressed are some long-standing concerns: How are reading skills acquired? What are the basic components of reading skill? How do skilled readers differ from less skilled ones? What are the best ways to approach instruction for different groups of readers—young beginning readers, poor readers with learning problems, and teenage and adult illiterates? How can reading skill best be measured—what standardized instruments and observational techniques are most useful? The large volume of textbooks and scholarly books that issue forth each year is clear evidence of the dynamic nature of the field.

The purpose of this volume is to survey some of the best work going on in the field today and reflect what we know about reading as it unfolds across the life span. Reading is clearly an activity that spans each of our lives. Yet most accounts of it focus on some narrow period of development and fail to consider the range of questions that serious scholarship needs to address for us to have a richer understanding of reading.

The book is divided into four parts. Part I considers the contexts in which people learn to read and the role of reading in these contexts. The initial chapter by JoBeth Allen and Donald Rubin tackles the ambitious question of how our culture shapes all of our acts in literacy, including reading. Their chapter reminds us that although it is useful to define the place and purpose for reading precisely (e.g., at home for recreation, at school for memorizing, at work to locate information), such concrete definitions of context may oversimplify more powerful forces at work, forces that derive from more general and ultimately powerful structures of culture. In other words, culture, broadly defined, is the context for reading and other literate acts. Cultures differ in the reasons that motivate their teaching of youngsters, for example, and these reasons likely vary with circumstances even within the culture. At times, learning to read is driven by the desire to transmit powerful moral lessons from adult to child; for most modern societies, reading also serves strong economic purposes—people's skill at it contributes to how they fare in school and later the opportunities available to them for work.

The chapter by Elfrieda Hiebert looks at two specific contexts for learning to read—home and school—and at the beginning stages of reading in early childhood. The chapter is rich with insightful ideas and generalizations about the lively field of emergent literacy. This is reason enough to read the essay. However, Hiebert also foreshadows a number of important themes that have clearcut parallels for later stages of reading. We'll mention two of our favorites. First, children carry around large amounts of knowledge, insights, and intuition about the world of language and print at a developmental moment when formal assessments of their reading reveal singularly unimpressive reading capabilities. There is a tendency to take this formal standard of reading as a performance that stands apart from and is discontinuous with all that has gone before. Ignoring the multitude of links and possible continuities results in a widespread educational practice, which illustrates the second theme of her chapter to be singled out for special mention. This is a tendency to ignore the powerful learning experiences and strategies that spawned the earlier base of knowledge in one context (e.g., home) and educators fashion novel instructional approaches and tactics to teach "real reading." Storybook reading, language play, and exposure to print, which worked so well before the onset of formal school give way to phonics and other foreign seeming learning activities.

The third chapter, by Jorie Phillippi, is concerned with workplace literacy. Phillippi describes the ecology of work environments and the literacy tasks most frequently encountered in them. Workplace literacy is subdivided into reading, writing, and mathematic strands with useful taxonomies of tasks in the separate strands. As in the chapter by Hiebert, it becomes clear that there is a literacy gap. Actually, it is more correct to say that there are two literacy gaps. First, there is a gap between the forms of literacy taught in school and the literacy tasks faced in many places of work. It is not surprising then, that so many people come to work ill-prepared to deal with the literacy tasks facing them. But, more surprising is the second gap between remedial programs crafted to correct these deficiencies and the hoped-for terminal skills. This second gap occurs because the remedial programs frequently teach overly general skills that don't transfer to specific workplace tasks.

The final chapter in this section, by Harvey Graff, considers the historical study of literacy over the past several centuries and most interestingly, from our perspective, it details the general themes that emerged with some consensus from it. Among the most important conclusions from our perspective are that: (a) There has been "a trend over time in the direction of a standardized and homogenized experience of literacy acquisition. Until the past century, although most literates learned their letters in childhood or youth, there was extensive variation in the relationship of age to the acquisition of skills" (p. 92); (b) "Despite regular shifts in reading pedagogical theories, persons young and old have regularly gained reading skills from every imaginable method as well as by self-learning" (p. 92); (c) "Only in the past 100 years have assumptions tying literacy learning to the earlier years of the life span and formal schooling come to dominate theory and practice" (p. 92); and, finally (d) "Historically, the abilities to read have dominated—in quantity as well as quality—over those of writing. Higher standing persons have been much more likely to be able to write as well as to read, as have males, members of dominant classes, ethnic groups and races, and urban residents" (p. 92).

Part II of this volume considers the child's discovery of the spelling-sound system in written language, how word recognition skills develop, and the nature of reading instruction for children and adolescents. The chapters by Connie Juel and Keith Stanovich serve as important reminders that there are requisite skills that children must acquire—regardless of whether they are instructed in traditional or whole language classrooms—in order to become proficient readers. Connie Juel describes four steps in the process of "breaking the code" of written language: the child must first recognize that print is encoded speech, must then acquire knowledge of the alphabet, develop phonemic awareness, and finally, discover the relationship between the visual and oral equivalents of words. Phonemic awareness is the most difficult step in this process, but is also perhaps the most important because it allows children to make distinctions between letters and sounds. Juel demonstrates that those children who fail to acquire spelling-sound knowledge face profound and enduring consequences. Juel's own research has shown that children with little phonemic awareness at entry into first grade fail to overcome their poor decoding skills and, by the end of fourth grade, lag three years behind their more able peers in decoding.

Keith Stanovich's chapter echoes that of Juel in its focus on the important basic processes in reading skill development, and brings us up to date in regards to recent work in word recognition. Stanovich also makes a key claim that serves as a thoughtful reminder of the discontinuity that often exists between basic research and instruction: Although we know a great deal about the processes of word recognition, little of this knowledge has made its way into curricular materials and teaching approaches. This discontinuity between research and practice is unfortunate because, although recent instructional trends have emphasized top-down processes of skill acquisition, crucial bottom-up processes may be ignored. Stanovich notes that several models of early reading acquisition capture both continuities and discontinuities in development. There is apparently great discontinuity between the initial paired-associate type learning stage and the subsequent "unnatural" cipher stage in which analytic grapheme-to-phoneme decoding emerges. Transitions among the remaining stages are thought to overlap to great degree, suggestive of greater continuity. What we know about the nature of children's learning how to decode words has important implications for reading instruction while not ordering specific instructional prescriptives. At base, children must first acquire functional spelling-to-sound knowledge, as suggested by Juel in her chapter, regardless of instructional approach. A knowledge base exists about the processes of word recognition. Stanovich does an admirable job of making this work accessible. Much work is yet to be done to convey this information to classroom teachers.

Judy Winn and Annemarie Palincsar focus on the nature of reading instruction in contemporary classrooms, with particular emphasis on critical literacy. That is, how do various models of reading instruction—direct instruction, explicit explanation, whole language, and reciprocal teaching—focus their goals and teaching approaches to foster the development of strategic skills that children need to become proficient and intelligent self-directed readers who can take charge of their own learning? Additionally, Winn and Palincsar examine four critical issues related to reading instruction: ease of implementing the various approaches, student assessment, working with students of varying abilities, and the role of differential instruction—particularly in regards to low achieving students. Finally, although they do not advocate one approach over the others, Winn and Palincsar believe that any form of instruction must foster students' strategic skills and the development of students' self-confidence in reading. These are obviously important goals for creating lifelong readers.

Part III of the volume offers a series of essays on the topic of reading in adulthood. The first chapter, by Bonnie Meyer, Carol Young, and Brendan Bartlett, synthesizes the vast literature on how well individuals from early to late adulthood remember and understand prose. The chapter addresses themes such as these: Are there declines in reading skills as people age? Are the declines widespread and inevitable? What is the nature of these declines? A short summary of the authors' answers to these and other questions is that there are some modest declines in memory and comprehension as people age, particularly when there is a premium placed on reading quickly and when the structure of the text does not highlight salient main points and supporting details. However, the more compelling generalization seems to be that highly verbal and educated older adults perform most reading-related tasks very well and with little difference from their younger adult peers matched on these background variables. The final section of the chapter reviews a number of programs designed to improve the comprehension skills of adults, with special attention to an invention which Meyer and her colleagues have implemented successfully with older adults.

The chapter by Roger Dixon and Lars Bäckman covers some of the same ground as the preceding chapter, but with a novel perspective that is gaining widespread endorsement in other areas of gerontological research. These authors begin with the insight that research on aging is replete with examples of different cognitive functions and skills as we get older; yet, equally compelling are the real world examples of the many older adults who function at very high levels of skill often in demanding and complex cognitive enterprises (e.g., teachers, lawyers, physicians, writers). What seems like a contradiction, the authors tell us, is readily explained by the following working hypothesis: Adults gain considerable knowledge, experience, and practice in specific domains as they get older, and they may readily be able to *compensate* for modest declines in information processing (such as slowed reaction times or lower working memory capacities) by a variety of means. They may put forth and devote correspondingly more attention, working memory, and active rehearsal and practice on a task; alternatively, they may take advantage of some latent skill to augment performance such as their knowledge about the topic, their experiences, or contextual clues provided for them. Finally, older adults may shift their processing mode to a different form, for example, by reading with the goal of connecting new ideas to their life experiences and belief systems as opposed to reading for verbatim memorization.

The third chapter, by Ruth Garner, considers relatively specific, yet provocative phenomena uncovered in recent work she and her colleagues have been pursuing on memory for prose. As the earlier chapters in this section amply document, there is considerable evidence that good readers, be they younger or older, tend to remember ideas (propositions) in a text that occupy a prominent place in some narrative or exposition—that is, the ideas are relatively *important* by virtue of being lead statements, topic sentences, and so forth. What Garner and her colleagues have discovered, however, is that memory for such prominent information can be mildly sabotaged (i.e., depressed) by inserting unusually compelling or riveting details— she calls them "seductive details." For example, hearing the important work of world famous physicist Stephen Hawking, on grand unification theory, subjects are less likely to remember the central point about his work on this theory if the text they read also includes a seductive detail about a bet Hawking made with colleague Kip Thorne.

The fourth and final chapter of this section by Richard Robinson surveys the work being done in the campaign to reduce adult illiteracy in our society. Although considerable debate centers around what it means to be literate, or specifically, to be a literate reader, the national effort to describe functional reading skills for adults includes tasks requiring skills that most of us would agree are essential to "function in society, to achieve one's goals, and to develop one's knowledge and potential" (Kirsch, 1986, p. 3, quoted in Robinson). NAEP (National Assessment of Educational Progress), in its prose literacy tests, asked samples of young adults, ages 21 to 25, to match information, produce or interpret information, or to generate a theme or main idea for texts such as newspaper editorials, news stories, and poems. The 1985 results reported here are disheartening. "While the majority of young adults adequately perform tasks at the lower levels ... sizeable numbers appear unable to do well on tasks of moderate complexity" (Kirsh & Jungeblat, 1986, p. 4, quoted in Robinson). The chapter then describes the typical remediation programs planned for adult illiterates in our contemporary society, some of the problems associated with these programs, and offers suggestions for new ways to assess the skills and limitations of illiterates in these programs.

Part IV returns us to the overriding theme of this volume—reading across the life span. The three chapters in this section examine reading and reading-related activities, such as studying and metacognitive behaviors, from somewhat different perspectives. John Thomas and William Rohwer report an ambitious and detailed investigation of studying and study-related reading across several years of secondary and postsecondary schooling. Again, continuities and discontinuities in such activities are apparent. Studying remains an intriguing activity to psychologists and educators because studying occurs throughout the life span, in a variety of contexts, and for a multitude of purposes—the primary purpose being to enhance one's knowledge. Study behavior is also much more complex than might be imagined, and effective studying requires the learner to behave in a mature, detective-like, problem-solving fashion, employing sophisticated strategies that are directed towards achieving self-determined learning goals. Thomas and Rohwer examined characteristics of courses taken by junior high, senior high, and college students, as well as their study activities. Discontinuities were apparent in the levels of demands, explicit supports or aids, and compensatory supports across the school years. As individuals move through school, there are increasing demands to become more autonomous learners and fewer explicit teacher-provided supports are available. By adulthood, of course, most study activities are self-initiated, self-directed, lacking in teacher-supplied supports, and require moderate to high demands on the generative processing of information, that is, strategic activities that render information more understandable and memorable. Unfortunately, schooling does little to prepare young people to become self-directed learners as adults—when they most need to be so.

Cecil Smith's chapter is an initial attempt to examine aspects of reading skill in adulthood from a life span orientation. The reading skills and attitudes among a sample of adults, ages 35 to 45, were evaluated. The research is interesting and unique because cognitive and achievement data were available from the adults' childhood school years following their participation in a longitudinal study. These data, and the data collected by Smith, allowed a longitudinal examination of the adults' reading progress from first grade to the middle years of adulthood. The study suggests again that continuity and discontinuity in reading skills acquisition are the norm. Continuity in both reading comprehension skills, from late adolescence to middle adulthood, appeared to be the rule despite whatever discontinuities may exist between school literacy and workplace literacy. Continuity was also apparent in the relationship between reading attitude and performance. Those persons who were above average achievers at both 1st and 12th grades had the most positive reading attitudes as adults, suggesting that early success in reading may lead to a lifetime of positive reading experiences. The data also support, however, the ideas presented in previous chapters that there is a qualitative shift from learning-to-read in early childhood to reading-to-learn in adulthood. There was also evidence of intra-individual discontinuity in metacognitive developments. That is, adults who could be considered to be proficient readers demonstrated great difficulty in understanding and remembering texts of moderate difficulty (somewhat echoing the findings of the NAEP study). Further, their ability to monitor their cognitive performances was very poor. Finally, to harken back to the ideas presented by Allen and Rubin concerning the role of context in reading, these findings illustrate the functional importance of context when studying reading skills: Individuals who are good readers in their everyday lives may function quite differently under unnatural experimental conditions.

Another line of research has provided several implications for understanding how people can best remember information contained in stories. The chapter by Steve Yussen and Randy Glysch surveys contemporary work in cognitive psychology that examines memory for narratives among young and old adults. Following a brief description of the key elements of a narrative, the authors summarize four major theories of story structure: scripts, story grammars, the causal connection model, and mental models. Each of these theories has guided contemporary research on narrative understanding and memory for text information. The authors conclude by describing a series of four recently complete studies. In total, these experiments demonstrate the powerful effect of *good story form* for enhancing young and old adults' memories of information contained in short narratives.

In sum, we believe that the current volume provides an excellent survey of much important work and ideas in the broad field of reading. We thank, and applaud, our fellow contributors to this volume who have shared their wisdom and, perhaps, have pointed to important new directions in the study of reading. We also wish to thank those persons who have played significant roles in bringing this volume to fruition. First, our thanks and appreciation to the editorial department at Springer-Verlag for its patience with our numerous missed deadlines and to the production staff at Springer-Verlag for their helpful suggestions regarding the final preparations of the manuscript. Thanks also to Nancy "Red" Cahill, Puhui Cho, Lin Nevitt, and Bettina Hass who helped proofread and prepare the manuscripts after we received them from our contributors, and particular appreciation is expressed to Debbie Holderness, who was responsible for getting the manuscript to appear in its final form. Gracious acknowledgement also goes to several of our students who assisted with proofreading, checking references, and tracking down errant sources—Wes Covalt, Nancy DeFrates-Densch, Paul Perrone, and Mary Ann Wham. Finally, thanks to our families for their love and support.

Steven R. Yussen
M Cecil Smith

Iowa City, Iowa
DeKalb, Illinois

Contents

Part III: Reading in Adulthood

Part IV: Reading Across the Lifespan

Contributors

JoBeth Allen, Department of Language Education, University of Georgia, Athens, Georgia, USA.

Lars Bäckman, Stockholm Gerontology Research Center, Karolinska Institute, Stockholm, Sweden.

Brendan J. Bartlett, Griffith University, Nathan, Queensland, Australia.

Roger A. Dixon, Department of Psychology, University of Victoria, Victoria, British Columbia, Canada.

Ruth Garner, Washington State University, Vancouver, Washington, USA.

Randall L. Glysch, Department of Educational Psychology, University of Wisconsin-Madison, Wisconsin, USA.

Harvey J. Graff, Programs in History and Humanities, University of Texas at Dallas, Richardson, Texas, USA.

Elfrieda H. Hiebert, School of Education, University of Colorado-Boulder, Colorado, USA.

Connie Juel, McGuffey Reading Center, University of Virginia, Charlottesville, Virginia, USA.

Bonnie J.F. Meyer, Department of Educational Psychology, The Pennsylvania State University, University Park, Pennsylvania, USA.

Annemarie S. Palincsar, School of Education, University of Michigan, Ann Arbor, Michigan, USA.

Jorie W. Philippi, Performance Plus Learning Consultants, Inc., Springfield, Virginia, USA.

Richard D. Robinson, Department of Curriculum and Instruction, University of Missouri-Columbia, Missouri, USA.

William D. Rohwer, Jr., Graduate School of Education, University of California-Berkeley, California, USA.

Donald L. Rubin, Department of Language Education, University of Georgia, Athens, Georgia, USA.

M. Cecil Smith, Department of Educational Psychology, Counseling, and Special Education, Northern Illinois University, DeKalb, Illinois, USA.

Keith Stanovich, Ontario Institute for Studies in Education, Toronto, Ontario, Canada.

John W. Thomas, Graduate School of Education, University of California-Berkeley, California, USA.

Judith A. Winn, Department of Exceptional of Education, University of Wisconsin-Milwaukee, Wisconsin, USA.

Carole J. Young, Bethel College, Roseville, Minnesota, USA.

Steven R. Yussen, School of Education, University of Iowa, Iowa City, Iowa, USA.

Part I:
The Contexts for Reading

1
Cross-Cultural Factors Affecting Initial Acquisition of Literacy Among Children and Adults

JoBeth Allen and Donald L. Rubin

Scenarios of Literacy Acquisition in Diverse Cultures

Haifa, Israel

In an absorption center situated on the grounds of a youth hostel overlooking the Mediterranean, a group of Ethiopian immigrants to Israel struggle during the summer and fall of 1985 to learn to read and write in Hebrew. Along with thousands of others, they are refugees from a deadly famine in their native land. Airlifted 10 months earlier from camps in neighboring Sudan, they are removed from their Third World subsistence life styles and deposited with the speed of jet transports into a technologically advanced society.

This particular center on the outskirts of Haifa houses unmarried young men and women mostly between the ages of 17 and 25, many of whom are presumed to be the only members of their families surviving the famine and the treacherous march to the Sudan. Most are experiencing little difficulty learning to read and write in their adopted language. Some have attended secondary school in Gondar and other large towns and have achieved advanced literacy in Amharic (itself a second language for a great number of the immigrants who were native Tigre speakers). Many more have achieved rudimentary literacy by virtue of their participation in the national literacy campaigns staged by the current Marxist regime in Ethiopia. (Demoz, 1986, describes the nature and outcomes of this mass instructional effort.)

But a handful of these young people hail from outlying areas ignored even by the Marxists' literacy campaign. For them, not only is Israeli society alien, not only is the Hebrew language alien, but the fundamental concepts of literacy are equally alien. By their teacher's accounts, students in this particular group began their instruction unaware of print conventions, unaware, for example, that white space signifies word boundaries. By the fall of 1985, they are exceedingly frustrated by what they perceive to be their lack of progress in learning to read and write.

In one observed class, the teacher attempts to capitalize upon these students' motivation to read a newspaper. Making extensive use of class vocabulary, referring to place names of sites visited on a recent outing, the teacher has composed and reproduced a facsimile of a newspaper article. Working cooperatively in small groups, the students manage with considerable difficulty, but also with considerable delight, to decode the text.

Following her usual procedure, the teacher presents the class with a set of written questions to which they are to write answers. Because the simulated newspaper article, accompanied by an illustration, is rather long, the text plus follow-up questions fill an entire sheet of paper from top to bottom. Unexpectedly, this results in complete befuddlement and even anger among the usually polite and cooperative students.

At first their teacher is puzzled by the students' reactions. After all, they are quite familiar with a routine of writing answers in spaces immediately following the questions. But they are apparently unable to extrapolate from that routine to this new situation in which no space for answers has been provided.

"How do we answer these questions? There's no place."
"Write the answers on another piece of paper."
"How is that possible?"

The teacher holds up a sheet of paper in each hand. "Read the question on this paper. Write the answer on that paper. Then go to the first paper to read the next question. Write the answer to the second question on the paper below your first answer."

"Reading on one paper and writing on another? Not possible! You are requiring too much to do." One young woman leaves the classroom in tears.

Athens, Georgia

Lumpkin Elementary School serves children from a wide range of socioeconomic and ethnic backgrounds. In one group of five African-American kindergarten children, parental incomes range from that of medical technician to that of welfare recipient, and parental educations range from minimal schooling to college educations. One thing that the children have in common, however, is extended interaction with other children at home, at play, and often in extended families. Much of their learning, including language learning and socialization, has taken place in the company of peers, learning from older children, teaching younger children, and negotiating with each other.

In Emily Carr's kindergarten, this natural learning environment of peer interaction is fostered during writing time. Children learn collaboratively how to make sense of print. They create and share texts daily in groups of five or six writers that operate autonomously much of the time, although the teacher is always available for conferences, dictation, and other assistance. The children know the routine well: They gather with the rest of the class on the floor to listen to Ms. Carr give a brief lesson; they go to their writing table to draw and write for about 30 minutes; and after the clean up signal from the teacher, they share their stories, letters, etc., and respond to questions from their fellow authors.

On one April afternoon, the group (mentioned earlier) consists of James, Latoya, Monica, Kevin, Cecily, and a participant-observer from the local university. James has waited, not at all patiently, for his turn to share. His writing is much more extensive than usual and has been painstakingly copied from the daily story the class had composed that morning. James, who usually pulls a dramatic action tale from an otherwise lifeless string of letters, has not copied, nor read from copy, before. When he has everyone's undivided attention, he begins:

"Today is Monday (pause)—what this say?" he asks Latoya, who is just beginning to make consistent print-to-speech connections.

"Uh—boys or girls," Latoya replies.

James, skeptical, turns to the participant-observer, who supplies "April."

"April the 8th, " Latoya prompts.

"April 9, 1987," James reads correctly. "It is sunny today. I see—" Again he turns to Latoya.

"Fourteen," she supplies.

"Fourteen boys and eight..."

"'and' -'and' start with 'a.'" Latoya interrupts.

"...and eight girls." James finishes, his bright eyes a challenge to would-be questioners. To his disappointment, there are none, and it is Cecily's turn. Cecily, who usually writes warm, early phonemic messages and dedicates them to her friends, has covered her page with scribbles today.

"This is my Spanish and my cursive," she announces. She proceeds to read, "Quarto, cinco, adios..."

"Amigos!" Monica chimes in.

"Burritos!" Kevin contributes.

"...ocho, and adios, and hasta la vista means see you later, alligator!" Cecily concludes.

The Cultural Bases of Literacy Acquisition

The contrasts between these scenarios are intended to highlight cultural differences in literacy acquisition. Among black youngsters in the southern United States who are learning to read and write in their native language, literacy learning is conditioned by their cultural norms for group process. Indeed, most children come to school with extensive learning through peer interaction, whether it be at home, in neighborhood play, or at the daycare or preschool (Cochran-Smith, 1984; DePardo & Freedman, 1987). Schools are successful, in part, to the degree with which they match the previous successful learning situations, or create school "ecologies" that parallel and interact with other social-ecological systems in which children learn (Bronfenbrenner, 1976). This may be particularly crucial for low-income African-American children (Heath, 1983; 1987). In this kindergarten classroom, which has supported collaborative learning (Allen & Carr, 1989), children negotiate meaning into and out of print just as they have learned to talk, to think, and to assert their community membership. They learn from and with their peers. Among young adult refugees from Ethiopia who are learning to read and write in a second language, literacy learning is likewise conditioned by their culture's discourse conventions. For them, abstracting discourse from conversation was foreign enough; separating answers from questions represented yet a greater distortion of language use.

Our thesis, however, is not limited to more-or-less nonmainstream social groups; culture impacts literacy acquisition across the life span for all individuals. Children of middle-class families, for example, often acquire literacy with relative ease, and not only because they attend schools with newer textbooks, better lighting, and more computers. Instead, the discourse norms of their speech communities contribute a strong foundation for understanding the language of schooled literacy. Middle-class family interaction patterns (e.g., "And what did we see way high up in the tree when we took our walk this morning?") provide children with subtle training in how to be responsive and loquacious, how to stick to a topic, how to assert the rights of monologue, and how to transform information from the here-and-now to the there-and-then (Bernstein, 1977; Heath, 1983).

As for those members of literate societies for whom literacy instruction for one reason or another did not "take" the first time around, learning to read and write as an adult entails far more than simply acquiring a technical skill. Rather, adult literacy instruction typically encompasses a strong dose of acculturative indoctrination even for adult learners who might not be readily labeled as culturally different by virtue of minority race or language. The acculturative force of adult education is evident in adult education instructional materials that seek to reproduce "culturally appropriate" roles and beliefs both through explicit messages, such as stories about national heroes, and also through a hidden curriculum, e.g., illustrations featuring manicured suburban scenes (Coles, 1977). In traditional oral cultures in which early literacy is rare, the coupling of adult literacy programs with sociopolitical indoctrination is yet more obvious (Kozol, 1978).

In short, for children as well as for adults and in highly literate as well as in traditionally oral-based settings, the way people acquire literacy is inextricably bound up with their cultures. In an influential work, Brian Street (1984) labels a similar position the "ideological" camp, and he lambastes a contrasting "autonomous" view of literacy. Street criticizes scholars such as David Olson (1986), operating from a psycholinguistic perspective, and Walter Ong (1982), operating from a historical/literary perspective, for supposing that some sort of monolithic literate thought—associated with alphabetic literacy in particular—

can be superimposed on diverse individuals and cultures. Street argues instead for the ideological position: Literacy practices are intrinsic aspects of cultural variation. It is a mistake to assume any homogenous patterns of literacy acquisition or cognitive consequences of literacy because each culture constructs literacy as a coherent part of its distinctive role structure, economy, and epistemology.

In analyzing cultural diversity in literacy acquisition, we are clearly allied with the view that literacy and literacy learning are embedded in culture—not superimposed upon it. We feel, however, that Street's (1984) dichotomization of the ideological and autonomous views of literacy is itself too extreme (see also Fuller, 1986). In agreement with Vygotsky (1978; see also Wertsch, 1985), we see mind and society interacting. Literacy can be regarded as a mental faculty, as a way of knowing. As such, its acquisition and development is governed by human maturational factors, but at the same time, literacy is constituted of social knowledge, and its meaning is negotiated in social contexts. Indeed, the development of reading and writing is a prime area for understanding the essential interactivity of individual cognitive development and social context (Harste, Woodward & Burke, 1984). Accordingly, we adopt a sociopsycholinguistic view of literacy acquisition (Langer, 1986) that acknowledges both genetic and cultural epistemology.

Numerous cross-national and cross-cultural studies of reading and writing education have compared achievement between groups (e.g., Purvis & Tahale, 1982; Thorndike, 1976). Rather than focusing on literacy as an *outcome* of acquiring some more-or-less discrete set of encoding and decoding skills, however, our purpose in this chapter demands that we emphasize literacy as socially constructed (Cook-Gumperz, 1986; Rubin, 1987). Literacy is socially constructed in that cultural forces ascribe meaning and valence to the very acts of reading and writing, to the situations in which reading and writing take place, to individuals who are distinguished as literates, and to the written code itself.

This chapter, then, presents a framework for conceptualizing how cultural differences in the ways reading and writing are construed affect patterns of literacy acquisition. For some cultures, cultures in which universal literacy has not been regarded as normative and perhaps not even desirable, initial literacy acquisition is an adult phenomenon. Thus cross-cultural studies of literacy naturally lead toward a life span developmental posture.

For the reader's convenience, an outline of the dimensions we discuss follows:

How Cultures Construe the Functions of Literacy
    Epistemic functions
        (reproducing, transforming knowledge)
    Social control functions
        (social stratification, national identity)
How Cultures Construe Occasions for Literacy
    Print-centered interaction
        (in families, larger social groups)
How Cultures Construe the Transmission of Literacy
    Institutionalization
        (religious, civic, informal)

Philosophy of teaching and learning
    (rote, learner centered, culturally compatible)
How Cultures Differ in Writing Systems
    Regularity of sound/symbol correspondence
    Correspondence between writing system correspondence
Universals in the Emergence of Literacy
How Teachers Adapt to the Cultural Bases of Literacy

How Cultures Construe the Functions of Literacy

Purposes for becoming literate vary within as well as across cultures, and these purposes often affect home, school, and community literacy practices and various measures of literacy achievement (Mason & Allen, 1986; see also Ferguson, 1978). Downing (1973a) pointed to specific literacy goals in several countries as affecting materials and instructional practices. Jewish children, especially in Israel, learn to read Hebrew early in order to read the Torah. In Japan, reading instruction emphasizes moral development through story selection and the teacher's focus on the moral of the story (Sakamoto 1976). Cultural values and socialization are stressed in India's primers (Blom & Wiberg, 1976). Even in the United States, which presents heterogenous cultural attributes, textbooks and instruction have at different periods emphasized religious, moral, or patriotic values (Smith, 1965), and a vocal contemporary movement advocates a return to literacy as a vehicle for inculcating morals (Hirsch, 1987).

Epistemic Functions

A number of theorists have characterized literate thought as favoring linear reasoning rather than simultaneous perception, abstract rather than concrete, paradigmatic rather than syntagmatic, metacognitive rather than intuitive (Scollon & Scollon, 1981). The pertinent literature, however, does not always agree in ascribing the locus of literate thought. Sometimes these properties of literate thought have been attributed to information processing in reading and writing as opposed to illiterate or preliterate individuals (Olson, 1977), and sometimes to literate as opposed to oral cultures (Goody & Watt, 1963; Ong, 1982).

Despite much plausible theory, attempts to verify the empirical cognitive consequences of literacy have not been notably successful. Although writing and reading processes can facilitate higher order thinking, often researchers have confounded written language with academic functions and oral language with expressive and interpersonal functions (Tannen, 1985). Comparisons between literate and illiterate individuals do not yield dramatic results in cultures where literates use writing and reading only for restricted purposes (Scribner & Cole,

1981), and historical evidence likewise suggests that the advent of literacy is itself only one cog in the machine that drives the evolution of thought (Clanchy, 1979).

Thought patterns, then, are not due to literacy per se, but to particular epistemic functions that literacy may play in particular contexts. In the form that is functionally closest to prototypical oral communication, writing may simply *reproduce knowledge*. Here, writing is a technique for recording information with great fidelity and longevity. The reproductive function of literacy is epitomized by the list. Lists, interestingly, appear to be among the earliest forms of writing both ontogenetically (Cook-Gumperz & Gumperz, 1981) and phylogenetically (Schmandt-Basserat, 1988).

In contrast to the reproductive function, writing and reading may *transform knowledge*. The transformational function capitalizes on the capability of print to sustain revision, to create new ways of seeing, and to create new perspectives. The expository essay epitomizes the transformational function, especially when we consider its origins in the personal journal (Heath, 1986), itself a transformation of the more "reproductive" diary. Imaginative literature relying on metaphorical and narrative language also transforms experience (Bruner, 1984; Scollon & Scollon, 1981).

The dominance of one or the other of the epistemic functions of literacy appears to be culturally linked. In accounting for results that failed, in the main, to find strong cognitive consequences of literacy among the Vai of Liberia, Scribner and Cole (1981) explain that the Vai practice "restricted literacy" aimed mainly at conducting commercial transactions or recounting family news. Other scholars have identified the parallel phenomenon of "Qu'aranic literacy" (Scollon & Scollon, 1981; Wilks, 1968). Here, creativity and generativeness in reading and writing are averred. One acquires literacy through rote repetition of formulaic material. The form of written texts is inviolate; "meaning-preserving errors" during reading aloud are errors nonetheless, for comprehension is of low priority. Similarly, learning to write is a matter of learning to scribe, not to compose.

Studies across cultures show both children and adults acquiring this sort of restricted literacy. The Vai disseminate their indigenous writing system through tutorial arrangements between adults (Scribner & Cole, 1981). Instruction in classical Arabic is made available to preteen and teenage boys in African villages (Wilks, 1968). Heath (1983) described parental interactions with white preschool working class children around print, which were marked by frequent labeling questions but relatively infrequent expectations for children to make inferences beyond the information given. Ferriero and Teberosky (1982) described the confusing and detrimental effects of early schooling in Latin America that emphasizes reading as sound production and writing as copying. Scollon and Scollon (1981) discuss Canadian Indian children who decode proficiently but who nevertheless cannot conceive of transcending their subjective experience by placing themselves in a third-person story frame; though possessing literacy skills, they function within a "bush consciousness."

Neither children nor adults who acquire literacy restricted to reproducing rather than transforming knowledge are likely to experience profound cognitive consequences. On the other hand, reading and writing can certainly become tools that facilitate higher order cognitive functioning. The interdependence of "critical consciousness" on transformational as opposed to restricted literacy is embodied in the philosophy of Paulo Freire (see, for example, Freire, 1970) whose work has exerted a powerful impact on adult literacy education in diverse settings (e.g., Fiore & Elssasser, 1981; Shor, 1980). In applying Freire's principles, learners engage in dialogue as a means of discovering and expressing their social realities. The sequence of acquisition begins with "generative words" that arise from the learners' emerging understanding of their worlds. For Friere and his adherents, acquiring literacy is part of a process, the primary focus of which is empowering individuals to construct their own world and their ways of seeing that world. Acquiring reading and writing skills is secondary.

Of the researchers who have attributed cognitive growth to literacy learning, Luria (1976) stands out. He studies adults selected for leadership roles as part of the Soviet agrarian and labor reform movement. His findings are somewhat difficult to interpret because of sparse details of methodology; results are reported anecdotally, elicitation procedures appear to have been unsystematic, and aspects of social status seem confounded with the distinction between literate and illiterate individuals. It is surprising that, according to Luria, the Russian peasants showed such radical apparent cognitive changes considering their brief exposure to literacy instruction. For example, literate peasants—including those described as "barely literate"—used abstract or functional or syntagmatic associations used by their illiterate comrades. On the other hand those findings become more plausible in light of the fact that their literacy learning was part of a literally revolutionary experience. For these adult learners, reading and writing were indeed introduced in the context of political and economic empowerment.

Social Control Functions

Freire's (1970) notion of literacy as empowering demonstrates that learning to read and write is not a value-neutral enterprise. Decisions about what kinds of literacy will be made available, to whom, and enshrouded in what rhetoric, determine the way that literacy acquisition is bound up with social control.

Forcing social stratification. One way in which literacy acquisition acts as an agent of social control is by playing a gatekeeper function. It is a matter of individual and cultural differences that some people may value literacy for themselves more highly than others do; the darker side of the issue is that some educational policymakers systematically discourage certain groups from learning to read and write. Historical accounts (e.g., Clifford, 1984) show that in many different epochs and in many different cultures, those who controlled the preservation and exchange of a group's information store controlled the group. Sometimes the privilege of literacy was intertwined with political power, sometimes religious, and sometimes economic. In Nepal, as in much of India, lower caste children, especially girls, are not encouraged to read or write (Junge & Sashi, 1984). Minority cultures have often received inadequate reading and writing instruction, if they receive any at all. For centuries, the full extent of the Chinese character system was mastered by only a few powerful "wise men" (Goody, 1968). With the recent national goal of increased literacy in the People's Republic of China, a simplified writing system is often introduced to beginning readers and writers (Jiang & Li, 1985). Withholding literacy, as American slave owners did, was a powerful means of oppression.

While possession of literacy (or illiteracy) acts as an agent for perpetuating caste in developing societies, social stratification in more advanced societies is promoted by selectively distributing different *kinds of literacy*. In primary grade reading instruction in the United States, for example, it is well documented that teachers direct more questions, and questions of a more complex nature, to students whom they expect to be proficient readers (Hansen & Pearson, 1983); and those expectations are likely to be conditioned by cultural stereotypes such that minority group children are likely to receive impoverished literacy instruction from the very start. These children will acquire the fundamentals of decoding and comprehension, but more advanced inferring skills will be reserved primarily for middle-class Anglos (Applebee, Langer, & Mullis, 1985). In addition, groups established for reading instruction may be based on the teacher's socioeconomic perceptions (Rist, 1973), and may perpetuate the existing social stratification (Grant & Rothenberg, 1986).

In the realm of adult literacy instruction in the United States, the movement to impart "functional literacy" skills has been widely touted. The clientele for functional literacy instruction is disproportionately black, Hispanic, or limited-English-proficient (see, for example, Rosenbaum, 1986). In such programs learners work with materials comprised of governmental and employment forms, work-related instruction manuals, public announcements, and the like. Other types of materials like classic and popular literature and extended essays are unlikely fare in adult developmental education because they are viewed as too challenging, too culturally remote, or otherwise non-motivating.

Critics have pointed out that functional literacy instruction of this kind may be well intentioned, but it serves only to foreclose learners from participation in the real sources of cultural and economic power, actually perpetuating social stratification (Hendrix, 1981; Levine, 1982). Indeed, a recent survey of adult literacy skills in the United States (Venezky, Kaestle, & Sum, 1987) did not uncover alarming numbers of illiterates, functional or otherwise. Up to 90% of the respondents were able to decode common instructions and commercial messages. Rather, the survey findings engender concern because of the inability of large numbers of Americans, especially from minority groups, to operate upon and extend the information they extract from written texts. These individuals, "literate" though they may be, are equipped to use reading and writing only for those purposes that maintain their status as compliant and effective producers and consumers. They have literacy skills, but are not literate (Heath, 1985).

Reinforcing national identity. In many societies, learning to read and write are associated with one's civic obligations, and the value system that literacy promotes is likely to extol nationalism. This was certainly evident in the patriotic materials included in the popular McGuffey readers in the United States. For the children of immigrant generations toward the turn of the Twentieth Century, learning to become literate in English was not only a matter of economic benefit, but also a badge of allegiance to the mainstream values of their adopted nation.

The association of literacy acquisition with nationalism is nowhere more evident, however, than in the mass literacy campaigns of revolutionary governments such as Cuba, Nicaragua, and Ethiopia (e.g., Demoz, 1986; Kozol, 1978). Aimed largely at adult peasant laborers who must be integrated into a continuing nationalistic movement, these literacy campaigns utilize materials that weave together practical knowledge and political rhetoric. Learners who acquire the power to read achieve a sense of personal liberation from ignorance; they are given tools–for example, information about crop rotation–intended to offer a degree of economic liberation; and all this is linked to the struggle to preserve national liberation. The effort to attain literacy can assume an aura of spiritual significance that unifies all segments into a single nationalistic identity.

Literacy acquisition can be associated with cementing a nationalistic identity in more subtle ways. The very existence of distinct writing systems reinforces distinctions in group membership; for example, the Arabic-based Urdu script of the Pakistanis and the Hindi script of the Indians are otherwise based on very similar oral languages (Ferguson, 1978). Where groups have developed indigenous writing systems–for example, the Vai of Liberia (Scribner & Cole, 1981)–these become a source of fierce cultural pride, and the transmission of these scripts comes to symbolize the preservation of group identity. Probably for this very reason, government-sponsored educational agencies never encouraged the use of the indigenous Cherokee writing system, a writing system that did indeed contribute to a sense of cultural self-esteem among its users (Basso, 1974). In multilingual or multidialectal nations, the selection of a standardized writing system usually reflects some decision about the ascendancy of one speech community over another. In Ethiopia, for example, the Amharic majority imposed their system over a number of sizable minority groups (Demoz, 1986; see also Fishman, 1988).

When written language standardization is imposed by politically and economically powerful forces, children from minority language groups are put in the position of affiliating with the dominant culture, or else failing at literacy. There is some evidence, however, that when standardization of an indigenous written language evolves gradually and consensually, a writing system can be a source of nationalistic cohesion even across differing dialect groups (e.g., in West Africa; Giesecke & Elwert, 1983). Literacy acquisition exercises a social control function in this sense by promoting a group or national identity among learners—whether children or adults. The converse is also true: Learners will succeed at the task of acquiring literacy only to the degree that they can find a way to accept identification with the associated value system.

How Cultures Construe Occasions for Literacy

Just as cultures differ in how they construe the functions of literacy, so do they differ in what counts as an occasion in which people typically or appropriately read or write. For members of some groups, print-based interaction permeates many aspects of life: recreation, child rearing, health care for example. For other groups, literacy occasions are more limited, circumscribed to just religious or just commercial settings, for example. Cultures differ also in the range of participation expected in literacy events—who participates, and in what roles. For example, some adults who serve as neighborhood "opinion leaders" might be expected to engage in more, and more varied, literacy events. Weinstein-Shr (1988) found Pao to play such a role in Hmong immigrant community in Philadelphia. For other members of the immediate community, their engagement with print lies primarily in being read to, in having the written word rendered intelligible to them by others (Taylor, Wade, Jackson, Blum, & Goold, 1980).

Print-Centered Instruction

In contrasting the more circumscribed occasions for literacy she observed in India as compared with Scotland and England, McCullough (1973) offers a telling personal anecdote: "Before my brother was born, my mother ate gristle and read a complete set of Shakespeare, hoping to make her baby physically strong and a person of taste and competence in reading" (p. 119). In her discussion of how parental attitudes affect home literacy practices, McCullough noted that British parents regularly helped their children with school reading assignments; in contrast, 40% of first-grade children in India dropped out of school to help their parents at home or in the fields. Numerous survey studies reveal a relationship between cultural group membership—socioeconomic status in particular—and reading achievement that seems to be mediated through home variables like number of books in the home and the number of magazine or newspaper subscriptions (e.g., Thorndike, 1976).

In a cross-national study which examined both home and societal factors related to reading achievement, Blom, Jansen, and Allerup (1976) surveyed reading professionals in Denmark, England, Finland, France, Greece, Iceland, Ireland, Norway, Scotland, Sweden, the United States, and West Germany. The researchers formulated a stability rating for home and school factors that included family moves, school changes during first grade, years with the same teacher, and uniformity of education throughout the country. The two countries with the lowest stability ratings, England and the United States, also had the highest child illiteracy and reading retardation rates. Another telling finding was that all countries gave children their beginning reading books to take home and keep—all countries except England and the United States. "This was a small but interesting finding which may have important implication as to a country's attitudes towards literacy and children" (Blom, et al., 1976, p. 486).

To be sure, however, the operative factors in determining patterns of literacy acquisition are not the number of books in a household nor the number of family relocations. These may be just marker variables, indicators of some factor of greater explanatory power. The variable exerting more direct impact on literacy acquisition seems to be the nature of interaction between learners and their caretakers during reading and writing events. Analyses of interactions during storybook reading episodes reveal a middle-class literate pattern in which caretakers use books to structure dialogue with learners, and those learners take progressively more active roles in supplying meaning (Snow, 1983; Wells, 1985).

In households that predictably produce effective readers and writers, the interactions with print seem geared in particular to heighten children's metalinguistic awareness, awareness of the concept of word, awareness of initial letters, and the like. For example, a parent reading *Goodnight Moon* (Brown, 1947) might say, "Okay, Paul, let's read this one together–you help me out at the end of each page," and proceed to leave out words the child can get from a combination of memory, rhyming, and syntactic patterns. Children learn terms such as *word*, *page*, and *read*, as well as the skills of remembering patterns, rhyming and analyzing language. Metalinguistic awareness of this type is a critical attainment for children learning to read and write across a wide variety of languages (Downing, 1987). Certain types of metalinguistic knowledge–accuracy in discerning word boundaries in speech, for example–likewise distinguish between adult literates and illiterates (Ferguson, 1981; Scribner & Cole, 1981).

Analyses comparing mainstream and nonmainstream cultures show how different social groups diverge from the typical middle-class pattern of interaction with print (Heath, 1983; Ninio, 1980). In many nonmainstream groups in which occasions for literacy are circumscribed rather than pervasive, caretakers construe reading aloud as calling for an oral rendering of the text and nothing more. Interaction with text in these groups is not especially an opportunity for dialogue or meaning making, and it is not likely to heighten metalinguistic awareness to the same extent as typical literate middle-class routines. In some instances, this limited interaction with print may be due in part to the limited literacy of the adult (Edwards, 1989).

Work on emergent literacy has established the powerful influence of reading and writing with children, talking with them about literacy events, and providing reading and writing materials (Teale & Sulzby, 1986). In developing countries such as Iran, Chile, and Hindi-speaking India, most homes do not or cannot provide this supportive literacy structure (Thorndike, 1976). In addition, Feitelson (1985) warns that in societies in transition, such as Israel, the literate tradition valued in some homes may be missing in others due to different traditions or situational factors such as the stress of poverty and/or relocation. Her fear is that recent studies which find that "well educated parents in mainstream cultures [who] help their young children make the transition to literacy" (p. 9) may prevent researchers from successfully working with children from other backgrounds.

Clay (1982) investigated several aspects of oral English development, reading, auditory memory, and visual perception in 5- and 6-year-old children with different language backgrounds. Two groups were Polynesian and two were Pakeha (the Maori word for New Zealand whites). One Polynesian group was the Maori, an indigenous rural people with little command of Maori, a dying language. The other Polynesian group was the Samoans, with 75% speaking fluent Samoan and a history of parental educational support. The Pakehas were categorized as English proficient or of average oral language development. All were students in classrooms where their own stories and other whole books were the basis for instruction.

Clay's (1982) most surprising finding was that although the Maori children had better oral language development than the Samoan children at 5 and 6 (and were about equal at 7), the Samoan children made significantly better progress in reading (approximately equal to the progress of average Pakeha group). The Maori did not progress at the rates of the other groups in areas of directionality, spatial orientation, and other visual aspects of print. Clay noted that language deficits have been blamed for delayed progress in reading but that her findings pointed to other factors as possible correlates.

Clay (1982) did not investigate home settings, so there is no account of interaction with print in the home. She did emphasize Samoan parental attitudes favoring education and their willingness to help their children. The Samoan parents also modeled literacy through their correspondence with friends and relatives in Samoa, as well as with church-related reading. It is quite possible that Samoan children were interacting with their parents around print, and that these interactions included such concepts as directionality and spatial orientation. Ferreiro and Teberosky (1982) point out that simple exposure to print is not sufficient for this type of learning; there must be interaction with a reader. If teachers assumed a certain level of visual perception development (and the Pakeha groups were higher than the Polynesian groups at school entry), they may have focused instruction solely on reading and interpreting texts. Samoan parents may have supplied the missing pieces; the less literate Maori parents may not have.

Another explanation for the differences in achievement between the English-speaking Maori and the Samoans, for whom English was a second language, speaks to attitudinal issues and the social control function of literacy discussed in the previous section. The Maori are an oppressed group in their own land, and they may harbor antipathy towards the values of school literacy, much like African-American adolescents in the United States (Labov, 1972; Ogbu, 1985). The Samoans, however, were not similarly burdened. As an immigrant group, they aspired towards the mainstream values, including literacy.

In a study directly examining the effect of parental involvement on reading achievement in the highly-literate Japanese society, Sakamoto (1976) found that the earlier the parents began to read to their children, the more fluently the children read by 5 years of age, a year before formal reading instruction begins. Japanese parents often read to their children from the time they are infants. Most parents buy books and subscribe to magazines aimed especially at the 4- to 6-year-old audience, around the time they are learning to read. Parents do not report "teaching" reading but believe it is important to read aloud, to give children their own books and letter/word/picture blocks, and to answer their children's questions. They also monitor and assist with extensive homework, including helping children learn the difficult Japanese writing system.

Research considering adult-child interactions with print in various cultural settings indicates that literacy acquisition is promoted by print-centered talk that is free ranging, dialogic, and situated in many everyday settings. What little work is available concerning interaction with print and adult nonreaders suggests the opposite: Most adult illiterates establish social networks that allow them to function in the society without substantial interaction with print (Avila, 1983; Fingeret, 1983). Sometimes these networks can be quite elaborate, with illiterate adults relying on a family member at one end of town to assist with medical forms and information and a co-worker at the other end of town to assist in reading and replying to school notices. Among immigrant adults who control only limited proficiency in their second language, parents and their second-language literate children may switch roles (Schieffelin & Cochran-Smith, 1984). In such cases, the children serve as mediators through whom the illiterate adults come to cope with the world of institutions that presents itself in print.

How Cultures Construe Transmission of Literacy

The wide variation between cultures in their occasions for literacy acquisition points to significant differences in the ways groups construe the proper transmission of literacy. In the literate mainstream mode, literacy acquisition is pervasive; it takes place in many home situations as well as in schools. In other cultures, literacy learning is more narrowly assigned to an institutional setting, and sometimes that institution is civic, sometimes religious. Concomitantly, cultures differ in the degree of formality or rigidity in what counts as a literacy lesson. In some groups, literacy may be seen as properly learned through informal apprenticeship involving a good deal of collaborative learning. In contrast, other groups' philosophy of teaching and learning may hold that literacy can be acquired properly only through heavily structured, rote recitation.

Institutionalization

It is clear that for many youngsters, a great deal of literacy learning takes place in the home, prior to and during the school years (Heath, 1983). This is not universally deemed appropriate, however. According to Oliva (1986):

> Hispanic illiterates show a cultural trait which particularly handicaps them. Most illiterate Hispanics—even those who are American citizens such as Puerto Ricans—originate from countries and cultures where education and instruction are viewed as functions of the educational institutions which are uniformly, centrally

andhierarchically operated by professionals without democratically fostered parental participation. Education is viewed as something belonging to teachers who know best and who must be respected. (1986, p. 80)

However when parents of young Hispanic children in U.S. schools are asked directly to become involved with their children's learning, they are willing, able, and successful (Goldenberg, 1989; see also Rodriguez, 1982, for discussion of cultural, social, and academic issues around such a recommendation).

Besides the mainstream North American norm of encouraging literacy learning to proceed and extend beyond the school, other models of deinstitutionalized literacy acquisition prevail in other cultures. Indigenously evolved writing systems like those of the Vai (Scribner & Cole, 1981) and the Tuareg (Ferguson, 1978) are taught through apprenticeships of sorts, apart from formal schooling. In other developing nations like Benin (Giesecke & Elwert, 1983) literacy "cells" may form in which small groups assemble for self-help sessions in literacy skills.

Where literacy instruction is organized into structures more closely resembling classes and schools, these may be under the aegis of civic or religious authorities. In much of the Moslem world, instruction in Qu'aranic literacy within the village-level institution of the maktab is well documented (Street, 1984; Wilks, 1968). Here, young boys (girls are once again excluded) receive religious instruction at the feet of a spiritual leader, to whom exclusive right to teach reading and writing is invested. These sessions are certainly less hierarchically structured than the Western concept of the graded elementary and secondary school.

Philosophy of Teaching and Learning

There is a wide range of literacy-related instructional styles even within mainstream North American classrooms (Applebee, 1981) and homes (Flood, 1977). There is a tension for many teachers between the belief that instruction should take into account the learner's interests and abilities, and the increasing imposition of systematic text-centered (and test-centered) curricula for which both teachers and students are accountable. Literacy testing is not only influencing the curriculum, it has become a part of it in some schools whose subjects now include reading, spelling, arithmetic, and ITBS (Iowa Test of Basic Skills). Teachers are, on the whole, dismayed by these legislative and administrative usurpations of teacher decision making and learner-centered instruction. In line with contemporary Western educational theory, some have been able to establish effective, meaningful literacy instruction that involves student as well as teacher-generated purposes for reading and writing (Gordon, 1984; Hansen, Newkirk, & Graves, 1985; Wigginton, 1985).

In contrast, some cultures embrace

a traditional method which does almost everything that all schools of reading instruction in the United States would agree does not work. They learn by rote memorization of unintelligible texts in a dead language, reading being learned separately from writing, and their literacy...is in effect an incidental byproduct of the process. (Ferguson, 1978, p. 586)

Such methods are common in both first- and second-language learning in many countries, including some regions in the United States. For these methods to change would entail more than an adjustment in instructional technology; it would entail a shift in the cultural view of what it means to impart and acquire literacy. Such change may also be highly political (Moffett, 1985).

Although there are many countries or sections of countries whose beginning reading and writing programs do not reflect knowledge of emergent literacy and appropriate instruction, Ferreiro and Teberosky (1982) have pinpointed the areas and implications of incompatibility most thoroughly in Argentina. Methods there, they assert, are based on erroneous concepts of what children know when they come to school, disregarding how they have learned about print up to the point of formal instruction. Children never, on their own, abandon meaning completely; the code-emphasis instruction "teaches" them that their strategies for getting and transmitting meaning must not be the way to approach reading and writing. Children are taught that reading is making sounds, not sense, and that writing is copying; "...children must forget all they know about their home language in order to learn to read, as if written language and the activity of reading had no relationship to real language functioning" (Ferreiro & Teberosky, 1982, p. 274).

There are countries where there is a commendable match between the natural emergence of literacy and beginning literacy instruction. A long tradition of compatible instruction in many European (especially Scandinavian) countries is consistent with child-centered, developmental views of early education. Malmquist (1973) summarizes this tradition in describing Swedish schools. There, the initial emphasis is on positive transfer from home to school environments, and on identifying what the learner knows in order to structure successful learning tasks. As Jansen (1973) describes this orientation, the school must be ready for the child, not vice versa.

Perhaps the best match between emergent literacy (concepts and behaviors children have developed through informal interactions around print) and beginning instruction exists where reading and writing are seen as related, mutually supportive processes. This match has grown out of observation of children at home as well as some common-sense notions about relationships among the language arts. Instructional integration is supported by Ferreiro and Teberosky's (1982) finding that reading and writing do not emerge sequentially, but concepts emerge differently in different individuals, going back and forth between reading and writing.

Looking again at Scandinavia, we learn that in Finland (Kyostio, 1973) children write what they read, and learning is accompanied by much talking and drama (oral language). Downing (1973a) describes writing in British schools as an important part of initial instruction, with an emphasis on communication rather than correct spelling. Encouraging young literacy learners to "invent" the language through various forms of reading and writing has gained substantial support in the United States in recent years (Harste, et al., 1984; Teale & Sulzby, 1986). There seems to be a parallel acceptance developing in China, where some schools are switching to a phonetic alphabet (pinyin) for beginning reading instruction. Although children move from pinyin to character reading and writing, Liu (1978, p. 158) notes that "in composition, if a word is needed for which the character has not been learned, the student is encouraged to write in pinyin." Other reports of curriculum that systematically integrates reading and writing come from Italy (Tutolo, 1983), Japan (Kurasawa, 1962), France (Ruthman, 1973), and Taiwan (Smith, 1982).

One example of a beginning reading program intentionally based on an understanding of emergent literacy is Denmark. Jansen (1973) explains that Danish reading methods have evolved from the observation of reading development. Observers over time noted that children went through a phase of word and picture reading with much guessing and necessary attention to words. Then there was often a rapid transition to reading larger units, with more attention to overall meaning. In writing, the shift was from concern with conventions to emphasis on the overall composition process. With these observations Danish schools moved toward "development of reading as a functional process" (Jansen, 1973, p. 292) by developing phases of instruction based on individual school-entry knowledge.

Although the emphasis is always on the teacher selecting instruction appropriate to the individual child, there are some general trends. Several months are devoted to oral language development, integrated instruction with words and sentences, and spelling and phonics development as the child has the need for them. The next few months bring rebus reading and word recognition supported by writing, basal readers with controlled vocabularies, and a variety of practice and creative activities including experience stories. At this point, the child is usually ready to move into much easy reading: to learn to read by reading. One reason this individualized, relaxed pace can be followed is that children in Danish schools often have the same teacher for several years, so there is no pressure to pass someone on or meet artificial curriculum goals.

How Cultures Differ in Writing Systems

The match (or lack thereof) between patterns of literacy emergence and philosophies of teaching and learning, we have claimed, affects literacy acquisition outcomes. Similarly, the match between writing system properties and educational practice can also affect literacy learning.

In contrasting writing systems, it is common to array them along a dimension that reflects the degree of isomorphism between the spoken and written language. On one end of the spectrum are writing systems based on a semantic system: ideographic or iconic writing systems in which each grapheme corresponds to a concept or a unit of meaning. On the other end of the spectrum are alphabetic writing systems in which each grapheme corresponds to one or more phonological units. In between lie syllabaries and various hybrid systems. Alphabets are most economical in the sense that they require the fewest number of written signs to represent the entirety of the lexicon. It is also claimed that only alphabets lay bare the distinction between what is said (the sign) and what is meant (the intention) and thus encourage reflective thought (metacognition) and reflexive language (metalinguistics; see Olson, 1986; Ong, 1982). Some writers attribute the ascendence of Western Civilization—including the birth of logic, science, and monotheism—to the evolution of alphabetic writing in the Mediterranean (Logan, 1986).

Regularity of Letter/Sound Correspondence

Because alphabets have a small number of characters, and because they are organized according to the logical principle of one letter/one sound (at least in some languages), they might be expected to promote literacy acquisition inherently. Learners should be able to attain mastery in alphabetic literacy quickly, and literacy should be accessible to broader segments of the population. The evidence bearing on these expectations, however, is mixed.

First, it appears that attempts to categorize writing systems as exclusively ideographic or alphabetic are mistaken. Much regularity in English spelling, for example, is at the level of morphology (meaning units), not phonology (sound units; Stubbs, 1980). By the same token, at least part of what is represented in Chinese characters is phonological, not semantic (Coulmas, 1983; DeFrancis, 1984). Because of these regularities in sound/letter correspondence, the memory burden in learning Chinese is not as great as was once believed (Downing, 1987).

A second reason to doubt the supposition that alphabetic writing systems inherently promote literacy acquisition lies in empirical studies of literacy learning. Although it is true that China, with its logographs, has had a rather high rate of illiteracy (Coulmas, 1983), this is not true for Japan, which has both a syllabary and an ideographic writing system, but no alphabet. Moreover, there is evidence that in experimental learning tasks, it is actually easier for American children— raised on alphabetic literacy—to acquire a new writing system based on semantic rather than syllabic principles, and a syllabary is easier to learn than a system based on the alphabetic principle (Gleitman & Gleitman, 1979).

Correspondence Between Writing System and Instruction

Although evidence does not support any inherent superiority of one kind of orthographic representation over another, some educators believe that literacy acquisition is facilitated when methods of instruction correspond with the manner in which the writing system represents the language. Emphasizing phonetic information and pattern would seem logical in languages with consistent letter-to-sound codes. To the degree that a writing system diverges from alphabeticity and approaches semanticity, a whole word/symbol emphasis would seem more suitable. Of course the elements of literacy learning can still be part of an overall program that keeps language whole and purposeful.

There is only a small body of research dealing with the match between ortho-graphic regularity and beginning reading methods. Many believe that language regularity influences literacy instruction in Japan (Sakamoto, 1976), Finland (Kyostio, 1973), Sweden (Malmquist, 1973), and Germany (Valtin, 1984) and that the children learn to read more easily because of the language characteristics. However, Downing stresses that hard data to support this contention is "almost non-existent" (1973a, p. 219). He points to some teachers' use of "a kind of atomistic decoding method" (1973b, p. 101) in Japan and China when teaching high meaning Japanese Kana (syllable characters) and Chinese logographs. In contrast, some countries with highly phonetic languages have traditionally been taught by global, meaning-centered methods. Feitelson (1973) found that Hebrew, a very regular language, was being taught by such a global method as a hold-over from the British reign, a method perhaps well suited to the irregular orthography of English, but inefficient for learning Hebrew.

Others have also noted this mismatch. Lee's (1960) international survey inves-tigating language regularity (spelling) on reading instruction led him to conclude that there was no close association between methods and regularity. Lee pointed to Finnish and Turkish, two of the most regularly spelled languages, as having different approaches. Holdaway (1979) pointed out that the initial teaching alphabet (ita) is a very efficient orthography, but in the first-grade studies it was not superior to other methods. (See Downing, 1973a, chapter 10 for alternative explanations of the ita studies.)

Downing (1973a; 1973b) discusses several reasons why "there seems to be no connection between linguistic characteristics and methods of reading instruction" (1973b, p. 99). There are usually dialectic differences within a language; for example, there are hundreds of dialects of the basic Han language spoken by most Chinese, and the differences in dialect may be greater than differences among Spanish, French, and Italian (Liu, 1978). Writing systems may code variables other than sounds; elements such as morphemes also carry meaning. Downing (1973a 1973b) also noted that although language may have influenced choice of methods, so have educational, social, and psychological issues.

Nevertheless, some researchers have developed instructional programs based on their belief that literacy acquisition is enhanced by methodology "matched" to features of the language. Elkonin (1973) developed a phonetic segmentation strategy based on the unique linguistic characteristics of Russian in which the consonant pronunciation (hard or soft) is determined by the following vowel. Although he was successful in teaching beginning readers the segmentation skills, no data have been reported to show long-term gains of students trained by his method. However, Clay's (1985) highly successful Reading Recovery Program in New Zealand includes a variation of Elkonin's technique to help children who need such work to hear sounds in words. Feitelson (1985) has reported success with spacing the introduction of letters and sounds away from those most similar in Hebrew, a language in which both auditory and visual features are easily confused.

Universals in the Emergence of Literacy

Conceiving of literacy as culturally embedded highlights differences in literacy acquisition. We have argued that literacy acquisition is developmentally as well as culturally determined. We extend this sociopsycholinguistic view in the following section, where we note consistent aspects of learning to read and write that, like language acquisition in general, seem to be influenced by human maturational processes.

Despite the considerable variation in literacy acquisition across different languages, researchers have noticed some universals in the ways children first come to recognize and produce written symbols. In general, these observations of similarities across language groups suggest that initial understandings of writing in young children do not stem from linguistic bases, but rather from graphic bases. For young children, development in writing is continuous—more like drawing than like spoken language (Dyson, 1983). Young children rereading their early scribblings do not at first manifest any recognition that one graphic unit separated from others by white space ought to correspond to one spoken word separated from other words by intonation or silence (Dyson, 1981). Written names and other early significant written words seem to function more as visual icons than as stand-ins for their spoken equivalents (Harste et al., 1984).

Cross-cultural studies of emergent literacy provide additional insights to children's developing concepts of print. Keislar, Hseih, and Bhasin (1971) studied the influence of environmental print on the discrimination of linguistic symbols among 153 four to five and one-half year old children from Taipei, Delhi, and Los Angeles. All were enrolled in nursery schools or kindergartens in middle-class neighborhoods, with no reported formal instruction at home or in school. Keislar et al. used a match-to-sample task of letters and words in the three languages. They found no significant differences between the ages 4 and 5, but significant discriminatory differences favoring the native language after 5. They concluded that while general form discrimination develops consistently from ages 4 to 5, the influence of environmental print is not seen until after age 5.

Tolchinsky and Levin (1981), in studying writing samples from middle-class Hebrew nursery schoolchildren, found that initially they too developed a set of general graphic features common across writing systems. Later, their writing reflected unique Hebrew characteristics. In a related finding, Muraisho (1976) noted that 4- and 5-year-old nonreaders in Japan did not draw characters according to stroke order, but followed a standard order: Curved lines preceded dots and straight lines, longer lines preceded shorter ones, and angular lines preceded nonangular lines.

Some of the most thorough research on emergent literacy to date was conducted in Argentina by Ferreiro and Teberosky (1982). They asked 108 subjects preschool (age 4) through first grade to perform various literacy tasks and to participate in interactive interviews regarding the tasks. Tasks included writing, distinguishing numbers from letters and pictures from text, spatial orientation, sentence reading with and without pictures, and concepts of oral and silent reading. Their major findings indicated developmental progressions in determining if something could be read, reading pictureless texts, and hierarchical writing levels.

They found that about two thirds of the children developed hypotheses that something could be read if it had a sufficient number of characters (three was the common minimum) with sufficient variability (e.g., "AAA" was not perceived as readable). Children held to these same beliefs in their own initial writing attempts. In reading texts without pictures, children moved from including just nouns (a single label or series of related nouns), to nouns and verbs, to complete sentences (nouns, verbs, and articles).

Ferreiro and Teberosky (1982) identified five levels of writing, not only in the preschool children who had received no instruction, but also in the first graders. The first level includes reproduction of writing features such as broken or connected lines. At this level children may include both writing and drawing, but can distinguish them if asked. At level 2, letter forms become more conventional, and children become aware of the importance of letter order. At the third level, children develop the syllabic hypothesis, which may conflict with the minimum number of characters hypothesis. Ferreiro (1979) identified the syllabic level as the first connection between oral and written speech. As children adhere to the syllabic principle more and more strictly, they may even erase letters that do not fit their one-sound per syllable system. At the fourth level, the alphabetic hypothesis is formed; young writers resolve the conflict between the syllabic and minimum number of characters hypothesis (if they get to this level—some do not). At the final level, the child uses conventional writing system's alphabetic principle and is more directly influenced by other print sources.

Clay's (1975; 1982) observation and analysis of the writing of New Zealand 5-year-olds led her to identify principles rather than hierarchical levels. The recurring, generative, sign, and inventory principles are used with increasing sophistication into adulthood, rather than abandoned in favor of higher level hypotheses, as Ferreiro and Teberosky (1982) contend. One reason for the discrepancy in these findings may be that Ferreiro and Teberosky included only structured writing tasks. In a year-long study of 183 kindergarten children in the United States, Allen (1989) and seven teachers found that most children did attempt more conventional writing as the year progressed (only 5% "regressed"). Children did not discard earlier forms, but added to their "writing repertoires" (Sulzby, 1985).

How Teachers Adapt to the Cultural Bases of Literacy

We close with several reports of how educators in various parts of the world have applied their insights about the key role of cultural factors in strengthening and facilitating literacy acquisition. These teachers and researchers have applied their understanding of both the universals of literacy acquisition and the complex impact of cultural factors on learning to read and write to create classrooms, and ideally even extended communities, where literacy learning is within reach for all people.

Chesterfield (1978) designed "environmentally specific" materials in an attempt to close the "cultural and language gulfs" between rural Brazilian children, texts, and teachers (usually from the cities). He changed the pictures and words (but not the basic structure or situations) in initial reading materials to reflect rural life. Subjects were 98 first-grade students in eight classes from eight schools; four classrooms had experimental texts, four the regular text. Students, ranging in age from 6 to 11 (some had repeated as many as three times), did not differ on a reading pretest. After 1 year of instruction the children, with culturally relevant texts scored significantly higher on a reading posttest and on total number of words used on a posttest writing sample ("Write about your best friend.").

The Kamehameha Early Education Project (KEEP) (Tharp et al., 1984) is one of the most comprehensive examples of attempts to adapt schooling to the cultural norms of its population. An interdisciplinary team of anthropologists, linguists, and educators have studied and worked with the native Hawaiian children, many of whom were experiencing pervasive failure in the public schools. The team first studied the socialization of children before they entered school, including at home and with peers in other settings. These patterns were compared with what was currently expected of children within the school setting in terms of adult interactions, peer interactions, language usage, and styles of learning. One finding that seemed to have strong implications for the classroom was that many native Hawaiian children were not used to learning from or with adults, but were much more likely to learn from peers. Children seldom were asked a question by an adult that they were expected to answer on their own, one of the most common school scripts. Instead, children often formed group responses.

Significant changes were made in the first 4 years of school for these children. A major difference was that now children were encouraged to work together, even in reading group time, to solve problems, answer questions, and make sense of texts. A group responding pattern called "talk story" has replaced the uncomfortable question/answer format. Learning centers encouraged cooperative work and social interaction.

This ongoing research/teaching project has been highly successful. By 1984, its 15th year, the 2,000 elementary children who had participated showed substantial improvement, with average standardized reading scores at the 50th percentile (Tharp et al., 1984). Further, it is not a static program, but one that is constantly evaluating its own efficacy as well as the sociocultural factors that impact its population of children.

Chesterfield's (1978) environmentally specific texts are an example of one cultural adaptation; the KEEP program involves multiple adaptations implemented and studied interactively over time. Teachers in both examples applied culturally relevant information to classroom literacy instruction. A third program with successful documentation is Reading Recovery. Reading Recovery grew out of years of close observation of children in homes and schools in New Zealand (Clay, 1979, 1982, 1985), and has now been successfully implemented in many schools in the United States (Pinnell, 1989), including inner city schools. It is a short-term remedial reading program for first-grade students that involves high teacher-child interaction around whole texts, including some student writing. Huck and Pinnell (1985) found the scaffolded, highly personalized instruction, which in many ways replaced the parent-child print interaction that may have been missing for many of the children, to be quite effective. The instruction was not so much culturally congruent as compensatory.

Pinnell and her colleagues (1985) have worried, however, that as successful as the program has been for these children, their efforts were limited. What happens to these children when they are in classrooms where the purposes and occasions for literacy are less clear and personal, and when reading means filling in blanks rather than laughing over the adventures of a dirty dog named Harry? Perhaps more importantly, what of the literacy norms and values of the society these children live in? Is a compensatory program that fails to replicate the cultural literacy norms ultimately effective? What is the place of a literate child in an otherwise illiterate or semiliterate family/social group?

These and other concerns about a broad-based, community view of literacy have led to a comprehensive program (Huck & Pinnell, 1985) for preservice and in-service teacher training and dissemination of literacy materials and information in children's homes. This program seeks careful consideration of the functions of literacy for varying social groups, and school-wide literacy instruction with an emphasis on meaningful engagement with texts. Such a comprehensive program creates literacy opportunities for broad (home and school), long-term (through elementary school) engagement. In this program, educators have a model for a two-way perspective: Literacy impacts culture just as culture impacts literacy. Just as we can no longer view the preliterate child or adult apart from that person's history, values, language, neither can we view the newly literate person as existing apart from the community.

We have come full circle now from the literacy learners in Israel and Georgia we described at the beginning of the chapter. We can see that the teacher at the absorption center valued the transforming function of literacy, encouraging her students to read to become informed citizens. She created realistic adult occasions for literacy and structured social interactions around print, and yet even this culturally sensitive teacher could not anticipate the strangeness to her students of the common school practice of writing answers on a sheet separate from their questions.

The kindergarten teacher in Georgia built on the communicative function of writing and the collaborative nature of young children's learning. She continued to study what children know about reading and writing, how they interact with adults and with each other, and what they value as emerging readers and writers. She learned from Cecily that her sister is learning Spanish in high school, so her "regression" to scribble writing actually reflected an exciting new aspect of language learning, one that was currently important in Cecily's home. For Cecily and James, as well as for the young woman in Haifa, culture–the entire macrostructure (Bronfenbrenner, 1976) of our nested personal, home, school, community and national cultures–impacts literacy.

References

Allen, J. (1989). Literacy development in whole language kindergartens. In J. Mason (Ed.), *Reading/writing connections: An instructional priority in elementary schools*. Medford, MA: Allyn & Bacon.

Allen, J., & Carr, E. (1989). Collaborative learning among kindergarten writers: James learns how to learn at school. In J. Allen & J. Mason (Eds.), *Risk makers, risk takers, risk breakers: Reducing the risks for young literacy learners* (pp. 30-47). Portsmouth, NH: Heinemann.

Applebee, A.N. (1981). *Writing in the secondary school: English and the content areas*. (Research Report No. 21). Urbana, IL: National Council of Teachers of English.

Applebee, A.N., Langer, J., & Mullis, I. (1985). *A reading report card*. Princeton, NJ: National Assessment of Educational Progress and Educational Testing Service.

Avila, M. (1983). Illiterate adults and readers: Their exchange system. *Adult Literacy and Basic Education, 7*(3), 117-128.

Basso, K. (1974). The ethnography of writing. In R. Baumann & J. Sherzer (Eds.), *Explorations in the ethnography of speaking*. Cambridge: Cambridge University Press.

Bernstein, B. (1977). Foreword. In D. Adlam (Ed.), *Code and context* (pp. vii-xv). London, England: Routledge & Kegan Paul.

Blom, C., Jansen, M., & Allerup, P. (1976). A cross-national study of factors related to reading achievement and reading disability. In J. Merritt (Ed.), *New horizons in reading* (pp. 479-493). Newark, DE: International Reading Association.

Blom, G., & Wiberg, L. (1976). Attitude contents in reading primers. In J. Downing (Ed.), *Comparative reading* (pp. 85-104). New York: Macmillan.

Bronfenbrenner, U. (1976). *The ecology of human development: Experiments by nature and design*. Cambridge: Harvard University Press.

Brown, M.W. (1947). *Goodnight moon*. New York: Harper & Row.

Bruner, J. (1984). Language, mind and reading. In H. Goelman, A. Oberg, & F. Smith (Eds.), *Awakening to literacy* (pp. 193-200). Portsmouth, NH: Heinemann.

Chesterfield, R. (1978). Effect of environmentally specific materials on reading in Brazilian rural primary schools. *The Reading Teacher, 32*(3), 312-315.

Clanchy, M. (1979). *From memory to written record 1066-1307*. London: Edward Arnold.

Clay, M. (1975). *What did I write?* Portsmouth, NH: Heinemann.

Clay, M. (1979). *Reading: The patterning of complex behavior*. Portsmouth, NH: Heinemann.

Clay, M. (1982). *Observing your readers*. Portsmouth, NH: Heinemann.

Clay, M. (1985). *Early detection of reading difficulties* (3rd ed.). Portsmouth, NH: Heinemann.

Clifford, G. (1984). Buch und lessen: Historical perspectives on literacy and schooling. *Review of Educational Research*, 54(4), 472-500.

Cochran-Smith, M. (1984). *The making of a reader*. Norwood, NJ: Ablex.

Coles, G.S. (1977). Dick and Jane grow up: Ideology in adult basic education readers. *Urban Education*, *12*, 37-54.

Cook-Gumperz, J. (Ed.). (1986). *The social construction of literacy*. Cambridge, England: Cambridge University Press.

Cook-Gumperz, J., & Gumperz, J.J. (1981). From oral to written culture: The transition to literacy. In M.F. Whiteman (Ed.), *Variation in writing: Functional and linguistic-cultural differences* (pp. 89-110). Hillsdale, NJ: Erlbaum.

Coulmas, F. (1983). Writing and literacy in China. In F. Coulmas & K. Ehlich (Eds.), *Writing in focus* (pp. 239-253).

DeFrancis, J. (1984). Phonetic versus semantic predictability in Chinese characters. *Journal of the Chinese Language Teachers Association, 9*(1), 1-21.

Demoz, A. (1986). Language, literacy, and society: The case of Ethiopia. In J. Fishman, A. Tabouret-Keller, M. Clyne, B. L. Krishnamurt, & M. Abdulaziz (Eds.), *The Fergusoriar impact: Vol. 1. From phonology to society* (pp. 343-366). Berlin: Mouton de Gruyter.

DePardo, A., & Freedman, S. (1987). *Historical overview: Groups in the writing classroom*. (Tech. Report No. 4). Berkeley, CA, Center for the Study of Writing.

Downing, J. (Ed.). (1973a). *Comparative reading: Cross-national studies of behavior and processes in reading and writing*. New York: Macmillan.

Downing, J. (1973b). Comparative reading: A fourteen nation study. In R. Karlin (Ed.), *Reading for all*. Newark, DE: International Reading Association.

Downing, J. (1987). Cognitive clarity: A unifying and cross-cultural theory for language awareness phenomena in reading. In D. Yaden & S. Templeton (Eds.), *Metalinguistics awareness and beginning literacy* (pp. 13-29). Portsmouth, NH: Heinemann.

Dyson, A.H. (1981). Oral language: The rooting system for learning to write. *Language Arts*, *58*(7), 776-784.

Dyson, A.H. (1983). The emergence of visible language: Inter-relationships between drawing and early writing. *Visible Language*, *16*(4), 360-381.

Edwards, P. (1989). Supporting lower SES mothers' attempts to provide scaffolding for bookreading. In J. Allen & J. Mason (Eds.), *Reducing the risks for young learners: Literacy practices and policies* (pp. 222-250). Portsmouth, NH: Heinemann.

Elkonin, D. B. (1973). USSR. In J. Downing (Ed.), *Comparative reading* (pp. 551-579). New York: Macmillan.

Feitelson, D. (1973). Israel. In J. Downing (Ed.), *Comparative reading* (pp 426-439). New York: Macmillan.

Feitelson, D. (1985). *Becoming literate in societies in transition*. Paper presented at the International Conference on the Future of Literacy in a Changing World, University of Pennsylvania, Philadelphia.

Ferguson, C.A. (1978). Patterns of literacy in multilingual situations. In J. Alatis (Ed.), *Georgetown University round table on languages and linguistics: international dimensions of bilingual education*. Washington, DC: Georgetown University Press.

Ferguson, C.A. (1981). *Cognitive effects of literacy: Linguistic awareness in adult nonreaders*. (Report No. NIE-G-80-0040). Stanford: Stanford University, Department of Linguistics. (ERIC Document Reproduction Service No. ED 222 857)

Ferriero, E. (1979). The relationship between oral and written language: The children's viewpoint. In Y. Goodman, M. Haussler, & D. Strickland (Eds.), *Oral and written language development research*. Urbana, IL: National Council of Teachers of English.

Ferriero, E., & Teberosky, A. (1982). *Literacy before schooling*. Portsmouth, NH: Heinemann.

Fingeret, A. (1983). Social network: A new perspective on independence and illiterate adults. *Adult Education Quarterly*, *33*, 133-146.

Fiore, K., & Elssasser, N. (1981). Through writing we transform our world: Third world women and literacy. *Humanities in Society*, *4*, 395-418.

Fishman, J. (1988). Ethnocultural issues in the creation, substitution, and revision of writing systems. In B. Raforth & D. Rubin (Eds.), *The social construction of written communication* (pp. 273-286). Norwood, NJ: Ablex.

Flood, J. (1977). Parental styles in reading episodes with young children. *The Reading Teacher*, *30*, 864-867.

Freire, P. (1970). Adult literacy process as cultural action for freedom. *Harvard Education Review*, *40*, 205-225.

Fuller, A. (1986). Review of Brian Street's literacy in theory and practice. *The Quarterly Newsletter of the Laboratory of Comparative Human Cognition*, *8*(3), 108-111.

Giesecke, M., & Elwert, G. (1983). Adult literacy in the context of cultural revolution: Structural parallels of the literacy process in sixteenth-century Germany and present-day Benin. In F. Coulmas & K. Ehlich (Eds.), *Writing in focus* (pp. 209-226). Berlin: Mouton Publishers.

Gleitman, H., & Gleitman, L. (1979). Language use and language judgments. In C. Moore, D. Templar, & W.S. Wang (Eds.), *Individual differences in language ability and language behavior* (pp. 203-231). New York: Academic Press.

Goldenberg, C. (1989). Making success a more common occurrence for children at risk for failure. In J. Allen & J. Mason (Eds.), *Risk makers, risk takers, risk breakers: Reducing the risks for young literacy learners* (pp. 48-79). Portsmouth, NH: Heineman.

Goody, J. (Ed.) (1968). *Literacy in traditional societies*. London, England: Cambridge University Press.

Goody, J., & Watt, I. (1963). The consequences of literacy. *Comparative Studies in Society and History*, *5*, 304-345.

Gordon, N. (1984). *Classroom experiences: The writing process in action*. Portsmouth, NH: Heinemann.

Grant, L., & Rothenberg, J. (1986). The social enhancement of ability differences: Teacher-student interactions in first- and second-grade reading groups. *The Elementary School Journal, 87*(1), 30-49.

Hansen, J., Newkirk, T., & Graves, D. (1985). *Breaking ground: Teachers relate dreading and writing in the elementary school*. Portsmouth, NH: Heinemann.

Hansen, J., & Pearson, P.D. (1983). An instructional study: Improving the inferential comprehension of good and poor fourth-grade readers. *Journal of Educational Psychology, 75*(6), 821-829.

Harste, J., Woodward, V.A., & Burke, C. (1984). *Language lessons and literacy stories*. Portsmouth, NH: Heinemann.

Heath, S.B. (1983). *Ways with words: Language, life and work in communities and classrooms*. New York: Cambridge University Press.

Heath, S.B. (1985). Being literate in America: A sociohistorical perspective. In J.A. Niles & R.V. Lalik (Eds.), *Issues in literacy: A research perspective* (pp. 1-18). Rochester, NY: The National Reading Conference.

Heath, S.B. (1986). Separating "things of the imagination" from life: Learning to read and write. In W. Teal & E. Sulzby (Eds.), *Emergent literacy: Writing and reading*. Norwood, NJ: Ablex.

Heath, S.B. (1987). A lot of talk about nothing. In D. Goswami & P.R. Stillman (Eds.), *Reclaiming the classroom: Teacher research as an agency for change* (pp. 39-48). Upper Montclair, NJ: Boynton-Cook.

Hendrix, R. (1981). The states and politics of writing instruction. In M.F. Whiteman (Ed.), *Variation in writing: Functional and linguistic-cultural differences* (pp. 53-70). Hillsdale, NJ: Erlbaum.

Hirsch, E.D. (1987). *Cultural literacy*. Boston: Houghton Mifflin.

Holdaway, D. (1979). *The foundations of literacy*. New York: Ashton Scholastic.

Huck, C., & Pinnell, G. S. (1985). *Reading recovery in Ohio: An early intervention effort to reduce reading failure*. Unpublished report.

Jansen, M. (1973). Denmark. In J. Downing (Ed.), *Comparative reading*. New York: Macmillan.

Jiang, S., & Li, B. (1985). A glimpse at reading instruction in China. *Reading Teacher, 38*, 762-766.

Junge, B., & Shrestha, S. (1984). Another barrier broken: Teaching village girls to read in Nepal. *Reading Teacher, 37*, 846-852.

Keislar, E.R., Hseih, H., & Bhasin, C. (1971). *An intercultural study of the development of a reading readiness skill* (Document No. FS 005 693). Washington, DC: Office of Economic Opportunity.

Kozol, J. (1978). A new look at the literacy campaign in Cuba. *Harvard Educational Review, 48*, 341-377.

Kurasawa, B. (1962). Reading instruction in Japan. *Reading Teacher, 16*, 13-17.

Kyostio, O.K. (1973). Finland. In J. Downing (Ed.), *Comparative reading*. New York: Macmillan.

Labov, W. (1972). The transformation of experience in narrative syntax. In *Language in the inner city* (pp. 354-396). Philadelphia: University of Pennsylvania Press.

Langer, J.A. (1986). *Children reading and writing: Structures and strategies.* Norwood, NJ: Ablex.

Lee, W.R. (1960). *Spelling irregularity and reading difficulty in English.* London: National Foundation for Educational Research.

Levine, K. (1982). Functional literacy: Fond illusions and false economies. *Harvard Educational Review, 52,* 249-266.

Liu, S. (1978). Decoding and comprehending in reading Chinese. In D. Feitelson (Ed.), *Cross-cultural perspectives on reading and reading research* (pp. 133-143). Newark, DE: International Reading Association.

Logan, R.K. (1986). *The alphabet effect.* New York: William Morrow.

Luria, A. (1976). *Cognitive development: Its cultural and social foundations.* Cambridge, MA: Harvard University Press.

Malmquist, E. (1973). Sweden. In J. Downing (Ed.), *Comparative reading* (pp. 466-487). New York: Macmillan.

Mason, J., & Allen, J. (1986). A review of emergent literacy with implications for research and practice in reading. In E. Rothkipf (Ed.), *Review of research in education* (pp. 3-47). Washington, DC: American Educational Research Association.

McCullough, C. (1973). Promoting reading ability at all levels. In R. Karlin (Ed.), *Reading for all.* Newark, DE: International Reading Association.

Moffett, J. (1985, September). Hidden impediments to improving English teaching. *Phi Delta Kappan,* 55-60.

Muraisho, S. (1976). The reading ability of preschool children in Japan. In J. Merritt (Ed.), *New horizons in reading* (pp. 255-268). Newark, DE: International Reading Association.

Ninio, A. (1980). Picture book reading in mother-infant dyads belonging to two sub-groups in Israel. *Child Development, 51,* 587-590.

Ogbu, J.U. (1985). *Minority education and caste: The American system in cross-cultural perspective.* New York: Harcourt Brace Jovanovich.

Oliva, J. (1986). Why parent tutors: Cultural reasons. In C. Simich-Dudgeon (Ed.), *Issues of parent involvement and literacy* (pp. 79-81). Washington: Trinity College.

Olson, D.R. (1977). From utterance to text: The bias of language in speech and writing. *Harvard Educational Review, 47,* 257-281.

Olson, D.R. (1986). The cognitive consequences of literacy. *Canadian Psychology, 27,* 109-121.

Ong, W.J. (1982). *Orality and literacy: The technologizing of the word.* New York: Methuen.

Pinnell, G.S. (1987). Helping teachers see how readers read. *Theory into Practice, 26,* 51-58.

Pinnell, G.S. (1989). A systemic approach to reducing the risk of reading failure. In J. Allen & J. Mason (Eds.), *Risk makers, risk takers, risk breakers: Reducing the risks for young literacy learners* (pp. 178-197). Portsmouth, NH: Heinemann.

Purvis, A., & Tahale, S. (Eds.). (1982). *An international perspective of the evaluation of written communication.* New York: Pergamon.

Rist, R. (1973). *The urban school: A factory for failure.* Cambridge, MA: M.I.T. Press.

Rodriguez, R. (1982). *Hunger of memory: The education of Richard Rodriguez.* New York: Bantam.

Rosenbaum, H. (1986). Basic skills education in the army. In C. Simich-Dugeon (Ed.), *Issues of parent involvement and literacy* (pp. 39-45). Washington: Trinity College.

Rubin, D.L. (1987). Divergence and convergence between oral and written communication. *Topics in Language Disorders, 7*(4), 1-18.

Ruthman, P. (1987). France. In J. Downing (Ed.), *Comparative reading* (pp. 319-341). New York: Macmillan.

Sakamoto, T. (1976). Writing systems in Japan. In J. Merritt (Ed.), *New horizons in reading.* Newark, DE: International Reading Association.

Schieffelin, B., & Cochran-Smith, M. (1984). Learning to read culturally: Literacy before schooling. In H. Goelman, A. Oberg, & F. Smith (Eds.), *Awakening to literacy.* Portsmouth, NH: Heinemann.

Schmandt-Basserat, J. (1988). From accounting to writing: Concrete and abstract representation in ancient Sumaria. In B. Raforth & D. Rubin (Eds.), *The social construction of written communication* (pp. 119-130). Norwood, NJ: Ablex.

Scollon, R., & Scollon, S. (1981). *Narrative, literacy, and face in interethnic communication.* Norwood, NJ: Ablex.

Scribner, S., & Cole, M. (1981). *The psychology of literacy.* Cambridge, England: Harvard University Press.

Shor, I. (1980). *Critical teaching and everyday life.* New York: South End Press.

Smith, N.B. (1965). *American reading instruction.* Newark, DE: International Reading Association.

Smith, N.B. (1982). Reading instruction in Taiwan: A model for using the reader effectively. *Reading Teacher, 36,* 34-37.

Snow, C.E. (1983). Literacy and language: Relationships during the preschool years. *Harvard Educational Review, 53,* 165-189.

Street, B. (1984). *Literacy in theory and practice.* Cambridge, England: Cambridge University Press.

Stubbs, M. (1980). *Language and literacy: The sociolinguistics of reading and writing.* London: Routledge & Kegan Paul.

Sulzby, B. (1985). Children's emergent reading of favorite storybooks: A developmental study. *Reading Research Quarterly, 20,* 458-481.

Tannen, D. (1985). Relative focus of involvement in oral and written discourse. In D. Olson, N. Torrance, & A. Hildyard (Eds.), *Literacy, language, and learning* (pp. 124-148). Cambridge, MA: Cambridge University Press.

Taylor, N., Wade, P., Jackson, S., Blum, I., & Goold, L. (1980). A study of low-literate adults: Personal, environmental and program considerations. *Urban Review, 12*(2), 69-77.

Teale, W.H., & Sulzby, E. (1986). *Emergent literacy: Writing and reading.* Norwood, NJ: Ablex.

Tharp, R., Jordan, C., Speidel, G., Au, K., Klein, T., Calkins, R., Sloat, K., & Gallimore, R. (1984). Product and process in applied developmental research: Education and the children of minority. In M. Lamb, A. Brown, & R. Rogoff (Eds.), *Advances in developmental psychology* (Vol. 3). Hillsdale, NJ: Erlbaum.

Thorndike, R. (1976). Reading comprehension in 15 countries. In J. Merritt (Ed.), *New horizons in reading* (pp. 500-507). Newark, DE: International Reading Association.

Tolchinsky, L., & Levin, I. (1981). *The development of the graphic and symbolic aspects of writing in preschoolers: A study in a Semitic language.* Paper presented at El Simposia Internacional Sobre Nuevas Perspectivas in los Procesos de Lectura y Escritura, Mexico City.

Tutolo, D. (183). Beginning reading in Italy. *Reading Teacher, 36,* 752-757.

Valtin, R. (1984). Awareness of features and functions of language. In J. Downing & R. Valtin (Eds.), *Language awareness and learning to read* (pp. 227-260). New York: Springer-Verlag.

Venezky, R.L., Kaestle, C.F., & Sum, A.M. (1987). *The subtle danger: Reflections on the literacy abilities of America's young adults.* Princeton: Educational Testing Service.

Vygotsky, L.S. (1978). *Mind in society.* Cambridge, MA: Harvard University Press.

Weinstein-Shr, G. (1988, January). *Ethnography and the study of literacy and social process: The case of a Hmong refugee community in Philadelphia.* Paper presented at the Qualitative Research in Education Conference, Athens, GA.

Wells, G. (1985). Preschool literacy-related activities and success in school. In D. Olson, N. Torrance, & A. Hildyard (Eds.), *Literacy, language, and learning* (pp. 229-255). Cambridge: Cambridge University Press.

Wertsch, J. (1985). *Vygotsky and the social formation of the mind.* Cambridge, MA: Harvard University Press.

Wigginton, E. (1985). *Sometimes a shining moment: The Foxfire experience.* Garden City, NY: Anchor Books.

Wilks, I. (1968). The transmission of Islamic learning in the Western Sudan. In J. Goody (Ed.), *Literacy in traditional societies* (pp. 161-197). New York: Cambridge University Press.

2
Young Children's Literacy Experiences in Home and School

Elfrieda H. Hiebert

For decades, young children's literacy development was viewed through the lenses associated with the reading readiness perspective. When young children were tested on reading readiness measures such as letter naming and auditory and visual discrimination, they were often seen as deficient in literacy skills. Reflecting a shift in paradigm, different questions began to be asked in the 1970s about young children's literacy development. When the early forms of literacy were viewed more broadly, it became apparent that many young children had a rich repertoire of strategies and concepts related to literacy. This broadened perspective on children's early reading and writing knowledge and ways of learning has come to be called "emergent literacy" (Teale & Sulzby, 1986).

The topic of what young children have learned has been treated quite comprehensively in several recent chapters and books (Adams, 1990; Dyson & Freedman, 1991; Juel, 1991a; Sulzby & Teale, 1991). Less attention has been given to how young children have acquired this knowledge, especially in connecting the learning contexts of home and school. It is to issues of literacy learning in home and school that attention is directed here.

Home Experiences

Studies of the effects of home variables on school achievement have a long history that predate the work on emergent literacy. White's (1982) meta-analysis of 200 studies showed the following factors to be associated with early reading achievement: (a) family characteristics, such as academic guidance, attitude toward education, and aspirations of parents for children, (b2) conversations in the home, and (c) reading materials and cultural activities. Studies in White's analysis used standardized tests of reading readiness and reading, rather than measures like storybook reading or storywriting which have been used by researchers of emergent literacy. The existing studies that trace the roots of emergent literacy in home settings, however, fall into three categories quite similar to White's: parents' personal literacy and aspirations for their children's literacy, parent-child interactions around literacy, and children's independent literacy activities.

Parents' Literacy and Aspirations for Their Children's Literacy

Quantity of parents' own literacy behaviors predict children's literacy learning even better than quantity of parent-child literacy interactions (Dunn, 1981; Hess, Holloway, Price, & Dickson, 1982; Hiebert, 1980). An explanation for this finding lies in Gough and Hillinger's (1980) identification of "cryptanalytic intent" as critical to literacy acquisition. Cryptanalytic intent refers to an understanding that print is encoded speech and that a systematic relationship exists between written and spoken words. Frequent, consistent opportunities to see adults using literacy provide children with an understanding of the existence of writing and its relationship to spoken language. Without such an understanding, young children may find the task of becoming fluent at reading ambiguous and even tedious. When children know what literacy is, they can respond as one kindergartner did when asked on his first day of school what he was going to learn, "To read! So that I can say the words in case my mom forgets how." (*Daily Camera*, 1987).

As adults use literacy, some explain their use to young children. Olson (1984) refers to this talk about language use as "metalanguage." For example, a parent who responds to a child's request for attention with the statement, "I have to finish writing this list for grocery shopping," is giving the child the language for labeling the writing process and an understanding of the functions of writing. Such talk about literacy enables an understanding of what needs to be learned and of the often technical language (e.g., word, letters) that surrounds reading instruction.

The predictive nature of parents' own literacy activities may also represent their commitment to literacy and a desire for their children to be literate. Not many children become knowledgeable about reading and writing in homes where adults do little to draw their attention to print. A strong relationship has been found between parents' aspirations for their children's literacy and children's literacy accomplishments (Hess et al., 1982). Dunn (1981) found that a measure of parental beliefs accounted for more variation in children's performances than the time parents spent reading to children.

Parents' own literacy weighs heavily in their children's reading and writing acquisition. Literate parents model literacy use for their children and have goals for their children to become literate. No matter how much a parent values literacy, however, at one point or another a child must be involved with reading and writing to become literate.

Parent-Child Literacy Interactions

Many kinds of interactions precipitate literacy learning. Storybook reading is the most commonly identified interaction but, especially for acquisition of word-level strategies, other events such as labeling letters and words in everyday contexts are also critical.

Storybook reading. Parents have long been encouraged to read to their children (Huey, 1908/1968) and heeding this advice pays off. Although storybook reading by parents does not ensure that children are early readers, and children who have not experienced home storybook reading learn to read in school (Hiebert, Colt, Catto, & Gury, 1991), reading aloud by parents consistently distinguishes children who are successful in school reading programs from those who are not (Edwards, 1991; Miller, Nemoianu, & DeJong, 1986; Teale, 1984). After a longitudinal analysis of preschool literacy-related activities and children's success in school, Wells (1985) concluded that storybook reading was the single best predictor of success in school reading. Storybook reading conveys information about the structure of stories, the nature of written language, and the comprehension process (Heath, 1982). All of these concepts are critical to school learning.

Several characteristics distinguish the storybook reading of parents whose children do well on reading and writing tasks. One is frequent, regular storybook reading that begins at an early age. This pattern has been confirmed among American families (Shanahan & Hogan, 1983), as well as in other cultures. Sakamoto (1976), studying the storybook reading patterns of Japanese families, reported that the earlier parents began reading to their children, the more fluently the children read by 5 years of age, a year before formal reading instruction. A study of storybook reading among Israeli families differing in socioeconomic status (Feitelson & Goldstein, 1986) showed extensive discrepancies in the number of books available in homes for kindergarten children and the amount of time parents spent reading to children. The number of children's books available in middle-class homes differed from those in working-class homes by a magnitude of one. Wheras many middle-class parents had begun reading for up to a half an hour a day to their children at age 1, 60% of the working-class parents did not read at all to their kindergarten children. The other 40% read infrequently and often had not started this practice until their child entered kindergarten.

Interaction around these literacy opportunities can differ substantially. A cogent argument for social interaction as a mechanism for children's literacy development comes from the work of Vygotsky (1962). Vygotsky saw social interaction as a primary means whereby practices and symbol systems of culture are acquired. Parents provide the support or "scaffolding" for conversations so that children can participate with new ideas (Ninio & Bruner, 1978). With this support, children move to the upper boundaries of their capabilities.

Studies have verified a strong relationship between certain features of storybook reading and literacy acquisition. Parental question-asking before, during, and after reading relates to reading acquisition (Flood, 1977). Parents of children who have a substantial literacy repertoire on entering school adjust their questions as children become more capable in comprehending. Heath (1983) found that middle-class mothers allowed their children to participate in dialogue during storybook reading up to approximately 3 years, at which point they were expected to listen during reading and to answer questions after reading. Furthermore, parents' ability to connect children's prior experiences with the content of stories, such as the reminder that the rabbit in the book is similar to one seen at the zoo or in another book, fosters children's involvement in book reading and, subsequently, their reading development (Shanahan & Hogan, 1983).

Interaction is not entirely one-sided as one interpretation of Heath's (1983) work might suggest. When encouraged, a preschooler can ask as many as 1,000 questions over a year of book reading episodes (Yaden & McGee, 1984). Parents' responsiveness to these questions strongly predicts children's reading development as well (Flood, 1977).

Recently, researchers have been using these findings as the basis for interventions with parents (Edwards, 1991; Whitehurst et al., 1988). Parents are guided in the types of questions they ask their children and their responses to children's comments. In Edwards' project, mothers who themselves had low literacy levels were shown how to model questions and responses during storybook reading through videotaped demonstrations and peer coaching. Efforts such as these can facilitate the literacy knowledge and participation of both parents and children.

The literature on parent-child storybook reading has grown considerably over the past decade. Substantive conclusions can be made about the nature of parent-child interaction that facilitates acquisition of reading and writing knowledge. These interactions focus on the meaning of the stories. In fact, storybook reading interactions might be viewed as a context for acquiring the prior knowledge base that has been emphasized so strongly as necessary for comprehension. However, there has been no evidence to date that parents teach children to identify words and to name letters in the context of storybook reading. Since many children enter kindergarten knowing letter names (Hiebert & Sawyer, 1984), children acquire this knowledge in one way or another in home settings. The source of this information should probably be best considered in everyday contexts.

Everyday interactions with written language. Even if there are not book reading events, there are literacy events in the homes of almost all children (Anderson & Stokes, 1984; Pellegrini, Perlmutter, Galda, & Brophy, 1990; Taylor & Dorsey-Gaines, 1988). Children see adults using print—recipe books, newspapers, prayer books, and hymnals in church; advertisements for movies; and street signs. Anderson and Stokes (1984) argue that storybook reading is often emphasized as the mechanism for young children's reading-related development at the expense of these everyday events. When this occurs, non-middle-class children are described as lacking literacy experiences although in reality their day-to-day life contains many examples of written language. Approximately 2000 hours of observations in the homes of Anglo-, African-, and Hispanic-American preschool children confirmed Anderson and Stokes' thesis. These observations showed eight types of literacy occasions, in addition to storybook time: daily living, entertainment, school-related activity, religion, general information, work, literacy techniques and skills, and interpersonal communication. Families spent approximately 8 minutes out of every hour of observation in one or more of these literacy events, with Anglo-American families having more but shorter episodes than African- or Hispanic-American families.

Despite the frequency of events that Anderson and Stokes (1984) describe, there is no evidence on how, and even if, parents in that sample involved their children in these events, nor did they demonstrate a relationship between the frequency of different types of events and children's literacy development.

Reports such as Torrey's (1969) case study of a child who learned to read through watching television commercials are rare. Children need guidance from someone who is sensitive to their needs and abilities, if they are to learn about print in everyday contexts. As Masonheimer, Drum, and Ehri (1984) demonstrated, children's familiarity with environmental print does not mean that they attend to the specific features of the print. Children's response to a stop sign with the name of a cola transposed on it is "Stop."

While formal instruction by parents is not efficacious with young children (Brzeinski, 1964), parental awareness and ability to capture opportunities to teach children informally seem necessary for development of concepts and skills related to written language. Hiebert and Adams (1987) found that parents of highly literate children could more accurately predict their children's performances on emergent literacy tasks than parents of children who scored less well on these tasks. With some parents, the effort seems to be quite extensive and definitely intentional, as is evident in Fowler's (1981) reexamination of the Terman (1918) genius studies. Fowler found two patterns among families: Parents who explicitly taught their children and acknowledged their roles; and parents who disavowed that role but devoted substantial time to reading to their children, answering children's questions, and interacting about language and literacy. In both groups, parents guided their children in educational experiences with reading a central part.

Several projects further describe the informal ways in which parents guide children's literacy learning at home. Taylor (1983), in studying the literacy events in the day-to-day lives of six children from the preschool years to school entry, reported that these children's literacy learning resulted from participating in literacy use that was part of the social activity of day-to-day life rather than from any direct teaching by parents. The mechanism in Taylor's study was clear: Parents drew their children into everyday literacy events. Bissex (1980), in a case study of her child's literacy development, similarly describes literacy learning in everyday events such as writing a grocery list or a get-well or birthday card to a friend.

Some parents create activities that are quite specifically oriented to literacy acquisition, such as games that enhance rhyming. Tobin (1981) found that parents of early readers were more likely to engage their children in informal, game-like activities that could be expected to promote mastery of phonics than parents of children who were not early readers when they entered kindergarten.

The level of specificity in parents' instruction of a skill like letter naming remains uncertain. It is clear, however, that parents of preschool children see instruction of letter naming as one of their obligations (Tobin & Pikulski, 1983). Since kindergarten teachers continue to maintain a stance that letter naming must precede other print-related activities (Education Research Service, 1986), a great service could be performed if data were provided on how this happens in homes. Undoubtedly, there are many activities that contribute to children's acquisition of letter naming and letter-sound matching in their home environments. It is most likely that the forms of written language are learned through everyday experiences, such as finding letters on signs, writing messages with preformed letters, and so on. This learning, however, can hardly be described as "natural" as Goodman and Goodman (1979) have claimed.

While the body of intervention studies on parent-child book reading is substantial, studies that guide parents in using everyday events to facilitate literacy learning are limited to a case study or two (e.g., Heath with Thomas, 1984). Anderson and Stokes' (1984) data on the frequency of literacy events in all homes point to a potentially rich resource for facilitating at-risk youngsters' literacy development.

Child Activities

All of literacy is not acquired through interactions with adults. Opportunities for children to use language in play, look at books, or to write by themselves or with peers are necessary for literacy acquisition. According to Vygotsky (1978), even the symbolic play that preschoolers engage in contributes to language and literacy development. Symbolic play and reading lessons both involve talking about words and using words to represent meaning. In a game of "family," children are using "linguistic verbs" when one says to the other, "You're the Mommy. 'You say, I'm home from work,'" and the other child replies, "O.K. You say the Daddy part, 'I watched television all day.'" In an examination of this theory, Pellegrini, Galda, Dresden, and Cox (1991) found that, indeed, heavier use of linguistic verbs in symbolic play as preschoolers predicted early reading performance and the writing of words as well. However, although solitary activities and play with peers contribute, the initial scaffolding and modeling of literacy occurs in interaction with adults.

Even though parents may not be immediately present when children scribble on chalkboards or leaf through books, they influence children's literacy development by providing them with toys and materials. Each year brings more sophisticated literacy-related toys such as dolls and stuffed animals with audiotapes that "read" to children. Voice synthesizers on computers provide another form of experience in that children's "invented spellings" can be read. Data are available on "Writing to Read", IBM's program for kindergarten and first-grade children, in school settings (Slavin, 1990). While results on children's reading are equivocal, children engaged in "Writing to Read" write more and better than peers in classrooms without the program, a result that may be explained by the lack of equivalent writing experiences in many of the comparison groups. Establishing the role of computers in preschool children's literacy development is also complicated by the high likelihood that access to computers is only one of many literacy experiences. With earlier generations, simple literacy props like paper and pencils, chalkboards, and books were more available in the homes of children who became early readers as compared to their nonreading peers who were matched on characteristics like socioeconomic status and intelligence (Durkin, 1966).

The routines that parents establish with materials are as important as the presence of the materials. Many of the children who were found to be avid readers lived in homes where parents had designated a time for reading, often just before bedtime (Fielding, Wilson, & Anderson, 1986). Studies of viewing "Sesame Street" consistently established that interaction with adults about show content enhanced children's learning (Bogatz & Ball, 1971).

Parents influence children's literacy development in another way, even though they are not immediately present—by their selection of preschools. As the following discussion of literacy experiences in preschools suggests, the likelihood of receiving frequent and supportive emergent literacy experiences in preschool or daycare settings are greater for children who already have rich literacy experiences at home than for children who do not (Schieffelin & Cochran-Smith, 1984).

School Instruction and Emergent Literacy

The agenda for literacy learning becomes quite explicit once children enter school. The laissez-faire approach to literacy acquisition that has been quite effective in homes is supplanted by formal reading programs in school, which are dictated by reading curricula of districts and states, commercial reading programs, and legislative mandates. Changes from home to school are inevitable, considering the adult to child ratio and the mandate of schools to teach children to read. In examining transitions across literacy contexts, Clay (1991) has questioned the continuity of literacy experiences from home to school. The issue of discontinuity becomes an urgent one as literacy instruction begins at earlier ages. Whereas in the 1960s and even 1970s reading instruction began in first grade, most children now receive formal reading instruction in kindergarten. For many children, this initiation into reading instruction is occurring in preschools and daycare centers, a phenomenon that Gallagher and Sigel (1987) have described as "hot-housing."

Some have argued that the techniques of the home should become those of the school, as is evident in Goodman and Goodman's (1979) argument that "learning to read is natural." Although direct extrapolations of home to school techniques may pose some difficulties, at minimum it would be expected that formal reading instruction would build on children's prior literacy knowledge and literacy experiences. A review of current beginning reading instruction shows that, most typically, adaptations of literacy instruction to accommodate young children's prior literacy or literacy experiences are infrequent.

Emergent Literacy and Current Beginning Reading Instruction

Ability of emergent literacy measures to predict performances in typical reading programs. Numerous studies on emergent literacy in the last decade have prompted some to examine the ability of these measures to predict success in beginning reading instruction. Dickinson and Snow (1987) found that ability to read contextualized print showed a weak relation to other measures of early reading and writing such as phonemic awareness, print decoding, and print production. In contrast, Lomax and McGee (1987) found that concepts about print component contributed to a model of word reading acquisition.

Equivocal patterns among emergent literacy measures to school achievement have prompted some to conclude that emergent literacy measures have little, if any, contribution to beginning reading programs. Chall (1983) designates emergent literacy as Stage 0 in a construct of reading stages, outside the realm of reading instruction in school that begins with Stage 1. According to Chall (1987), the emergent literacy perspective may describe the way some children move into literacy in the home environment but may not be relevant to children who acquire literacy in school.

Counter arguments are also possible. If typical reading instruction pays no heed to the knowledge about reading and writing that children have acquired prior to school, a relationship between emergent literacy measures and achievement in traditional reading instruction would hardly be expected. Part of the explanation may also lay in the idiosyncrasies and lack of reliability data for many of the emergent literacy measures (Scott, Hiebert, & Anderson, 1988).

Analyses of current beginning reading instruction. The great debate that Chall (1967/1983) described had to do with the role of phonics and whole word instruction in beginning reading instruction, but the reading readiness phase, which has preceded formal reading instruction since the 1920s when the term "reading readiness" was first used (NSSE, 1925), has inspired little debate. The reading readiness perspective is based on the premise that there is an ideal point at which a proficiency such as reading is acquired. Until that happens, children are engaged in readiness activities that provide them with prerequisites such as discrimination of letters, sounds, shapes, and colors and letter naming. These ideas were based on the Gesellian psychology of the 1920s and 1930s and have remained largely unchallenged as the guiding force for children's introduction into reading. Although the age for participation in reading readiness activities has moved lower, the idea that children must master a series of prerequisites before being involved in reading activities continues to underlie reading instruction, as is evident from analyses of textbook materials and observations of classroom practices.

Despite many criticisms and calls for alternatives, textbooks continue to influence American reading instruction (Woodward, 1987). Many kindergarten teachers report use of the kindergarten and readiness components of basal reading series (Education Research Service, 1986). Consequently, Hiebert and Papierz (1990) analyzed kindergarten and readiness books of four series. Auditory discrimination (including letter-sound matching) and visual discrimination (including letter naming) together accounted for about one half of the activities in students' books across series. The remaining textbook pages were allocated to listening comprehension and a cluster of activities called readiness, which included identification of colors and shapes. Little attention was devoted to reading words and none to reading stories. When listening activities involved a story, the stories came from the teacher's manual and consisted of dense print and no pictures. Unlike typical storybook reading episodes, children are unable to follow along with the print or use pictures to gain an insight into the story.

Descriptions of kindergarten classrooms replicate these patterns in textbooks. In observations of 42 kindergarten classrooms, Durkin (1987a) found that 25% of the class day was devoted to academic activities. Almost 90% of the "academic" activities was related to reading, and at least half of these activities (and even more, if activities like alphabetical order, spelling, and handwriting are added) involved letter naming and letter-sound matching. Even though a substantial number of children entering kindergarten may have mastered this traditional curriculum of naming letters and matching letters and sounds (Hiebert & Sawyer, 1984), few of the kindergarten teachers in Durkin's project assessed children on these specific tasks of the curriculum, leaving assessment to general readiness tests such as the Metropolitan Readiness Test (Durkin, 1987b).

In many contexts, young children's abilities seem to be viewed from the perspective of a set of prerequisites, gained through logical analyses of the reading task rather than summaries of young children's emergent literacy. This pattern is similar to Kagan's (1990) observation that school readiness is viewed as residing in children and is their responsibility, rather than being something that schools accommodate and even create.

Literacy experiences in preschools and daycare centers have been documented even less than the limited descriptions of kindergarten programs. The few available indications suggest that the daycare or preschool programs for the majority of children mirror the experiences of typical kindergartens. A preliminary study of three preschool institutions (university laboratory school, a cooperative nursery school, and a daycare franchise) by Hiebert, Stacy, & Jordan (1985), and a second study of two preschools (university-related school and daycare franchise) in another site by Papierz, Hiebert, and DiStefano (1990) found that children in the university-related schools were more likely to receive experiences similar to those in homes that facilitate literacy. In the university-related preschools, teachers read books to children, drew children's attention to labels around the classrooms (such as children's names on cubbies), and encouraged children to dictate or write (e.g., titles and labels for their artwork). For the children in the daycare franchises, experiences were quite different. Even 3- and 4-year-olds received phonics and letter naming instruction that resembled rather closely the instruction in readiness and kindergarten books of basal reading series. During one observation period of a 3-year-old class, children needed to copy the letter *B* on a sheet of paper and to identify pictures that began with /b/. Children had to successfully complete the worksheets before they could go to the play corner.

These two descriptions of literacy in preschools and daycares were limited in scope (since there are many contexts in which preschool children spend their time) and duration. Even so, these findings are provocative in suggesting that the very children with limited literacy experiences at home, such as those in daycare franchises, may be experiencing developmentally inappropriate reading experiences at early ages. In theoretically sound preschool programs, such as ones described by Schweinhart and Weikart (1988) and Rowe (1989), a premium is placed on language development and literacy as part of various activities such as dress-up, painting, storytime, and even snacktime. The university-related preschools and the cooperative nursery school followed that route but many more children spend their days in settings like the daycare franchises.

Implementations of Emergent Literacy Programs

While researchers of emergent literacy spent considerable time during the late 1970s and early 1980s describing children's development of various forms and functions of literacy, a more recent emphasis has been on working with teachers in implementing instruction compatible with the emergent literacy perspective. Two types of programs can be distinguished — those that work to transform entire classrooms and those that provide intensive interventions for children whom schools have frequently failed.

Efforts at transforming the practices of entire classrooms have taken one of two directions. The first is to implement a comprehensive program (Martinez, Cheyney, McBroom, Hemmeter, & Teale, 1989; Schickedanz, 1986; Taylor, Blum, & Logsdon, 1986). Martinez et al. describe Kindergarten Emergent Literacy Program (KELP) where teachers work with university-based educators on two clusters of activities — reading and writing. Both components involve teacher-led and emergent, or student application activities. In reading, teacher-led activities consist primarily of repeated reading of storybooks with discussion and extensions of the literature. For example, a science lesson might be conducted around Eric Carle's (1984) *The Very Busy Spider* or a visit to the grocery store for ingredients might follow the reading of *Stone Soup* (Brown, 1947). Occasions that further emergent readings of storybooks, using Sulzby's (1985) term for young children's talk as they examine books, are frequent as well, with books that have been read by teachers readily accessible and props like flannel board figures or puppets for retelling stories. Writing is fostered through daily whole class sessions where teachers record children's dictated news or their adaptation of a pattern from a book, like "Sometimes it looked like a witch/But it wasn't a witch," modeled after *It Looked Like Split Milk* (Shaw, 1947). A writing center that children could visit daily was designed to further their emergent writing. The case studies that Martinez et al. (1989) describe confirm the movement of children from at risk to having a solid foundation in reading and writing.

A second group of researchers have concentrated on changing or increasing the amount of student time in a particular activity. The initiation of writing centers has been common (Allen & Carr, 1989; Dyson & Freedman, 1991). Other writing interventions have been more elaborate like Greene's (1985) study of a "postal" system in a classroom.

In many more projects, book reading has been at the forefront. Some of the projects have been aimed at increasing children's independent interactions with books. Morrow and Weinstein (1982) found that simply presenting books more attractively in a library center increased children's use of library books during free play. Increasing the amount of time that teachers read aloud to children reaps benefits on children's reading acquisition as well (Feitelson, Kita, & Goldstein, 1986).

Several groups of researchers have worked to establish features of effective bookreading by teachers (e.g., Green & Harker, 1982; Mason, Peterman, Powell, & Kerr, 1989; Teale & Martinez, 1991). Similar to the work on parent book reading, findings from this work have been applied in interventions. For example, in a series of studies, Mason and colleagues (Mason, McCormick, & Bhavnagri, 1986; Peterman, Dunning, Eckerty, & Mason, 1987) have worked to restructure book reading interactions, such as giving students more opportunities to ask questions or guiding teachers in using questions that elicit responses from children other than "yes" or "no." Such changes can bring about higher levels of understanding about particular stories and also about books in general.

Others have fostered student reading along with big or enlarged books (Holdaway, 1979). Bridge, Winograd, and Haley (1983) found that children's learning of sight words increased from participation with enlarged books, but that project was of limited duration and follow-through. Shared reading of enlarged books in kindergarten classrooms over a somewhat longer period of time resulted in improvement on a first-grade readiness test and an increase of placement of children in top reading groups (Brown, Cromer, & Weinberg, 1986). Similarly, Dickinson (1989) reports that a shared book experience dramatically increased Head Start children's engagement with books and print in particular.

Interventions aimed at children for whom the match to academic or school literacy is not high have also been based on the emergent literacy literature. Clay's (1985) Reading Recovery, developed in New Zealand, applied her extensive research on book reading and writing to a one-to-one tutoring context. Since its first year of United States implementation at Ohio State University in 1984, Reading Recovery has proliferated. Forty-three of the 50 states had Reading Recovery sites in the fall of 1991. At the Ohio State site, reading levels of children who receive the tutoring are, from all indications, very high, with students maintaining their proficiency into at least fourth-grade (Pinnell, 1989). Although in some sites like New York City success rates may be somewhat lower than the 93% and above that was reported in Ohio State (Smith-Burke, 1991), Madden and Slavin's

(1989) conclusion that Reading Recovery to date is the best treatment seems to hold true.

The tutoring model has also been translated into different contexts. For instance, Juel's (1991b) adaptation uses university athletes with literacy problems as tutors for first- and second-grade at-risk students. Slavin's Success for All (Slavin, Madden, Karweit, Livermon, & Dolan, 1990) uses the tutoring model but as part of the entire restructuring of primary reading instruction. Work done over a 4-year period in seven schools shows that Success for All (Slavin, Madden, Karweit, Dolan, & Wasik, 1992) students read far better than matched control students, although effects for comprehension appear not to be as strong as those for decoding. Effects are particularly large for those students who were in the lowest 25% of their classes on the pretest. Slavin et al. (1992) also report that schools with full implementation of the project have reduced retentions to near zero and have cut special education placements in half.

Although the success of Reading Recovery is clear, the ability of a tutoring model to solve all literacy problems in many districts can be raised. Success for All provides an alternative model for transforming entire schools but there is also a need to consider how some fundamental instructional structures in classrooms and Chapter 1 settings can be restructured to provide better literacy instruction. One such structure is the small group, which has often been equated with ability grouping. Reviews have criticized long-term ability grouping, leading to a current misinterpretation among teachers that all small group instruction should be abandoned in favor of individual conferencing or whole class lessons. Hiebert et al. (1991) worked with Chapter 1 teachers in redesigning their small group instruction. Results of a year-long project where Chapter 1 teachers worked with small groups of first-grade children for 15-week periods showed that two thirds of the children in the intervention had become successful readers, as measured by an informal reading inventory and by the standardized test that the district used to determine Chapter 1 eligibility. By contrast, 12% of the children in the nonparticipating Chapter 1 classrooms had attained similar levels.

Taylor, Frye, Short, and Shearer (1990) have worked with first-grade teachers to provide 15 or 20 minutes a day of supplemental reading instruction to a group of the six or seven lowest achieving students in their classrooms. Students also read individually to a trained aide for about 5 minutes a day. This project has demonstrated a high level of success. In one site, 73% of the children in the treatment were reading a first-grade text or higher at the end of first grade, whereas 20% of the control children were reading at that level.

The last 5 years have seen much activity in transforming early childhood experiences under the aegis of emergent literacy or the broader term often used for constructivist pedagogy in literacy—whole language. Although available evidence shows that whole language classrooms provide more opportunities for higher level cognitive processing and student participation than skill-oriented classrooms (Fisher & Hiebert, 1990), the breadth of these changes are unclear. Projects have proliferated. The degree to which they have impacted the majority of classrooms remains a question for further study.

Issues Related to Implementing Findings From Emergent Literacy Research in School Settings

The construct of emergent literacy derives primarily from research on young children's development in naturalistic settings. The call for applications of this research to school settings assumes that learning in educational settings matches development in naturalistic settings. Basing educational models on developmental theories poses problems (Resnick, 1981). Fein and Schwartz (1982) describe the difference between theories of development and of education in the following manner. Theories of development consider the normal course of growth and change within an environment; educational theories deal with practice related to particular individuals in particular settings aimed at maximizing the benefits of deliberate interventions. Developmental theory views change in the individual as a function of multiple influences, whereas educational theory looks essentially at the influence of practice on individuals. One type of theory can inform the other but one cannot be derived totally from the other.

The contributions of a theory of development, such as the emergent literacy construct, can inform educators in a number of ways. For example, developmental theory provides information on the ways in which young children act on the world, which guides the kinds of educational activities appropriately used in early childhood settings. However, to suggest the extrapolation of research from home to school, as many in the emergent literacy field have done, disregards some critical issues that are discussed next.

The Nature of Knowledge

Chall's (1987) critique of emergent literacy research raises an unanswered question about emergent literacy research: Does knowledge acquisition take a different course in a naturalistic setting such as the home than in a structured setting such as the school? This question particularly deserves attention in light of researchers' claims of developmental progressions or stage constructs in several facets of emergent literacy (e.g., Ferreiro & Teberosky, 1982). These progressions have been based on research done primarily with middle-class children. Children who come to school without this knowledge, it has been suggested (Temple, Nathan, Burris, & Temple, 1988), should have experiences that enhance movement through these stages. There is absolutely no empirical proof, however, that 5- and 6-year-olds who have not passed through stages of drawing, scribbling, and invented spelling need to simulate the learning experiences and progression of 3- and 4-year-olds. The development of young children in their home environments may be somewhat haphazard. Even though some 6-year-olds may not be very knowledgeable about written language, they may have ways of acting on the world that are more sophisticated than those of 3-year-olds.

A shortcoming of the emergent literacy research to date is that researchers have failed to document the mechanisms for and nature of movement from emergent literacy to literacy, as commonly recognized by adults. Although a child's pretend reading of a story reflects knowledge of story structure and the tenor of written language, this production is a far cry from reading precisely what is on the page. Even those children who have been read to frequently at home generally do not become adept at decontextualized word identification (i.e., reading what is on the page) prior to formal reading instruction. Ehri and Wilce (1984) suggest that learning to read may require acquisition of prerequisite skills such as phonemic awareness that are not spontaneously learned by most preschoolers. Whether this is indeed so remains uncertain because researchers of emergent literacy have tended to ignore issues related to more formal word identification, claiming that this knowledge will naturally develop in school settings as in homes (Goodman, 1986). The frequent dismissal of measures that have been verified in study after study as characterizing effective beginning readers such as phonemic awareness needs to be rectified in the emergent literacy field. As Teale (1987) notes, issues related to word-level strategies have often been swept under the rug in deference to storybook reading or invented spelling — a reaction to the exclusive concentration on letter naming and letter-sound correspondence training in traditional reading readiness and beginning reading instruction. For emergent literacy programs to prove their worth to teachers and policy-makers, the ways in which word identification strategies develop through emergent literacy techniques require verification (Scott et al., 1988). What is especially needed are descriptions of the progressions followed by children coming to school from literacy-rich environments as well as children with few preschool literacy experiences.

Mechanisms of Learning

Calls for educational practice based on the developmental perspective of emergent literacy also disregard discrepancies in the educational environments of home and school. The presence of a teacher, mandated by society to "teach" children, makes the environment of the school much different than that of the home. Differences in goals and mandates are exacerbated by very different adult to child mandates and contexts. Advice such as providing relevant information about letters and sounds to children when they have questions about them (Goodman, 1986) may work when a parent interacts intimately with a child at home. How one teacher adheres to this advice when he or she is confronted with 30 or more youngsters, all of them presumably at different places in their reading acquisition, is not at all certain.

Teachers' beliefs about reading instruction have probably as strong a role in predicting children's early reading experiences as parents' beliefs. In Taylor et al.'s (1986) intervention, only half of the teachers fully implemented the instructional treatment. This occurred even in the face of a careful training program and participation by only volunteer teachers. Unfortunately, teachers were not interviewed in Taylor et al.'s (1986) study so their verbalized reasons for implementing or not implementing the treatment remain unclear. However, Taylor et al.'s findings are hardly surprising when viewed from the perspective of research on teachers' beliefs about beginning reading instruction. A survey by the Education Research Service (1986) shows that most kindergarten teachers are opposed to teaching reading but not opposed to teaching readiness. Teachers associate learning of words and reading in books as "reading," whereas "readiness" is defined as learning letters and letter-sound correspondences. Interestingly, of the teachers in Taylor et al.'s (1986) study who did not implement the treatment, over half were found to be using the emergent literacy activities more in the year following the study than during the treatment period. As the adage goes, things take time.

The characteristics of parent-child interaction, especially around storybook reading, are frequently cited as the model for instruction of reading in school (Mason & Allen, 1987). Large-scale or long-term implementations beyond a several-occasion intervention have not been reported, and so numerous questions about parent-child storybook reading as the model for classroom literacy acquisition remain. For example, shared reading of big books can involve a large group of children with text to a greater extent than occurs in the typical storybook reading where the teacher reads from a regular sized book. However, a shared book experience with even 10 children (much less than the 25 or 30 children in many kindergarten classes) cannot accommodate even some of the questions of some children in the group. This situation is very different than the one-to-one interaction of parent-child storybook reading, where a child asks questions freely and has the undivided attention of an adult in answering and asking questions. Whether listening to the interaction of teacher and peers is as effective as asking one's own questions and having these answered remains uncertain, although research on children's learning from turns in a reading group suggests that one learns most during one's own turn (Anderson, Mason, & Shirey, 1984-1985).

In the home environment, the middle-class preschool child engages in independent interactions with literacy as well as parent-child storybook reading. School is characterized by time for independent interactions, frequently called "seatwork." Whether the independent times of school can be restructured to emulate the independent experiences of children at home is unclear. In middle-class homes, preschool children frequently accumulate countless hours scribbling on chalkboards and leafing through books. Can the years of scribbling on chalkboards, magic slates, and writing with preformed letters be simulated in the classroom? Can computers with voice synthesizers provide such experiences and accomplish in a short time what happens in the home environment over an extended period of exploration? It makes good sense that writing a message and hearing that message immediately would foster a sense of the relationship between the written message and speech, but the research evidence backing up this idea is lacking at this point.

Efforts to apply emergent literacy research in classroom settings must be tempered with the realization that the routes followed by children differ. McCormick and Mason (1989) in reporting their "little book" treatment and Slavin et al. (1992) in describing the results of their intervention, noted that children with low literacy performances on entering the program benefitted most from the treatment. Studies need to take into account the entry level of children as the effects of different treatments are examined. Such a comment does not imply that children who have had less literacy experiences should be deprived of book reading and writing occasions, which has frequently been the response to some groups of children in the past (Moll, Estrada, Diaz, & Lopes, 1980), nor should the "nonsolutions" of retention or ability grouping (Shepard, 1991) be the response. Immersion in classroom events with intensive support such as that described by Clay (1985) requires careful design in contexts where large numbers of children depend on schools to become literate.

Conclusion

The emergent literacy perspective has brought fresh insights into understanding the nature and extent of young children's literacy learning. Many young children have a rather extensive repertoire of concepts and strategies about literacy, even though they are not formally reading. There can be little dispute that children's existing knowledge should become the basis for teaching children to read in school. Examinations of the instruction in the school setting, even at preschool level, indicate that current instructional programs are not taking this knowledge into account. The curriculum and instructional modes of early childhood programs have been modeled on the elementary school rather than the home. Research on children's learning in the home shows that the means whereby children acquire emergent literacy differ dramatically from the instructional tasks of school. Some have suggested that the home be used as the model for school instruction (Silvern, 1988). Homes and schools do not match perfectly on goals and contexts, which makes extrapolations from home to school learning difficult. Existing research on classroom applications of the emergent literacy research show, however, that the match can be made more advantageous to children's learning. A substantial research effort has gone into describing the domain of emergent literacy and the ways in which this knowledge is acquired. A similar effort on instructional applications in preschools and kindergartens is needed if young children's existing knowledge and ways of learning are to become the basis for lifelong literacy.

References

Adams, M. (1990). *Beginning to read: Thinking and learning about print.* Cambridge, MA: M.I.T. Press.

Allen, J., & Carr, E. (1989). Collaborative learning among kindergarten writers: James learns how to write at school. In J. Allen & J.M. Mason (Eds.), *Risk makers, risk takers, risk breakers: Reducing the risks for young literacy learners* (pp. 30-47). Portsmouth, NH: Heinemann.

Anderson, A.A., & Stokes, S.J. (1984). Social and institutional influences on the development and practice of literacy. In H. Goelman, A. Oberg, & F. Smith (Eds.), *Awakening to literacy* (pp. 24-37). Portsmouth, NH: Heinemann Educational Books.

Anderson, R.C., Mason, J., & Shirey, L. (1984-85). The reading group: An experimental investigation of a labyrinth. *Reading Research Quarterly, 20,* 6-38.

Bissex, G.L. (1980). *Gnys at wrk: A child learns to write and read.* Cambridge, MA: Harvard University Press.

Bogatz, G.A., & Ball, S. (1971). *The second year of "Sesame Street": A continuing evaluation.* Princeton, NJ: Educational Testing Service.

Bridge, C.A., Winograd, P.N., & Haley, D. (1983). Using predictable materials vs. preprimers to teach beginning sight words. *Reading Teacher, 36,* 884-891.

Brown, M. (1947). *Stone soup.* New York: Scribners.

Brown, M.H., Cromer, P.S., & Weinberg, S.H. (1986). Shared book experiences in kindergarten: Helping children come to literacy. *Early Childhood Research Quarterly, 1,* 397-406.

Brzeinski, J.E. (1964). Beginning reading in Denver. *The Reading Teacher, 18,* 16-21.

Carle, E. (1984). *The very busy spider.* New York: Scholastic Books.

Chall, J.S. (1982). *Learning to read: The great debate* (2nd ed.). New York: McGraw-Hill.

Chall, J.S. (1983). *Stages of reading development.* New York: McGraw-Hill.

Chall, J.S. (1987). The "new" literacy: From infancy to high technology [Reviews of *Toward a new understanding of literacy* and *Emergent literacy: Writing and reading*]. *Contemporary Psychology.*

Clay, M.M. (1985). *Early detection of reading difficulty* (3rd ed.). Portsmouth, NH: Heinemann.

Clay, M.M. (1991). *Becoming literate: The construction of inner control.* Portsmouth, NH: Heinemann.

Daily Camera (August 26, 1987). The first day of school. Boulder, CO.

Dickinson, D.K. (1989). Effects of a shared reading program on one Head Start language and literacy environment. In J. Allen & J.M. Mason (Eds.), *Risk makers, risk takers, risk breaks: Reducing the risks for young literacy learners* (pp. 125-153). Portsmouth, NH: Heinemann Educational Books.

Dickinson, D.K., & Snow, C.E. (1987). Interrelationships among prereading and oral language skills in kindergartners from two social classes. *Early Childhood Research Quarterly, 2,* 1-25.

Dunn, N.E. (1981). Children's achievement at school-entry age as a function of mothers' and fathers' teaching sets. *Elementary School Journal, 81,* 245-253.

Durkin, D. (1966). *Children who read early.* New York: Teachers College Press.

Durkin, D. (1987a). A classroom-observation study of reading instruction in kindergarten. *Early Childhood Research Quarterly, 2,* 275-300.

Durkin, D. (1987b). Testing the kindergarten. *The Reading Teacher, 40,* 766-770.

Dyson, A.H., & Freedman, S.W. (1991). Writing. In J. Flood, J.M. Jensen, D. Lapp, & J.R. Squire (Eds.), *Handbook of research on teaching the English language arts* (pp. 754-774). New York: Macmillan.

Education Research Service (1986). *Kindergarten programs and practices in public schools.* Arlington, VA: Educational Research Service.

Edwards, P.A. (1991). Fostering early literacy through parent coaching. In E.H. Hiebert (Ed.), *Literacy for a diverse society: Perspectives, practices, and policies* (pp. 199-213). New York: Teachers College Press.

Ehri, L., & Wilce, L. (1984). Movement into reading: Is the first stage of printed word learning visual or phonetic? *Reading Research Quarterly, 20,* 163-179.

Fein, G., & Schwartz, P.M. (1982). Developmental theories in early childhood education. In B. Spodek (Ed.), *Handbook of research in early childhood education* (pp. 82-104). New York: Free Press.

Feitelson, D., & Goldstein, Z. (1986). Patterns of book ownership and reading to young children in Israeli school-oriented and non-school-oriented families. *Reading Teacher, 39,* 924-930.

Feitelson, D., Kita, B., and Goldstein, Z. (1986). Effects of listening to series stories on first graders' comprehension and use of language. *Research in the Teaching of English, 20,* 339-356.

Ferreiro, E., & Teberosky, A. (1982). *Literacy before schooling.* Portsmouth, NH: Heinemann Educational Books.

Fielding, L.G., Wilson, P.T., & Anderson, R.C. (1986). A new focus on free reading: The role of trade books in reading instruction. In T. Raphael (Ed.), *Contexts of school-based literacy* (pp. 149-162). New York: Longman.

Fisher, C.W., & Hiebert, E.H. (1990). Characteristics of tasks in two approaches to literacy instruction. *Elementary School Journal, 91,* 6-13.

Flood, J. (1977). Parental styles in reading episodes with young children. *The Reading Teacher, 31,* 864-867.

Fowler, W. (1981). Case studies of cognitive precocity: The role of exogenous and endogenous stimulation in early mental development. *Journal of Applied Developmental Psychology, 2,* 319-367.

Gallagher, J.M., & Sigel, I.E. (1987). Introduction to special issue: Hothousing of young children. *Early Childhood Research Quarterly, 2,* 201-202.

Goodman, K. (1986). *What's whole in whole language?* Portsmouth, NH: Heinemann.

Goodman, K.S., & Goodman, Y.M. (1979). Learning to read is natural. In L.B. Resnick & P. Weaver (Eds.), *Theory and practice of early reading* (pp. 137-154). Hillsdale, NJ: Erlbaum.

Gough, P., & Hillinger, M.L. (1980). Learning to read: An unnatural act. *Bulletin of the Orton Society, 30,* 179-196.

Green, J.L., & Harker, J. (1982). Reading to children: A communicative process. In J.A. Langer & M.T. Smith-Burke (Eds.), *Reader meets author/Bridging the gap: A psycholinguistic and sociolinguistic perspective* (pp. 196-221). Newark, DE: IRA.

Greene, J. (1985). Children's writing in an elementary school postal system. In M. Farr (Ed.), *Advances in writing research*: Vol 1. *Children's early writing development* (pp. 201-296). Norwood, NJ: Ablex.

Heath, S.B. (1982). What no bedtime story means: Narrative skills at home and school. *Language in Society, 11*, 49-76.

Heath, S.B. (1983). *Ways with words: Language, life and work in communities and classrooms*. Cambridge: Cambridge University Press.

Heath, S.B., with Thomas, C. (1984). The achievement of preschool literacy for mother and child. In H. Goelman, A. Oberg, & F. Smith (Eds.), *Awakening to literacy*. Portsmouth, NH: Heinemann.

Hess, R., Holloway, S., Price, G., & Dickson, W. (1982). Family environments and the acquisition of reading skills. In L. Laosa & I. Sigel (Eds.), *Families as learning environments for children*. New York: Plenum Press.

Hiebert, E.H. (1980). The relationship of logical reasoning ability, oral language comprehension, and home experiences to preschool children's print awareness. *Journal of Reading Behavior, 12*, 313-324.

Hiebert, E.H., & Adams, C.S. (1987). Fathers' and mothers' perceptions of their preschool children's emergent literacy. *Journal of Experimental Child Psychology, 44*, 25-37.

Hiebert, E.H., Colt, J.M., Catto, S., & Gury, E. (1991, December). *The impact of consistent, authentic literacy experiences on Chapter 1 students' literacy.* Paper presented at the annual meeting of the National Reading Conference, Palm Springs, CA.

Hiebert, E.H., & Papierz, J. (1990). The content of kindergarten and readiness books in four basal reading programs. *Early Childhood Research Quarterly, 5*, 317-334.

Hiebert, E.H., & Sawyer, C.C. (1984, April). *Young children's concurrent abilities in reading and spelling.* Paper presented at the annual meeting of the American Educational Research Association, New Orleans.

Hiebert, E.H., Stacy, B., & Jordan, L. (1985). *An analysis of literacy experiences in preschool settings.* Unpublished manuscript, University of Kentucky, Lexington, KY.

Holdaway, D. (1979). *The foundations of literacy*. Sydney: Ashton Scholastic.

Huey, E.B. (1968). *The psychology and pedagogy of reading*. Cambridge, MA: M.I.T. Press. (Original work published 1909)

Juel, C. (1991a). Beginning reading. In R. Barr, M.L. Kamil, P.B. Mosenthal, & P.D. Pearson (Eds.), *Handbook of reading research* (Vol. 2, pp. 759-788). New York: Longman.

Juel, C. (1991b). Cross-age tutoring between student-athletes and at-risk children. *Reading Teacher, 45*, 178-186.

Kagan, S.L. (1990). Readiness 2000: Rethinking rhetoric and responsibility. *Phi Delta Kappan, 72*, 272-279.

Lomax, R.G., & McGee, L.M. (1987). Young children's concepts about print and reading: Toward a model of word reading acquisition. *Reading Research Quarterly, 22,* 237-256.

Madden, N.A., & Slavin, R.E. (1989). Effective pullout programs for students at risk. In R.E. Slavin, N.L. Karweit, & N.A. Madden (Eds.), *Effective programs for students at risk* (pp. 52-72). Boston: Allyn & Bacon.

Martinez, M.G., Cheyney, M., McBroom, C., Hemmeter, A., & Teale, W.H. (1989). No-risk kindergarten literacy environments for at-risk children. In J. Allen & J.M. Mason (Eds.), *Risk makers, risk takers, risk breakers: Reducing the risks for young literacy learners* (pp. 93-124). Portsmouth, NH: Heinemann.

Mason, J.M., & Allen, J. (1987). A review of emergent literacy with implications for research and practice in reading. In E.Z. Rothkopf (Ed.), *Review of research in education* (Vol. 13, pp. 3-47). Washington, DC: American Educational Research Association.

Mason, J.M., McCormick, C., & Bhavnagri, N. (1986). How are you going to help me learn? Lesson negotiations between a teacher and preschool children. In D. Yaden & S. Templeton (Eds.), *Metalinguistic awareness and beginning literacy: Conceptualizing what it means to read and write* (pp. 159-172). Portsmouth,NH: Heinemann.

Mason, J.M., Peterman, C.L., Powell, B.M., & Kerr, B.M. (1989). Reading and writing attempts by kindergartners after book reading by teachers. In J.M. Mason (Ed.), *Reading and writing connections* (pp. 105-120). Needham Heights, MA: Allyn & Bacon.

Masonheimer, P.E., Drum, P.A., & Ehri, L.C. (1984). Does environmental print identification lead children into word reading? *Journal of Reading Behavior, 14,* 257-271.

McCormick, C.E., & Mason, J.M. (1989). Fostering reading for Head Start children with little books. In J. Allen & J.M. Mason (Eds.), *Risk makers, risk takers, risk breakers: Reducing the risks for young literacy learners* (pp. 125-153). Portsmouth, NH: Heinemann Educational Books.

Miller, P., Nemoianu, A., & DeJong, J. (1986). Early reading at home: Its practice and meanings in a working class community. In B. Schieffelin & P. Gilmore (Eds.), *The acquisition of literacy: Ethnographic perspectives* (pp. 3-15). Norwood, NJ: Ablex.

Moll, L.C., Estrada, E., Diaz, E., & Lopes, L.M. (1980). The organization of bilingual lessons: Implications for schooling. *The Quarterly Newsletter of the Laboratory of Comparative Human Cognition, 2,* 53-58.

Morrow, L.M., & Weinstein, C.S. (1982). Increasing the children's use of literature through program and physical design changes. *Elementary School Journal, 83,* 131-137.

National Society for the Study of Education (1925). *Report of the National Committee on Reading: 24th yearbook of the National Society for the Study of Education.* Bloomington, IN: Public School Publishing.

Ninio, A., & Bruner, J. (1978). The achievement and antecedents of labelling. *Journal of Child Language, 5,* 5-15.

Olson, D.R. (1984). "See! Jumping!" Some oral language antecedents of literacy. In H. Goelman, A.A. Oberg, & F. Smith (Eds.), *Awakening to literacy.* Portsmouth, NH: Heinemann Educational Books.

Papierz, J.M., Hiebert, E.H., & DiStefano, D.D. (1990, December). *Literacy experiences of preschool children.* Paper presented at the annual meeting of the National Reading Conference, Miami, FL.

Pellegrini, A.D., Golda, L., Dresden, J., & Cox, S. (1991). A longitudinal study of the predictive relations among symbolic play, linguistic verbs, and early literacy. Research in the Teaching of English, 25, 219-235.

Pellegrini, A.D., Perlmutter, J.C., Galda, L., & Brophy, G.H. (1990). Joint book reading between black Head Start children and their mothers. *Child Development, 61,* 443-453.

Peterman, C.L., Dunning, D., Eckerty, C., & Mason, J.M. (1987, April). *The effects of story reading procedures collaboratively designed by teacher and researcher on kindergartners' literacy learning.* Paper presented at the annual meeting of the American Educational Research Association, Washington, DC.

Pinnell, G.S. (1989). Reading Recovery: Helping at-risk children learn to read. *The Elementary School Journal, 90,* 161-183.

Resnick, L.B. (1981). Social assumptions as a context for science: Some reflections on psychology and education. *Educational Psychologist, 16,* 1-10.

Rowe, D.W. (1989). Author/audience interaction in the preschool: The role of social interaction in literacy learning. *Journal of Reading Behavior, 21,* 311-347.

Sakamoto, T. (1976). Writing systems in Japan. In J. Merritt (Ed.), *New horizons in reading.* Newark, DE: International Reading Association.

Schickedanz, J.A. (1986). *More than the ABCs.* Washington, DC: National Association for the Education of Young Children.

Schieffelin, B.B., & Cochran-Smith, M. (1984). Learning to read culturally: Literacy before schooling. In H. Goelman, A.A. Oberg, & F. Smith (Eds.), *Awakening to literacy* (pp. 3-23). Portsmouth, NH: Heinemann Educational Books.

Schweinhart, L.J., & Weikart, D.P. (1988). Early childhood education for children living in poverty: Child-initiated learning or teacher-directed instruction? *Elementary School Journal, 89,* 213-225.

Scott, J.A., Hiebert, E.H., & Anderson, R.C. (1988). *From present to future: Beyond becoming a nation of readers* (Technical Report 443). Champaign-Urbana, IL: Center for the Study of Reading.

Shanahan, T., & Hogan, V. (1983). Parent reading style and children's print awareness. In J.A. Niles & L.A. Harris (Eds.), *Searches for meaning in reading/language processing and instruction* (pp. 212-218). Rochester, NY: National Reading Conference.

Shaw, C.G. (1947). *It looked like split milk.* New York: Harper & Row.

Shepard, L.A. (1991). Negative policies for dealing with diversity: When does assessment and diagnosis turn into sorting and segregation? In E.H. Hiebert (Ed.), *Literacy for a diverse society: Perspectives, practices, and policies* (pp. 279-298). New York: Teachers College Press.

Silvern, S.B. (1988). Continuity/discontinuity between home and early childhood environments. *Elementary School Journal, 89,* 147-160.

Slavin, R.E. (1990). IBM's Writing to Read: Is it right for reading? *Phi Delta Kappan, 72,* 214-16.

Slavin, R.E., Madden, N.A., Karweit, N.L., Dolan, L.J., & Wasik, B.A. (1992, April). *Success for all: Getting reading right the first time.* Paper presented at the annual meeting of the American Educational Research Association, San Francisco.

Slavin, R.E., Madden, N.A., Karweit, N.L., Livermon, B.J., & Dolan, L. (1990). Success for all: First-year outcomes of a comprehensive plan for reforming urban education. *American Educational Research Journal, 27,* 255-278.

Smith-Burke, T. (1991, December). *Meeting the needs of young at-risk children in urban schools.* Paper presented at the annual meeting of the National Reading Conference, Palm Springs, CA.

Sulzby, E. (1985). Children's emergent reading of favorite storybooks: A developmental study. *Reading Research Quarterly, 20,* 458-481.

Sulzby, E., & Teale, W.H. (1991). Emergent literacy. In R. Barr, M.L. Kamil, P. Mosenthal, & P.D. Pearson (Eds.), *Handbook of reading research* (Vol. 2, pp. 727-757). New York: Longman.

Taylor, B.M., Frye, B.J., Short, R., & Shearer, B. (1990). *Early intervention in reading: Preventing reading failure among low-achieving first-grade students.* Unpublished paper, University of Minnesota, Minneapolis, MN.

Taylor, D. (1983). *Family literacy: Young children learning to read and write.* Exeter, NH: Heinemann.

Taylor, D., & Dorsey-Gaines, C. (1988). *Growing up literate: Learning from inner-city families.* Portsmouth, NH: Heinemann.

Taylor, N., Blum, I.H., & Logsdon, D.M. (1986). The development of written language awareness: Environmental aspects and program characteristics. *Reading Research Quarterly, 21,* 131-149.

Teale, W.H. (1984). Reading to young children: Its significance for literacy development. In H. Goelman, A. Oberg, & F. Smith (Eds.), *Awakening to literacy* (pp. 110-121). Portsmouth, NH: Heinemann Educational Books.

Teale, W.H. (1987). Emergent literacy: Reading and writing development in early childhood. In J.E. Readence & R.S. Baldwin (Eds.), *Research in literacy: Merging perspectives: 36th yearbook of the National Reading Conference* (pp. 45-74). Rochester, NY: National Reading Conference.

Teale, W.H., & Martinez, M.G. (1991). *Teacher storybook reading style: A comparison of six teachers.* San Antonio, TX: University of Texas at San Antonio.

Teale, W.H., & Sulzby, E. (Eds.). (1986). *Emergent literacy: Writing and reading.* Norwood, NJ: Ablex.

Temple, C., Nathan, R., Burris, N., & Temple, F. (1988). *The beginnings of writing* (2nd ed.). Boston: Allyn & Bacon.

Terman, L.M. (1918). *Genetic studies of genius.* Stanford: Stanford University Press.

Tobin, A.W. (1981). *A multiple discriminant cross-validation of the factors associated with the development of precocious reading achievement.* Unpublished doctoral dissertation, University of Delaware, Wilmington, DE.

Tobin, A.W., & Pikulski, J.J. (1983, April). *Parent and teacher attitudes toward early reading instruction.* Paper presented at the annual meeting of the American Educational Research Association, Montreal.

Torrey, J.W. (1969). Learning to read without a teacher: A case study. *Elementary English, 46* (550-556), 658.

Vygotsky, L.S. (1962). *Thought and language.* Cambridge, MA: M.I.T. Press.

Vygotsky, L.S. (1978). *Mind in society.* Cambridge, MA: Harvard University Press.

Wells, G. (1985). Preschool literacy-related activities and success in school. In D.R. Olson, N. Torrance, & A. Hilyard (Eds.), *Literacy, language, and learning: The nature and consequences of reading and writing* (pp. 229-255). Cambridge: Cambridge University Press.

Woodward, A. (1987, April). *From the professional teacher to activities manager: The changing role of the teacher in Reading Teachers' Guides, 1920-1985.* Paper presented at the annual meeting of the American Educational Research Association, Washington, DC.

White, K. (1982). The relation between socioeconomic status and academic achievement. *Psychological Bulletin, 91,* 461-481.

Whitehurst, G.J., Falco, F.L., Lonigan, C.J., Fischel, J.E., DeBaryshe, B.D., Valdez-Menchac, M.C., & Caulfield, M. (1988). Accelerating language development through picturebook reading. *Developmental Psychology, 24,* 552-559.

Yaden, D.B., & McGee, L.M. (1984). Reading as a meaning-seeking activity: What children's questions reveal. In J.A. Niles & L.A. Harris (Eds.), *Changing perspectives on research in reading/language processing and instruction. Thirty-third yearbook of the National Reading Conference* (pp. 101-109). Rochester, NY: National Reading Conference.

3
Acquiring and Using Literacy Skills in the Workplace

Jorie W. Philippi

The economy and the workplace are changing rapidly, accelerating the need for workers to use literacy skills as they perform job tasks. The shifts toward self-directed teamwork and emphasis on quality production that are necessary for competing in a global economy have created job tasks that employ applications of literacy skills. Job-specific literacy tasks require different applications of skills from those taught and used in academic contexts. Competent workers now must be able to use (a) job reading processes for locating information and for using higher level thinking strategies to problem solve; (b) occupational writing processes for organizing clear, readable writing and for mastering those thinking skills that enable analysis, elaboration, and extension of written ideas; and (c) workplace applications of mathematical processes for calculating information and solving problems that go beyond basic number concepts and computation skill drill and enable workers to acquire proficiency levels in reasoning and interpretation. These skill applications all require the use of cognitive strategies and are seldom used in isolation, but generally cluster in combinations related to the performance of specific job tasks. Using a functional context approach (i.e., using job materials and scenarios to provide instruction and training in such workplace literacy applications) promotes transfer of learning to improved performance on job tasks.

Acquiring and Using Literacy Skills in the Workplace

For the past 2 decades, there has been a growing awareness of the need to upgrade the basic skills of the workforce. National concern over the rapidly shrinking pool of qualified applicants for entry level jobs has focused attention on the need for job literacy training. Experts reporting on current demographics indicate a workforce that is unskilled or at a skill level too low to compete for entry or reentry level positions (Brock, 1987; Montague, 1987; Semerad, 1987). At the same time they report both the elimination of many unskilled jobs and an increase in skill level requirements for remaining positions due to technological advances and management restructuring. Changes now taking place in the workplace center around improvements in product and service quality and increased worker responsibility. Both large and small companies are requiring numerous new tasks of their employees in efforts to remain in business and to leapfrog their competition in a global economy.

Most companies attempt to make processes more efficient and profitable through: (a) shifts in responsibility such as downsizing, cross-training with accompanying certification processes, and self-directed work teams; (b) upgrades in technically sophisticated equipment, such as computer terminals, robotics and program logic controlled machinery; and (c) collection and analysis of product and service quality statistics to measure cycle time, scrap, reworked materials, consistent quality and customer satisfaction. The impetus in all of these efforts is a company's bottom line—and many businesses are "running scared." Risking survival on a new piece of equipment or a shift in management structure causes more and more companies concern as they operate with leaner staff resources and tighter timelines. Companies are increasingly uncertain of the capacity of their current workforce and of prospective new hires to master the skills necessary to accomplish these critical changes. In many cases, organizations must rely on a workforce that includes incumbent employees who ranked academically in the bottom third of high school classes to assume these responsibilities. Additionally, companies are looking for ways to improve job performance to cut costs already being incurred, due to accidents, waste, and unnecessary reworks.

Concurrently, in many parts of the United States, employers are experiencing a labor shortfall due to demographic shifts in the available pool of entry level hires. Figures from a recent educational assessment (Kirsch & Jungeblut, 1986) indicate that almost 85% of the millions of young adults in the United States possess actual literacy skills equivalent to the fourth- to eighth-grade level. This group of "intermediate literates," who may or may not be high school graduates, and who have not obtained a currently functional or *employable* level of literacy, will make up as much as 65% of those who enter the workforce over the next 15 years (Semerad, 1987). Assuming these trends continue, the predicted outcome is that by the year 2000 there will be more jobs than there are qualified workers. Less than adequately skilled workers can no longer be rejected, replaced, or rehired elsewhere. Instead, there is a need to retool new and existing workers to prepare them to function successfully, both now and in the future. An investment in workplace basic skills training by employers and workers ensures joint survival of employers and employees (Fields, 1986).

To accomplish new workplace tasks effectively and to improve current job performance, employers have begun to realize the necessity for providing workers with training in job literacy skills. Most employees also feel the need for, and often ask for a "brush up" or special training to prepare themselves to assume control of their work environment. For every job there are tasks that are critical to its performance. The varying degrees to which workers can perform these critical tasks determine their levels of job proficiency and, collectively, determine the quality of the workforce. Competent performance of job tasks requires more than knowledge of job content. Superior workers are those who are able to identify job needs and efficiently use basic skills applications (i.e., reading, writing, speaking, listening, computation, problem solving) to complete job tasks (Mikulecky, 1987). Collectively, these skill applications are known as "workplace literacy."

Impact of Academic Literacy Skills Training on Workplace Performance

Initial efforts to provide workplace basic skills training have often resulted in the relocation of adult academic remedial education programs onto the worksite. Traditionally, remedial instruction for adult learners has addressed the nonreader or marginal literate and has been job related only to the extent that reading materials thematically explored occupational career possibilities. For many years basic skills teachers have provided this type of general instruction for low achieving employees enrolled in community education or vocational/industrial training programs. It was theorized that raising the reading grade levels, general math, and writing abilities of adult learners would improve their job skills performance and opportunities for employment and promotion. Instruction focused on improving academic performance, as it is measured by standardized tests, and on assisting students in their preparation for passing the General Education Development (GED) test. In fact, increasing adult students' general basic skills levels in this way appears to build their self-confidence and to enable them to better function in a literate society, but it does not necessarily improve their performance of on-the-job literacy tasks. This is because improvement of general literacy skills with generic materials in a classroom setting does not transfer to the kinds of literacy skill applications found in the workplace.

The similarity of processing performed in instruction and in the tasks to which learning is to be transferred must be high in order to achieve subsequent retrieval and application of knowledge; if the processes are different, procedures learned in training yield no transfer, or even negative transfer (Bransford & Franks, 1976; Tulving & Thomson, 1973). In a recent study of the cognitive basis of knowledge transfer, Gick and Holyoak point out:

> Some of the most spectacular and widely decried failures of transfer—failures to apply knowledge learned in school to practical problems encountered in everyday life—may largely reflect the fact that the material taught in school is often disconnected from any clear goal and hence lacks a primary cue for retrieval in potentially relevant problem contexts. (1987, p. 31)

Observations stemming from a recent study of workplace literacy skills conducted by the National Center for Research in Adult Education (Fields, 1986) indicate that this is so. Data demonstrated the lack of skill transfer to job performance from traditional tuition reimbursement plans for employees enrolled in basic skills programs or company-sponsored GED programs. Benefits that resulted were only indirectly applicable to the companies' needs and offered little return on initial investments. When companies provided individuals or groups of employees with direct, contextual literacy skills instruction needed to perform current jobs, or as a prerequisite for the adoption of new technology, however, the programs were tied to company survival, with measurable performance results, and perceived to be mutually beneficial to employer and employees.

Research provides strong evidence that the basic skills applications employed in workplace contexts differ significantly from generic basic skills taught in academic environments (Diehl & Mikulecky, 1980; Philippi, 1988; Sticht, 1975a). For example, classroom reading is generally engaged in for the purpose of adding to the store of information in memory (reading-to-remember), wheras reading on the job often involves locating information to apply to the performance of a particular task (reading-to-do). Additionally, basic skills applications used in job contexts tend to appear as integrated clusters embedded in the performance of job tasks. Reading, writing and computation on the job are not discrete acts practiced in isolation from one another, as are the separately taught subjects traditionally found in academic settings. These ideas will be discussed in more detail in the following sections of this chapter.

Some Common Workplace Reading Skill Applications

On the job, workers spend an average of 1.5 to 2.0 hours per workday engaged in reading forms, graphs, charts, schematics, manuals and computer screens (Diehl, 1980; Mikulecky, Shanklin, & Caverly, 1979; Philippi, 1987; Rush, Moe, & Storlie, 1986; Sharon, 1973-74; Sticht, 1975b). The emphases of on-the-job reading are on locating information for immediate use and utilizing inferential processes for problem solving.

The act of reading, in which one acquires information from the printed page or screen, is primarily dependent on the background knowledge that the reader brings to the page. Understanding, or comprehension, relies on the reader's ability to make sense of what he is reading by fitting the printed information into the context of what he already knows about the topic. Without the interplay between the reader's stored prior knowledge and the new knowledge presented on the page, the printed words cannot impart meaning to the reader. Reading comprehension is a constructive process in which the reader constructs his own meaning or interpretation of what the writer is communicating. The reader must use his prior knowledge held in memory in order to succeed in the acquisition of meaning from printed materials. In the workplace, comprehension of printed job materials or computer screen displays is thus greatly dependent upon the worker's prior knowledge of his work environment and job tasks.

During workplace reading, another layer of information processing is also added: in text search applications, a type of reading-to-do that is frequently used in the workplace to locate information for immediate use, the reader must perform cognitive operations that allow him to create categories and selectively search by rapidly scanning to identify and match requested information structures (Dreher & Guthrie, 1990; Kirsch & Guthrie, 1984; Kirsch & Mosenthal, 1990). It is only by using innate language of spelling patterns (orthography), word order (syntax), word meaning (semantics), and prior knowledge of the subject retrieved from memory (schemata) that the competent reader understands and interacts with the ideas presented on the page or screen.

Job reading tasks regularly require workers to be proficient in setting purposes, defining categories, self-questioning, summarizing information, and monitoring comprehension as they read. Researchers have found that the ability to use these higher level (metacognitive) reading processes correlates with superior job performance (Mikulecky & Winchester, 1983). Specific applications of reading skills often used to perform job tasks in many occupations are listed in Figure 3.1. These applications of reading processes are very different from the goals of traditional classroom reading instruction, which is designed to teach discrete reading skills in isolation for the purpose of increasing students' ability to follow directions, to internalize content for future recall, and to respond correctly to general vocabulary and comprehension questions on standardized tests (Diehl & Mikulecky, 1980; Mikulecky, 1982; Mikulecky & Ehlinger, 1986; Sticht, 1977).

Some Common Workplace Writing Skill Applications

To be literate in the workplace is not just dependent on mastery of reading skills for locating information and making decisions. Reading is normally only one single step, or subtask, within performing the job task as a whole. The act of reading almost always results in the worker doing something with the information gained from print—writing a summary statement or memo, calculating machine specifications for recalibration, entering information onto a form or computer data base, and so on. The application of reading skills to subsequent performance of a complete job task usually involves the use of literacy skills in writing and mathematics, as well.

The applications of workplace writing skills also differ significantly from those taught in the traditional classroom. In 1980, Diehl reported that the majority of occupational writing tasks involve completing simple forms or preparing brief memoranda. A study by Mikulecky in 1982 confirms this. Mikulecky (1982) found that out of 276 writing tasks required to perform jobs listed in the *Dictionary of Occupational Titles*, 42.4% involved filling out prepared forms and 22.5% generating memoranda or letters. Another 25% of the job writing tasks required recording, summarizing, or noting work completed. Task-related writing, such as producing blueprints, accounted for yet another 11% of job writing, and only 10.5% involved writing reports or articles like those students are taught to produce in academic settings. (Because many writing tasks for work overlap, these percentages are greater than 100%.) In 1986, Rush, Moe, and Storlie reported that, other than those writing tasks performed by secretarial employees, clarity is the chief

Vocabulary:

- Recognizing common words and meanings, task-related words with technical meanings, and meanings of common abbreviations and acronyms.

Literal Comprehension:

- Identifying factual details and specifications within text, following sequential directions to complete a task, and determining the main idea of a paragraph or section.

Locating Information Within a Text:

- Using table of contents, index, appendices, glossary, systems, or subsystems.

- Locating pages, titles, paragraphs, figures, or charts needed to answer questions or solve problems.

- Skimming or scanning to determine whether or not text contains relevant information.

- Cross-referencing within and across source materials to select information to perform a routine.

- Using a completed form to locate information to complete a task.

Comparing and Contrasting:

- Combining information from multiple sources that contribute to the completion of a task.

- Selecting parts of text or visual materials to complete a task.

- Identifying similarities and differences in objects.

- Determining the presence of a defect or extent of damage.

- Classifying or matching objects by color, size, or significant marking.

- Distinguishing between relevant and irrelevant information in text or visuals.

Recognizing Cause and Effect; Predicting Outcomes:

- Using common knowledge for safety.

- Applying preventative measures prior to a task to minimize problems.

- Selecting appropriate course of action in emergency.

Using Charts, Diagrams, Schematics:

- Reading two or more column charts to obtain information.

- Locating chart information at intersections of rows and columns.

- Cross-referencing charted material with text.

- Applying information from tables or graphs to locate malfunctions or select actions.

- Using flow charts and organizational charts to sequence events, arrive at a decision, or problem solve.

- Identifying components within a schematic.

- Isolating problem components in schematics, tracing to cause of problem, and interpreting symbols.

- Identifying details, labels, numbers, parts of an illustration, parts from a key or legend.

- Following sequenced illustrations as a guide.

- Interpreting three dimensional drawings of objects for assembly or disassembly.

Inferential Comprehension:

- Determining meaning of figurative, idiomatic, or technical usage of terms, using context clues as reference.

- Making inferences from text; organizing information from multiple sources in a series; interpreting codes and symbols.

Figure 3.1. Applications of reading skills found in the workplace. Phillipi, J.W. (1988). Matching literacy to job training: Some applications from military programs. *Reading, 31,* 658-666. Copyright 1988. Reprinted by permission, United Kingdom Reading Association.

requirement of on-the-job writing. Information often must be translated to concise communication which contains only the essentials. For example, a production line operator may have to enter information into a computer problem log in 144 characters or use a specified format to send electronic mail to another department. In job training situations, too, Rush et al. (1986) found that accuracy of information is considered more important than standard English usage. The United States Department of the Army (1986) also has recently disseminated new regulations emphasizing the need for clarity and brevity in soldiers' writing, similar to the "telegraphic" style frequently used in business and industry communications.

The seemingly simplistic style workers must use to complete forms or produce brief memoranda or summaries should not be misleading as to the nature of most occupational writing tasks. Highly complex processing is required to perform such tasks successfully. To communicate effectively, whether in limited space on prepared forms, in summary statements, or in condensed, telegraphic terms, workers must employ a problem-solving process in which they activate mental schema to: (a) define their anticipated audience and purpose; (b) determine what form of communication is appropriate; (c) generate and organize ideas; (d) translate their message to a concise, accurate form; and (e) review the written product by evaluating and revising (Mikulecky, Ehlinger, & Meenan, 1987).

Recent studies of the writing process have identified a prewriting period, which may only last for as long as 1 minute, but which is a critical part of the writing process during which the writer utilizes mental strategies to activate topic background information (schemata), organize the writing task into manageable pieces, and select out relevant information for inclusion in the written product (Perl, 1979). In 1981, Graves detailed the writing process as comprising the ingredients of "topic selection, rehearsing (i.e., the conscious or unconscious preparation for writing), information access, organizing, spelling, handwriting, or keyboarding, reading, editing, and revising" (p. 6). Graves also found that experienced writers employ selectivity criteria during the prewriting period that include the mental information analysis categories of standard, process, information, experience, verification, audience, topic limitations, language, and length.

Other research findings support the writer's use of mental schema (established thinking patterns, categories, and connections built from experience and held in long-term memory) through the initial production and revision stages of the writing process as well as during prewriting (Hayes & Flower, 1980; Rumelhart, 1980; Stein & Glenn, 1979). Throughout the entire writing process, competent writers move back and forth from the abstract (high level plans) to the concrete (specific sentences and language), mentally keeping track of a variety of plans and schemata, simultaneously. (See Figure 3.2 for a list of specific workplace writing skill applications frequently used in many occupations.) As in the case of workplace reading skill applications, analysis of workplace writing skill applications goes well beyond correct grammar or standard memorandum formatting. Rather, it indicates the presence of a strong undercurrent of cognitive strategies used by competent workers.

Production:

- Writing key technical words accurately on forms.
- Spelling task-related words and abbreviations correctly.

Information Transfer (Single Step/Source):

- Entering appropriate information onto a form.
- Recording essential information that involves more than one sentence.
- Recording essential information in phrases or simple sentence form accurately and precisely.

Information Transfer (Multiple Step/Sources):

- Transferring numbers, codes, dates, figures from equipment or written sources onto appropriate sections of forms.
- Writing a report including necessary support documentation or classification.

Translation:

- Writing brief, descriptive accounts of activities or transactions performed.
- Outlining a situation by identifying key ideas and supporting details.
- Summarizing essential details for a written communication, using a problem-solving or news-writing heuristic.
- Selecting relevant details for a written communication.
- Stating general impressions of an event or situations as they relate to specific reporting goals.
- Summarizing events and precise dialogue in an accurate, complete, and objective manner.
- Summarizing the major points presented in a written communication.
- Generalizing a written communication according to a specific format (e.g., memorandum, telex, or letter).

Extension/Interpretation:

- Identifying objectives, intent, target audience, and all essential and supporting details of a written communication.
- Generating a written communication, arranging events sequentially.
- Writing brief justification for actions taken and providing good reasons for rejecting alternative action.
- Appraising a written communication and making adjustments to improve clarity.

Figure 3.2. Applications of writing skills found in the workplace. Philippi, J.W. (1989). Basic skills in the workplace. In L. Nadler & Z. Nadler (Eds.), *Handbook for human resource development* (2nd ed.). College Park, MD: J. Wiley & Sons. Copyright 1989. Reprinted by permission.

Companies commonly identify "grammar" as what they want to be taught in employee writing courses. By this they normally mean "correct writing that is clear and readable," rather than the study of scientific rules of the language. Frequently organizations classify as "bad grammar" in employee-produced writing the symptoms of vague diction, faulty punctuation, lack of clarity, lack of focus, wordiness,or lack of purpose. In fact, these common errors are directly related to the workers' inability to use the processing and organizational skills as outlined above (Anderson, 1986). To be effective, writing instruction in the workplace should not be centered around grammar exercises that treat the inaccurately labeled symptoms, but should address the cause of the problem by focusing on teaching employees the mental processes needed to perform job writing tasks correctly.

Literacy skills for the workplace involve not only reading and writing. Often, in many types of work, workers must apply mathematical competencies to accomplish job-related tasks. The next section describes some of the typical mathematic skills applications that are required in the workplace.

Some Common Workplace Mathematical Skill Applications

Although some researchers would argue that workplace literacy should limit itself to reading and writing skill applications, the nature of job performance requirements generally combines applications of reading, writing, and mathematic skills in completing one job task or subtask. Because research demonstrates that transfer of learning is dependent on a high degree of similarity between processes used in instructional tasks and in performance tasks, mathematical skills are inseparable from job tasks and should remain an integral part of any workplace literacy discussion or instructional design.

In its recent report, *Basic Skills in the U.S. Work Force*, the Center for Public Resources (CPR) points out the constant need in the business world for employees who possess skills in reasoning and calculation (Henry & Raymond, 1982). Business executives reported that medium to high levels of mathematics skills are required across job categories with consistently high levels required in the manufacturing, utilities, and finance industries. Employees must use calculation to correctly conduct inventories, complete accurate reports of production levels, measure machine parts or specifications, and so on. They must be able to reason through problems logically in order to anticipate the consequences of their actions and decrease the need for excessive supervision. Employers also viewed problem-solving abilities and knowing "how to learn" as the keys to successful retraining efforts.

Employers frequently complain that their workers are deficient in computational skills, particularly those evidenced in miscalculations of decimals and fractions, which result in costly production errors (Henry & Raymond, 1982). However, upon further investigation, employers confirmed that workers can, in fact, perform basic computation algorithms (addition, subtraction, multiplication, and division). The report from the National Assessment of Educational Progress study, conducted by Kirsch & Jungeblut (1986) supports this with the finding that approximately 75% of the young adults tested performed quantitative literacy tasks at the intermediate to adept levels or beyond. The real problem lies in workers' inability to decide which computation algorithm(s) to apply to a particular job problem or to recognize errors resulting from inappropriate applications because they do not understand why specific computations are used (Kloosterman & Harty, 1986). Neither time-consuming computation skill drills nor the use of calculators is an effective remedy, because, although both methods can correct the problem of computational errors, neither one assists the individual in knowing which computation is needed to solve an on-the-job problem (Kloosterman & Gillie, 1987-1988). The difficulty level of the computational task is also increased when workers must apply more than one numerical operation in the appropriate sequence or use information that is embedded in print materials (Kirsch & Jungeblut, 1986).

Workplace applications of mathematical skills require employees to acquire proficiency levels in reasoning and problem solving beyond the basic use of computational algorithms. Figure 3.3 lists specific mathematical skill applications frequently used in the workplace. Those items marked with an asterisk (*) in Figure 3.3 indicate skills directly involving the use of problem solving or interpretation. Pratzner (1978), in a report prepared for the National Center for Research in Vocational Education, lists diagnosis, estimating and problem solving (to include determining relevant information and selecting alternative solutions) as "generic," or basic reasoning skills used in the workplace. Supporting his position with citations from studies by Singer (1977) and Altman (1976), he points out that "application and practice of these skills under a variety of realistic life and work performance conditions should facilitate subsequent application or transfer of skills, knowledge, and attitudes... to work settings" (pp. 34-35). Wiant, in *Transferrable Skills: The Employer's Viewpoint*, (1977), also identifies problem solving, analyzing, organizing, and decision making as skills most frequently mentioned as desired by employers. Resnick (1987), too, states that, In mathematics, recent research suggests the most successful learners ... understand the task to be one of *interpreting* numbers, not just doing routine calculations.... Failure to engage in "higher order reasoning" about quantities is related to failures in learning the "basic" skills of calculation and number usage (p. 10).

Workplace problem solving can be defined as critical- or logical-thinking (Kloosterman & Gillie, 1987-1988), which uses brainstorming, activates learner's schema, and involves group cooperation (Karmos & Karmos, 1986). Good problem solvers are those who can clearly define the problem, state the goal, limit the "search space" for the solution, and access prior knowledge (schema) appropriately (Chi & Glaser, 1985).

Recommendations for Providing Effective Instruction in Workplace Literacy Skills

Based on the information above, one can readily conclude that even those adults who have mastered academic literacy skills are seldom prepared for the ways they will need to use those skills to competently perform current and future job tasks in which they are found embedded in the workplace. The Conference Board of New York City Lund & McGuire, (1990) reports that approximately 90% of the employed United States workforce are, in fact, academically literate. Only 10% of the employees of the companies surveyed were reported to be nonliterates or low level literates, that is, reading below a fourth grade ability level, yet only 25% of all the workers were described as "advanced level literates." Of the remaining 65% of the employed United States workforce, many have GEDs or high school diplomas. The average worker today is almost 40 years old. For years these workers have performed the same job tasks, but as their job responsibilities change with upgrades in technology and shifts in management structure, they find themselves no longer equipped with the skills needed to tackle new job tasks. Such workers

---

Performing Whole Number Operations

- ● Reading, writing, and counting single and multiple digit whole numbers to complete a task or subtask.

- ● Adding, subtracting, multiplying, and dividing single and multiple digit numbers to complete a task or subtask.

- * Using addition, subtraction, multiplication, and division to solve problems with single and multiple digit whole numbers.

- * Rounding off single and multiple digit numbers to complete a task or subtask.

Using Fractions

- ● Reading and writing common fractions to complete a task or subtask.

- * Adding, subtracting, multiplying, and dividing common fractions to solve problems.

Using Decimals

- ● Carrying out arithmetic computations involving dollars and cents.

- ● Reading and writing decimals in one and more places to complete a task or subtask.

- * Rounding of decimals in one and more places to complete a task or subtask.

- * Adding, subtracting, multiplying and dividing decimals in one and more places to solve a problem.

Using Percents

- ● Reading, writing, and computing percents to complete a task or subtask.

Performing Mixed Operations

- * Converting fractions to decimals, percents to fractions, fractions to percents, percents to decimals, common fractions or mixed numbers to decimal fractions, and decimal fractions to common fractions or mixed numbers to complete a task or subtask.

- * Solve problems by selecting and using correct order of operations.

- ● Computing averages, ranges, or ratios to complete a task or subtask.

Measurements and Calculation

- * Reading numbers or symbols from time, weight, distance, and volume measuring scales.

- * Using a measuring device to determine an object's weight, distance, or volume in standard (English) units or metric units.

- * Performing basic metric conversions involving weight, distance, and volume.

- * Using a calculator to perform basic arithmetic operations to solve problems

Estimations

- * Determining if a solution to a mathematical problem is reasonable.

(*Indicates skills directly involved with using problem-solving strategies or interpretation.)

Figure 3.3. Applications of computation and problem-solving skills in the workplace. Philippi, J.W. (1988). *Job literacy: Computation and problem-solving.* Report for the United States Department of Labor and American Society for Training & Development, Alexandria, VA. Copyright 1990, Performance Plus Learning Consultants. Reprinted by permission.

may be classified as intermediate level literates, no longer able to be competently functional in the workplace environment without additional literacy skills training.

To solve this problem, many employers and labor organizations have begun to offer literacy skills training programs to supplement technical training on new job tasks. The most successful of these are the programs that are designed to facilitate maximum transfer from the learning situation to job performance. These are programs that are built on actual job scenarios and that utilize job materials as a vehicle to teach the metacognitive and cognitive strategies that competent workers use. To develop such programs, a technique called "literacy task analysis" is often used for identifying the literacy skill applications embedded in the performance of job tasks. Literacy task analysis (LTA) involves the simultaneous observation and interviewing of competent workers performing their job tasks. Questions are asked to clarify the procedure that is being observed and to obtain correct technical terminology. This protocol assists the curriculum developer with accurate portrayals of the tasks as a vehicle for delivering instruction, that is, in creating job scenarios or job-related exercises. Questions are also asked of competent workers to determine what thinking strategies or mental steps are being used while the job tasks are being performed. These responses then become the instructional objectives for the subsequent development of "functional context" curriculum materials (Philippi, 1991).

Because functional context curriculum is an outgrowth of the ways in which competent workers perform job tasks, its impact on the learner's job performance can be measured. Employers and employees must first identify those job tasks that are critical to the organization's survival. The reasons such tasks are critical generally is due to concerns about current or future productivity, quality, and amounts of waste. Base line measures can usually be obtained for these indicators from data already collected by the company. Then, literacy task analyses are conducted with competent employees who perform these critical job tasks. A functional context curriculum is then developed from the results of the LTAs and instruction may be implemented. Because the instructional tasks used to teach each task's embedded cognitive strategies are representative of the actual job task performance, transfer from training to actual job performance is able to be evaluated and its impact on the company's bottom line can then be calculated. This adaptation of instructional systems design is acceptable to both management and organized labor because it focuses on a problem situation, that is, critical job task(s) in the workplace, rather than on individual worker skill deficits. This approach is also readily embraced by worker program participants because, in using their workplace materials and building on their workplace experiences, it validates what they already know and is perceived as relevant to their immediate needs.

Summary

Literacy skills in the workplace are comprised of those particular applications of cognitive strategies that enable transfer of traditional reading, writing, computation and problem-solving skills to the performance of job tasks. Competent performance of these job tasks enables the joint survival of both employees and companies. Research demonstrates that workplace applications of literacy skills differ significantly from those used in academic contexts.

Providing effective training in workplace literacy skills requires the development of instructional tasks that closely resemble actual job tasks so that positive transfer of learning to job performance can occur. A functional context curriculum development approach can be employed to create such instruction. Utilizing various techniques to identify the cognitive strategies embedded in job task performance, the resulting functional context curricula make use of job simulations and materials as vehicles for teaching workplace literacy skills.

References

Altman, J.W. (1976). *Transferability of vocational skills: Review of literature and research* (Information Series No. 103). Columbus: Ohio State University, Center for Vocational Education.

Anderson, W.S. (1986, March 13-15). *Opportunities for consultants.* Paper presented at the 37th annual meeting of the Conference on College Composition and Communication, New Orleans, LA. (ERIC Document Reproduction Service No. ED 271 761)

Bransford, J.D., & Franks, J.J. (1976). Toward a framework for understanding learning. In G.H. Bower (Ed.), *The psychology of learning and motivation* (Vol. 10). New York: Academic Press.

Brock, W.E. (1987). Future shock: The American work force in the year 2000. *American Association for Community, Technical & Junior Colleges Journal, 57*(4), 25-26.

Chi, M.T.H., & Glaser, R. (1985). *Problem-solving ability.* (Report No. LRDC-1985/6) Washington, DC: National Institute of Education, Psychological Services Division. (ERIC Document Reproduction Service No. ED 257 630)

Diehl, W.A. (1980). *Functional literacy as a variable construct: An examination of attitudes, behaviors, and strategies related to occupational literacy.* Unpublished doctoral dissertation, Indiana University, Bloomington, IN.

Diehl, W.A., & Mikulecky, L.J. (1980). The nature of reading at work. *Journal of Reading, 24,* 221-227.

Dreher, M.J., & Guthrie, J.T. (1990). Cognitive processes in textbook search tasks. *Reading Research Quarterly, 25,* 323-339.

Fields, E.L. (1986). Industry-based programs: A growing source for adult literacy development. *Lifelong Learning: An Omnibus of Practice and Research, 10*(10), 7-9.

Fields, E.L., Hull, W.L., & Sechler, J.A. (1987). *Adult literacy: Industry-based training programs* (Research & Development Series No. 265C). (ERIC Document Reproduction Service No. ED 284 981)

Gick, M.L., & Holyoak, K.J. (1987). The cognitive basis of knowledge transfer. In S.M. Cormier & J.D. Hagman (Eds.), *Transfer of learning: Contemporary research and applications* (Educational Technology Series). Alexandria, VA: United States Army Research Institute for the Behavioral and Social Sciences.

Graves, D.H. (1981). *A case study observing the development of primary children's composing, spelling, and motor behaviors during the writing process: Final report* (National Institute of Education, Grant No. G-78-0714). Durham:

University of New Hampshire. (ERIC Document Reproduction Service No. ED 218 653)

Hayes, J.R., & Flower, L.S. (1980). Identifying the organization of writing processes. In L.W. Gregg & E.R. Steinberg (Eds.), *Cognitive processes in writing* (pp. 3-30). Hillsdale, NJ: Lawrence Erlbaum.

Henry, J.F., & Raymond, S. (1982). *Basic skills in the U.S. workforce.* New York: Center for Public Resources.

Karmos, J., & Karmos, A. (1986). *Strategies for problem-solving.* Springfield, IL: Illinois State Board of Education, Department of Adult, Vocational, and Technical Education. (ERIC Document Reproduction Service No. 274 784)

Kirsch, I.S., & Guthrie, J.T. (1984). Prose comprehension and text search as a function of reading volume. *Reading Research Quarterly, 19,* 331-342.

Kirsch, I.S., & Jungeblut, A. (1986). *Literacy: Profiles of America's young adults.* (Report No. 16-PL-02) Princeton, NJ: Educational Testing Service.

Kirsch, I.S., & Mosenthal, P.B. (1990). Exploring document literacy: Variables underlying the performance of young adults. *Reading Research Quarterly, 25,* 5-31.

Kloosterman, P., & Gillie, S. (1987-1988). Basic mathematical skills for vocational education. In H. Harty, P. Kloosterman, L. Mikulecky, & J. Pershing (Dirs.), *The impact and potential of basic skills applications in vocational/technical education: The basic skills work-education bridge (WEB).* (Project No. 395-87-47000). Indianapolis: Indiana State Board of Vocational and Technical Education.

Kloosterman, P., & Harty, H. (1986). *Need sensing, assessing, and validation for science, mathematics, computer, and foreign language education in the state of Indiana: Final report.* Bloomington: Indiana University School of Education. (ERIC Document Reproduction Service No. ED 272 391)

Lund, L., & McGuire, E.P. (1990). *Literacy in the work force.* New York: The Conference Board.

Mikulecky, L.J. (1982). Functional writing in the workplace. In L. Gentry (Ed.), *Research and instruction in practical writing.* Los Alamitos, CA: Southwest Regional Laboratories.

Mikulecky, L.J. (1987). The status of literacy in our society. In J. Readance & S. Baldwin (Eds.), *Research in literacy: Merging perspectives* (pp. 211-235). New York: National Reading Conference.

Mikulecky, L.J., & Ehlinger, J. (1986). The influence of metacognitive aspects of literacy on job performance of electronics technicians. *Journal of Reading Behavior, 18*(1), 41-62.

Mikulecky, L.J., Ehlinger, J., & Meenan, A.L. (1987). *Training for job literacy demands: What research applies to practice.* University Park: Pennsylvania State University, Institute for the Study of Adult Literacy.

Mikulecky, L.J., Shanklin, N.L., & Caverly, D.C. (1979). *Adult reading habits, attitudes, and motivations: A cross-sectional study. Monograph in Language and Reading Series, 2.*

Mikulecky, L.J., & Winchester, D. (1983). Job literacy and job performance among nurses at varying employment levels. *Adult Education Quarterly, 34*, 1-15.

Montague, W. (1987, May 13). More coordination in job training seen. *Education Week*, p. *13*.

Perl, S. (1979). The composing process of unskilled college writers. *Research in the Teaching of English, 13*, 317-336.

Philippi, J.W. (1987). Formative evaluation of basis skills education program/career skills education program reading. In *Self-evaluation of the HSCP and BSEP/CSEP contract, 22 September '86-31 March '87*, (Report presented to Army Continuing Education Services, United States Army Europe, Leimen, West Germany). (Contract No. DAJA37-86-D-008). Available from Big Bend Community College, European Division, Central Services: Bad Kreuznach, West Germany.

Philippi, J.W. (1988). Matching literacy to job training: Some applications from military programs. *Journal of Reading, 31*(7), 658-666.

Pratzner, F.C. (1978). *Occupational adaptability and transferable skills: Project final report* (Information Series No. 129). Columbus: Ohio State University National Center for Research in Vocational Education. (ERIC Document Reproduction Service No. ED 186 717)

Resnick, L.B. (1987, October 5). *Skilled workers are thinking workers: The new basics in American education.* Testimony before the Congress of the United States Subcommittee on Education and Health, Joint Economic Committee, Washington, DC.

Rumelhart, D.E. (1980). Schemata: The building blocks of cognition. In R. Spiro, B. Bruce, & W. Brewer (Eds.), *Theoretical issues in reading comprehension* (pp. 33-58). Hillsdale, NJ: Lawrence Erlbaum.

Rush, R.T., Moe, A.J., & Storlie, R.L. (1986). *Occupational literacy education.* Newark, DE: International Reading Association.

Semerad, R.D. (1987). Workers in the year 2000: Why we're in trouble. *American Teacher, 71*(8), 7-12.

Sharon, A. (1973-1974). What do adults read? *Reading Research Quarterly, 9*, 148-169.

Singer, R.N. (1977). To err or not to err: A question for the instruction of psychometric skills. *Review of Educational Research, 47*(3), 479-498.

Stein, N.L., & Glenn, C.G. (1979). An analysis of story comprehension in elementary school children. In R.O. Freedle (Ed.), *New directions in discourses processing* (Vol. 2, pp. 53-120). Norwood, NJ: Ablex.

Sticht, T.G. (1975a). *A program of Army functional job reading training: Development, implementation, and delivery systems: Final report* (HumRRO Report No. FR-WD [CA]-75-7). Alexandria, VA: Human Resources and Research Organization. (ERIC Document Reproduction Service No. ED 116 161)

Sticht, T.G. (1975b). *Reading for working: A functional literacy anthology.* Alexandria, VA: Human Resources and Research Organization.

Sticht, T.G. (1987). *Functional context education*. San Diego, CA: Applied Behavioral and Cognitive Sciences.

Tulving, E., & Thomson, D.M. (1973). Encoding specificity and retrieval processes in episodic memory. *Psychological Review, 80*, 352-373.

United States Department of the Army. (1986, June 2). *Effective writing for Army leaders* (Department of the Army Pamphlet No. 600-67). Washington, DC: Headquarters, U.S. Government Printing Office.

Wiant, A.A. (1977). *Transferable skills: The employers' viewpoint*. Columbus: Ohio State University National Center for Research in Vocational Education. (ERIC Document Reproduction Service No. ED 174 809)

4
Literacy Patterns in Historical Perspective

Harvey J. Graff

The history of literacy, as a regular, formal, significant, and sometimes central concern of historians having a wide range of topical, chronological, and methodological inclinations, in the 1990s is certainly well established. Its relevance transcends the interests of historians and educational researchers alone, as the inclusion of a historical chapter in a volume on *Reading Across the Life Span* attests. Nevertheless, this also raises key questions about the necessary relationships between the historical study of literacy and those of reading and life course studies, either past *or* present. They cannot fairly be said to have commenced, let alone grown to fruition. Bridges between historical and contemporary literacy students and those between historians of literacy and reading researchers are joined much too rarely for the active, mutually enriching and reinforcing development of all sides of the possible equations. The active thrust and exceptional growth in historical literacy studies over the past 2 decades have propelled the subject to new prominence; yet, basic linkages among and between subjects and students, by discipline and interdisciplines, barely have advanced (Note 1).

The maturation of the historical study of literacy has been enormously beneficial, inside the academy and on occasion, beyond its walls. Nevertheless, this significant body of scholarship demands more attention: both in terms of what it may contribute to other researchers, planners, and thinkers, and in terms of its own growing needs for interdisciplinary cooperation and constructive criticism. For example, historical literacy studies have been marked by their attention to the exploitation of quantitative data and to issues of quantity and measurement. As important as that has been to initial advances, that emphasis has also been, or begins to become, a limitation toward new conceptualizations and, especially, interpretations. (There are instructive parallels here with reading and with life course studies.)

My principal concern in this essay is the present state of historical literacy studies, and their possible relations to those of reading viewed across the span of lives. For literacy, I term this something of an "awkward age," or stage of development. That I should sense this aspect of the present moment is perhaps not surprising, for historical studies in general after almost 2 decades of proliferating "new histories" are themselves in something of an awkward age. The recent appearance of a hefty number of books and articles surveying the state of the craft, searching for trends, and sometimes proposing new emphases and directions all underscore this condition (e.g., Stone's (1979) call for retreats from social scientific and quantitative studies and hopes for "new narratives," attacks on social history, among many others). As the history of literacy joins the historiographic mainstream, it suffers from similar challenges and questions. Reading research writ large offers a parallel situation, and literacy's students may well sit, more or less uncomfortably, between these two (and perhaps other) disciplines. Literacy studies, though, may be an exceptional case: for example, the distinctions between *quantities* and *qualities*, to use one dichotomy, exacerbate all questions of interpretation and meaning. Here, the quantitative record, no matter how essential to literacy's complete study and no matter how cleverly exploited, may have inherent limits at least as severe as those in other areas of historical or reading analysis.

I referred to an awkward age for the historical study of literacy. I am tempted to conceive of the field's development itself in terms of life courses or cycles, at least metaphorically in the present volume, and to posit the present situation as one of late adolescence or youthfulness. I do think, more seriously, that perhaps a *generational* perspective is more apt than a life cycle one. In these terms, for the purposes of discussion and assessment, we might conceive of three *modern* generations of historical literacy studies.

A *first generation* includes principally the late-1960s work of Stone (1969), Cipolla (1969), and Schofield (1968), and was foreshadowed by the 1950s studies by Fleury and Valmary (1957) in France. The contributions here were several: to advance a strong case for the historical study of literacy–its direct study, that is, and for its import and significance as a historical factor; to review the general course of literacy's chronological trends and principal transitions and passages; to identify sources for fuller, systematic exploitation–primarily but not exclusively, numerical sources; to advance the case(s) for the utility of routinely generated, systematic, and sometimes comparable and "direct" measures; and to posit, sometimes speculatively, the factors most closely tied to and responsible for changes in the course of literacy over time—its dynamics, distributions, impacts, and consequences. As far as reading was concerned, no attention fell on the question of its place in the life span, and overall caution was emphasized in drawing relations between trends in basic literacy levels and implications for those in reading patterns. In part, this stemmed from an effort to limit cavalier generalizations about reading, on one hand, and an attempt to establish with literacy levels parameters for a more refined discussion of reading practices and their presumptive impacts.

A *second generation* grew directly from and was clearly stimulated by the first more sweeping and speculative students. It includes, for example, among major studies, Schofield's (1973) later work, Egil Johansson's (1977, 1981, 1985) studies, and book-length reports by Cressay (1980), Furet and Ozouf

(1983), Graff(1981c; 1986; 1987), Rab Houston (1983; 1985), Lockridge (1974), and Soltow and Stevens (1981). In addition, there exist numerous articles, monographs, local and regional studies, and theses and dissertations, mostly unpublished, especially in Great Britain and France.

The emphasis became a larger, more detailed erection and exploitation of the quantitative record, usually but not always from signatory or census sources: greater concern for a more evidentially and sometimes more contextually grounded historical interpretation of changing patterns–especially of distributions and differentiations in levels of literacy; relation of literacy's trends to social and economic development, institutional interventions, and state activities–especially, the availability of formal schooling and public school systems, political transformations, and events like the French Revolution, ideological aspects of the subject, among such factors; concern with class formation; uses of literacy in terms both of patterns of reading and individual and group attitudinal and psychological changes; increased awareness of the contradictory nature of the subject and alertness to the difficulties in building historical interpretations upon a quantitative analysis of secular trendlines and patterns of distributions and differentiations (among many other aspects). The value of comparative frameworks was also recognized, if only occasionally formally attempted or practiced. If we know much more about literacy's social patterns over time and the fairly systematic and patterned variations in its distributions over time and place, we are perhaps also more hesitant and cautious in explanation and attribution of meaning.

At the same time as the maturing of this second generation, literacy also was "discovered" by an increasing number of historians, especially those employing quantitative methods and numerical sources that included some information on literacy (either on an aggregative, ecological, or an individual level) or that were fairly easily linked to information sources on literacy. Thus, literacy increasingly featured in studies of economic change, demographic behavior, cultural development and conflict, class formation and stratification, collective actions of all kinds, family formation and structures, and the like, as the literature on all these key subjects now reflects. Interestingly, in this sphere of studies, literacy tended to be conceptualized most often as an independent variable, presumably useful in the explanation of another, dependent variable, which was itself the object of more direct and sustained study. The history of reading, in partial but not complete contrast, lagged behind especially in terms of its relations to literacy directly and the contexts of acquisition and usage across lives and their experiential dimensions. Problems of evidence and of epistemology in part explain this lacunae.

In the growing number of studies that took literacy itself as the central object of study and discussion, literacy could be and was conceptualized as either or both dependent or independent variable. At once a source of analytic and conceptual flexibility, this could also be a problem and a source of interpretive confusion and weakness: The nature of literacy as a (historical) variable insufficiently is examined critically. Indeed, that also relates to the generally tardy, lesser developed, and somewhat isolated studies of reading.

New concern about the (potential and actual) "uses" of literacy and about the terms and consequences of its acquisition brought the question of reading and reading in the life course to occasional attention (Davis, 1975; Graff, 1979; Calhoun, 1973; Cressy, 1980; Darnton, 1983, 1984; Hall, 1983, 1984, 1985; Gilmore, 1989, are among the major examples; see Kaestle, 1985). Overall, the history of reading, as Hall (1983, 1984, 1985) and Kaestle (1985) recently underscore, emerged as a minor theme in the historical study of literacy. The more historians learned about literacy the less we found ourselves above to impute simply and directly its uses. Nevertheless, from diverse places and times there came hints of certain overarching generalizations, including several of great interest and potential importance to students of reading and the life span.

Principally, these include:

1. A trend over time in the direction of a standardized and homogenized experience of literacy acquisition. Until the past century, although most literates learned their letters in childhood or youth, there was extensive variation in the relationship of age to the acquisition of skills. Historians of the early modern era, for example, now debate the degree to which literacy was tied commonly to childhood learning. (See, for example, Cressy, 1980; Galenson, 1981; Laqueur, 1976.)

2. Only with the development of modern, comprehensive schooling institutions and educational systems can we speak firmly of a life-course specific learning experience for literacy (Graff, 1979, 1986), although the relationship has never been perfect.

3. Literacy, importantly, has been gained historically at virtually all ages, and in situations ranging from the most informal of circumstances to highly structured pedagogical environments. At all points over, say, the last millennium, diverse modes and situations for gaining the skills of reading and writing have coexisted.

4. Despite regular shifts in reading pedagogical theories, persons young and old have regularly gained reading skills from every imaginable method, as well as by self-learning (Graff, 1979, 1986; Calhoun, 1973; Soltow and Stevens, 1981).

5. Only in the past 100 years have assumptions tying literacy learning to the earlier years of the life span and formal schooling come to dominate theory and practice. Experiences of individuals and groups and pedagogical theory have always differed greatly in practice–in patterns of learning and common habits of use (Graff, 1979, 1986; Calhoun, 1973; Laqueur, 1976; Galenson, 1981; Spufford, 1981).

6. Ages and circumstances of learning have varied directly with social class and its concommitants to the effect that higher placed persons (especially but not exclusively males) have tended to gain their letters earlier–and to be taught a higher valuation of the skills.

7. Historically, the abilities to read have dominated–in quantity as well as in quality–over those of writing. Higher standing persons have been much more likely (since the late Middle Ages at least) to be able to write as well as to read, as have males, members of dominant classes, ethnic groups and races, and urban residents.

8. Quality–in terms of popular abilities to use one's literacy, especially the skills of reading–has always varied from quantity–the level of mass elementary literacy in a society. On one hand, this makes it difficult to generalize from levels of popular literacy to actual patterns of its employment; on the other hand, this seems consistently to be a striking divergence between "approved" or promoted uses of literacy–for religious or improving literacy, for example–and common uses. In part, this pivots on questions of the quality of ability levels, but at least as important have been motivations and interests that led regularly to more frequent reading for recreation than for more "serious" or "useful" practices. This is not of course to deny the importance of historical examples of the latter. Key cases of class and individual employment of literacy–for political, social and cultural, and economic advance–punctuate the historical experience.

9. Two major patterns for the achievement of mounting levels of literacy intertwine historically: those of individual, class, or familial motivations—often in terms of perceptions of the utilities of literacy (a push and a pull factor)—and those of social control and cultural hegemony. An intricate and often blurred dialectic ties the two sides of this tricky equation. (See Calhoun, 1973; Clanchy, 1979; Cressy, 1980; Davis, 1975; Gilmore, 1989; Graff, 1979, 1981, 1986; Hall, 1979, 1982, 1983, 1984, 1985; Houston, 1983, 1985; Johansson, 1977, 1981; Kett & McClung, 1984; Laqueur, 1976; Noakes, 1981; Spufford, 1979, 1981; and Webb, 1955.)

10. Among the diverse consequences of such complex connections are the regular disappointment of those who expect "higher" uses and practices of reading and, perhaps more importantly, the imputation of a cyclical history of regular literacy "declines."

11. Given all of the above, it is perhaps not surprising to discover occasional evidence of underutilized, even atrophying abilities to read over the individual life span. (These generalizations draw widely upon the literature cited in the reference list.)

Another group of historians, interested in cultural, publishing, and/or literary topics, have increasingly tended to consider literacy within their purview. Although they least often directly studied literacy levels and patterns, they took it as a central factor or parameter for their own work: here one thinks of press and newspaper histories, *l'histoire du livre*, studies of popular culture that include new interest in oral culture and its interaction with literacy, and historians of print and publishing (Note 2). Some of this work, such as that of Robert Darnton (1982, 1983, 1984) and Elizabeth Eisenstein (1979), is more closely allied to considerations of reading than others. We have learned much from such work, too much to summarize (see the following citations). Most of it, unfortunately, often remains unconnected to that mentioned here, that is, directly to literacy itself; therefore assumptions about its use–in terms of reading and reading over the life span–tend to remain disconnected and unpersuasive. Some historians, however, have begun to consider age, class, gender, ethnic, regional and other group-specific bodies of reading materials and their audiences. (For an interesting effort, see Gilmore, 1989.)

If unrealized thus far, the potential for such linkages remains great (see Darnton, 1983; Kaestle, 1985). Carl Kaestle is one scholar currently investigating the history of reading in relation to that of print and literacy; he is attempting, as part of this project, the historical estimation of levels of reading difficulties (Kaestle & Trollinger, 1986). More generally, Robert Darnton (1983) embraces the point:

> Despite a considerable literature on its psychology, phenomenology, textology, and sociology, reading remains mysterious. How do readers decode the signs on the printed page? What are the social effects of that experience? And how has it varied? Literary scholars like Wayne Booth, Stanley Fish, Wolfgang Iser, Walter Ong, and Jonathan Culler have made reading a central concern of textual criticism because they understand literature as an activity, the construal of meaning within a system of communication, rather than as a canon of texts. The book historian could make use of their notions of fictitious audiences, implicit readers, and interpretive communities, but may find their observations somewhat time-bound. Although the critics know their way around literary history... they seem to assume that texts have always worked on the sensibilities of readers in the same way. But a seventeenth-century London burgher inhabited a different mental universe from that of a twentieth-century American professor. Reading itself has changed over time (p. 18) (See also, in the reference list, Darnton, 1984; the works of Holub (1984), Iser (1974), Jauss (1982), Suleiman & Crosman (1980), Tompkins (1978), among the relevant literature.)

Darnton (1984, chapter 6) essayed a "reader response" history of a contemporary French bourgeois reading of Rousseau; Ginzburg (1980) interpreted the reading of a 16th-century Italian miller; Spufford (1981) considered "popular" reading in 17th-century England. From such studies, we gain a deeper sense of the fundamental "historicity" of reading, a requisite to its comprehension as a cultural and social psychological, indeed as an active human interaction: with reader shaping the textual meaning and text shaping reader meaning. Major novel research avenues that tie historians of literacy and reading to those of print, culture, and ideas, and in turn both groups to students of psychology, reading, literature, and philosophy are before us. Yet, the tendentiousness of much of this work, and limits of evidence on one hand and theory on the other, should make us cautious, too.

Virtually all such work, it should be underscored, has labored under the specter and shadows of "modernization theories" with their strong assumptions of literacy's role, powers, and provenance–an issue that must be confronted critically. Students have chosen alternatively to challenge the assumptions of modernization's links to and impacts upon literacy (or vice versa) or to assimilate their work within its traditions, suffering conceptual and interpretive difficulties, which the empirical record alone seldom meets squarely and which remain to be examined. In some cases, the latter assumption actually substitutes for empirical, as well as critical research. Problems also include the persisting presence of obstructive dichotomies such as literate versus illiterate, print versus script, written versus oral, and the like, none of which are interpretively rich or complex enough to advance our understanding (Cipolla, 1969; Graff, 1979, 1981c, 1986; Houston, 1983, 1985; Lockridge, 1974; Soltow & Stevens, 1981; Stone, 1969).

Reading history is no different. Despite the fruits of recent research, it remains easy to fall into a "great divide" or "transition" approach to its historical sweep. A ready formulation, parallelling that of script to print or illiterate to literate may be: *from* oral, collective, and intensive (the term of German scholar Rolf Engelsing, 1973, 1974; used also by Darnton, 1983; Hall, 1984; Gilmore, 1989), *to* silent, individual, and extensive reading habits. This dichotomy can no more be accepted than any of the others; in fact, the fundamental historicity of reading—with its great variability and its refusal to develop linearly—requires a rejection of any such view (see Calhoun, 1973; Cressy, 1980; Davis, 1975; Graff, 1979, 1986; Houston, 1985; Gilmore, 1989; Noakes, 1981; Saenger, 1982; for important evidence and interpretations). Darnton (1983) comments

> The history of reading will have to take into account the ways that texts constrain readers as well as the ways that readers take liberties with texts. The tension between those tendencies has existed wherever readers confronted books and has produced some extraordinary results....Though it may be possible to recapture the great rereadings of the past, the inner experience of ordinary readers will always elude us. But at least we should be able to reconstruct a good deal of the social context of reading. The debate about silent reading during the Middle Ages has produced some impressive evidence about reading habits, and studies of reading societies in Germany...have shown the importance of reading in the development of a distinct bourgeois cultural style. (p. 19-20)

There is no reason that life span issues cannot be added to these considerations, especially when focus falls upon literacy acquisition and literacy use across the life course.

The *third generation* now awaits us. It has barely raised its head, although I shall relate my thoughts about its agendas and emphases. In part, I believe, discussion must now focus upon the needs and opportunities—questions, sources, methods—of a third generation. In fact, the most recent studies begin to point the way (Johansson, 1985; Stevens, 1985); ground-breaking work in contemporary studies usefully demonstrates basic areas and aspects of interdisciplinary collaboration, especially respecting historians of literacy and students of reading.

In part, two new and original directions in the social scientific study of literacy offer intriguing and tantalizing leads to historians (as well as to contemporary students). Here I think, in particular, of the socio-psychological work, which is sometimes brilliant and often path; breaking in its implications—of the experimental, ethnographic and comparative cognitive psychologists, Sylvia Scribner and Michael Cole, especially in their *The Psychology of Literacy* (1981); and of Sylvia Scribner's (1984) continuing studies of the skills, including reading and writing, required and utilized in different kinds of work settings and demands. The collateral fields of the psychology of everyday experience and cognitive psychology form another part of the third domain. I also refer to the community-based ethnographies of literacy and education brought together by anthropologist and linguist Shirley Heath in *Ways with Words: Language, Life and Work in Communities and Classrooms* (1983; see also Cook-Gumperz, 1986; Schieffelin & Gilmore, 1986; Tannen,

1982; Whiteman, 1981). Together, they underscore the import for literacy of *context* of learning and use, nature of acquisition, culture and traditions, and the like. Especially striking, in similarities and in differences, are their relationship to an explicit–even if not cast in such terms–focus on reading as a dynamic, human social and cultural activity, in theory and in practice, and on ethnography as a mode of its location and study. In so doing, they offer much to historians and other students of reading by example, analogy, and conceptualization and emphasize one key path for an agenda for the third generation.

Several other recent studies underscore these directions as they also lead us into different and wider terrains. Radway's *Reading the Romance: Women, Patriarchy, and Popular Literature* (1984; see also Radway, 1986) proposes, and with a contemporary group of romance readers illustrates, that reading *can* be usefully and critically (and as her work in particular evidences, sympathetically) studied in social, cultural, and political-economic contexts. Potential connections to the life span are also discerned, as is the case in Heath's community-based ethnographies. Radway's (1986) imaginative practice is jointly informed by anthropological and literary critical perspectives; she also hints at the possibilities for historical efforts in this direction. In fact, creative research by Vincent (1981) and Mitchell (1981) shows potential for historical applications via autobiographical and literary sources, for the working class and middle-class women, respectively. In this respect, the pioneering and idiosyncratic, if not always persuasive, writings of Ginzburg (1980) and Darnton (1984) suggest the depths and insights that close study of reading practices set into socioculturally-informed communicative contexts may yield. In these examples, I note, the limits of the work are as rich as the real achievements. (See also Burke, 1978; Gilmore, 1989; Isaacs, 1976a, 1976b, 1982; Kaplan, 1984; Scribner, 1981, 1984; Spufford, 1979, 1981; Stout, 1977; for additional examples.)

The occasion for these reflections, happily, coincides with a highly significant moment for historical studies of literacy–and perhaps for reading (and life span) research, too. If my surmises are at least partially accurate, the field of inquiry is today at a crossroads. We ask, not at all frivolously or lightly: whither historians of literacy and reading? If the second generation–having firmly established the field of the history of literacy–is winding down now, if my sensing a diminishing of new researchers and research projects focused directly on literacy is also an accurate reading, and if we assume that literacy deserves and demands further study and consideration, we also recognize that (a) many gaps in the record remain to be completed; (b) many questions–some only relatively recently posed–remain to be answered; and (c) key problems in conceptualization, interpretation, and explanation mark these efforts. Consideration of the outlines and agendas of a perhaps currently, only hypothetically viewed, third generation is of more than academic interest. (See also Darnton, 1983; Hall, 1985; Kaestle, 1985).

In part, we need to shift our dialogue from quantitative methods to qualitative results and critical questions. We do well to ponder the links in terms of both continuities and changes between the second generation (represented so strongly in the literature) and my proposed third generation. I propose that we do more than take stock and assess, but also undertake those activities with an aim toward future

studies conceived and designed in novel ways. That is the discussion these reflections aim at stimulating.

The achievements of historical literacy studies are many and clear. No simple
summary of that richness is possible here (but see Graff, 1981a, 1986; Houston,
1983). Persisting patterns of limitations also mark the field. Increasingly, we
recognize limits of quantitative analysis alone–and of aggregative and ecological
methods and research designs. In some ways, I aver, we are only now coming to
the most important questions and issues: That, perhaps, in addition to time series
and patterns of variation, will be seen as one of the major contributions of
generations 1 and especially 2. In part, there has been a shattering of "received
wisdom" (as in "literacy myths"), expectations, and assumptions–that, it should
be understood, is no small accomplishment. The obverse, however, is the question
of what will replace it–in part a theoretical issue. The "great debates" about
literacy's relationships to economic (ie., commercial and/or industrial) and social
development, political mobilization, religion, social mobility, social class formation, work and leisure patterns, and social change all generally reflect this. Questions about method, such as those of dependent versus independent variables, levels
of aggregation, and problems of correlational analysis, follow. The demand for
critical reflection now falls upon conceptualization, method, and interpretation.

Historian Rab Houston (1983) captures the spirit of this moment when he
usefully comments,

> If attempts to explain structures and trends in illiteracy have been less satisfactory
> than simple expositions of them, analysis of the meaning of literacy is even more
> rudimentary. The field has seen a proliferation of merely statistical analyses of which
> it seems trite to say that the well-established structural measures such as regional or
> male-female difference must be seen in the context of social and political institutions,
> attitudes surrounding class and gender, but above all of the ways in which power is
> ordered and preserved....The study of education and literacy has become less anec-
> dotal and parochial but the lack of a proper context prevents us from understanding
> its place in social development. Education is dealt with too much in its own terms.
> Even those studies which purport to analyze the interaction of education, literacy and
> society tend to select only a few simple aspects such as the way educational provision
> reflected the demands of different groups or how wealth, status and literacy overlap.
> Literacy can certainly be used as a valuable indicator of social divisions, but in what
> way did it help to preserve and perpetuate them? (p. 279)

In one way, the path lies in moving beyond literacy as a dichotomous variable, as
perceived as either conservative and controlling or as liberating. This might
constitute moving toward a cultural politic and a political economy of literacy in
history. There are a number of possible avenues. Very synoptically, I will suggest
some now, with an eye toward setting an agenda for the elusive third generation–
and toward bridging historians to other students of literacy and reading.

Most generally, historical literacy studies must build upon their own past while
also breaking away from it. The work of the second generation, such as that of Furet
and Ozuf (1983), Cressy (1980), or Soltow and Stevens (1981), delineates parameters, base lines, and key interrelationships that offer opportunities to investigate

more precisely the linkages and to seek refinements in the specification of factors and their interactions. These range from literacy's relations with class, sex, age, and culture to larger themes of economic development, social order, mobility and stratification, education and schooling, the actual uses of literacy, language, and culture, etcetera. One demand falls upon sharper contextual grounding, often in clearly delineated localities. Others encompass the completion of time series, among other quantitative analyses.

Second is the advancement of comparative study, requiring a greater apprecia- tion and emphasis on source criticism and recognition of the different meanings of different measures of literacy among different populations as evidenced from varying sources. Contextualization here is also critical for comparisons, as Johans- son's (1981) and Houston's (1983) work in particular illustrates, so is the further search for indicators of the levels and the quality of literacy: allowing us to advance beyond the limiting dichotomy of literate versus illiterate. Novel approaches to the combination of records–which may also include data on reading over the life span–and to record linkage stand out on the agenda (Graff, 1979, 1986; Houston, 1985).

Third is the major need for new conceptualizations of context in the historical study of literacy. Recognizing that literacy only acquires meaning and significance within specified historical contexts does not in itself reduce the risks of abstracted analysis. Novel work in anthropology and psychology, like that of Heath (1983) and Scribner and Cole (1981), mentioned earlier, provides important suggestions and guidelines for historians. The tasks lie not only in defining and specifying contexts for study and interpretation but also in delineating the varying levels of context–vertically or horizontally, for example–and in experimenting with ways to operationalize them. Stevens' focus on illiterates in judicial settings and Johans- son's (1977, 1981) perspective on church and community suggest two opportuni- ties to probe more intensively. Ginzburg's (1980) writings may provide another; so too may those of Darnton (1982, 1983), Mitchell (1981), Radway (1986), and Vincent (1981). Gilmore's (1989) local case study reiterates the richness of the records, for the recent past, oral histories, library use records, and participant observation, or ethnographies of communications, offer other possibilities (Note 3).

Contexts for analysis are many and diverse. They range from those of acquisi- tion, use, and action, to those of individual, family, group or community, gender, age, or social class. The scope for defined study is itself variable, but should include material conditions, motivations, opportunities, needs and demands, traditions, and transformations. In this way, linguistic forms, dialects, communication channels and networks, "pushes" and "pulls" from religion, culture, politics, the economy, etcetera, may be incorporated. Literacy's relationship to personal and/or collective efficacy and activism–a source of much debate–may also be further explored, in part in analysis of specific events and processes and in part in terms of patterns of communications and mobilization within defined contexts. Class formation and vital behavior are just two of the many key topics calling for attention.

Are "historical ethnographies" of literacy–conceptualized fully in terms of literacy among the modes and relations of communications–possible? Recent work, such as that noted here, contains fascinating hints in that direction, which merit fuller examination in the terms of a highly contextualized ethnographic and communicative approach to literacy. In this respect, a number of recent studies in popular culture–for example, those of Burke (1978), Ginzburg (1980), Isaacs (1982), LeRoy Ladurie (1978), R. Scribner (1984), Wrightson and Levine (1979), and Stout (1977)–may prove stimulating beginning models. Clearly, the subject and its significance mandate a fair test. The current interest within anthropology and movement toward an anthropology of communications based on ethnographies of reading and writing at varying levels of context and generality are guides to follow. (See Cook-Gumperz, 1986; Heath, 1983; Schieffelin & Gilmore, 1986; Tannen, 1982; Whiteman, 1981.)

On one hand, literacy may be viewed as one among other "media" and its roles and impacts evaluated. On the other hand, ethnographic and (cultural and technological) communicative approaches have the potential to expand perspectives while grounding them more precisely for meaningful interpretation. Novel contextualization can also be a boost to the renewal and refinement of quantitative studies. Context, in sum, offers both new and better cases for study, opportunities for explanation, and approaches to literacy's changing and variable historical meanings and contributions.

Reading–conceptualized and studied in part in terms of its life span and other key distinctions–is itself central to such approaches. Kaestle (1985) notes,

> As we seek to understand the purposes and consequences of literacy, we must reach out into more general histories of education, culture, publication, and communication, and to contemporary theoretical works that might inform a synthesis of these materials....Broadening the history of literacy to consider the uses of reading by adults.... (p. 36-46)

Joining with other recent calls by Darnton (1984), Gilmore (1989), and Hall (1985), in particular, he urges that historians of literacy require greater efforts at synthesis, based in larger degree on "mov[ing] beyond the history of texts to the history of readers" (Kaestle, 1985). Reading, after all, is *the* predominant use of literacy, and as such demands a central place in sophisticated studies of the uses of reading in everyday life. Only a recent interest among present-day students, this ranks highly on the new agenda of historians. Given the problems that complicate its direct study, the demands for clear contextualization and critical analysis are great. As Kaestle (1985) concludes:

> It is very difficult to trace printed works to their readers and still more difficult to trace meaning from the text to the reader. Even where we have some evidence about the uses of literacy, there is no way to summarize for a whole society the significance of so commonplace and pervasive an activity as reading. There will be, then, no comprehensive theory to explain the entire history of texts and readers. There is an open field, however, for new, detailed research on the individual items of an immense, exciting research agenda. There is also a need for broadly synthetic works that will

relate different genres to each other, to readers from different groups, to other forms of communication, and to key developments in cultural and social history. (p. 45) (See also Darnton's "model," 1983; Hall, 1985.)

A fourth consideration follows. This is the difficult but special demand for critical examination of the conceptualization of literacy itself. The second generation has taught the contradictions central to literacy's history. It has also revealed the problems in treating literacy as either or both dependent and independent (Graff, 1979). Questions of contextualization may well limit analysis of literacy as independent; they will also, I think, stimulate new formulations of the nature of literacy as a dependent factor. In the process, new considerations about levels and quality of literacy must transcend the related limits of the tradition of conceptualizing literacy, and reading too, as a dichotomous variable. The psychological and anthropological studies promise to contribute here too. The body of work of the second generation collectively underscores the special complications whose resolution ranks high on any agenda. To transcend it requires excavation of other relevant aspects of communicative culture–always including the oral and the visual–among which literacy and reading, in shifting degrees and mediations, takes its place.

Fifth is the question of literacy and what might well be termed the "creation of meaning." Historical study of literacy has been little influenced by recent debates in intellectual and cultural history, literary criticism, cognitive psychology, cultural anthropology and ethnography, or critical theories of communication. In some manner, the origins of these current emphases stem from dissatisfaction with traditional approaches to "texts," their understanding, and their communication. More recently, the entire enterprise of grasping the creation, maintenance, and communication of meaning has changed in major respects potentially relevant to issues central to literacy and reading. Cultural and intellectual history are themselves, along with major areas of the humanities and the social sciences–together, the human sciences–in a significant time of ferment and wider exploration of their parameters; so too, are literary criticism, cognitive and cultural psychology, and some areas of philosophy. Concerns about interactions between readers and texts, responses to writing and print, shaping of individual and collective processes of cognition, and ways in which meaning is created, influenced, transmitted, and changed are common, if not always clarified (Note 4). Possibly to its detriment, the history of literacy and reading stands in isolation from them. Now perhaps is the moment to at least consider the grounds for interdisciplinary rapprochement. Questions about literacy's contribution to individual, class, and collective awareness, patterns of cognition (and also noncognitive attitudinal formation), and cultural behavior–including their role over the life course–more generally all underscore this need. The nagging issue of the uses of literacy–of reading–and their consequences, deserves new exploration.

The need for a sharper theoretical awareness of the relevance of the history of literacy for many important aspects of social, economic, and psychological theory, constitutes a sixth point. This is implied in the foregoing. Historical studies of literacy do provide significant opportunities for testing theories, and insofar as their results continue to raise criticisms of "normative" theoretical expectations and assumptions, there may be prospects for essaying new formulations. Reading–in terms of theory, study, and practice can only gain from this encounter.

A seventh consideration, raised as a question of methodology, indeed of epistemology, links all of the above. Has the tradition, from two generations of studies, of taking literacy as primary object of analysis–"the history of literacy" per se–approached an end point? Should a third generation, rooted at least in part in the foregoing, refocus itself in terms of literacy as a significant–a necessary–aspect of other relevant investigations? The question, simply put, is that of shifting from "historical studies of literacy" to "histories that encompass literacy within their context and conceptualization," from "the history of literacy" to "literacy–and reading–in history"? There is reason to argue, I think, that the limits of the second generation's conceptualization encourage the exploration of what transformation would entail. To move in this direction, it should be grasped, is no simple task: I call for the reconceptualization and the mutual interaction not only of the history of literacy and reading but of the history of communications, culture, and society as well.

Finally, I call attention to the relevance of the history of literacy for a number of policy areas in societies developed and underdeveloped today, and to the additional contributions that reconceptualization might bring. Historical analysis can contribute to understanding and fashioning new responses to deal with those problems that are sometimes deemed "literacy crises." In grasping that there are many paths to literacy, that literacy's relations to social and economic development are complex, that the quantity and the quality of literacy (and literacy's possession and its use) are not linearly or simply related, that the consequences of literacy are neither simple nor direct, and that literacy is never neutral, historians have much to share with their fellow students and to offer those who formulate social policies (Arnove & Graff, 1987; Graff, 1981b, 1981c). Historians also have much to learn. Neither, in the end, constitute small contributions.

Notes

[1]These reflections on the state of research in the historical study of literacy stem from my research and thinking over the last decade and a half. For reasons of economy and space limitations, I can not consider in detail all the relevant issues, nor can I present complete bibliographic references for the text; interested readers may consult my *The Literacy Myth: Literacy and Social Structure in the Nineteenth-Century City; Literacy in History: An Interdisciplinary Research Bibliography; The Legacies of Literacy: Continuities and Contradictions in Western Society and Culture*; and *The Labyrinths of Literacy*. Some of the major examples of historical scholarship are collected in my *Literacy and Social Development in the West: A Reader*, wheras historical and more recent parallels are explored in *National Literacy Campaigns: Historical and Comparative Perspectives* (Arnove & Graff, 1987).

[2]See for example, Martin (1968-1970, 1977); Burke (1978); Febvre and Martin (1958); Eisenstein (1979); Joyce (1983); Carpenter (1983); the journals *Revue francaise d'histoire du livre* and *Publishing History*; Feather (1985); and critiques by Davis (1975); Darnton (1972, 1982, 1983, 1984). See now Kaestle (1985); Kaestle and Trollinger (1986); Gilmore (1989).

[3]See Johansson (1985) and Stevens (1985) based on their contributions to the Bellagio Conference. See also Scribner (1981, 1984); LeRoy Ladurie (1978); Graff (1979, 1981c, 1986); Isaacs (1976a, 1976b); Ginzburg (1980); Stout (1977).

On the possibilities from oral history, see the continuing work and the data base developed by Paul Thompson at the University of Essex, described in Thompson (1975, 1978). In a similar vein, see Radway (1984); Heath (1983); Whiteman (1981).

[4]This literature—actually several different copies of it—is much too vast to cite here. See for introductions, Higham and Conkin (1979); Rabb and Rotberg (1982); and such journals as *Critical Inquiry*; *New Literary History; Representations*. Access to relevant literary criticism may be gained easily from the works of Holub (1984), Iser (1978), Jauss (1982), Suleiman and Crosman (1980). See also, Kaplan (1984); Darnton (1983); Kaestle (1985); Hall (1983, 1984, 1985).

References

Abrams, P. (1980). History, sociology, historical sociology. *Past & Present, 87*, 3-16.

Arnove, R.F., & Graff, H.J. (Eds.). (1987). *National literacy campaigns: Historical and comparative perspectives*. New York: Plenum.

Burke, P. (1978). *Popular culture in early modern Europe*. New York: Harper and Row.

Calhoun, D. (1973). *The intelligence of a people*. Princeton: Princeton University Press.

Carpenter, K.E. (Ed.). (1983). *Books and society in history*. New York: R.R. Bowker.

Cipolla, C. (1969). *Literacy and development in the west*. Harmondsworth: Penguin.

Clanchy, M.T. (1979). *From memory to written record: England, 1066-1307*. Cambridge, MA: Harvard University Press.

Cook-Gumperz, J. (Ed.). (1986). *The social construction of literacy*. Cambridge: Cambridge University Press.

Cressy, D. (1980). *Literacy and the social order*. Cambridge: Cambridge University Press.

Darnton, R. (1972). Reading, writing, and publishing in 18th-century France. In F. Gilbert & S.R. Graubard (Eds.), *Historical studies today* (pp. 238-250). New York: Norton.

Darnton, R. (1982). *The literacy underground of the old regime*. Cambridge, MA: Harvard University Press.

Darnton, R. (1983). What is the history of books? In K.E. Carpenter (Ed.), *Books and society in history* (pp. 3-28). New York: R.R. Bowker.

Darnton, R. (1985). Readers respond to Rousseau: The fabrication of romantic sensitivity. In R. Darton (Ed.), *The great cat massacre and other episodes in French cultural history* (pp. 215-256).

Davis, N.Z. (1975). Printing and the people. In N.Z. Davis (Ed.), *Society and culture in early modern France* (pp. 189-226). Stanford: Stanford University Press.

Eisenstein, E. (1979). *The printing press as an agent of change* (2 vols.). Cambridge: Cambridge University Press.

Engelsing, R. (1973). Analphabetentum und lektrue. *Zue sozialgeschichte des lesen in Deuschland zwichen feudaler und industrieller Gesellschaft.* Stuttgart.

Engelsing, R. (1974). *Der burger als leser: Lesergeschichte in Deutschland, 1500-1800.* Stuttgart.

Feather, J. (1985). *The provincial book trade in 18th-century England.* Cambridge: Cambridge University Press.

Febvre, L., & Martin, H. (1958). *L'apparition du livre.* Paris: Editions Albin Michel.

Febvre, L., & Martin, H. (1976). *The coming of the book.* London: New Left Books.

Flueury, M., & Valmary, P. (1957). Les progres de l'instruction elementaire de Louis XIV a Napoleon III. *Population, 12,* 71-92.

Furet, F., & Ozouf, J. (1977). *Lire et ecrire* (2 vols.). Paris: Editions de Minuit.

Furet, F., & Ozouf, J. (1983). *Reading and writing.* Cambridge: Cambridge University Press.

Galenson, D. (1981). Literacy and age in preindustrial England: Quantitative evidence and implications. *Economic Development and Cultural Change, 29,* 823-829.

Garcia, H.D. (1977). *Communications in the migration to Kentucky, 1769-1792.* Unpublished doctoral dissertation, University of Wisconsin, Madison.

Gilmore, W.J. (1989). *Reading becomes a necessity of life.* Knoxville: University of Tennessee Press.

Ginzburg, C. (1980). *The cheese and the worms.* Baltimore: Johns Hopkins University Press.

Graff, H.J. (1979). *The literacy myth: Literacy and social structure in the 19th-century city.* New York: Academic Press.

Graff, H.J. (1981a). *Literacy in history: An interdisciplinary research bibliography.* New York: Garland.

Graff, H.J. (Ed.). (1981b). *Literacy and social development in the west.* Cambridge: Cambridge University Press.

Graff, H.J. (1981c). Reflections on history of literacy: Overview, critique, and proposals. *Humanities in Society, 4,* 303-333.

Graff, H.J. (1986). *The legacies of literacy: Continuities and contradictions in western culture and society.* Bloomington: Indiana University Press.

Graff, H.J. (1987). *The labyrinths of literacy: Reflections on past and present.* Sussex: Falmer Press.

Hall, D.D. (1979). The world of print and collective mentality in seventeenth-century New England. In J. Higham & P.K. Conklin (Eds.), *New directions in American intellectual history* (pp. 166-180).

Hall, D.D. (1982). Literacy, religion and the plain style. In *New England begins: The 17th century: 2. Mentality and environment* (pp. 102-112). Boston: Museum of Fine Art.

Hall, D.D. (1983). The uses of literacy in New England, 1660-1850. In W.L. Joyce, D.D. Hall, R.D. Brown, & J.B. Hench (Eds.), *Printing and society in early America* (1-47). Worcester, MA: American Antiquarian Society.

Hall, D.D. (1984). On native ground: From the history of printing to the history of the book. *Proceedings, American Antiquarian Society, 92*, 313-336.

Hall, D.D. (1985). A report on the 1984 conference on needs and opportunities in the history of the book in American culture. *Proceedings, American Antiquarian Society, 95*, 101-112.

Heath, S.B. (1980). The functions and uses of literacy. *Journal of Communication, 30*, 123-133.

Heath, S.B. (1983). *Ways with words: Language, life and work in communities and classrooms.* Cambridge: Cambridge University Press.

Higham, J., & Conkin, P. (Eds.). (1979). *New directions in American intellectual history.* Baltimore: Johns Hopkins University Press.

Hobsbawm, E.J. (1980). The revival of narrative: Some comments. *Past & Present, 86*, 3-8.

Holub, R.C. (1984). *Reception theory: A critical introduction.* London: Metheun.

Houston, R. (1983). Literacy and society in the west, 1500-1800. *Social History, 8*, 269-293.

Houston, R. (1985). *Scottish literacy and the Scottish identity: Illiteracy and society in Scotland and Northern England, 1600-1800.* Cambridge: Cambridge University Press.

Isaacs, R. (1976a). Dramatizing the ideology of revolution: Popular mobilization in Virginia, 1774 to 1776. *William and Mary Quarterly, 33*, 357-385.

Isaacs, R. (1976b). Preachers and patriots: Popular culture and the revolution in Virginia. In A.F. Young (Ed.), *The American revolution* (pp. 125-156). DeKalb: Northern Illinois University Press.

Isaacs, R. (1982). *The transformation of Virginia.* Chapel Hill: University of North Carolina Press.

Iser, W. (1974). *The implied reader: Patterns of communication in prose fiction from Bunyan to Beckett.* Baltimore: Johns Hopkins University Press.

Iser, W. (1978). *The act of reading: A theory of aesthetic response.* Baltimore: Johns Hopkins Press.

Jauss, H.R. (1982). *Toward an aesthetic of reception.* (T. Bahti, Trans.). Minneapolis: University of Minnesota Press. (Original work published 1975)

Johansson, E. (1977). *The history of literacy in Sweden.* (Educational Report, No. 12. Umea, Sweden: Umea University and School of Education.

Johansson, E. (1981). The history of literacy in Sweden. In H.J. Graff (Ed.), *Literacy and social development in the west* (pp. 151-182).

Johansson, E. (1985). Popular literacy in Scandinavia about 1600-1900. *Historical Social Research, 34,* 60-64.

Joyce, W.L., Hall, D.D., Brown, R.D., & Hench, J.B. (Eds.). (1983). *Printing and society in early America.* Worcester, MA: American Antiquarian Society.

Kaestle, C.F. (1985). The history of literacy and the history of readers. *Review of Educational Research, 12,* 11-53.

Kaestle, C.F., & Trollinger, W.V. (1986, August). *Difficulty of text as a factor in the history of reading* (Program Report No. 86-13). Madison: University of Wisconsin, Wisconsin Center for Education Research.

Kammen, M. (Ed.). (1980). *The past before us.* Ithaca, NY: Cornell University Press.

Kaplan, S.L. (Ed.). (1984). *Understanding popular culture: Europe from middle ages to 19th century.* Berlin: Mouton.

Kett, J.F., & McClung, P.A. (1984). Book culture in post-revolutionary Virginia. *Proceedings, American Antiquarian Society, 94,* 97-147.

LaCapra, D., & Kaplan, S.L. (Eds.). (1982). *Modern European intellectual history.* Ithaca, NY: Cornell University Press.

Laqueur, T.W. (1976). The cultural origins of popular literacy in England, 1500-1800. *Oxford Review of Education, 2,* 255-272.

LeRoy Laudrie, E. (1978). *Montaillou: Promised land of error.* New York: Braziller.

Levine, D. (1979). Education and family life in early industrial England. *Journal of Family History, 4,* 368-380.

Lockridge, K.A. (1974). *Literacy in colonial New England.* New York: Norton.

Martin, H.J. (1968-1970). *Le livre et la civilisation ecrite* (3 vols.). Paris: Ecole Nationale Superieure des Biblioteques.

Martin, H.J. (1975). Culture ecrite et culture orale, culture savante et culture opulaire dans la France d'ancien regime. *Journale des Savants,* 225-282.

Mitchell, S. (1981). *The fallen angel: Chastity, class and women's reading, 1835-1880.* Bowling Green, OH: Popular Press.

Noakes, S. (1977, Winter). The 15th Oes, the *Disticha Catonis,* Marculfius, and Dick, Jane, and Sally. *University of Chicago Library Bulletin,* pp. 2-15.

Noakes, S. (1981). The development of the book market in late Quattrocento Italy: Printers' failures and the role of the middleman. *Journal of Medieval and Renaissance Studies, 11,* 23-55.

Rabb, T.K., & Rotberg, R.I. (Eds.). (1982). *The new history: 1980s and beyond.* Princeton: Princeton University Press.

Radway, J.A. (1984). *Reading the romance: Women, patriarchy, and popular literature.* Chapel Hill: University of North Carolina Press.

Radway, J.A. (1986). Identifying ideological seams: Mass culture, analytic method, and political practice. *Communication, 9,* 93-123.

Saenger, P. (1982). Silent reading: Its impact on late medieval script and society. *Viator, 53*, 367-414.

Schieffelin, B.B., & Gilmore, P. (Eds.). (1986). *The acquisition of literacy: Ethnographic perspectives*. Norwood, NJ: Ablex.

Schofield, R.S. (1968). The measurement of literacy in pre-industrial England. In J. Goody (Ed.), *Literacy in traditional society* (pp. 311-325). Cambridge: Cambridge University Press.

Schofield, R.S. (1973). The dimensions of illiteracy in England, 1750-1850. *Explorations in Economic History, 10*, 437-454.

Scribner, R.W. (1981). *For the sake of simple folk: Popular propaganda for the German reformation*. Cambridge: Cambridge University Press.

Scribner, S. (1984). Studying working intelligence. In B. Rogoff & J. Lowe (Eds.), *Everyday cognition: Its development in social context* (pp. 9-40). Cambridge, MA: Harvard University Press.

Scribner, R.W. (1984). Oral culture and the diffusion of reformation ideas. *History of European Ideas, 5*, 237-256.

Scribner, S., & Cole, M. (1981). *The psychology of literacy*. Cambridge, MA: Harvard University Press.

Soltow, L., & Steven, E. (1981). *The rise of literacy and the common school in the United States*. Chicago: University of Chicago Press.

Spufford, M. (1979). First steps in literacy: The reading and writing experience of the humblest 17th century spiritual autobiographers. *Social History, 4*, 407-435.

Spufford, M. (1981). *Small books and pleasant histories: Popular fiction and its readership in 17th-century England*. London: Methuen.

Stevens, E. (1985). Literacy and the worth of liberty. *Historical Social Research, 34*, 65-81.

Stevens, J.D., & Garcia, H.D. (1980). *Communication history*. Beverly Hills: Sage.

Stone, L. (1969). Literacy and education in England, 1640-1900. *Past & Present, 42*, 69-139.

Stone, L. (1979). The rival of narrative: Reflection on a new old history. *Past & Present, 85*, 3-24.

Stout, H.S. (1977). Religion, communications, and the ideological origins of the American revolution. *William and Mary Quarterly, 34*, 519-541.

Strauss, G. (1978). *Luther's house of learning*. Baltimore, MD: Johns Hopkins University Press.

Strauss, G. (1984). Lutheranism and literacy: A reassessment. In K. von Greyerz (Ed.), *Religion and society in early modern Europe* (pp. 109-123). London: Allen and Unwin

Strayssm, G., & Gawthorp, R. (1984). Protestantism and literacy in early modern Germany. *Past & Present, 104*, 31-55.

Suleiman, S.R., & Crosman, I. (Eds.). (1980). *The reader in the text: Essays on audience and interpretation*. Princeton: Princeton University Press.

Tannen, D. (Ed.). (1982). *Spoken and written language: Exploring orality and literacy*. Norwood, NJ: Ablex.

Thompkins, J.P. (Ed.). (1980). *Reader-response criticism: From formalism to post-structuralism*. Baltimore: Johns Hopkins University Press.

Thompson, P. (1975). *The Edwardians*. Bloomington: Indiana University Press.

Thompson, P. (1978). *The voice of the past: Oral history*. Oxford: Oxford University Press.

Vincent, D. (1981). *Bread, knowledge and freedom: A study of 19th-century working class autobiography*. London: Europa.

Webb, R.K. (1955). *The British working class reader*. London: Allen and Urwin.

Whiteman, M.F. (Ed.). (1981). *Writing: The nature, development and teaching of written composition: Vol. 1. Variation in writing*. Hillsdale, NJ: Lawrence Erlbaum.

Winchester, I. (1978, 1980). *How many ways to universal literacy?* Paper presented to the Ninth World Congress of Sociology, 1978, and Seminar on the History of Literacy in Post-Reformation Europe, University of Leicester, 1980.

Wrightson, K., & Levine, D. (1979). *Poverty and piety*. New York: Academic Press.

Part II:
Reading in Childhood

5
The Spelling-Sound Code in Reading

Connie Juel

Imagine you are a child in the first grade. You have learned to recognize a few words (/¥ = *the*; ¶•/ = *cat*; [= *down*). You have learned the "sounds" of some letters (• = the sound at the start of *apple*; $ = the sound at the start of *sun*). Now you are sitting in a circle around your teacher with several other children when the big moment finally arrives. Your first real school book is passed out, and the teacher calls on you to read the first sentence. All eyes are upon you as you start to read aloud:

/¥ ¶•/ $•/ [.

If you, the adult, try to read the previous sentence you may concentrate attention on identifying each word, and your slow, word-by-word attempts will sound much like those of the beginner. As adults we forget that the process by which we learned to recognize thousands of words in print more than likely had a slow and labored start.

Children appear to approach word learning much as they approach any new labeling task: They look for cues that distinguish the new object from other objects they already know. We know, for example, that when learning to identify a dog, children frequently seize upon one of the more salient visual features of dogs, that they have four legs. This may lead a child to temporarily label other creatures with four legs as dogs. Eventually the child learns additional distinguishing features of dogs after comparing them to other animals with four legs that have different labels, such as cats. The child learns that dogs are four-legged and large, whereas cats are four-legged and small.

This same process of finding distinguishing features occurs as children learn to identify printed words. At first the child may not even know to look at the print itself for such features. Such children "read" the McDonald's sign by the golden arches or the stop sign through its color. My colleague, Phil Gough (Gough & Hillenger, 1980), performed a simple experiment with preschool children that demonstrates this point. He taught a group of nonreaders to identify 10 words, which were printed on flashcards. These words were high frequency nouns taken from a popular preprimer reader. On one of the flashcards there was a noticeable thumbprint. He had simply taken his thumb, stuck it on an ink pad, and pressed it at the bottom of one of the cards. After the children had learned to read the 10 flashcards, he had them read them with 2 new flashcards snuck in. One card had nothing but a thumbprint on it, and 1 card had the old word without the thumbprint. Although most of the children read the card with only the thumbprint as the old word, most missed the correct word when it appeared without the thumbprint.

When environmental cues such as the thumbprint or the color of a sign no longer suffice, the child will begin to focus on the print. Initially the child will grasp the more salient visual features of the printed word, such as the *oo* in *moon* or the dot in the middle of *pig* or the length of *elephant* (Gates & Boeker, 1923). First and last letters frequently are used as recall cues (Samuels & Jeffrey, 1966). When the teacher introduces the new words for a story on the board a child may remember that the one that starts with a *c* is *cat*, whereas the long one is *sidewalk*. Unfortunately this arbitrary recall approach is doomed. The next day the child may forget what were the likely candidates for the words in her story. That is, she may forget the words introduced the day before, and/or the child may encounter another word that starts with *c* or is long (or, as in the introductory example, "•" for "¶•/" will no longer suffice when "•/" is introduced). At this point each new word that the child needs to learn will be harder to remember than the one before it, as more distinguishing features have to be found and recalled (Gough & Hillinger, 1980).

Unlike telling the difference between a dog and a cat, the differences distinguishing between printed words can be very subtle, resting on a single letter in a particular position. When the child must quickly learn to distinguish many words, as in first grade, reading can become an increasingly frustrating activity if the child continues to use arbitrary cues. To advance, children need to discover a more efficient, less arbitrary, cue system for word identification. One of the roles of reading teachers, then is to guide children towards useful cues and to make sure teaching practices and materials don't encourage the use of irrelevant cues.

Only three useful cue systems exist. The child can memorize the visual sequence of letters in a word, the child can make use of spelling-sound correspondences, or sometimes the child can fashion a hybrid system, using story context, usually in conjunction with the memorization of some letters or sounds, to identify words. Although some words can (and some must) be memorized as visual letter sequences, the great advantage of alphabetic languages is that there is a degree of correspondence between visual letter sequences and sounds. These spelling-sound correspondences allow an alternative route for the reader to use to identify a word that is not immediately recognized on the basis of well rehearsed visual sequences (i.e., words never seen before or words infrequently seen). The inexperienced reader is more likely to actively use spelling-sound correspondences to identify words than the experienced reader (Doctor & Coltheart, 1980; Juel, 1983; Shankweiler & Liberman, 1972; Soderberg, 1977). To progress in reading, the child must discover the spelling-sound cue system and break the "code" of the written language.

Prerequisites to Discovering Spelling-Sound Correspondences

In order to break the code of the written language, Gough and Hillinger (1980) suggest that four conditions must be met. First, the child must have cryptanalytic intent; that is, he or she must understand that print is encoded speech. Second, the child must have alphabet knowledge; that is the child must be aware of the letters in a word and their order. Third, the child must have phonemic awareness; he or she must be aware that words are composed of phonemes. Fourth, the child must have data for cryptanalysis; the child must have seen enough words paired with their spoken counterparts to discover the relations between the visual and oral equivalents.

Of the above, phonemic awareness may be the most difficult condition to meet. Phonemic awareness is the realization that oral words are sequences of meaningless sounds (i.e., phonemes) that can be independently manipulated. This realization is not necessary for understanding or producing speech. In speech production there is no clear distinction between phonemes, as one phoneme may overlap another. In understanding speech it is even necessary at some level to "ignore" individual phonemes (e.g, to understand that *kinda* means *kind of*). The speaker and listener both focus on the contextual meaning of the communication. Prior knowledge of people and objects in conversation, as well as features of conversations such as intonation and gesture, usually provide substantial contextual support for the overall message.

Many young children seem oblivious to even the most elemental form of phonemic awareness, that is, the acoustic duration of words. Rozin, Bressman, and Taft (1974) had children pronounce with a tester two words that varied considerably in length (e.g, *mow* and *motorcycle*). Then children indicated which of two printed words was the spoken word. Even a child who cannot read could do this task by matching the long printed word to the long spoken word, but preschool and kindergarten children were not very good at this task. Lundberg and Tornéus (1978) found that even 6-year-old Swedish children did not perform well on this task. Compulsory education does not start in Sweden until the child is 7 years old. This finding suggests that print exposure, which is inherent to the school environment, may actually induce or foster phonemic awareness. Indeed, on the basis of a longitudinal study of first-grade children, Perfetti, Beck, and Hughes (1981) found that some phonemic awareness abilities (such as phoneme blending) are prerequisites to learning to read, whereas other abilities (such as identifying the number of phonemes in a word) are augmented by print exposure.

Besides print exposure, there are language activities that may stimulate phonemic awareness. These activities may vary among cultures. Calfee, Chapman, and Venezky (1972) found, for example, that most American kindergarten children are quite unable to rhyme words. Yet, at a recent symposium on phonemic awareness held at the University of Virginia (1987), Peter Byrant indicated that many British 4-year-olds are quite good at rhyming. (It should be noted here that compulsory education starts at age 5 in Britain). Barbara Foorman (1987) suggested that the emphasis on the memorization of traditional English nursery rhymes in British preschools may contribute to this advantage. It would certainly seem that in homes or school where adults engage in frequent word play with children (i.e., through rhymes, Dr. Seuss books) children may be stimulated to attend to the phonetic level of speech—a level which is otherwise easy to ignore.

Activities which foster phonemic awareness at home or in the school are worth exploring as there is compelling evidence from both experimental and longitudinal studies from several countries that some form of phonemic awareness is necessary for successfully learning to read alphabetic languages (e.g., Blachman & James, 1985, United States; Bradley & Bryant, 1983, Great Britain; Elkonin, 1963, 1973, Soviet Union; Fox & Routh, 1975, United States; Juel, Griffith, & Gough, 1986, United States; Lundberg, Oloffson, & Wall, 1980, Sweden; Share, Jorm, Maclean, & Matthews, 1984, Australia; Tornéus, 1984, Sweden; Treiman & Baron, 1982, United States; Tunmer & Nesdale, 1985, Australia; Williams, 1984, review of studies from several countries).

Instruction and Growth in Spelling-Sound Knowledge

With phonemic awareness the child can begin to make connections between letters and sounds. In school, phonic instruction will attempt to make letter-sound correspondences explicit. We have found, though, that phonics instruction is not effective unless children already have (or quickly develop) some phonemic awareness at the beginning of first grade (Juel, Griffith, & Gough, 1986).

In one aspect of the above study we identified two groups of first-grade children, both of whom had been exposed to fairly large amounts of print in their readers and also had received a year's phonics instruction, but who differed in their levels of phonemic awareness (i.e., high phonemic awareness vs. low phonemic awareness). We tested them for spelling-sound knowledge by having them read a list of 50 pseudowords (Bryant Test of Basic Decoding Skill). The first 20 pseudowords on the Bryant are CVC's (e.g., *buf, dit, nuv*), and most of the remaining items are slightly more complex single syllable or two syllable pseudowords (e.g., *yode, shi, cleef, consuv*). We found a significant difference between the two groups on performance on the Bryant test. At the end of first grade, the low phonemic awareness group had a mean score on the Bryant of 3.7, with a modal score of zero. Despite having been exposed to large amounts of print and a year of phonics instruction, many of the low phonemic awareness children could not read a single nonsense word at the end of first grade. In contrast, the mean score for the high phonemic awareness group was 27.9, and the mode was 21.

It appears that only children with phonemic awareness can readily benefit from phonics instruction. Assuming the child has phonemic awareness, phonics instruction may teach some letter-sound correspondences. There is an inexact match between the actual sounds of letter(s) and the sounds that are taught in phonics, however. The letter *b*, for example, does not make a *buh* sound, as is usually ascribed to it in phonics. Rather the child must learn that the teacher only approximates the sound, that *b* makes a sound like that heard at the beginning of *buh* and not like the *uh* at the end. In doing this the child is being directed to one of the most relevant cues for identifying words, that is, their constituent sounds. Also, the child is learning that the printed form of a word is not random—that there is some correspondence between letters and sounds. Rather than trying to memorize some arbitrary visual cue to remember a word, the child learns to search for letter-sound cues in words, and by so doing induces the *real* spelling-sound correspondences. This type of induction will be necessary in any case, for it also appears that the rules covered by phonics instruction cannot account for the mastery of several hundred "rules" by the skilled reader (Honeycutt, undated; Venezky, 1967).

That children can induce phonic generalizations without explicit instruction has been shown (Durkin, 1966; Ehri, 1978; Goodman, 1980), but it is also apparent that phonics instruction can hasten acquisition of these generalizations and influence word recognition strategies (Barr, 1972, 1974, 1974-1975; Chall, 1967; DeLawter, 1970; Elder, 1971; Evans & Carr, 1983; MacKinnon, 1959). When phonics instruction is paired with initial reading texts that contain mainly regular decodable words, we find that more rapid learning of the taught phonic generalizations occurs and that children more rapidly induce *un*taught generalizations (Juel & Roper/Schneider, 1985). Unfortunately many basal series treat phonics lessons as if they had no relation to story reading (Beck, 1981). That is, children may receive a phonics lesson on the short *o* sound (e.g., as in *cop*) and then read text with few short *o* words to practice upon—and even worse, encounter words that violate what they were just taught (e.g., *come*). Children in such a situation frequently abandon their attempts to "sound out" words (Juel & Roper/Schneider, 1985).

Children who do not or cannot apply spelling-sound knowledge are not taking advantage of the alphabetic nature of English. They both recognize and write words in qualitatively different ways than children who possess such knowledge (Gough, Juel, & Roper/Schneider, 1983; Juel, et al., 1985). Let's illustrate this difference with some actual data from Juel, Griffith, and Gough (1985). In that study we asked 120 children in February of first grade to pronounce the Bryant list of 50 pseudowords. Twenty children were unable to pronounce a single nonsense word. We then compared word recognition and spelling performance of these 20 children with the 20 children who correctly pronounced the most pseudowords on the Bryant. We identified 69 words that were on the core vocabulary lists of their basal readers. We asked the 40 children to do two tasks: (a) read the 69 words and tell how they knew what the word was and (b) spell each word after it was pronounced orally and used in a sentence. These two tasks were, of course, separated by a few weeks.

We expected that children who scored high on the Bryant would be much better readers and spellers. The data confirmed this. We also expected and found a qualitative difference in the types of errors they made on the word recognition and spelling tasks. The word recognition errors of the poor Bryant scorers were usually real word substitutions. In particular, these children frequently substituted a real word that started with the same letter as the target word *and* was a word that had been in their basal reader. In other words, they reached into the bag of words stored in their head that they knew were likely candidates for a printed word and pulled one out that contained some of the letters of the unrecognizable word. In response to the word *rain*, for example, the reading errors of the poor spelling-sound children were: *ring, in, runs, with, ride, art, are, on, reds, running, why*, and three *ran*'s. When the high Bryant scorers (the children with good spelling-sound knowledge) made a word recognition error, they frequently substituted a nonsense word reflecting unsuccessful attempts to sound out the target. Only two of these children incorrectly read *rain*; one said *running* and one said *rannin*.

When we asked the children to tell us how they knew the words they correctly (or incorrectly) read, there were differences in what the two groups said. The spelling-sound children referred both to a specific letter or letters in the word (e.g., "the *sk* in *ask*"), to all the letters in the word (e.g., "because it has: *c, o, m, e*"), and to particular locations where the word appeared (e.g., "because it's on the bulletin board"). The good spelling-sound children more often mentioned particular sounds (e.g., "because the *er* says /r/ in *her*").

We expected the spelling-sound knowledge of the high Bryant scorers to be even more apparent in spelling. It was thought that these children would frequently spell a word by segmenting it into phonemes, and then apply spelling-sound knowledge to arrive at a spelling. We predicted and found that most of the spelling errors of these children were homophonous errors. The spelling errors of good spelling-sound knowledge children to *rain*, for example, were: *rian, raing, raine*, and five *rane*'s.

The children with poor spelling-sound knowledge, by contrast, could only spell a word by recalling a "visual" image or by guessing. Their errors were thus unlikely to be homophonous. If they could not locate a complete image of a word they would substitute another real word; or , if they located an incomplete image and recalled approximate length, they would fill it in with random letters. In response to *rain* used in a sentence, the spelling errors of these children were: *weir, rach, yes, uan, ramt, fen, rur, Rambl, wetn* (a possible blend of the word *wet* which the child knew and the letter *n*, which was what he could recall of *rain*), *wnishire, Rup*, five *ran*'s, and one drawing of raindrops.

My colleague, Nancy Roser, shared with me a conversation she had with her daughter, Erin, who at the time had been in first grade for about a month. Nancy was driving her daughter to school when Erin started to tell her about learning to read. Being a reading researcher, Nancy pulled the car over, took out her notepad and recorded.

Erin: I figured out how to learn to read. If you know how to spell, you take apart the letters. And then you sound out those letters and you make a word. Then you can read something with it.

Nancy: Like what?

Erin: A book

Nancy: Is there another way to read?

Erin: Not that I can think of (pause). Oh, you can just read out of books. Just remember those words. Read them in a book. Memorize it. But that's a lot harder.

Indeed it would appear that attempting to remember either distinctive visual cues or all the letters in a word would be difficult for the beginner. In the very first reading books in first grade (the preprimers), which are usually completed between September and December, the child is exposed to between 300 and 600 *different* words in running text of well over 5,000 words (Juel & Roper/Schneider, 1985). The beginning reader is constantly encountering words that have not been seen before and words that may not be repeated for awhile. At this early stage, spelling-sound knowledge will be quite useful, if not essential.

Sounding out words cannot only allow the child some independence in reading, but the concentrated attention on the letters during that process may eventually allow the child to circumvent sounding out altogether. Either the application of letter-sound information becomes rapid and automatic, or it is not needed as the visual/orthographic representation of the word has now been amalgamated to its sound and meaning (Ehri, 1984, 1985). The speed at which good readers can name pseudowords (e.g., *dit, cleef*) suggests just how automatic the process of phonological recoding can become. Moreover, speed of pseudoword naming is a task that clearly differentiates good from poor readers (Perfetti & Hagaboam, 1975). Venezky (1976) indicates that spelling-sound knowledge continues to grow at least through eighth grade—long after formal instruction in such knowledge has ceased.

The automatic recognition of a large corpus of high frequency words seems to appear by second or third grade (Doehring, 1976; Golinkoff & Rosinski, 1976; Guttentag & Haith, 1978, 1979, 1980; Rosinski, 1977; Rosinski, Golinkoff, & Kukish, 1975; West & Stanovich, 1979). There appears a shift from the primary to the upper elementary grades from phonological recoding to direct lexical access of many words (Backman, Bruck, Hebert, & Seidenberg, 1984; Doctor & Coltheart, 1980; Juel, 1983). In comparing the impact of spelling-sound (i.e., cipher knowledge) and word specific (i.e., lexical knowledge) on word recognition skill, we found that cipher knowledge predominated in first grade, whereas lexical information had the edge by the end of second grade (Juel et. al, 1986).

The process of learning to read words would appear frequently to be something like this: (a) the child laboriously sounds out words; (b) a corpus of words the child has frequently seen and sounded out elicit either automatic phonological processing or become recognizable purely on the basis of orthographic features; (c) the child can now read more words "automatically," which leads to wider reading; (d) with wide reading the child learns even more spelling-sound information, which can be applied to new words until they too become automatically recognized.

Consequences of Poor Spelling-Sound Knowledge

The importance of early phonemic awareness and spelling-sound knowledge lies in their impact on later reading achievement. Through the use of path analysis, Tunmer and Nesdale (1985) showed that in first grade phonological analysis affects reading comprehension indirectly, through phonological recoding (as measured by pseudoword naming). With path analysis we found the same relationship (Juel, Griffith, & Gough, 1986).

We examined the literacy development of approximately 120 children and, in particular, the relation between phonemic awareness, spelling-sound knowledge (as measured by the Bryant pseudoword test), and reading comprehension at the end of first grade. Sixty-three children scored at or above grade level on the Iowa TBS Reading Comprehension subtest at the end of first grade. Spelling-sound knowledge was measured by the Bryant test of pseudoword reading. Phonemic awareness was measured through a test developed by Roper/Schneider (1984). We found that there were almost no children at the end of first grade with low phonemic awareness who had average or above average performance on the Bryant decoding test. There were, however, some children with average or above average phonemic awareness at the end of first grade who had poor spelling-sound knowledge. Phonemic awareness would thus appear to be a necessary, but not sufficient, prerequisite to growth in spelling-sound knowledge.

Only four children with above average spelling-sound knowledge had below average reading comprehension at the end of first grade; all other children who were at or above average in spelling-sound knowledge had at least average reading comprehension. It may be that those children with poor spelling-sound knowledge (and who have at least average reading comprehension at the end of first grade) have been successful in memorizing enough visual orthographic cues about particular words to have a minimal first-grade reading vocabulary. We would, however, expect them to be reading in a qualitatively different way than those children with good spelling-sound knowledge.

Thus the poor reading comprehenders at the end of first grade were mainly children below the mean on the Bryant decoding test. Many of these children entered first grade with little phonemic awareness. We were interested in what would happen to these children in subsequent years; we wanted to know if they would remain poor readers.

To study this point, I looked at what happened to the bottom quartile of children on the TBS Iowa Reading Comprehension subtest at the end of first grade. The mean of the group was only K6 on the TBS, and none of the children scored above a 1.2 grade equivalent. There were 29 of these children of which 24 remained at the school through fourth grade. Of the 24, all but 3 were still poor readers in fourth grade. They had a group mean of 3.5 on the TBS with no student scoring higher than grade equivalent 4.2 (Juel, 1988).

Of the 24 children who remained poor readers through the four grades, only 2 had average decoding skills. At the end of fourth grade, the other 22 children were at least one standard deviation below their average and good reader peers on the Bryant pseudoword test. These 22 children could not decode all the monosyllable pseudowords (e.g., *dit, cleef, yode*) on the Bryant, *despite 4 years of reading instruction*.

Most of the children who became poor decoders entered first grade with little phonemic awareness. Although their phonemic awareness steadily grew in first grade, they left first grade with less phonemic awareness than that which the children who became average or good readers possessed upon *entering* first grade. This appeared to contribute to a very slow start in learning spelling-sound correspondences. Nine of the poor readers could not read a single pseudoword on the Bryant at the end of first grade—despite a year of phonics instruction. By the end of fourth grade the poor decoders had still not achieved the level of decoding that the average and good readers had achieved by the beginning of second grade.

The depressing finding about the poor readers in our study is quite similar to one found by Lundberg (1984) in a longitudinal study of children learning to read in Sweden. Lundberg found that linguistic awareness of words and phonemes in first grade correlated .70 with reading achievement in sixth grade. Moreover, of the 46 Swedish children in this study with low linguistic awareness and low reading achievement in first grade, 40 were still poor readers in sixth grade.

The findings from Lundberg's (1984) and our own longitudinal study certainly suggest both that children who begin school with phonemic awareness are at a distinct advantage in learning to read an alphabetic language and that this early advantage yields long-term benefits. Children with phonemic awareness can both realize the alphabetic principle and better learn taught letter-sound relations and/or induce them from print, leading to much more rapid text exposure.

One encouraging note for the child who is a poor decoder in first grade comes from Calfee and Piontkowski (1981). They studied the reading development of 50 first grade children from 10 classrooms in four schools. They then compared end-of-year first grade development with end-of-year reading achievement in second grade. Although overall they found a moderately strong correlation between decoding skill in first grade and reading achievement in second grade ($r = .65$), there was considerable variation in this relation among the 4 schools. In 1 school, the relation was virtually impossible to measure as so few children learned to decode; in another school the ranking on the decoding test was almost identical to that on the reading achievement test. The one hopeful case was a school in which the reading program in second grade appeared to promote a uniformly high level of reading achievement by the end of the year—despite the student's success or lack of success in learning letter-sound correspondences in first grade (pp. 369-370). Unfortunately we don't know the specific processes that made the second grade program at this school so successful.

It also appears that poor early decoding leads to additional problems. Faulty decoding skill prevents poor decoders from reading as much as good decoders. By the end of first grade, the good readers in our study had seen approximately 18,681 words in running text in their basal readers. The poor readers, however, had seen only about half as many—9,975. Other researchers have found similar differences among ability groups to exposure to print (Allington, 1984; Biemiller, 1977-1978). The difference in exposure to print in first grade continues in subsequent grades, and by at least the end of second grade is further compounded by differences in the amount of time spent reading outside of school (Juel, 1988). In this 4 year study, children who had been poor readers in first and second grade expressed a very real dislike of reading by third and fourth grade, and so it is relatively easy to understand why they read little after school.

One of the most surprising findings in my longitudinal study, however, was the difference in listening comprehension (i.e, difference in vocabulary, syntax, concepts, and pragmatics in understanding text that is orally read) that emerged between the children who early on in first grade learned to decode, and those who did not. We have hypothesized that in spite of certain differences in form between speech and written text (cf. Rubin, 1980), a single underlying process directs both reading and listening comprehension. This implies that, given perfect decoding, a child will read and comprehend a written text exactly as well as the child will comprehend the text if it is spoken (Gough & Tunmer, 1986; Juel et al., 1986). The difference in listening comprehension that emerged between the good and poor decoders, then, would be expected to further distance the reading comprehension of the two groups.

The longitudinal study occurred in a low SES neighborhood school with a racially mixed population of children. Whether due to the predominant (i.e., home) language being Spanish, or dialect differences, or other factors associated with low SES, those children who became average to good readers *and* those who became poor readers started first grade with scores on the Metropolitan Readiness Test, School Language and Listening Comprehension subtest that averaged below the 39th percentile. At the end of first grade both groups were still low average on the TBS Listening Comprehension subtest.

The children who became good decoders and therefore good readers in first grade made considerable growth in listening comprehension after first grade, however. These children had a mean grade equivalent on the TBS Listening Comprehension subtest of 5.2 at the end of fourth grade. The children who were poor readers, however, made almost no growth in listening comprehension on this subtest after second grade. They ended fourth grade with a mean grade equivalent on the TBS Listening Comprehension subtest of only 2.6.

In my longitudinal study, the poor readers in fourth grade (i.e., children who scored below a 4.2 grade equivalent on the TBS Reading Comprehension subtest) were mainly children who were neither competent at decoding nor competent listeners. Although in each grade, skill in word recognition was more predictive of reading comprehension than was skill in listening comprehension, the impact of listening comprehension rose steadily with each grade level (Juel, 1988). It is likely that the impact of listening comprehension would only continue to grow with each higher grade (cf. Curtis, 1980; Singer, 1976).

Nagy and Anderson (1984) postulate: "Beginning in about third grade, the major determinant of vocabulary growth is amount of free reading" (p. 327). Stanovich (1986) has labeled this type of phenomenon the "Matthew effects." Stanovich states:

> The effect of reading volume on vocabulary growth, combined with the large skill difference in reading volume, could mean a "rich get richer" or cumulative advantage phenomenon is almost inextricably embedded within the developmental course of reading progress. The very children who are reading well and who have good

vocabularies will read more, learn more word meanings, and hence read even better. Children with inadequate vocabularies—who read slowly and without enjoyment— read less, and as a result have slower development of vocabulary knowledge, which inhibits further growth in reading ability. (p. 381)

This statement certainly found support in my longitudinal study. Listening comprehension—and subsequently reading comprehension—appears to be bolstered by the vocabulary, etcetera, that is learned through reading, and, children who do not learn to decode easily, read much less than good decoders both in and out of school (Juel, 1988).

There is much attention in the literature to increasing the reading comprehension skills of older students, yet, a review by Carver (1987) of some studies that had attempted to teach comprehension, found little evidence that the efforts had much payoff. Many studies have attempted to improve students' reading comprehension through development of vocabulary and/or metacognitive comprehension strategies. The reason that these studies may show very little effect could be that it is very difficult to make up for years of lost experiences with the words and concepts found in print through relatively short-term treatments.

What seems essential is to insure that children learn to decode in first grade. If decoding skill arrives too much later, it may be very hard to change the direction that reading achievement will take: Poor decoding skill leads to little reading and little opportunity to increase one's basic vocabulary and knowledge, leaving a shaky foundation for later reading comprehension.

References

Allington, R.L. (1984). Content coverage and contextual reading in reading groups. *Journal of Reading Behavior, 16*, 85-96.

Backman, J., Bruck, M., Hebert, M., & Seidenberg, M.S. (1984). Acquisition and use of spelling-sound correspondences in reading. *Journal of Experimental Child Psychology, 38*, 114-133.

Barr, R. (1972). The influence of instructional conditions on word recognition errors. *Reading Research Quarterly, 7*, 509-529.

Barr, R. (1974). Influence of instruction on early reading. *Interchange, 5*(4), 13-2.

Barr, R. (1974-1975). The effect of instruction on pupil reading strategies. *Reading Research Quarterly, 4*, 55-582.

Beck, I.L. (1981). Reading problems and instructional practices. In G.E. MacKinnon & T.G. Waller (Eds.), *Reading research advances in theory and practice* (Vol. 2, pp. 53-95). New York: Academic Press.

Biemiller, A. (1977-1978). Relationships between oral reading rates for letters, words, and simple text in the development of reading achievement. *Reading Research Quarterly, 13*, 223-253.

Blachman, B.A., & James, S.L. (1985). Metalinguistic abilities and reading achievement in first-grade children. In J. Niles & R. Lalik (Eds.), *Issues in literacy: A research perspective* (pp. 280-286). Rochester, NY: National Reading Conference.

Bradley, L., & Bryant, P.E. (1983). Categorizing sounds and learning to read—a causal connection. *Nature, 301*, 419-421.

Bryant, N.D. (1975). *Diagnostic test of basic decoding skills.* New York: Teachers College, Columbia University.

Bryant, P. (1987, April). *International symposium on phonemic awareness.* Symposium conducted at the George Graham Lectures. University of Virginia, Charlottesville, VA.

Calfee, R.C., Chapman, R., & Venezky, R. (1972). How a child needs to think to learn to read. In L. W. Gross (Ed.), *Cognition in learning and memory* (pp. 139-182). New York: John Wiley & Sons.

Calfee, R.C., & Piontkowski, D.C. (1981). The reading diary: Acquisition of decoding. *Reading Research Quarterly, 16*, 346-373.

Carver, R.P. (1987). Should reading comprehension skills be taught? In J.E. Readence & R.S. Baldwin (Eds.), *Research in literacy: Merging perspectives: National Reading Conference* (pp. 115-126). Rochester, NY: National Reading Conference.

Chall, J.S. (1967). *Learning to read: The great debate.* New York: McGraw Hill.

Curtis, M. (1980). Development of components of reading skill. *Journal of Educational Psychology, 72*, 656-669.

DeLawter, J. (1970). *Oral reading errors of second grade children exposed to two different reading approaches.* Unpublished doctoral dissertation, Columbia University, Teachers College, New York, NY.

Doctor, E., & Coltheart, M. (1980). Children's use of phonological encoding when reading for meaning. *Memory and Cognition, 8*, 195-209.

Doehring, D.G. (1976). Acquisition of rapid responses. *Monographs of the Society for Research in Child Development, 41* (2, Serial No. 165).

Durkin, D. (1966). *Children who read early.* New York: Teachers College Press.

Ehri, L.C. (1978). Beginning reading from a psycholinguistic perspective: Amalgamation of word identities. In F.B. Murray (Ed.), *The development of the reading process.* (International Reading Association Monograph No. 3 pp. 1-33). Newark, DE: International Reading Association.

Ehri, L. (1984). How orthography alters spoken language competencies in children learning to read and spell. In J. Downing & R. Valtin (Eds.), *Language awareness and learning to read* (pp. 119-147). New York: Springer-Verlag.

Ehri, L. (1985). Effects of printed language acquisition on speech. In D. Olson, N. Torrance, & A. Hildyard (Eds.), *Literacy, language, and learning* (pp. 333-367). New York: Cambridge University Press.

Elder, R.D. (1971). Oral reading achievement of Scottish and American children. *Elementary School Journal, 71*, 216-230.

Elkonin, D.B. (1963). The psychology of mastering the elements of reading. In B. Simon & J. Simon (Eds.), *Educational psychology in the U.S.S.R.* (pp. 165-179). London: Routledge & Kegan Paul.

Elkonin, D.B. (1973). U.S.S.R. In J. Downing (Ed.), *Comparative reading* (pp. 551-579). New York: Macmillan.

Evans, M.A., & Carr, T.H. (1983). *Curricular emphasis and reading development: Focus on language or focus on script.* Symposium conducted at the biennial meeting of the Society for Research on Child Development, Detroit, MI.

Foorman, B. (1987, April). *International symposium on phonemic awareness.* Symposium conducted at the George Graham Lectures, Charlottesville, VA.

Fox, B., & Routh, D.K. (1975). Analyzing spoken language into words, syllables, and phonemes: A developmental study. *Journal of Psycholinguistic Research, 4*, 331-342.

Gates, A.I., & Boeker, E. (1923). A study of initial stages in reading by preschool children. *Teachers College Record, 24*, 469-488.

Golinkoff, R.M., & Rosinski, R.R. (1976). Decoding, semantic processing, and reading comprehension skill. *Child Development, 47*, 252-258.

Goodman, Y. (1980). The roots of literacy. In M. P. Douglas (Ed.), *Forty-fourth yearbook of the Claremont Reading Conference* (pp. 1-32). Claremont, CA: Claremont Reading Conference.

Gough, P.B., & Hillinger, M.L. (1980). Learning to read: An unnatural act. *Bulletin of the Orton Society, 30*, 179-196.

Gough, P.B., Juel, C., & Roper/Schneider, D. (1983). Code and cipher: A two stage conception of initial reading acquisition. In J.A. Niles & L.A. Harris (Eds.), *Searches for meaning in reading/language processing and instruction* (pp. 207-211). Rochester, NY: The National Reading Conference.

Gough, P.B., & Tunmer, W.E. (1986). Decoding, reading, and reading disability. *Remedial and Special Education, 7*(1), 6-10.

Guttentag, R.E., & Haith, M.M. (1978). Automatic processing as a function of age and reading ability. *Child Development, 49*, 707-716.

Guttentag, R.E., & Haith, M.M. (1979). A developmental study of automatic word processing in a picture classification task. *Child Development, 50*, 894-896.

Guttentag, R.E, & Haith, M.M. (1980). A longitudinal study of word processing by first-grade children. *Journal of Educational Psychology, 72*, 701-705.

Honeycutt, S. *Phonological rules for a text-to-speech system.* M.I.T. Natural Language Processing Group, Cambridge, MA. Undated manuscript.

Juel, C. (1983). The development of mediated word identification. *Reading Research Quarterly, 18*, 306-327.

Juel, C. (1988). Learning to read and write: A longitudinal study of 54 children from first through fourth grades. *Journal of Educational Psychology, 80*, 437-447.

Juel C., Griffith, P.L., & Gough, P.B. (1985). Reading and spelling strategies of first grade children. In J.A. Niles & R. Lalik (Eds.), *Issues in literacy: A research perspective* (pp. 306-309). Rochester, NY: The National Reading Conference.

Juel, C., Griffith, P.L., & Gough, P.B. (1986). Acquisition of literacy: A longitudinal study of children in first and second grade. *Journal of Educational Psychology, 78*, 243-255.

Juel, C., & Roper/Schneider, D. (1985). The influence of basal readers on first grade reading. *Reading Research Quarterly, 20*, 134-152.

Lundberg, I. (1984, August). Learning to read. *School Research Newsletter.*

Lundberg, I., Oloffson, A., & Wall, S. (1980). Reading and spelling skills in the first school years predicted from phonemic awareness skills in kindergarten. *Scandinavian Journal of Psychology, 21*, 628-636.

Lundberg, I., & Tornéus, M. (1978). Nonreaders' awareness of the basic relationship between spoken and written words. *Journal of Experimental Child Psychology, 25*, 404-412.

MacKinnon, A.B. (1959). *How do children learn to read?* Toronto: Copp Clark.

Nagy, W.E., & Anderson, R.C. (1984). How many words are there in printed school English? *Reading Research Quarterly, 19*, 304-330.

Perfetti, C.A., Beck, I.L., & Hughes, C. (1981). *Phonemic knowledge and learning to read: A longitudinal study of first graders.* Paper presented at the biennial meeting of the Society for Research in Child Development, Boston.

Perfetti, C.A., & Hagaboam, T. (1975). Relationship between single word decoding and reading comprehension skill. *Journal of Educational Psychology, 67*, 461-469.

Roper-Schneider, H.D.W. (1984). *Spelling, word recognition, and phonemic awareness among first grade children.* Unpublished doctoral dissertation, University of Texas, Austin.

Rosinski, R.R. (1977). Picture-word inference is semantically based. *Child Development, 48*, 643-647.

Rosinski, R.R., Golinkoff, R.M., & Kukish, R.S. (1975). Automatic semantic processing in a picture-word interference task. *Child Development, 48*, 643-647.

Rozin, P., Bressman, B., & Taft, M. (1974). Do children understand the basic relationship between speech and writing? The Mow-Motorcycle test. *Journal of Reading Behavior, 6*, 327-334.

Rubin, A. (1980). A theoretical taxonomy of the differences between oral and written language. In R.J. Spiro, B.C. Bruce, & W.F. Brewer (Eds.), *Theoretical issues in reading comprehension* (pp. 411-438). Hillsdale, NJ: Erlbaum.

Samuels, S.J., & Jeffrey, W.E. (1966). Discriminability of words and letter cues used in learning to read. *Journal of Educational Psychology, 57*, 337-340.

Shankweiler, D., & Liberman, I.Y. (1972). Misreading: A search for causes. In J.F. Kavanaugh & I.G. Mattingly (Eds.), *Language by ear and by eye* (pp. 293-317). Cambridge, MA: The M.I.T. Press.

Share, D.L., Jorm, A.F., Maclean, R., & Matthews, R. (1984). Sources of individual differences in reading achievement. *Journal of Educational Psychology, 76*, 1309-1324.

Singer, H. (1976). Substrata-factor theory of reading: Theoretical design for teaching reading. In H. Singer & R. Ruddell (Eds.), *Theoretical models and precesses of reading* (2nd ed., pp. 681-689). Newark, DE: International Reading Association.

Soderberg, R. (1977). *Reading in early childhood: A linguistic study of a preschool child's gradual acquisition of reading ability*. Washington, DC: Georgetown University Press.

Stanovich, K.E. (1986). Matthew effects in reading: Some consequences of individual differences in the acquisition of literacy. *Reading Research Quarterly, 21*, 360-406.

Torneus, M. (1984). Phonological awareness and reading: A chicken and egg problem? *Journal of Educational Psychology, 76*, 1346-1358.

Treiman, R.A., & Baron, J. (1982). Segmental analysis ability: Development and relation to reading ability. In T.G. Waller & G.E. MacKinnon (Eds.), *Reading research: Advances in theory and practice* (Vol. 3, 159-198). New York: Academic Press.

Tunmer, W.E., & Nesdale, A.R. (1985). Phonemic segmentation skill and beginning reading. *Journal of Educational Psychology, 77*, 417-427.

Venezky, R.L. (1967). English orthography: Its graphical structure and its relation to sound. *Reading Research Quarterly, 2*, 75-106.

Venezky, R.L. (1976). *Theoretical and experimental base for teaching reading*. The Hague, The Netherlands: Mouton.

West, R.G., & Stanovich, K.E. (1979). The development of automatic word recognition skills. *Journal of Reading Behavior, 11*, 211-219.

Williams, J.P. (1984). Phonemic analysis and how it relates to reading. *Journal of Learning Disabilities, 17*, 240-245.

6
The Language Code: Issues in Word Recognition

Keith E. Stanovich

Just 20 years ago writings about word recognition in textbooks and in curriculum materials were nine parts speculation to one part information. There were so few established facts about word recognition that many authors simply started out with a theoretical view on the nature of reading and then developed the implications of their theory for word recognition. Thus, it is not surprising that the reading literature came to contain much theoretical speculation masquerading as established scientific fact.

A 20-year perspective is sufficient to reveal the encouraging amount of progress that has been made in studying the word recognition process. Far more is known now, and many of the issues that just 2 decades ago were in the realm of speculation have been empirically resolved and are the subject of a broad-based scientific consensus. Nevertheless, this optimistic picture must be tempered by the realization that this knowledge has not always been efficiently transmitted to teachers through textbooks and curriculum materials. Practitioners still often labor under misinformation promulgated during the "speculative era" of debates about global models of reading, much of it displaying a classic characteristic of pseudoscience: It is not altered by new empirical facts.

Although this survey will document important advances in our knowledge about decoding and word recognition processes, it is important to understand that these conclusions do not *directly* dictate particular instructional strategies. Knowledge of basic processes is only one part of what is needed to prescribe an instructional strategy. The facts about basic processes must still be integrated with data and theory on the instructional environment. However, even if the facts themselves do not directly prescribe an instructional strategy, they can still be diagnostic for the practitioner as a "truth in advertising" mechanism. Any educational program, curriculum, and/or instructional strategy that misrepresents the basic facts about the word recognition process has signaled either that (a) its developers have an unscientific approach, or that (b) the program's developers are simply unaware of the latest evidence. Either of these is sufficient to warn the practitioner to be skeptical.

The Importance of Word Recognition Skill

It is well documented that word recognition skill is a critically important factor in the reading process and in understanding individual differences in reading ability. There is now overwhelming evidence that problems at the word recognition level of processing are a critical factor in most cases of dyslexia (Bertelson, 1986; Bruck, 1990; Morrison, 1984, 1987; Morrison & Manis, 1982; Olson, Kliegl, Davidson, & Foltz, 1985; Siegel, 1985; Vellutino, 1979) and that word recognition efficiency accounts for a large proportion of the variance in reading ability in the early elementary grades (Adams, 1990; Chall, 1983b; Curtis, 1980; Gough & Tunmer, 1986; Perfetti, 1985; Richardson, DiBenedetto, & Adler, 1982; Stanovich, 1986). In later grades, comprehension strategies and schema-based knowledge structures play a much larger role in determining individual differences in reading ability. However, even among adults, word recognition efficiency accounts for a sizeable amount of variance in reading ability (Byrne & Ledez, 1983; Cunningham, Stanovich, & Wilson, 1990; Liberman, Rubin, Duques, & Carlisle, 1985; Perfetti, 1985; Read & Ruyter, 1985; Scarborough, 1984).

As the evidence linking word recognition skill to reading ability became more and more overwhelming, the debate about how to conceptualize word recognition in reading shifted from questioning the linkage itself to a dispute about what psychological mechanisms were responsible for the superior word recognition skill of the better reader. This dispute evolved into the famous top-down versus bottom-up debate in reading theory. The debate boiled down to the question of whether the superior word recognition efficiency of the skilled reader was due to skill at bottom-up processes of spelling-to-sound decoding and direct visual recognition or whether it was due to superior top-down processes of expectancy generation and contextual prediction. Evidence is now strongly on the side of the former view. Poorer readers are markedly inferior at the bottom-up skills of word recognition but appear to be relatively competent at using top-down processes to facilitate decoding. Several reviews and summaries of the large literature on this issue have been published (see Gough, 1983; Leu, DeGroff, & Simons, 1986; Liberman, 1982; Mitchell, 1982; Perfetti, 1985; Perfetti & McCutchen, 1987; Stanovich, 1980, 1984, 1986, 1991). The consensus in this research area has recently been bolstered by developments in two additional areas: the study of eye movements and advances in computer simulation and artificial intelligence.

What Eye Movement Studies Reveal About Word Recognition

Recent work with more advanced eye movement technologies than were available to earlier investigators has established several important facts about eye movements in reading that have implications for models of word recognition. Although, as previously discussed, these facts do not dictate instructional practice–nor do they completely circumscribe theory–they represent important basic information about the reading process that practitioners should know. Indeed, it is puzzling that this fundamental work on eye movements in reading is ignored in most educational texts that contain speculation about precisely those processes that the current empirical work illuminates.

Research is consistent in indicating that the vast majority of content words in text receive a direct visual fixation (Balota, Pollatsek, & Rayner, 1985; Ehrlich & Rayner, 1981; Hogaboam, 1983; Just & Carpenter, 1980, 1987; Perfetti, 1985; Pollatsek, Rayner, & Balota, 1986; Rayner & Pollatsek, 1989). Short function words and highly predictable words are more likely to be skipped, but even the majority of these are fixated. In short, the sampling of visual information in reading, as indicated by fixation points, is relatively dense. Readers do not engage in the wholesale skipping of words that is sometimes implied in presentations of top-down models.

The study of the processing of visual information within a fixation has indicated that the visual array is rather completely processed during each fixation. It appears that visual features are not minimally sampled in order to confirm "hypotheses," but instead are rather exhaustively processed, even when the word is highly predictable (Balota et al., 1985; Ehrlich & Rayner, 1981; McConkie & Zola, 1981; Zola, 1984). An important study by Rayner and Bertera (1979) demonstrated that efficient reading is dependent on a detailed sampling of the visual information in the text. Using the contingent display possibilities afforded by modern computer technology, they had subjects read text while a computer masked one letter in their foveal vision on each fixation. The loss of this *single letter* reduced reading speed by 50%. Clearly, efficient reading depended on the visual information contained in each of the individual letters that were within foveal vision.

In summary, research indicates: (a) Sampling of the text during reading, as indicated by fixation points, is relatively dense, (b) even nonfixated words are processed to some extent (Just & Carpenter, 1987), and (c) visual feature extraction during a fixation is relatively complete. Summarizing their experiments on the processing of words varying in predictability, Balota et al. (1985) stated that: There is little doubt (as indicated by the present production task norms) that subjects could have guessed the next word in our example sentence to be *cake* based on relatively ambiguous parafoveal information (*cahc*). However, because of the dynamics of the eye-movement system in reading, the subjects usually waited until their eyes directly fixated the target to identify it....It appears that subjects were not likely to make a strong commitment about ambiguous parafoveal information even when the target words were highly predictable from the sentence context....Thus, the data contradict a view of reading wherein expectations and predictions about forthcoming information are primary and visual information is there merely for confirmation. (pp. 387-388)

These research findings indicate that the implication of some of the early top-down models of reading—that the visual information in text is almost of secondary importance (e.g., "it is clear that the better reader barely looks at the individual words on the page", Smith, 1973, p. 190)—is quite patently false. Nevertheless, a critical point emphasized in the early top-down writings–that efficient reading occurs when the reader expends processing capacity on higher level comprehension processes rather than on word recognition–is shared by bottom-up models and appears to be a valid insight. We now, however, know *how* this occurs: Via efficient decoding processes, rather than by using context to speed word recognition. Where the top-down models went wrong was in their tendency to conflate the use of the visual features in the text with the cognitive resources necessary to process those features. It is not that the good reader relies less on visual information, but that the visual analysis mechanisms of the good reader use less capacity. Good readers are efficient processors in every sense: They completely sample the visual array *and* use fewer resources to do so.

Reading and Models in Cognitive Science

Models of word recognition in reading have always been heavily influenced by theoretical developments within the interrelated fields of cognitive science. For example, early models of word recognition were heavily influenced by the analysis-by-synthesis models of speech perception and by the highly interactive computer models that were popular in artificial intelligence work. For example, Rumelhart's (1977) interactive model has had considerable influence on reading theory. Drawing on work in artificial intelligence during the preceding 10 years (the Hearsay speech recognition system, for example), his model emphasized top-down influences and hypothesis testing at every level of the processing hierarchy, including the lexical and letter levels.

The problem for reading theory–and especially for top-down theories that rested their case primarily on the then-current consensus in AI research–is that the worm has turned. The current vogue is not top-down, hypothesis-testing models, but parallel-architecture connectionist models (McClelland & Rumelhart, 1986; Rumelhart & McClelland, 1986; Schneider, 1987; Tanenhaus, Dell, & Carlson, 1988) that have a heavy bottom-up emphasis. There are no explicit hypotheses in such models at all. Learning and recognition do not occur via hypothesis testing but by the updating of connection strengths in the network and by a settling of activation after a stimulus has been presented. Solutions to problems emerge from patterns of activation generated by incoming information and previously established connections; they are not expressed as hypotheses put forth by an executive processor. One such model, NETtalk (Sejnowski & Rosenberg, 1986), "learned" to read by being exposed to pairings of letter strings and phoneme strings. The simulation contained no orthographic rules, made no use of contextual information beyond the word level, and had no executive processors to make hypotheses or generate expectancies. The network learned simply by readjusting connections between units after being exposed to input. It learned to recognize a medium-sized corpus of words with 90% accuracy and had a limited ability to generalize to novel words.

A similar example occurs in the psychology of perception. Some of the first top-down models of the reading process (e.g., Smith, 1971) were influenced by developments in what has been termed the *New Look* in perceptual research, a theoretical framework that emphasized the influence of context and expectancies on perception. However, the current vogue in the study of perception is completely antithetical to the New Look framework. The popular concept is now modularity (Fodor, 1983, 1985; Seidenberg, 1985; Tanenhaus, Dell, & Carlson, 1988; Tanenhaus & Lucas, 1987)–the idea that basic perceptual processes are "informationally encapsulated": that they are not driven by higher level hypotheses and real world knowledge.

Both of these examples indicate that current models in artificial intelligence and cognitive science provide no sustenance at all for top-down models of word recognition in reading. Nevertheless, the purpose of highlighting these examples is not to argue for one class of model over another. Considering them does serve as a caution, however, that theories of reading should probably always rest more on empirical facts about the process of reading than on the latest theoretical fashion in cognitive psychology and artificial intelligence.

Clearing up Confusions: Word Calling and Oral Reading Errors

The resolution of the top-down versus bottom-up debate has helped to clarify several other related puzzles and confusions in the reading literature. For example, the term *word caller* frequently occurs in the educational literature on reading. A dose of operationism would have precluded much of the confusion and uncertainty that has accumulated around the term, because it is almost always used without specifying criteria for its application. The term's popularity arises as a natural consequence of its operational uncertainty: Every researcher and practitioner is free to match it to their own, inevitably different, criteria. In an attempt to clarify this confusion, I have attempted (see Stanovich, 1986) to develop a prototype definition of what most writers appear to imply by their use of the term. An amalgamation of the many uses of the term reveals that the implicit assumptions behind its use seem to be: (a) Word calling occurs when the words in the text are efficiently decoded into their spoken forms without comprehension of the passage taking place, (b) this is a bad thing, because it means that the child does not understand the purpose of reading, which is comprehension, (c) children engaging in word calling do so because they have learned inappropriate reading strategies, and (d) the strategic difficulty is one of overreliance on phonic strategies.

The idea of a word-calling phenomenon embodying these assumptions is frequently encountered in educational writings despite the lack of evidence indicating that it applies to an appreciable number of poor readers. For example, there is no research evidence indicating that decoding a word into phonological form often takes place without meaning extraction, even in poor readers. To the contrary, a substantial body of evidence indicates that even for young children, word decoding automatically leads to semantic activation *when the meaning of the word is adequately established in memory* (Ehri, 1977; Goodman, Haith, Guttentag, & Rao, 1985; Guttentag, 1984; Guttentag & Haith, 1978, 1980; Kraut & Smothergill,

1980; Rosinski, 1977). The latter qualification is of course critical, but it is quite often ignored. Reports of word calling rarely definitively establish whether the words that are called are actually in the child's listening vocabulary. If the child would not understand the meaning of the passage when listening to it, then overuse of decoding strategies can hardly be blamed if the child does not understand the written words. In short, a minimal requirement for establishing word calling, as defined by the assumptions outlined earlier, is the demonstration that the written material being called is within the listening comprehension abilities of the child (see Gough & Tunmer, 1986; Hood & Dubert, 1983; Hoover & Gough, 1990).

It is additionally necessary to show that the word calling is not simply a consequence of poor decoding. Although reasonably efficient decoding would appear to be an integral part of any meaningful definition of word calling, decoding skills are rarely carefully assessed when this label is applied. Instead, a rough index of decoding accuracy is usually employed, and any child near the normal range is considered a candidate for the label. However, as other investigators have previously noted (e.g., LaBerge & Samuels, 1974; Perfetti, 1985, 1986), a clear picture of a child's decoding abilities is not obtained unless speed and automaticity criteria are also employed. It is quite possible for accurate decoding to be so slow and capacity demanding that it strains available cognitive resources and causes comprehension breakdowns. Such accurate but capacity-demanding decoding with little comprehension should not be considered word calling as defined above. To the contrary, it is a qualitatively different type of phenomenon. Comprehension fails not because of overreliance on decoding, but because decoding skills are not developed *enough*.

A related confusion surrounds the interpretation of data from studies of oral reading errors (see Kibby, 1979; Simons & Leu, 1987; Stanovich, 1986). When skilled and less skilled readers are reading the same passages, the less skilled readers are processing material that is relatively more difficult. Because it is well known that the syntactic and semantic appropriateness of errors decreases with increases in text difficulty (Biemiller, 1979; Leu, 1982; Wixson, 1979), it should not be surprising that in such designs poor readers show less effects of contextual constraint. In short, when poor readers are in difficult materials their slow and inaccurate word-decoding processes may degrade the contextual information available to them, rendering it unusable. The observation that, under such conditions, poor readers do not rely on context should not be viewed as indicating that they cannot, or will not, use context to facilitate word recognition. To the contrary, there is voluminous evidence indicating that when contextual information is functionally available, poor readers tend to use it at least as much as good readers (see Perfetti, 1985, and Stanovich, 1986, 1991, for reviews).

Phonological Sensitivity and Early Reading Acquisition

One exciting outcome of research in reading during the last 20 years is that researchers have isolated a process that is a major determinant of the early acquisition of reading skill and one of the keys to the prevention of reading disability. Although there are many correlates of the ease of initial reading acquisition, a large number of studies have demonstrated that phonological abilities stand out as the most potent specific predictor (Adams, 1990; Bradley & Bryant, 1985; Juel, 1988; Juel, Griffith, Gough, 1986; Kamhi & Catts, 1989; Lomax & McGee, 1987; Mann, Tobin, & Wilson, 1987; Share, Jorm, Maclean, & Matthews, 1984; Stanovich, Cunningham, & Cramer, 1984; Tunmer & Nesdale, 1985; Vellutino & Scanlon, 1987; Wagner & Torgesen, 1987; Williams, 1984).

Although the strength of the observed relationship serves to draw attention to phonological abilities, it is not proof that these abilities are causally implicated in early reading acquisition. However, an increasing amount of converging evidence serves to suggest such a causal link. First, there are several studies showing that measures of phonological sensitivity predict reading ability even when the former are assessed before reading skills have developed (Bradley & Bryant, 1985; Bryant, Bradley, Maclean, & Crossland, 1989; Fox & Routh, 1975; Lundberg & Hoien, 1989; Lundberg, Olofsson, & Wall, 1980; Maclean, Bryant, & Bradley, 1987; Share et al., 1984). Second, the results of some longitudinal studies where cross-lagged correlational methods and/or structural equation modeling have been employed have led to the conclusion that the early development of phonological sensitivity leads to superior reading achievement (Perfetti, Beck, Bell, & Hughes, 1987; Torneus, 1984). Evidence supporting this conclusion has also come from reading-level match designs (Bradley & Bryant, 1978; Bruck, 1990; Bruck & Treiman, 1990; Olson, Wise, Conners, Rack, & Fulker, 1989; Siegel & Faux, 1989; Snowling, 1980, 1981). Finally, and of course most convincing, are the results of several studies where phonological skills were manipulated via training and resulted in significant experimental group advantages in reading, word recognition, and spelling (Bradley & Bryant, 1985; Cunningham, 1990; Fox & Routh, 1984; Lundberg, Frost, & Peterson, 1988; Olofsson & Lundberg, 1985; Torneus, 1984; Treiman & Baron, 1983; Vellutino & Scanlon, 1987).

It should be noted that several of the studies cited above have also supported Ehri's (1979, 1985, 1987) position that reading acquisition itself increases phonological sensitivity (see also, Morais, Alegria, & Content, 1987; Perfetti, 1985; Perfetti et al., 1987), so the proper model appears to be one of reciprocal causation. Such situations can have important bootstrapping effects on achievement (see Stanovich, 1986).

Ehri's (1979) early work also presaged the current controversy over precisely what level of phonological sensitivity is a prerequisite to acquiring alphabetic literacy (Bertelson, Morais, Alegria, & Content, 1985; Bryant & Bradley, 1985; Morais et al., 1987; Perfetti et al., 1987). In order to understand this controversy, certain terminological distinctions and clarifications must be made. First, researchers have used the term *phonemic awareness* to refer to conscious access to phonemic representations and the ability to consciously manipulate representations at this level. Perhaps, though, the emphasis on the concepts of *consciousness* and *awareness* in these definitions has unnecessarily confused discussions in the domain of phonological abilities. Despite the repeated accolades to cognitive psychology for reintroducing these terms back into psychology, they still have no consensual usage in any of the disciplines that employ them. Indeed, discussions of awareness and consciousness are notoriously contentious and confused, and it is not at all clear that a final scientific/philosophical resolution will retain these terms in anything like current folk conceptualizations (Armstrong & Malcolm, 1984; P. M. Churchland, 1989; P. S. Churchland, 1983, 1986; Holender, 1986; Stanovich, 1990; Stich, 1983; Wilkes, 1984, 1988). Thus, it is probably preferable to adopt a more operational stance.

I would suggest that the generic term *phonological sensitivity* be used to cover the set of processing constructs being tapped by the various tasks utilized in research. Phonological sensitivity should be viewed as a continuum ranging from "deep" sensitivity to "shallow" sensitivity. Tasks indicating deeper levels of sensitivity require more explicit reports of smaller sized units (e.g., phonemes versus onset/rimes or syllables). The phoneme segmentation and sound isolation tasks studied by Yopp (1988) would fall on the deep end of the continuum. In contrast, examples of tasks tapping the most shallow forms of phonological sensitivity might be oddity tasks of rhyming stimuli. Tasks intermediate in phonological depth might be those like phoneme deletion (see Yopp, 1988), where the response is not a phoneme-sized unit, but segmentation has clearly been demonstrated.

If these rough distinctions are made, then a rough consensus becomes apparent in the literature, which has been characterized by the use of increasingly imaginative longitudinal and cross-cultural designs (Maclean et al., 1987; Mann, 1986; Morais et al., 1987; Morais, Bertelson, Cary, & Alegria, 1986; Read, Zhang, Nie, & Ding, 1986). Deep phonological sensitivity, in the sense defined above, appears not to be an absolute prerequisite to reading progress, but is itself fostered by the analytic attitude developed during initial learning of an alphabetic orthography (Morais et al., 1987). It should be emphasized that even if this conclusion is true, early development of deep phonological sensitivity *is* a powerful bootstrapping mechanism to further reading progress in stages that are *still* very early in the child's acquisition history. Just because the deeper forms of phonological sensitivity are not absolute prerequisites to any reading progress at all does not mean that they are not powerful facilitators in critically early stages of reading acquisition (during first grade, for example).

In addition, it seems that a more shallow type of phonological sensitivity *does* serve as a prerequisite in acquiring alphabetic literacy (Bryant, Maclean, Bradley, & Crossland, 1990). This shallow phonological sensitivity may also be in a reciprocal relationship with reading, but the time course of its developmental effects may be different. These tentative conclusions do no grave injustices to the longitudinal studies, experiments comparing literates to illiterates, and the cross-cultural research.

Research on phonological processing has recently moved from merely documenting the causal connection with reading and has begun to address more specific questions. For example, researchers are currently linking experiences prior to school entry–such as experience with nursery rhymes–to the development of phonological sensitivity (e.g., Maclean et al., 1987) and are speculating on how to model phonological process training on what is known about syllable structure (Treiman, 1991; Wise, Olson, & Treiman, 1990).

Why Phonological Abilities? Decoding in an Alphabetic Orthography

Researchers are largely agreed on why phonological abilities are so important in the early stages of reading. To enable the powerful self-teaching mechanism inherent in an alphabetic orthography (Gough & Hillinger, 1980; Jorm & Share, 1983), the child must learn the general principle that spelling corresponds to sound and then must learn sufficient exemplars of spelling-to-sound correspondences to support efficient decoding. In order to utilize the alphabetic principle, the child must adopt an analytic attitude toward both written words and the spoken words they represent; that is, the child must discover and exploit the fact that the mapping takes place at the level of letters and phonemes. Segmenting visual words into letter units is well within the perceptual capabilities of every nonimpaired school-age child, but the development of the tendency to exhaustively process all of the visual detail in words (particularly the sequence of interior letters) may be difficult for some children (Frith, 1985; Gough & Hillinger, 1980). However, an even greater source of individual differences resides in the sounds to which the letters map. Segmenting speech at the level of phonemes is notoriously difficult for young children (Bruce, 1964; Calfee, Chapman, & Venezky, 1972; Lewkowitz, 1980; Liberman, Shankweiler, Fischer, & Carter, 1974; Williams, 1984). The phonological sensitivity tasks utilized in the research reviewed previously relate to reading acquisition because they predict the ease or difficulty with which a child will learn to segment spoken words at levels below the syllable (Treiman, 1991).

In a seminal and provocative paper, Gough and Hillinger (1980) asserted that we should consider learning to read to be an "unnatural act." This characterization followed from their two-stage model of the earliest stages of reading acquisition. Gough and Hillinger posited that the first stage was one of paired-associate learning utilizing minimal cues. That is, children initially begin to associate spoken words with particularly salient cues in the visual array. For example, *dog* might be associated with the initial letter, "hole in the middle", or "tail at the end"; in short, visual distinctiveness is a key factor at this stage. Gough and Hillinger hypothesize that this paired-associate procedure works well for the first few items but quickly breaks down because of the difficulty in finding a unique distinctive visual cue for each new word encountered. Paired-associate learning of this type becomes more difficult as the number of items to be learned increases (Otto & Pizillo, 1970). The paired-associate procedure based on distinctive visual cues is not generative (i.e., it is of no help in recognizing unfamiliar words), eventually results in confusion, and inevitably must be discarded. Normal progress in reading dictates that the child make the transition to the next stage of acquisition: that characterized by fully analytic processing–where words are fully segmented, both visually and phonologically. Unlike the first stage, where the child acquires words naturally and often spontaneously, the fully analytic stage (what Gough and Hillinger term the *cipher stage*) is not natural and almost always requires intervention by an outsider (teacher, parent, sibling) who gives cues to support analytic processing and/or presents words in ways that foster such processing (Adams, 1990). Thus, a basic discontinuity in word acquisition is proposed.

Subsequent research has tended to support Gough and Hillinger's (1980) conceptualization. Byrne (1991) has presented evidence indicating that fully analytic processing of words is not the natural processing set of preliterate 4-year-old children. He demonstrated that learning to discriminate *fat* from *bat* did not enable the children to discriminate *fun* from *bun* with greater than chance accuracy. Their performance illustrates what would be expected from a child who had not passed beyond Gough and Hillinger's paired-associate stage. Byrne argues that it might be instructive to view reading disability–the failure to develop reliable spelling-to-sound decoding skills–as functional fixation of the unbiased acquisition procedure of all beginning readers, namely, nonanalytic processing. Since this "natural" set is precisely what must be overcome in learning to read, Byrne's results support the characterization of Gough and Hillinger.

Young preliterate children often spontaneously learn to name words on television, advertisements, cereal boxes, and billboards. This particular phenomenon has frequently spawned characterizations of reading diametrically opposed to that of Gough and Hillinger (1980), characterizations that view learning to read as a natural act, directly analogous to learning spoken language. (In order to consider other evidence, we will put aside the obvious objection that many children require extensive adult intervention in order to acquire reading skills and that some children fail in the acquisition process despite herculean efforts on the part of teachers and parents–a situation vastly unlike that of spoken language; see Liberman & Liberman, 1990; Perfetti, 1991.) However, the results of a study by Masonheimer, Drum, and Ehri (1984) indicate that this type of word learning is like that of Gough and Hillinger's paired-associate stage, and that later stages of beginning reading are not continuous extensions of this type of spontaneous word learning.

Masonheimer et al. (1984) studied 3- to 5-year-old children who were environmental print "experts": those who, based on a preliminary survey, could identify at least 8 of the 10 most commonly known environmental labels (McDonald's, K Mart, Crayola Crayons, the Incredible Hulk, Pepsi, etc.). Most of these children (n=96) had virtually no ability to read words outside of the set of labels that they knew. Since a few children (n=6) read all of the test words, the distribution of reading ability was markedly bimodal and "was not distributed continuously as one might expect if it were true that the accumulation of environmental print experience leads children into word reading" (1984, p. 268). The 96 prereaders were completely unable to report anything wrong with labels that had letter alterations (e.g., *Xepsi*). In addition, the ability to read the labels dropped dramatically when the logos were removed, indicating that the children were "reading the environment" rather than the print.

It is important, though, not to misinterpret the results of this study. Masonheimer et al. emphasize that the correct interpretation of their results is not to deny that preschoolers acquire some information about print from their environmental experiences....What children do not appear to do as a consequence of exposure to environmental print is learn to distinguish and identify the graphic cues as separate units. Very likely, some other types of learning experiences are required to achieve this skill. (1984, p. 269) Thus, Masonheimer et al. are careful to point out that their conclusions refer directly only to the information-processing characteristics of two adjacent stages in early reading acquisition, and to one particular experiential variable: knowledge of the labels of common environmental signs. Their results should not be read as arguing against the general efficacy of early literacy experiences.

Gough, Juel, and Griffith (1991) report several intriguing tests of the nature of the paired-associate learning-by-selective-cues stage in early reading acquisition. They had a group of 5-year olds learn sets of words written on flashcards to a criterion of two successive correct trials. One of the flashcards was deliberately marred by a thumbprint on the corner. During the test phase, when the children were shown the thumbprinted word on a clean card, less than half could identify the word. Almost all of them, however, produced the word when shown a thumbprinted card with no word on it. As an additional test, children were shown a thumbprinted card containing a word other than the one that accompanied it during training. Almost all children named the word that accompanied the thumbprint during training, rather than the word that was presently on the card.

The results of Gough et al. (1991) clearly converge nicely with those of Byrne (1991) and Masonheimer et al. (1984) and are consistent with the idea that learning fully analytic spelling-to-sound correspondences is an unnatural act for young children. Results from an important classroom study also support this conclusion. Seymour and Elder (1986) studied a class of new entrants into a Scottish primary school where the emphasis was on the development of a sight vocabulary via whole-word methods, and no phonics training occurred during the first 2 terms. An examination of their subsequently developed word recognition skills indicated that they were not generative: The children could not recognize unfamiliar words that they had not been taught. Unlike the case of children who have developed some spelling-to-sound decoding skills (see Gough et al., 1991), the error responses of these children were drawn only from the set of words that they had been taught. The characteristics of their discrimination performance were similar to those that would be expected from Gough and Hillinger's (1980) selective cue learning. Bertelson (1986) has argued that the most important implication of the results of Seymour and Elder (1986) is "that there is no continuity between early logographic reading and the direct orthographic reading of the skilled adult, where typically all the available orthographic evidence is taken into account" (p. 19).

Models of Early Reading Acquisition

Gough and Hillinger's (1980) basic model has been elaborated and extended in subsequent stage models of early reading acquisition. Frith's (1985, 1986) stage model incorporates an initial logographic stage similar to Gough and Hillinger's paired-associate learning stage. In this stage the child relies on particularly salient graphic features, eschewing a full analysis of the letters and their order. Phonological factors are also not operative in this stage. Frith's (1985) alphabetic stage is similar to Gough and Hillinger's cipher learning stage. Here, letter order and phonological recoding on the basis of grapheme-phoneme correspondences play a critical role. Frith's (1985) orthographic stage characterizes the more fluent reading that results from efficient passage through the alphabetic stage and from extensive exposure and practice (see Cunningham & Stanovich, 1990; Stanovich, 1986; Stanovich & West, 1989). In this stage, the child uses familiar orthographic sequences to aid in accessing (Backman, Bruck, Hebert, & Seidenberg, 1984; Barron, 1986; Ehri, 1985; Juel, 1983; Stanovich, 1986; Stanovich & West, 1989).

Ehri (1987; Ehri & Wilce, 1985, 1987) has presented evidence in support of an acquisition stage between the paired-associate stage and the cipher/alphabetic stage. Termed *phonetic-cue reading*, this stage usually is entered after the child knows the alphabet and a few words. Phonetic-cue reading involves reading words by forming and storing associations between some of the letters in words' spellings and some of the sounds in their pronunciations. The phonetic cues selected are based on readers' knowledge of letter names, sounds, or both. (Ehri & Wilce, 1987, p. 4) This stage is different from Gough and Hillinger's (1980) paired-associate stage in that letter-sound units are the cues rather than generic visual features. The phonetic-cue stage also does not represent completely analytic cipher reading because the alphabetic principle of phonemic letter-sound mapping is not completely understood and all letter-sound relationships are not represented. This stage is more efficient than the visual-cue learning of the paired-associate stage because letter-sound relationships are systematic in a way that purely visual-cues are not. However, phonetic-cue learning is less efficient than the exhaustive decoding of the cipher stage because it is not fully generative. Because it is still cue learning, the children cannot read words they have not encountered before, nor can they verify matches between the letter string and what they articulate, as can children in the more advanced cipher stage. Elegant experimental tests of the existence of the phonetic-cue stage are contained in a series of experiments by Ehri (1987; Ehri & Wilce, 1985, 1987).

There is clearly a considerable degree of convergence in the models of early reading acquisition developed by Gough and Hillinger (1980), Frith (1985, 1986), and Ehri (1987), and it seems not unreasonable to concatenate their ideas into a general framework for conceptualizing early reading acquisition. Such a framework would encompass four sequential reading stages: an early paired-associate learning stage conceptualized along the lines of Gough and Hillinger (1980), a phonetic-cue stage conceptualized as in Ehri and Wilce (1987), a cipher stage characterized by fully analytic grapheme-to-phoneme decoding (Frith, 1985;

Gough & Hillinger, 1980), and an orthographic stage characterizing more advanced levels of reading fluency (Frith, 1985). Current evidence would appear to indicate that the transitions between Stages 2, 3, and 4 are continuous and overlapping, reflecting quantitative change; whereas there are some indications that the transition between Stages 1 and 2 may be more discontinuous, perhaps reflecting qualitative change (Ehri & Wilce, 1987).

Controversies About Decoding and the Regularity of English

How does the recent research on word recognition and early reading acquisition that is described above relate to some of the oldest controversies in reading instruction? First, there is obviously no contradiction between the conclusions in Chall's classic work (1967; and update,1983a) and the basic research outlined here (see also, Adams, 1990). Word recognition is a critical component of the reading process; individual differences in this component account for substantial variance at all levels of reading, and in order to become fluent, all readers must have stored in memory spelling-sound correspondences that can function as efficient recognition mechanisms. Nevertheless, it is necessary to reiterate that none of these basic conclusions necessarily dictates specific instructional practices. This is something that is often forgotten by phonics advocates in the educational literature, who often uncritically view the results of research like that outlined previously as providing justification for their particular methods of instruction.

It is important to understand just what can and cannot be concluded from this research. For example, it could well be the case that language experience or whole-language approaches might provide the child with the optimum amount of exposure for the induction of spelling-sound correspondences (although research does seem to indicate that the explicit teaching of specific letter-sound correspondences does facilitate reading acquisition [Anderson, Hiebert, Scott, & Wilkinson, 1985; Chall, 1983a; Share & Jorm, 1987; Williams, 1985]). Regardless, the point to be emphasized here is the avoidance of too hasty a jump from basic research and theoretical models of reading to instructional implications. Similarly, the conclusion that all readers must acquire functional spelling-to-sound knowledge is not the same as saying that all children must learn phonics rules. The child needs to associate orthographic with phonological patterns in memory, but this need not be done by the learning of rules. Somewhat of an existence proof for this point is contained in the previously mentioned work of Sejnowski and Rosenberg (1986). They have designed a connectionist computer model that learns to read English words after being exposed to a large number of pairings of letter strings and phoneme strings. This parallel model contains no rules at all, but simply learns by updating–based on new input–the stengths of connections between elements.

Likewise, however, opponents of phonics as an instructional method have also on occasion jumped too hastily from basic research models of reading and theoretical work in other disciplines to instructional conclusions. One example, the overgeneralization of the early top-down cognitive models, was discussed previously. Another example that recurs in the writings of those hostile to phonics is a tendency to overemphasize the irregularity of the spelling-sound correspondences in English. It is a common ploy in such writings to litter the text with examples of correspondences that are ambiguous in reading (e.g., *ea* can be pronounced as in *teach, bread, great,* or *create*) or spelling (e.g., /f/ can be written as in *frog, phone, tough, stuff,* etc.). Although it is true that English is one of the most irregular of the alphabetic orthographies, it is misleading to imply that the regularities that are present are not sufficient to support a substantial role in reading acquisition for spelling-sound correspondences.

First, it is important to distinguish the use of spelling-sound correspondences in reading from the use of sound-spelling correspondences for spelling (Berndt, Reggia, & Mitchum, 1987; Haas, 1970; Henderson, 1982). The distinction is important because the spelling-sound correspondences of English are more regular than the sound-spelling correspondences (Cronnell, 1978; Henderson, 1982; Henderson & Chard, 1980; Read, 1983). For example, while the phoneme /f/ can map to *f, ff, ph,* or *gh,* the letter *f* regularly maps to /f/, with the exception of the high frequency *of.* Likewise, *k* maps to /k/ in the vast majority of cases, and is silent in the initial position before *n* (e.g., *knee*). In contrast, in the sound-spelling direction /k/ can map to *k, c, cc, ck, ch, q,* and others (Henderson & Chard, 1980). Thus, an emphasis on spelling irregularities is somewhat misleading. Most of the consonants of English, like *f* and *k,* have regular reading correspondences (Berndt et al., 1987; Cronnell, 1973; Venezky, 1970). The most notorious irregularities virtually all concern vowels. This fact interacts with the tacit assumption in many critiques that if the correspondences do not yield a unique pronunciation, then they are useless. To the contrary, partially diagnostic cues can indeed be useful. The c-ns-n-nts -r- th- m-st -mp-rt-nt c-mp-n-nts -f w-rds -nd -t -s p-ss-bl- t- r-d w-th-t th-m provided you have some context. Thus, even if a child could only decode the regular consonants, this would be a considerable aid in early reading.

Other critiques ignore the fact that the English orthography is considerably more regular if the positions of letters are taken into account or if units larger than the letter are considered. George Bernard Shaw's famous example, that *ghoti* could be pronounced the same as *fish* (gh as in *tough,* o as in *women,* ti as in *nation*), ignores the position-specific constraints of the orthography: *gh* is never pronounced /f/ when word initial and *ti* never as /s/ when word final. Furthermore, all analyses of the orthography indicate that there is considerable regularity when groups of letters are considered (Treiman, 1991), particularly when a medial vowel is combined with the following consonant or consonant cluster (*ea* can map as in *great, stream,* or *bread*; but *ead* almost always maps as in *bread*; the *ight, ook, ind* families, etc.; see Mason, 1977; Wylie & Durrell, 1970).

Treiman (1991) has imaginatively linked the VC(C) regularity of English orthography with experimental demonstrations of the psychological reality of intrasyllabic speech units (onset and rime–units intermediate between the phoneme and syllable; see also Treiman, 1986) for young children. The onset of a syllable is its initial consonant (or cluster) and the rime is its vowel plus any consonants that follow. Treiman has found that young children's segmentation skills pass through an intermediate stage where they are much more sensitive to the onset/rime distinction than to the phoneme distinction. She speculated that the English writing system developed in such a way that the following consonant has more influence on the vowel than a preceding consonant (VCs are more regular than CVs) precisely because spoken syllables have an onset/rime structure. She has proposed that at certain points in reading acquisition, working with onset/rime (and corresponding C and VC[C] structures) might be optimal because these intrasyllabic units are more generative than syllables, but do not require the phonemic segmentation ability that may not be developed in some children until later reading stages where more experience with reading and spelling has been acquired (see Ehri, 1984, 1987; Ehri, Wilce, & Taylor, 1987). Treiman's (1991) hypotheses are supported by Ryder and Pearson's (1980) finding that the pronunciation of vowel digraphs was more predictable by a final consonant model than by an invariant response model or a type-token model (see also Johnson & Venezky, 1976). The larger point reinforced by Treiman's (1991) work is that there may be more ways to exploit the regularities that exist in the English orthography than is commonly recognized (see also, Bryant & Goswami, 1987; Goswami, 1986, 1988, 1990; Goswami & Bryant, 1991). Treiman's (1991) suggestions neatly bypass the biggest problem with the orthography–irregularities at the individual letter level–because they necessitate working with larger units that are considerably more regular.

Conclusion

This is an exciting time in reading research. Important discoveries are being made. Issues that have been debated for decades are finally yielding to empirical methods, and scientific consensus is developing in several areas. However, researchers still need to do a much better job of disseminating their results in an understandable way. The diffusion of findings throughout the community of practitioners is still much too slow. Perhaps even more important, more effort must be made to communicate the basic philosophy and logic of the scientific method so that researchers and teachers will have more of a common base for discussion. Misunderstandings between researchers and practitioners often occur because the foundational assumptions of science are still insufficiently understood (see Singer & Stanovich, 1982; Bryant & Bradley, 1987, for examples in the educational literature). In short, scientific interchange entails a concern for communicating the attitudes inherent in the process of science (Bronowski, 1977) as a well as its content in a particular area. Nowhere is this more apparent than in the relationship between the psychology of reading and reading education.

The standard scientific criteria for evaluating knowledge claims are actually few in number. Many of these are things that teachers, as "consumers" of research evidence, should become aware of. These scientific criteria are not complicated. They include the publication of findings in refereed journals (scientific publications that employ a process of peer review), the duplication of the results by disinterested investigators in different research laboratories or classroom settings, and a consensus within a particular research community on whether or not a critical mass of studies that point toward a particular conclusion has been reached (see Stanovich, 1989). These are some of the best "consumer protections" that a teacher can have in an age and culture in which a spirit of laissez faire rules in the domain of educational techniques.

References

Adams, M.J. (1990). *Beginning to read: Thinking and learning about print.* Cambridge, MA: M.I.T. Press.

Anderson, R.C., Hiebert, E.H., Scott, J., & Wilkinson, I. (1985). *Becoming a nation of readers.* Washington, DC: National Institute of Education.

Armstrong, D.M., & Malcolm, N. (1984). *Consciousness & causality.* Oxford: Basil Blackwell.

Backman, J., Bruck, M., Hebert, M., & Siedenberg, M. (1984). Acquisition and use of spelling-sound correspondences in reading. *Journal of Experimental Child Psychology, 38,* 114-133.

Balota, D., Pollatsek, A., & Rayner, K. (1985). The interaction of contextual constraints and parafoveal visual information in reading. *Cognitive Psychology, 17,* 364-390.

Barron, R. (1986). Word recognition in early reading: A review of the direct and indirect access hypothesis. *Cognition, 24,* 93-119.

Berndt, R., Reggia, J., & Mitchum, C. (1987). Empirically derived probabilities for grapheme-to-phoneme correspondences in English. *Behavior Research Methods, Instruments, & Computers, 19,* 1-9.

Bertelson, P. (1986). The onset of literacy: Liminal remarks. *Cognition, 24,* 1-30.

Bertelson, P., Morais, J., Alegria, J., & Content, A. (1985). Phonetic analysis capacity and learning to read. *Nature, 313,* 73-74.

Biemiller, A. (1979). Changes in the use of graphic and contextual information as functions of passage difficulty and reading achievement level. *Journal of Reading Behavior, 11,* 307-319.

Bradley, L., & Bryant, P.E. (1978). Difficulties in auditory organization as a possible cause of reading backwardness. *Nature, 271,* 746-747.

Bradley, L., & Bryant, P.E. (1983). Categorizing sounds and learning to read–a causal connection. *Nature, 301,* 419-421.

Bradley, L., & Bryant, P.E. (1985). *Rhyme and reason in reading and spelling.* Ann Arbor: University of Michigan Press.

Bronowski, J. (1977). *A sense of the future.* Cambridge: M.I.T. Press.

Bruce, D. (1964). The analysis of word sounds by young children. *British Journal of Educational Psychology, 34,* 158-170.

Bruck, M. (1990). Word-recognition skills of adults with childhood diagnoses of dyslexia. *Developmental Psychology, 26,* 439-454.

Bruck, M., & Treiman, R. (1990). Phonological awareness and spelling in normal children and dyslexics: The case of initial consonant clusters. *Journal of Experimental Child Psychology, 50,* 156-178.

Bryant, P.E., & Bradley, L. (1985). Reply to Bertelson et al. *Nature, 313,* 74.

Bryant, P.E., & Bradley, L. (1987). "Knowing" and empirical research. *British Journal of Educational Psychology, 57,* 249-252.

Bryant, P.E., Bradley, L., Maclean, M., & Crossland, J. (1989). Nursery rhymes, phonological skills and reading. *Journal of Child Language, 16,* 407-428.

Bryant, P.E., & Goswami, U. (1987). Beyond grapheme-phoneme correspondence. *Cahiers de Psychologie Cognitive, 7,* 439-443.

Bryant, P.E., Maclean, M., Bradley, L., & Crossland, J. (1990). Rhyme and alliteration, phoneme detection, and learning to read. *Developmental Psychology, 26,* 429-438.

Byrne, B. (1991). Learning to read the first few items: Evidence of a nonanalytic acquisition procedure in adults and children. In P. Gough, L. Ehri, & R. Treiman (Eds.), *Reading acquisition.* Hillsdale, NJ: Erlbaum Associates.

Byrne, B., & Ledez, J. (1983). Phonological awareness in reading-disabled adults. *Australian Journal of Psychology, 35,* 185-197.

Calfee, R.C., Chapman, R., & Venezky, R. (1972). How a child needs to think to learn to read. In L. Gregg (Ed.), *Cognition in learning and memory* (pp. 139-182). New York: John Wiley.

Chall, J.S. (1967). *Learning to read: The great debate.* New York: McGraw-Hill.

Chall, J.S. (1983a). *Learning to read: The great debate.* New York: McGraw-Hill.

Chall, J.S. (1983b). *Stages of reading development.* New York: McGraw-Hill.

Churchland, P.M. (1989). *A neurocomputational perspective: The nature of mind and the structure of science.* Cambridge: M.I.T. Press.

Churchland, P.S. (1983). Consciousness: The transmutation of a concept. *Pacific Philosophical Quarterly, 64,* 80-95.

Churchland, P.S. (1986). *Neurophilosophy: Toward a unified science of the mind/brain.* Cambridge: M.I.T. Press.

Cronnell, B. (1973). Designing a reading program based on research findings in orthography. *Elementary English, 50,* 27-34.

Cronnell, B. (1978). Phonics for reading vs. phonics for spelling. *The Reading Teacher, 31,* 337-340.

Cunningham, A.E. (1990). Explicit versus implicit instruction in phonemic awareness. *Journal of Experimental Child Psychology, 50,* 429-444.

Cunningham, A.E., & Stanovich, K.E. (1990). Assessing print exposure and orthographic processing skill in children: A quick measure of reading experience. *Journal of Educational Psychology, 82,* 733-740.

Cunningham, A.E., Stanovich, K.E., Wilson, M.R. (1990). Cognitive variation in adult students differing in reading ability. In T. Carr & B.A. Levy (Eds.), *Reading and development: Component skills approaches* (pp. 129-159). San Diego: Academic Press.

Curtis, M. (1980). Development of components of reading skill. *Journal of Educational Psychology, 72*, 656-669.

Ehri, L.C. (1977). Do adjectives and functors interfere as much as nouns in naming pictures? *Child Development, 48*, 697-701.

Ehri, L.C. (1979). Linguistic insight: Threshold of reading acquisition. In T. Waller & G. MacKinnon (Eds.), *Reading research: Advances in research and theory* (Vol. 1, pp. 63-114). New York: Academic Press.

Ehri, L.C. (1984). How orthography alters spoken language competencies in children learning to read and spell. In J. Downing & R. Valtin (Eds.), *Language awareness and learning to read* (pp. 119-147). New York: Springer-Verlag.

Ehri, L.C. (1985). Effects of printed language acquisition on speech. In D. Olson, N. Torrance, & A. Hildyard (Eds.), *Literacy, language, and learning* (pp. 333-367). Cambridge: Cambridge University Press.

Ehri, L.C. (1987). Learning to read and spell words. *Journal of Reading Behavior, 19*, 5-31.

Ehri, L.C., & Wilce, L. (1985). Movement into reading: Is the first stage of printed word learning visual or phonetic? *Reading Research Quarterly, 20*, 163-179.

Ehri, L.C., & Wilce, L. (1987). Cipher versus cue reading: An experiment in decoding acquisition. *Journal of Educational Psychology, 79*, 3-13.

Ehri, L.C., Wilce, L., & Taylor, B.B. (1987). Children's categorization of short vowels in words and the influence of spellings. *Merrill-Palmer Quarterly, 33*, 393-421.

Ehrlich, S., & Rayner, K. (1981). Contextual effects on word perception and eye movements during reading. *Journal of Verbal Learning and Verbal Behavior, 20*, 641-655.

Fodor, J. (1983). *Modularity of mind.* Cambridge: M.I.T. Press.

Fodor, J.A. (1985). Pr'ecis of "The Modularity of Mind". *Behavioral and Brain Sciences, 8*, 1-42.

Fox, B., & Routh, D.K. (1975). Analyzing spoken language into words, syllables, and phonemes: A developmental study. *Journal of Psycholinguistic Research, 4*, 331-342.

Fox, B., & Routh, D.K. (1984). Phonemic analysis and synthesis as word attack skills: Revisited. *Journal of Educational Psychology, 76*, 1059-1064.

Frith, U. (1985). Beneath the surface of developmental dyslexia. In K. Patterson, J. Marshall, & M. Coltheart (Eds.), *Surface dyslexia* (pp. 301-330). London: Erlbaum.

Frith, U. (1986). A developmental framework for developmental dyslexia. *Annals of Dyslexia, 36*, 69-81.

Goodman, G., Haith, M., Guttentag, R., & Rao, S. (1985). Automatic processing of word meaning: Intralingual and interlingual interference. *Child Development, 56*, 103-118.

Goswami, U. (1986). Children's use of analogy in learning to read: A developmental study. *Journal of Experimental Child Psychology, 42*, 73-83.

Goswami, U. (1988). Orthographic analogies and reading development. *Quarterly Journal of Experimental Psychology, 40A*, 239-268.

Goswami, U. (1990). A special link between rhyming skills and the use of orthographic analogies by beginning readers. *Journal of Child Psychology and Psychiatry, 31*, 301-311.

Goswami, U., & Bryant, P.B. (1991). Rhyme, analogy, and children's reading. In P. Gough, L. Ehri, & R. Treiman (Eds.), *Reading acquisition.* Hillsdale, NJ: Erlbaum.

Gough, P.B. (1983). Context, form, and interaction. In K. Rayner (Ed.), *Eye movements in reading* (pp. 203-211). New York: Academic Press.

Gough, P.B., & Hillinger, M.L. (1980). Learning to read: An unnatural act. *Bulletin of the Orton Society, 30*, 171-176.

Gough. P.B., Juel, C., & Griffith, P. (1991). Reading, spelling, and the orthographic cipher. In P. Gough, L. Ehri, & R. Treiman (Eds.), *Reading acquisition.* Hillsdale, NJ: Erlbaum.

Gough, P.B., & Tunmer, W.E. (1986). Decoding, reading, and reading disability. *Remedial and Special Education, 7*, 6-10.

Guttentag, R. (1984). Semantic memory organization in second graders and adults. *Journal of General Psychology, 110*, 81-86.

Guttentag, R., & Haith, M. (1978). Automatic processing as a function of age and reading ability. *Child Development, 49*, 707-716.

Guttentag, R., & Haith, M. (1980). A longitudinal study of word processing by first-grade children. *Journal of Educational Psychology, 72*, 701-705.

Haas, W. (1970). *Phono-graphic translation.* Manchester, England: Manchester University Press.

Henderson, L. (1982). *Orthography and word recognition in reading.* London: Academic Press.

Henderson, L., & Chard, J. (1980). The reader's implicit knowledge of orthographic structure. In U. Frith (Ed.), *Cognitive processes in spelling* (pp. 85-116). London: Academic Press.

Hogaboam, T.W. (1983). Reading patterns in eye movement data. In K. Rayner (Ed.), *Eye movements in reading: Perceptual and language processes* (pp. 309-332). New York: Academic Press.

Holender, D. (1986). Semantic activation without conscious identification in dichotic listening, parafoveal vision, and visual masking: A survey and appraisal. *Behavioral and Brain Sciences, 9*, 1-66.

Hood, J., & Dubert, L. (1983). Decoding as a component of reading comprehension among secondary students. *Journal of Reading Behavior, 15*, 51-61.

Hoover, W.A., & Gough, P.B. (1990). The simple view of reading. *Reading and Writing: An Interdisciplinary Journal, 2*, 127-160.

Johnson, D.D., & Venezky, R.L. (1976). Models for predicting how adults pronounce vowel digraph spellings in unfamiliar words. *Visible Language, 10*, 257-268.

Jorm, A., & Share, D. (1983). Phonological recoding and reading acquisition. *Applied Psycholinguistics, 4,* 103-147.

Juel, C. (1983). The development and use of mediated word identification. *Reading Research Quarterly, 18,* 306-327.

Juel, C. (1988). Learning to read and write: A longitudinal study of 54 children from first through fourth grades. *Journal of Educational Psychology, 80,* 437-447.

Juel, C., Griffith, P.L., & Gough, P.B. (1986). Acquisition of literacy: A longitudinal study of children in first and second grade. *Journal of Educational Psychology, 78,* 243-255.

Just, M.A., & Carpenter, P.A. (1980). A theory of reading: From eye fixations to comprehension. *Psychological Review, 4,* 329-354.

Just, M.A., & Carpenter, P.A. (1987). *The psychology of reading and language comprehension.* Boston: Allyn & Bacon.

Kamhi, A., & Catts, H. (1989). *Reading disabilities: A developmental language perspective.* Boston: College-Hill Press.

Kibby, M.W. (1979). Passage readability affects the oral reading strategies of disabled readers. *The Reading Teacher, 32,* 390-396.

Kraut, A., & Smothergill, D.W. (1980). New method for studying semantic encoding in children. *Developmental Psychology, 16,* 149-150.

LaBerge, D., & Samuels, S. (1974). Toward a theory of automatic information processing in reading. *Cognitive Psychology, 6,* 293-323.

Leu, D. (1982). Oral reading error analysis: A critical review of research and application. *Reading Research Quarterly, 17,* 420-437.

Leu, D.J., DeGroff, L., & Simons, H.D. (1986). Predictable texts and interactive-compensatory hypotheses: Evaluating individual differences in reading ability, context use, and comprehension. *Journal of Educational Psychology, 78,* 347-352.

Lewkowitz, N. (1980). Phonemic awareness training: What to teach and how to teach it. *Journal of Educational Psychology, 72,* 686-700.

Liberman, I. (1982). A language-oriented view of reading and its disabilities. In H. Mykelbust (Ed.), *Progress in learning disabilities* (Vol. 5, pp. 81-101). New York: Grune & Stratton.

Liberman, I.Y., & Liberman, A.M. (1990). Whole language versus code emphasis: Underlying assumptions and their implications for reading instruction. *Annals of Dyslexia, 40,* 51-76.

Liberman, I.Y., Rubin, H., Duques, S., & Carlisle, J. (1985). Linguistic abilities and spelling proficiency in kindergarteners and adult poor spellers. In D. Gray & J. Kavanagh (Eds.), *Biobehavioral measures of dyslexia* (pp. 163-175). Parkton, MD: York Press.

Liberman, I.Y., Shankweiler, D., Fischer, F., & Carter, B. (1974). Explicit syllable and phoneme segmentation in the young child. *Journal of Experimental Child Psychology, 18,* 201-212.

Lomax, R.G., & McGee, L.M. (1987). Young children's concepts about print and reading: Toward a model of word reading acquisition. *Reading Research Quarterly, 22,* 237-256.

Lundberg, I., Frost, J., & Peterson, O. (1988). Effects of an extensive program for stimulating phonological awareness in preschool children. *Reading Research Quarterly, 23,* 263-284.

Lundberg, I., & Hoien, T. (1989). Phonemic deficits: A core symptom of developmental dyslexia? *Irish Journal of Psychology, 10,* 579-592.

Lundberg, I., Oloffson, A., & Wall, S. (1980). Reading and spelling skills in the first school years predicted from phonemic awareness skills in kindergarten. *Scandinavian Journal of Psychology, 21,* 159-173.

Maclean, M., Bryant, P., & Bradley, L. (1987). Rhymes, nursery rhymes, and reading in early childhood. *Merrill-Palmer Quarterly, 33,* 255-281.

Mann, V. (1986). Phonological awareness: The role of reading experience. *Cognition, 24,* 65-92.

Mann, V., Tobin, P., & Wilson, R. (1987). Measuring phonological awareness through the invented spelling of kindergarten children. *Merrill-Palmer Quarterly, 33,* 365-391.

Mason, J.M. (1977). Refining phonics for teaching beginning reading. *The Reading Teacher, 30,* 179-184.

Masonheimer, P.E., Drum, P.A., & Ehri, L.C. (1984). Does environmental print identification lead children into word reading? *Journal of Reading Behavior, 16,* 257-271.

McClelland, J.L., & Rumelhart, D.E. (1986). *Parallel distributed processing: Explorations in the microstructure of cognition* (Vol. 2). Cambridge: M.I.T. Press.

McConkie, G.W., & Zola, D. (1981). Language constraints and the functional stimulus in reading. In A.M. Lesgold & C.A. Perfetti (Eds.), *Interactive processes in reading* (pp. 155-175). Hillsdale, NJ: Erlbaum.

Mitchell, D. (1982). *The process of reading: A cognitive analysis of fluent reading and learning to read.* Chichester: John Wiley.

Morais, J., Alegria, J., & Content, A. (1987) The relationships between segmental analysis and alphabetic literacy: An interactive view. *Cahiers de Psychologie Cognitive, 7,* 415-438.

Morais, J., Bertelson, P., Cary, L., & Alegria, J. (1986). Literacy training and speech segmentation. *Cognition, 24,* 45-64.

Morrison, F. (1984). Word decoding and rule-learning in normal and disabled readers. *Remedial and Special Education, 5,* 20-27.

Morrison, F.J. (1987). The nature of reading disability: Toward an integrative framework. In S. Ceci (Ed.), *Handbook of cognitive, social, and neuropsychological aspects of learning disabilities* (pp. 33-62). Hillsdale, NJ: Erlbaum.

Morrison, F.J., & Manis, F. (1982). Cognitive processes and reading disability: A critique and proposal. In C. Brainerd & M. Pressley (Eds.), *Program in cognitive development research* (Vol. 2, pp. 59-94). New York: Springer-Verlag.

Olofsson, A., & Lundberg, I. (1985). Evaluation of long-term effects of phonemic awareness training in kindergarten. *Scandanavian Journal of Psychology, 26,* 21-34.

Olson, R., Kliegl, R., Davidson, B., & Foltz, G. (1985). Individual and developmental differences in reading disability. In T. Waller (Ed.), *Reading research: Advances in theory and practice* (Vol. 4, pp. 1-64). London: Academic Press.

Olson, R.K., Wise, B., Conners, F., Rack, J., & Fulker, D. (1989). Specific deficits in component reading and language skills: Genetic and environmental influences. *Journal of Learning Disabilities, 22,* 339-348.

Otto, H., & Pizillo, C. (1970). Effect of intralist similarity on kindergarten pupils' rate of word acquisition and transfer. *Journal of Reading Behavior, 3,* 14-19.

Perfetti, C. A. (1985). *Reading ability.* New York: Oxford University Press.

Perfetti, C. A. (1986). Continuities in reading acquisition, reading skill, and reading disability. *Remedial and Special Education, 7,* 11-21.

Perfetti, C. A. (1991). The psychology, pedagogy, and politics of reading. *Psychological Science, 2,* 70-76.

Perfetti, C. A., Beck, I., Bell, L., & Hughes, C. (1987). Phonemic knowledge and learning to read are reciprocal: A longitudinal study of first-grade children. *Merrill-Palmer Quarterly, 33,* 283-319.

Perfetti, C. A., & McCutchen, D. (1987). Schooled language competence: Linguistic abilities in reading and writing. In S. Rosenberg (Ed.), *Advances in applied psycholinguistics* (Vol. 2, pp. 105-141). Cambridge: Cambridge University Press.

Pollatsek, A., Rayner, K., & Balota, D. A. (1986). Inferences about eye movement control from the perceptual span in reading. *Perception & Psychophysics, 40,* 123-130.

Rayner, K., & Bertera, J. H. (1979). Reading without a fovea. *Science, 206,* 468-469.

Rayner, K., & Pollatsek, A. (1989). *The psychology of reading.* Englewood Cliffs, NJ: Prentice Hall.

Read, C. (1983). Orthography. In M. Martlew (Ed.), *The psychology of written language* (pp. 143-161). Chichester, England: John Wiley.

Read, C., & Ruyter, L. (1985). Reading and spelling skills in adults of low literacy. *Remedial and Special Education, 6,* 43-52.

Read, C.A., Zhang, Y., Nie, H., & Ding, B. (1986). The ability to manipulate speech sounds depends on knowing alphabetic reading. *Cognition, 24,* 31-44.

Richardson, E., DiBenedetto, B., & Adler, A. (1982). Use of the decoding skills test to study differences between good and poor readers. In K. Gadow & I. Bialer (Eds.), *Advances in learning and behavioral disabilities* (Vol. 1, pp 25-74). Greenwich, CT: JAI Press.

Rosinski, R. (1977). Picture-word interference is semantically based. *Child Development, 48,* 643-647.

Rumelhart, D.E. (1977). Toward an interactive model of reading. In S. Dornic (Ed.), *Attention and performance* (Vol. 6, pp. 573-603). New York: Academic Press.

Rumelhart, D.E., & McClelland, J.L. (1986). *Parallel distributed processing: Explorations in the microstructure of cognition* (Vol. 1). Cambridge: M.I.T. Press.

Ryder, R., & Pearson, P.D. (1980). Influence of type-token frequencies and final consonants on adults' internalization of vowel digraphs. *Journal of Educational Psychology, 72*, 618-624.

Scarborough, H.S. (1984). Continuity between childhood dyslexia and adult reading. *British Journal of Psychology, 75*, 329-348.

Schneider, W. (1987). Connectionism: Is it a paradigm shift for psychology? *Behavior Research Methods, Instruments, & Computers, 19*, 73-83.

Seidenberg, M. (1985). The time course of information activation and utilization in visual word recognition. In D. Besner, T. Waller, & G. MacKinnon (Eds.), *Reading research: Advances in theory and practice* (Vol. 5, pp. 199-252). New York: Academic Press.

Sejnowski, T.J., & Rosenberg, C.R. (1986). *NETtalk: A parallel network that learns to read aloud.* (Tech. Rep. No. JHU/EECS-86/01). Baltimore, MD: Johns Hopkins University, Department of Electrical Engineering and Computer Science.

Seymour, P.H.K., & Elder, L. (1986). Beginning reading without phonology. *Cognitive Neuropsychology, 3*, 1-36.

Share, D.L., & Jorm, A.F. (1987). Segmental analysis: Co-requisite to reading, vital for self-teaching, requiring phonological memory. *Cahiers de Psychologie Cognitive, 7*, 509-513.

Share, D.L., Jorm, A.F., Maclean, R., & Matthews, R. (1984). Sources of individual differences in reading acquisition. *Journal of Educational Psychology, 76*, 1309-1324.

Siegel, L.S. (1985). Psycholinguistic aspects of reading disabilities. In L. Siegel & F. Morrison (Eds.), *Cognitive development in atypical children* (pp. 45-65). New York: Springer-Verlag.

Siegel, L.S., & Faux, D. (1989). Acquisition of certain grapheme-phoneme correspondences in normally achieving and disabled readers. *Reading and Writing: An Interdisciplinary Journal, 1*, 37-52.

Simons, H.D., & Leu, D.J. (1987). The use of contextual and graphic information in word recognition by second-, fourth-, and sixth-grade readers. *Journal of Reading Behavior, 19*, 33-47.

Singer, M. H., & Stanovich, K. E. (1982). Introduction: Reading disability. In M. Singer (Ed.), *Competent reader, disabled reader* (pp. 33-37). Hillsdale, NJ: Erlbaum.

Smith, F. (1971). *Understanding reading.* New York: Holt, Rinehart & Winston.

Smith, F. (1973). *Psycholinguistics and reading.* New York: Holt, Rinehart & Winston.

Snowling, M. (1980). The development of grapheme-phoneme correspondence in normal and dyslexic readers. *Journal of Experimental Child Psychology, 29*, 294-305.

Snowling, M. (1981). Phonemic deficits in developmental dyslexia. *Psychological Research*, *43*, 219-234.

Stanovich, K.E. (1980). Toward an interactive-compensatory model of individual differences in the development of reading fluency. *Reading Research Quarterly*, *16*, 32-71.

Stanovich, K.E. (1984). The interactive-compensatory model of reading: A confluence of developmental, experimental, and educational psychology. *Remedial and Special Education*, *5*, 11-19.

Stanovich, K.E. (1986). Matthew effects in reading: Some consequences of individual differences in the acquisition of literacy. *Reading Research Quarterly*, *21*, 360-407.

Stanovich, K.E. (1989). *How to think straight about psychology* (2nd ed.). Glenview, IL: Scott Foresman.

Stanovich, K.E. (1990). Concepts in developmental theories of reading skill: Cognitive resources, automaticity, and modularity. *Developmental Review*, *10*, 72-100.

Stanovich, K.E. (1991). Word recognition: Changing perspectives. In R. Barr, M.L. Kamil, P. Mosenthal, & P.D. Pearson (Eds.), *Handbook of reading research* (Vol. 2, pp. 418-452). New York: Longman.

Stanovich, K.E., Cunningham, A.E., & Cramer, B. (1984). Assessing phonological awareness in kindergarten children: Issues of task comparability. *Journal of Experimental Child Psychology*, *38*, 175-190.

Stanovich, K.E., & West, R.F. (1989). Exposure to print and orthographic processing. *Reading Research Quarterly*, *24*, 402-433.

Stich, S. (1983). *From folk psychology to cognitive science*. Cambridge: M.I.T. Press.

Tanenhaus, M.K., Dell, G.S., & Carlson, G. (1988). Context effects in lexical processing: A connectionist approach to modularity. In J. Garfield (Ed.), *Modularity in knowledge representation and natural language understanding*. Cambridge, MA: M.I.T. Press.

Tanenhaus, M.K., & Lucas, M.M. (1987). Context effects in lexical processing. *Cognition*, *25*, 213-234.

Torneus, M. (1984). Phonological awareness and reading: A chicken and egg problem? *Journal of Educational Psychology*, *70*, 1346-1358.

Treiman, R. (1986). The division between onsets and rimes in English syllables. *Journal of Memory and Language*, *25*, 476-491.

Treiman, R. (1991). The role of intrasyllabic units in learning to read and spell. In P. Gough, L. Ehri, & R. Treiman (Eds.), *Reading acquisition*. Hillsdale, NJ: Erlbaum.

Trieman, R., & Baron, J. (1983). Phonemic-analysis training helps children benefit from spelling-sound rules. *Memory & Cognition*, *11*, 382-389.

Tunmer, W.E., & Nesdale, A.R. (1985). Phonemic segmentation skill and beginning reading. *Journal of Educational Psychology*, *77*, 417-427.

Vellutino, F. (1979). *Dyslexia: Theory and research.* Cambridge, MA: M.I.T. Press.

Vellutino, F., & Scanlon, D. (1987). Phonological coding, phonological awareness, and reading ability: Evidence from a longitudinal and experimental study. *Merrill-Palmer Quarterly, 33,* 321-363.

Venezky, R.L. (1970). *The structure of English orthography.* The Hague, The Netherlands: Mouton.

Wagner, R.K., & Torgesen, J.K. (1987). The nature of phonological processing and its causal role in the acquisition of reading skills. *Psychological Bulletin, 101,* 192-212.

Wilkes, K.V. (1984). Is consciousness important? *British Journal of Philosophy of Science, 35,* 223-243.

Wilkes, K.V. (1988). *Real people: Personal identity without thought experiments.* Oxford: Oxford University Press.

Williams, J. (1984). Phonemic analysis and how it relates to reading. *Journal of Learning Disabilities, 17,* 240-245.

Wise, B.W., Olson, R.K., & Treiman, R. (1990). Subsyllabic units in computerized reading instruction: Onset-rime versus postvowel segmentation. *Journal of Experimental Child Psychology, 49,* 1-19.

Wixson, K.L. (1979). Miscue analysis: A critical review. *Journal of Reading Behavior, 11,* 163-175.

Wylie, R., & Durrell, D.D. (1970). Teaching vowels through phonograms. *Elementary English, 47,* 787-791.

Yopp, H.K. (1988). The validity and reliability of phonemic awareness tests. *Reading Research Quarterly, 23,* 159-177.

Zola, D. (1984). Redundancy and word perception during reading. *Perception & Psychophysics, 36,* 277-284.

7
Reading Instruction in Childhood and Adolescence

Judith A. Winn and Annemarie Sullivan Palincsar

Perhaps no other area of instruction has profited as much from the "cognitive revolution" as has reading. Research regarding the constructive nature of reading activity, individual differences among skilled and less skilled readers, and various approaches to both preventing and remediating reading difficulties offers a mere sampling of the reading issues that have emerged over the past several decades.

We will begin our discussion by considering the goals of reading instruction as they are currently being defined. Following this, we will address the content of instruction (what is taught) as well as the ways in which teachers share that content with students.

Discussions of the goals of reading instruction today reflect the fact that our definitions of literacy have been expanded to include increasingly lofty goals. Where literacy was once defined as the ability to read and write, today the goals of literacy include the ability to use reading and writing for the purpose of reasoning and problem-solving activity, to go beyond adapting to the goals of the prevailing culture (Bereiter & Scardamalia, 1987), and to make sense of one's life (McGinley, 1991).

Essential to students' attaining the goals of critical literacy is their ability to engage in intentional, self-regulated reading. Over the past 15 years, cognitive and instructional research (e.g., Anderson & Pearson, 1984; Anderson, Reynolds, Schallert, & Goetz, 1977; Brown, Bransford, Ferrara, & Campione, 1983; Meyers & Paris, 1978; Paris, Lipson, & Wixon, 1983; Paris & Oka, 1986) has provided us a characterization of expert readers as having the knowledge and beliefs that facilitate self-regulation. What have we learned from this research about self-regulated readers that has informed and can further inform our instructional goals?

Students who are self-regulated readers approach tasks with a repertoire of strategies, which they are able to use purposefully and flexibly. Self-regulated readers identify the need for planful activity in reading and are able to apply strategies in a manner suited to themselves as learners as well as to the demands of the task (Palincsar & Brown, 1989b; Paris, Lipson, & Wixon, 1983; Paris & Oka, 1986). Such students use their knowledge of strategies in concert with metacognitive and real world knowledge (Pressley, Borkowski, & Schneider, 1987) to control their reading. They understand what reading strategies are (declarative knowledge about strategies) and how to use them (procedural knowledge). Flexible use of strategies also involves students' conditional knowledge of strategies (Paris, Lipson, & Wixon, 1983) or their knowing why strategies are important and when to use them. Self-regulated readers are aware of characteristics of their own learning (e.g., "I have difficulty remembering important parts of social studies chapters"; "I understand this material better when I know a lot about the topic") as well as characteristics of the task (e.g., reading for gist, studying for a multiple choice test). They identify goals for their reading, utilize strategies accordingly, monitor whether or not their goals are being met, and take corrective action when necessary.

Self-regulation is fostered by a conception of reading as meaning seeking. Through the use of interviews, it has been found that younger and poorer readers have a less developed notion of the purpose and demands of reading. For example, Meyers and Paris (1978) interviewed second and sixth graders about their knowledge of person, task, and strategy variables involved in reading. The second graders more often expressed a view of reading as decoding, identifying the goal of reading as "sounding out the words correctly." These students were also much less aware than the sixth graders were that reading requires specialized skills. Forrest and Waller (1980) not only looked at age differences, but also differences in achievement level, interviewing students of three different reading levels in grades 3 and 6. They found developmental and ability differences with the older and higher achieving readers being more aware of reading as meaning seeking.

Let us take a quick look at what we know about the activities the self-regulated reader might be engaged in before, during and after reading. Prior to reading, self-regulated readers engage in several specific strategic behaviors (Palincsar, Jones, Ogle, & Carr, 1986). They are aware of and actively set purposes for reading. Along with this, they activate relevant background knowledge. From their knowledge of the purposes for reading as well as their background knowledge, self-regulated readers develop expectancies for the content of the text—expectancies that will guide their reading and that they will alter and modify while reading. To further guide their reading, self-regulated readers identify a probable text structure, based on their knowledge of how texts are organized. Finally, based on knowledge obtained from all of the aforementioned sources, self-regulated readers select appropriate reading strategies.

While reading, self-regulated readers continually use strategies to monitor and guide their reading (Palincsar et al., 1986). They use all cue systems (graphophonemic, syntactic, semantic, text structure) to identify and define words. In addition, they monitor for sense-making through the use of strategies such as predicting, self-questioning, and visualizing. As confusing concepts or vocabulary are encountered, self-regulated readers seek clarifications through the use of such strategies as rereading, checking the context, or discussion. Self-regulated readers are continually checking and modifying their predictions as they read.

Finally, following reading, self-regulated readers continue to confirm or alter their predictions. They work to assimilate or accommodate their prior knowledge with the text. Based on their purposes for reading, they identify important information and evaluate their comprehension, in the process organizing information into superordinate and subordinate categories (Palincsar et al., 1986).

Knowledge and behavior-promoting self-regulation strategies have motivational correlates. Poor readers have often been characterized as lacking the knowledge and behavior associated with self-regulation (August, Flavell, & Clift, 1984; Baker & Brown, 1984; Garner, 1980, 1987; Garner, Wagoner, & Smith, 1983; Meyers & Paris, 1978); similarly, they have been described as lacking beliefs in themselves and their ability to control their learning that more expert, self-regulated readers display (Butkowsky & Willows, 1980; Johnson & Winograd, 1985; Paris & Winograd, 1991). As students become more able to engage in self-regulated reading, they develop a greater sense of self-efficacy and willingness to take risks, which in turn further enables self-regulation. Our instructional agenda therefore must address the development of students' beliefs and pride in their ability to monitor and direct their reading as well as the development of their confidence in doing so.

Whereas historically our instructional goals have been based on mastery of discrete subskills of reading (see Paris, Wixon, & Palincsar, 1986; Venezky, 1986, for historical reviews of reading instruction), current instructional goals focus on the development of cognitive and motivational processes that will enable students to monitor and regulate their reading. Thus the goals of reading instruction are to develop students':

(a)   knowledge of reading tasks;
(b)   knowledge of themselves as learners; and,
(c)   declarative, procedural, and conditional knowledge about strategies that they can use to monitor and regulate their reading.

Along with these is the goal of students developing the ability to use the aforementioned knowledge purposefully and flexibly while reading. Finally, instructional goals must include the development of students' beliefs in their ability to control their reading and appropriate motivation to do so.

Instruction focused on goals of self-regulation has been endorsed on both the national and state level. For example, the *Guide to Curriculum Planning in Reading*, published by the Wisconsin Department of Public Instruction (1986) states:

The major goal of an effective reading program is the development of strategic readers who are knowledgeable about reading and who:

• construct meaning from print

• apply strategies to learn from print

• develop an interest in reading as a life-long source of enjoyment

• analyze reading tasks

- monitor understanding while reading
- establish reading purposes
- regulate by making appropriate corrections
- plan appropriate strategies
- reflect upon task completion (p. 6).

What Do We Teach to Reach Our Goals?

Although strategies are means rather than ends to self-regulation and must be taught as such, they form an important core of our reading instruction. Before preceding, let us clarify the difference between reading skills and strategies.

Dole, Duffy, Roehler, and Pearson (1991) provide four useful criteria for distinguishing skills and strategies. The first centers on intentionality. Reading skills are seen as "automatic routines" or actions that are not employed deliberately and planfully; strategies, however, are selected and employed as indicated by task demands and reader characteristics. The second criterion is cognitive sophistication. Skills are fairly low level, requiring little reasoning or problem solving whereas strategies involve both of these processes. Dole et al.'s third criterion is flexibility. Whereas skills are applied rather rigidly, without adaptation based on text, task, and reader characteristics, strategies are continually being modified by the reader. The last criterion is awareness. Employing skills requires little awareness and reflection; employing strategies involves at least the ability to reflect on the effectiveness of them.

Although scope and sequence charts often indicate that there are a plethora of skills to be learned, the research on strategic reading has pointed to the value of teaching a limited number of strategies. Guidelines have been suggested for selecting which strategies to teach (Dole et al., 1991; Palincsar & Brown, 1989a; Pressley, Johnson, Symons, McGoldrick, & Kurita, 1989) with criteria including: (a) consistency with a cognitively based view of the reading process, (b) differentiation between skilled readers and novices, (c) generalizability, (d) instructional amenability, and (e) results of research. Pressley et. al (1989) have identified the following strategies as receiving support in the reading research literature for students 8 years of age or older: summarization; representational and mnemonic imagery; use of story grammar; question generation; question answering; and use of prior knowledge to make predictions, inferences, and monitoring adequacy of responses to questions.

We suggest that the above guidelines be used as general criteria in selecting strategies to be emphasized in reading instruction. The personal nature of strategy use and the need to stress knowledge of reader characteristics indicates attention to the criteria of usefulness to students. Strategies that are effective for certain readers to accomplish reading purposes may not be effective for others working on the same task. Certainly, adult readers use a variety of personally helpful strategies for reading tasks such as studying for tests. We must address flexibility and utility of strategy use as we address the strategies themselves to help students learn to think about and employ strategies in personally meaningful ways.

Are reading comprehension strategies the sum of what to teach if our goal is to develop self-regulated readers? Instruction focused on declarative, procedural and conditional knowledge about comprehension strategies is necessary but not sufficient to reach our goals. Along with a focus on flexible and purposeful uses of comprehension strategies, instruction must also address word recognition and vocabulary identification strategies as well as continual building and reflection upon background knowledge. Finally, instruction must involve exposure to and development of attitudes toward a wide variety of text genres. Instruction in these areas is beyond the scope of this chapter; however, we emphasize the importance of thinking about and presenting all aspects of reading instruction to students in the context of meaning seeking and the development of independent monitoring and regulation of reading to meet task demands.

Before proceeding to our discussion of how we teach to reach our goals, we need to emphasize that our end goal in teaching reading strategies is *not* learning strategies for the sake of learning the strategies, but rather as a route to comprehension and learning from text (Paris & Winograd, 1991). We know from interview data with students (e.g., Roehler & Duffy, 1986) that their notions of what they are learning and why they are learning are important and reflect, at least in part, what the teacher emphasizes. If the instructional emphasis is mainly on strategies themselves, students are likely to focus on learning what the strategies are (in other words, learning a list of strategies), rather than how to use them; in turn, they will be less likely to employ the strategies in the service of understanding and learning from text. If, however, emphasis is placed on using strategies to set purposes and to monitor and regulate reading according to these purposes, students are more likely to become self-regulated readers.

How Do We Teach to Reach Our Goals?

Given the goal of developing strategic readers who purposefully and flexibly monitor and regulate their interactions with text and thus achieve critical literacy, and the content of instruction for self-regulation as outlined in the previous section, we will now turn our attention to the ways in which instruction can be provided.

We will first discuss the role of the teacher as he or she interacts with students and texts in the classroom. Traditionally (Dole et al., 1991; Durkin, 1978-1979), the teacher's activities have focused on either: (a) asking comprehension questions during and following the reading of particular passages or (b) providing direct instruction in discrete subskills of reading. Although teachers often engage students in activities such as asking them what they know about topics and making predictions, they often do not point out the value of engaging in these activities or encourage students to do so on their own. All too often, little attention is drawn, explicitly or implicitly, to students' reflections on or understanding of what they need to do to understand and remember text.

What can teachers do to help students to become independent strategic readers? To address this question, we will survey four current instructional approaches to reading instruction. All four involve the teacher focusing attention on students' reading for meaning seeking rather than on mastery of skills and correct responses to comprehension questions pertaining to particular stories. One important way in which these four differ is in the degree to which the teacher focuses on, defines, and directs strategic interactions of students and texts. In our survey of each model, we will consider: (a) the basic tenets of each, (b) the manner in which the teacher shares knowledge about ways of controlling and regulating comprehension with the students, and (c) representative implementation research. The approaches we will review are Direct Instruction, Explicit Explanation, Cognitive Apprenticeship, and Whole Language.

Direct Instruction

The first approach to reading instruction to be considered, Direct Instruction, was introduced as a result of the process-product research on effective teaching practices (Rosenshine, 1979). This research pointed to the importance of teacher behaviors and the relationship of these to student achievement. Direct Instruction of reading strategies is characterized by systematic, explicit teaching of reading strategies (Gersten, Woodward, & Darch, 1986). Strategies are presented in a sequential fashion, generally based on task analysis in which the strategies are broken down and presented to students from simple to complex steps. The teacher, typically using scripts for lesson presentation and systematic correction procedures, defines each step of a reading strategy and models its use. The students are explicitly taught the steps, often through rules and heuristics (Baumann, 1988). Students practice these steps with the teacher providing and gradually fading prompts. Each step of the strategy is practiced until students reach mastery criteria before the next step is introduced. Evaluation of performance is based on whether or not students are following stated procedures. As such, there is little room for personalizing strategy use.

A typical Direct Instruction lesson in a reading strategy, as defined by Baumann (1988) includes: (a) an introductory statement, (b) direct, explicit instruction in the strategy, (c) heuristics or visual displays, (d) constructive responses by the students (e.g., writing summaries), (e) gradual transfer of responsibility for strategy use through guided practice, and (f) teacher provision of conditional knowledge.

Critical to Direct Instruction, and to some (e.g., Baumann, 1988), the most important characteristic is the active and directive role played by the teacher:

> ...the teacher, in a face-to-face, reasonably formal manner, tells, shows, models, demonstrates, *teaches* the skill to be learned. The key word here is *teacher*, for it is the teacher who is in command of the learning situation and leads the lesson, as opposed to having instruction "directed" by a worksheet, kit, learning center, or workbook. (Baumann, 1988, p. 714)

Throughout instruction, the teacher maintains control of the pace, sequence, and content of the lessons (Kierstead, 1985). He or she identifies and defines strategies and situates their use such that there is little ambiguity or uncertainty about how and when to use them; consequently, however, there is little room for students to personalize their use or to adapt them to different texts and tasks.

The outcomes of Direct Instruction have been studied with students learning a variety of comprehension strategies such as identifying main ideas, understanding anaphoric relations, and using study skills to remember information. In much of the work to date, Direct Instruction has been compared to more traditional instruction such as that associated with a language arts curriculum.

Baumann (1984) compared Direct Instruction of main idea comprehension (strategy group) with main idea instruction as presented in a traditional basal reader series (basal group) and vocabulary instruction (control group) with sixth graders. Using a posttest-only design, he found the strategy group to be superior to the basal and control groups in recognizing explicit and implicit main ideas at the paragraph and passage level and in composing outlines of passage and paragraph main ideas. The treatment groups did not differ, however, in their free recalls of passages, something that was not directly taught.

Patching, Kameenui, Carnine, Gersten, and Colvin (1983) utilized a Direct Instruction model to teach critical reading skills (detecting instances of faulty generalization, false causality, and invalid testimonials) to fifth graders. Instruction was conducted on an individual basis over a 3-day period. Posttest performance was compared to that of students using a workbook and corrective feedback approach as well as to that of students receiving no instruction. Students receiving Direct Instruction scored higher than the other two groups on a test in which they had to determine if they could be sure whether statements following passages were true or not. There were no significant differences among the groups on two other measures, one requiring students to detect invalid arguments and reasoning and one in which they had to identify which of three given rules could be applied to identify invalid arguments. This study was modified and replicated with fourth- through sixth-grade learning disabled students (Darch & Kameenui, 1987). Students in the Direct Instruction group scored higher than those in the contrast group on all three dependent measures.

Direct Instruction, an approach rooted in behaviorism, involves systematic presentation of strategies and skills in a hierarchically sequenced manner. There is a high degree of teacher control in identifying and defining strategies as well as evaluating their use. More attention is given to the strategies themselves than to reader or task characteristics. Direct Instruction has been found to be effective in increasing targeted strategies and skills. Less clear, however, is the effect on comprehension and recall of text related to the increase in strategy proficiency.

Explicit Explanation

Explicit explanation (Duffy & Roehler, 1987; Duffy et al., 1986; Duffy et al., 1987; Pearson & Raphael, 1990) is an approach to reading instruction in which reading skills are recast as strategies and the reasoning involved in employing these is emphasized. Initially, the teacher provides declarative, conditional and procedural knowledge about reading strategies to the students. In presenting a strategy, the teacher "thinks aloud"; this involves sharing his or her thinking with students about such aspects of reading as: (a) the mental processes he or she uses when having difficulty understanding text, (b) the ways in which application of a strategy can help him or her remove the difficulty, and (c) the mental steps he or she uses to implement the strategy.

Lessons within this model proceed in a five-step sequence (Pearson & Raphael, 1990). First, the teacher models the use of a strategy, focusing on the mental processes involved. This is followed by guided practice in which the students attempt to use the strategy while the teacher continues to model his or her use of it in response to difficulties the students may have. Guided practice is followed by independent practice, consolidation (discussing strategy use with other students), and application to authentic texts.

Two major studies of this approach to reading instruction have been conducted by Duffy and his associates (1986; 1987). In both, teachers were working with their low reading groups. The first study (Duffy et al., 1986) was focused on: (a) whether teachers who were trained to be more explicit with their low achieving reading groups were in fact so, (b) whether students in the low reading groups whose teachers were trained to provide explicit instruction were more aware of the skills they had been taught and how to use those skills strategically, and (c) whether those same students achieved higher scores on a standardized reading comprehension subtest.

The participants were 22 fifth-grade teachers and their low achieving reading groups. Half of the teachers were assigned to the treatment group and half to the control group. The treatment group teachers participated in 10 hours of instruction in which they were taught how to recast reading skills as strategies, how to provide explicit information about the skills including how and when to apply them, and how to organize their lesson presentations. Emphasis was placed on teachers modeling their mental processes. The teachers were told to present the skills in the context of reading rather than in an isolated manner. Training for control teachers focused on effective management principles.

The teachers were observed four times throughout the school year and randomly selected students were interviewed after each observation. Based on ratings of the observations, the teachers in the treatment group were more explicit in their explanations. The students in these groups showed significantly higher levels of awareness of what they had learned. However, there were no significant differences between the students in the treatment and control groups on the standardized measure of comprehension.

Using modified teacher instruction and a wider variety of student outcome measures, Duffy et al. (1987) addressed the same research questions in a follow-up study, this time involving third graders. Treatment and control teachers were instructed in behavior management principles, the use of Uninterrupted Sustained Silent Reading, and on preparing students to take standardized tests. The treatment teachers were also instructed in providing explicit information. In addition, they were given extra coaching in the provision of explicit information after their observations.

Students in the treatment groups were found to be significantly higher in procedural and conditional knowledge about strategies as well as in their awareness of the strategic nature of reading. Their scores on an achievement measure designed to assess reasoning while they performed skill tasks were also significantly higher than the scores of the control group although there were not significant differences in their ability to perform the skills. Differences favoring the treatment groups were found on other measures, including scores on the Michigan Educational Assessment Program test (MEAP), which was administered 5 months after the study was completed.

Explicit explanation attends to teaching reading strategies in a more holistic fashion than does Direct Instruction. In addition, more emphasis is placed on the thinking processes involved in flexibly applying strategies rather than on following procedures as defined by the teacher (Duffy & Roehler, 1989). Although the teacher's role is quite directive, his or her interactions with the students are less prescribed and more broadly focused than within Direct Instruction.

Cognitive Apprenticeship

The term *cognitive apprenticeship* refers to learning processes that experts use to accomplish complex tasks in the context of using these processes (Collins, Brown, & Newman, 1989). Students must come to understand and be able to carry out tasks through engaging in them before they are capable of doing so independently. The teacher's role is to model expert processes, challenge students to engage in these, and provide the support that will enable them to do so. This support has been referred to as *scaffolding* (Wood, Bruner, & Ross, 1976) due to its temporary and adjustable nature; the level and type of support the teacher provides is determined by the students' proficiency in utilizing expert processes as demanded by particular tasks. Cognitive processes are made explicit and thus can be reflected upon as they are used.

Reciprocal Teaching (Brown & Palincsar, 1985, 1989; Palincsar, 1985; Palincsar & Brown, 1984, 1989a, 1989b) is an approach to reading instruction that exemplifies cognitive apprenticeship. In reciprocal teaching, students and the teacher engage in a dialogue while reading text. The dialogue is structured, but not dominated by, the use of four strategies: summarizing, self-questioning, predicting, and clarifying. The teacher provides support for the students, through the dialogue, as they gradually acquire the ability to use the strategies independently.

For the first several days of reciprocal teaching, the students receive direct instruction regarding the strategies. The teacher explains and models the four strategies for the purpose of acquainting the students with the language of the dialogues. Following this, the students and teacher take turns leading discussions, using the strategies to help them understand the text. At all times, the students are asked to competently use the strategies and given the support needed to do so. For example, during the first few days of the discussions, the teacher may model a summary or question for the student leader to repeat or supply a partial question for the leader to complete. As students become more able to use the strategies independently, the teacher provides less support. Throughout the dialogues, the level of support is adjusted to each child's needs with particular texts. Although children take turns in the role of discussion leader, they are encouraged to join in the discussions at any time, adding to others' summaries and questions, making their own predictions, and asking for clarifications. The teacher provides support through collaborating with the students as they work together to make sense of the text through the use of the four strategies.

Brown and Palincsar (1985) present the following principles upon which reciprocal teaching is based:

(a) The teacher should make the underlying processes of the strategies overt, explicit, and concrete through modeling;

(b) the strategies should be modeled in appropriate contexts, not as isolated, decontextualized skills;

(c) the students should be informed about the needs for the strategies and about situations in which they can use them;

(d) the students should come to recognize the utility of the strategies;

(e) responsibility for task completion should be transferred as soon as the students are ready;

(f) transfer of responsibility should be gradual; and

(e) feedback should be adjusted to each student's level and always encourage progression toward independent competence.

Reciprocal Teaching has been extensively studied with students in both elementary and junior high school. The initial research (Palincsar & Brown, 1984) with junior high students was conducted by Palincsar; this was followed by studies in which junior high classroom teachers conducted the instruction. In all of these, the students in reciprocal teaching showed increased ability to use the targeted strategies as well as increased comprehension, as assessed by performance on criterion-referenced measures. These gains were found to generalize to classrooms and to maintain over time.

Reciprocal Teaching has also been found to be effective in promoting listening comprehension. Palincsar (1987) conducted a study in which classroom teachers used reciprocal teaching with groups of six students—five of the six in each group being at risk for potential school difficulty. Instruction proceeded as described except the teacher read the text to the students. The experimental group's performance on the comprehension assessment was significantly higher than that of the control group following the first half of intervention. In addition, these students scored significantly higher on analogy questions and measures of strategy knowledge.

The Reciprocal Teaching approach has been compared to: (a) instruction identical to the first 4 days of reciprocal teaching and then written practice of the strategies with minimal feedback, (b) demonstration of the strategies with minimal opportunity for the students to practice them, (c) worksheet activities in which the students practiced the strategies and received teacher feedback on their performance but did not practice the strategies in the context of naturalistic reading, and (d) no instruction (Palincsar, 1985). Reciprocal Teaching was found to produce greater comprehension gains than any of the other conditions. Demonstration alone (Item b in former list) was the least effective.

Reciprocal Teaching emphasizes students' learning strategies in the context of using them to monitor and regulate their reading of naturalistic text. The teacher scaffolds the students as they gradually learn to assume responsibility for independently employing the strategies, providing this support in the context of the dialogues through modeling, prompting, and providing informative feedback. The strategies are learned in the context of application, and all students have the opportunity to comment on the strategies. These conditions allow for flexibility in strategy use and is an integral part of instruction.

Whole Language

Whole language is perhaps better termed a philosophy of instruction rather than a model or approach. It also has been characterized as a "grass roots movement" (Y. Goodman, 1989; Watson, 1989) as many of the practices and articulated beliefs have been developed by teachers working collaboratively. Watson (1989) offers the following definition of whole language: "Whole language is a perspective on education that is supported by beliefs about learners and learning, teachers and teaching, language, and curriculum" (p. 133).

Throughout whole language classrooms, there is a focus on the process of reading and writing that is carried out within authentic, personally meaningful contexts. Students pursue their own interests, generally selecting their own texts and writing topics, focusing on these individually or in small groups.

What type of activities occur within a whole language classroom? One is likely to find students engaged in any of the following activities: (a) sustained independent reading of self-selected texts (Atwell, 1987); (b) writing responses to literature they have selected through dialogue journals (McWhirter, 1990) or responding to texts through drama, art, music, or searching out other books by the same author (Watson, 1990); (c) composing, sharing, and publishing original stories (Atwell, 1987; Graves, 1983); and (d) extended meaningful writing in forms such as notes, letters, orders, and newspapers (Atwell, 1987).

Of all of the approaches discussed, it is most difficult to define the role of the teacher within whole language. One description (Newman, 1986) is that the teacher "leads from behind," setting the environment and social norms so that students can learn, and then providing instruction as the need naturally occurs while children pursue their interests in reading and writing. It can be argued, however, that the teacher, in arranging the environment and norms, is also "leading ahead" in his or her creation of an environment that will facilitate insights about reading and writing texts.

Questions have arisen about the teacher's role (e.g., Pearson, 1989), questions that seem difficult to answer as whole language is not as well defined in terms of instruction as are the other approaches reviewed here. Some have questioned whether the teacher instructs at all. This "myth" received the following response from Newman and Church (1990):

> Teachers working from a whole language perspective are active participants in the learning context. We continually work at structuring an environment in which learners can engage in purposeful activities. We collect curriculum resources such as trade books, magazines, science, math and social studies support materials, and we consider and reconsider their location in the classroom. We initiate learning activities. We pose questions, offer procedural suggestions, and suggest explorations. We are ever on the alert for opportunities to present learners with challenges that push them beyond their current strategies and understanding. We are constantly observing our students, asking questions, and inviting contributions from all members of the class in order to judge when learners can best use particular information. We make time to reflect on how learning is proceeding and change direction when it becomes apparent that things aren't going as well as expected or when students propose better alternatives. All of these activities are integral aspects of teaching. (p.22)

There are accounts of fairly teacher-directed instruction within whole language. Slaughter (1988), for example, in describing Chapter 1 whole language programs, found that, although indirect instruction was emphasized, direct teaching activities also occurred. What seems critical is that the teaching is in the context of making sense of text. Staab (1990), for example, discusses a teacher's use of FYIs (for your information): "information presented briefly at a time when it is relevant to needs of the children" (p. 549).

Nancie Atwell (1987), in discussing the use of reading workshops with eighth graders, describes daily reading mini-lessons. In these lessons, conducted at the beginning of the workshops, she focuses on procedural aspects of reading sessions (keeping reading logs, etc.), genres of literature, publishing conventions, and what she refers to as skills. Her attention to the latter involves her explaining and demonstrating Frank Smith's psycholinguistic theory (e.g., 1984), focusing on how good readers sample print. She guides students to "unlearn" many skills they had previously been taught such as underlining and rereading, showing them how this interferes with focusing on large samples of print.

Most of the research that has been conducted utilizing whole language has been descriptive in nature, often involving teachers' documentation of students' reading behaviors and attitudes. McWhirter (1990), for example, documents changes in her eighth-grade students from boredom with and disinterest in reading to a sense of excitement and ownership. Don, a student who initially "hated to read," wrote in his dialogue journal:

Dear Ms. M.,
I'm reading that book *Buster Bear*. And its really easy, so I'm going to read the hole thing. Maybe it will improve me some more so I can go to a little harder book. It's a funny book and nice, because it deal with animals, and how they get along. It makes you think that harmful animals are really not harmful.
Don (p. 564).

Atwell's (1987) book, *In the Middle: Reading, Writing, and Learning with Adolescents*, chronicles in depth the ways in which her eighth-grade students developed engagement in and positive attitudes towards reading and writing. For example, she discusses Lori, a student who wrote:

I can't really believe that I've read so many books this year. At the beginning of the year I just read so that I would pass reading but now I read because it's fun. Now that I've stopped moving my lips it seems like I'm just going right through the books. And you were right. Taking Terri Mueller has really picked up and now it's really interesting I'm at the part where she first goes to see her mother and it's really great. And I'm almost done so that will be 21 this spring. (p. 158).

Accounts such as the above have been presented by teachers throughout the country (e.g., Klein, 1989) and most often involve students developing heightened enthusiasm for reading and writing as well as confidence in their ability to participate in both of these processes.

Overall, teachers within whole language provide less explicit attention to strategic behaviors than do teachers within the other approaches discussed. K. Goodman (1986) cautions against talking *about* language first (outside of the context of using it). One of the teacher's main roles is to model the use and utility of reading and writing in their own lives. Within whole language, there is instruction in conventions of print as well as in strategies to guide reading; however, this often (although not always, as exemplified by Atwell's (1987) mini-lessons) is in the context of "teachable moments" as indicated by the students' pursuits and is in the context of authentic reading and writing tasks.

Comparisons of Teacher's Activities Within the Four Approaches to Reading Instruction

All four approaches reviewed involve the teacher's drawing attention to reading as a process of meaning making requiring active self-monitoring and regulation on the part of the reader. A main difference, one that opens questions about how we should be instructing for self-regulation, is the way in which strategies are identified, defined and evaluated. Within Direct Instruction, the teacher has maximum degree of control: He or she identifies particular strategies as well defines consistent procedures to be used in employing them. There is little room for negotiation with students about strategy utilization or for flexibility in the way the strategies are used to meet differing text and task demands. Explicit explanation also involves a high degree of teacher control in selecting and defining strategies; however, as the focus is on reasoning in using strategies, the teacher-guided procedures are more flexible than within direct instruction, with less emphasis on following set procedures. The teacher in reciprocal teaching initially identifies the four strategies that frame the dialogue; as the control of strategy utilization switches to students, the teacher becomes less directive. Throughout the dialogues, emphasis is placed on negotiation between students and teachers as the strategies are used to make sense of the text; little attention is placed on procedures or heuristics. The negotiation involves attention to text characteristics and utility to particular readers. The teacher's role, in terms of addressing strategies, is least definable within whole language as there is less attention to strategies. What is critical is that the attention given is integrated with and stems from the needs and interests of students as they interact with texts.

Another important way in which the teacher's activities differ among these approaches is the extent to which they involve explicit attention to strategies. Strategies are in the forefront of lessons in Direct Instruction: much of the instruction and talk in the lessons focuses on students' ability to use them according to the given heuristics; discussion of content is secondary. Explicit explanation also involves much focus on the strategies themselves; however, there is more attention to content as the strategies are employed with naturally occurring text and discussed relative to this. Explicit attention to strategies fades over time within Reciprocal Teaching; as the students become more proficient in using the strategies to discuss the text, the dialogues become more focused on content and less so on the strategies themselves (Palincsar, 1986). Whole language involves the least amount of explicit attention to strategies with the teacher's attention much more focused on arranging the environment to foster students' engagement in authentic reading and writing tasks.

Which approach to instruction is most conducive to the development of self-regulation? Are certain approaches more suited to particular students? Delpit (1988), in discussing literacy instruction for minority children, questions the lack of teacher explicitness found in process-oriented approaches such as whole language. She argues that children who do not come from mainstream backgrounds may be denied the access to full participation in this culture if they are not given explicit instruction in the conventions of communication within it. Although not addressing strategic reading per se, Delpit does raise concern about the fairness of teachers assuming a lead-from-behind role with students who do not enter school with the literacy experiences or background of cultural communication patterns that will enable them to benefit from this.

Others (Carver, 1987; Pearson & Dole, 1987; Tierney & Cunningham, 1984) have questioned the need for any explicit attention to strategies. Tierney and Cunningham (1984) use the metaphor of gardening, asking whether we attend to the tools rather than the vegetables. There are also questions with regard to understanding the nature of the strategies that students spontaneously generate, given real reasons to engage in reading and writing. Regardless of one's perspective on the issues of strategy instruction, it has become clear that, as educators, we need to have a clearer understanding of the ways in which learners represent problems before we can determine the nature and extent of strategy instruction in which to engage. At this point, little comparative research has been done among the approaches to reading instruction. Although it is difficult to draw conclusions from comparative research, as well as to determine how to most meaningfully compare approaches, examining differential outcomes over time may help us to plan instruction for diverse learners and to address questions such as those raised by Delpit (1988) and others. In addition, studies of different approaches can identify implementation issues that may not become apparent when the approaches are considered in isolation.

Palincsar and colleagues (1989; 1990; 1991; in press) examined the differential effects of three approaches to strategy instruction with two classes of third graders. The approaches represented a continuum with teacher control of instruction on one end and student control on the other. On the highly teacher-controlled end was Direct Instruction, whereas on the highly student-controlled end was collaborative problem solving; more towards the middle was Reciprocal Teaching.

Direct Instruction and Reciprocal Teaching have been described earlier in this chapter and were implemented as described. The teacher in the Direct Instruction groups, following scripted lesson plans, explained what the targeted strategies were and how they could be helpful;, demonstrated their use; and presented explicit steps to be followed in carrying them out, making use of rules and heuristics. Students practiced the steps as directed by the teacher and received immediate feedback on their performance. Evaluation was in terms of the teacher leading the students to state whether or not the steps were carried out as directed (e.g., "Did you leave out unimportant information in your summary?"). Students practiced the lessons independently through the use of worksheets.

In Reciprocal Teaching, the students received guided practice in applying strategies as they and the teacher engaged in dialogues about the content of the text. The dialogues were guided by the use of summarizing, questioning, predicting, and clarifying. The teacher provided support to the students as they attempted to use the strategies while reading connected text. In comparison to Direct Instruction, the teacher attended more to the students' understanding of the strategies' use rather than their ability to carry out procedural steps.

The third approach, one designed for this study, represented the least amount of teacher control in identifying and defining strategies and evaluating their use. Collaborative problem solving focused on students, through collaboration with their peers, maintaining maximum involvement in all of these aspects. The students suggested strategies to use, tried to employ them as a group or in pairs, evaluated their helpfulness, and in so doing, developed procedures for using the strategies. Thus procedural knowledge was developed in the context of fulfilling purposes for using the strategies.

After engaging in activities to facilitate group problem solving (See Palincsar, Winn, David, & Stevens, in press, for a more complete description of the activities), the students read the same texts used in the other approaches, a section at a time. Before reading each section, they selected a strategy to use as a group or in pairs. They read the section, employed the strategy, and then evaluated its effectiveness. The teacher initially observed what the students could do working collaboratively and unassisted, and then provided a series of prompts through further questioning and suggestions. She had a marginal role in evaluating the use of strategies; the students were not given a clear standard for determining strategy effectiveness.

The study was carried out in 2 third-grade classrooms ($N=41$). In each classroom, there were three groups of students, with each group participating in instruction utilizing one of the approaches. The strategies covered in all groups were summarizing, self-questioning, and prediction. The same expository texts were used in all instructional groups. A variety of outcome measures were utilized including criterion-referenced tests of comprehension; metacognitive interviews about conceptions of reading, characterizations of skillful reading, awareness of text features and text demands, and strategy knowledge; a "think-aloud" in which students shared their thinking while reading ambiguous stories; and strategy use measures.

The results indicated that instruction had a significant positive effect on criterion-referenced, metacognitive, and strategy use measures (but not on a "think-aloud" measure) across the three approaches. Only one measure was sensitive to differential outcomes; the students in the collaborative problem solving groups showed more positive changes on the criterion-referenced comprehension measure. When the student outcome data was analyzed according to achievement levels of the students, it was found that the higher achieving students in the collaborative problem solving and Reciprocal Teaching groups made more gains in the strategy use measure than did the higher achieving students in the Direct Instruction groups.

In reflecting on their experiences in conducting instruction utilizing the three approaches, the researchers in the Palincsar et al. study (1989, 1990; 1991; in press) identified several implementation issues that have implications for the feasibility of using these approaches in classrooms; in addition, these issues are relevant to thinking about approaches such as whole language and explicit explanation that were not focused on in this particular study. Three of these issues are ease of implementation, assessment, and the role of heterogeneity.

Ease of Implementation

Ease of implementation refers to the ongoing decisions that teachers make while conducting instruction. The fewer ongoing decisions, the easier instruction is to implement. Of the three approaches in the Palincsar et al. study, Direct Instruction had the greatest degree of ease of implementation. The lessons contained embedded guidelines for determining correct or incorrect student performance as well as procedures for correction. The ease of implementation was less in Reciprocal Teaching; scaffolding students' use of strategies could not be planned in advance and required the teacher to attend to multiple variables. In addition, the teacher's decisions had to be made in the course of instruction and could not be planned beforehand. All of the implementation difficulties of Reciprocal Teaching were present in collaborative problem solving. In addition, the high degree of ambiguity;

lack of structure in the tasks; and emphasis on student control in strategy selection, definition, and evaluation added further difficulties.

The guided practice phase of explicit explanation involves a greater degree of ambiguity than within Direct Instruction because the teacher shares her reasoning with the students and responds to theirs as they employ the strategies. Implementation can be managed by carefully considering the nature of the reasoning to share with students previous to instruction. However, the interactions within guided practice will vary depending on the students' use of the strategies. Ease of implementation, in terms of instruction for self-regulation, may be most difficult within a whole language approach, especially one that strives to lead from behind. Arranging the environment so that opportunities for discussion and reflection on reading activities occur to a sufficient degree and are able to be capitalized on is quite challenging.

Assessment

The second issue that emerged in discussions about the three instructional approaches was assessment. This issue is twofold: (a) the level at which assessment can occur and (b) the focus of assessment. Assessment at an individual level was built into the independent practice of Direct Instruction but was more elusive in the other two approaches, especially collaborative problem solving. In Direct Instruction, students were assessed through the use of individual worksheets, providing a clear record of their performance. The dialogues of Reciprocal Teaching provided the teachers opportunities to assess each student's level of competence in using the strategies. This type of assessment was more complex than assessment in Direct Instruction; however, the students were using the strategies in a way in which it was expected that they would need assistance. Collaborative problem solving provided little opportunity for individual assessment as the focus was on group problem solving; there was not a structure for individual participation.

The focus of assessment was most constrained in Direct Instruction, with emphasis solely on mastery of the strategies focused on in instruction. Both in Reciprocal Teaching and collaborative problem solving, there were opportunities to assess strategy use in the service of content, and concurrently, to assess comprehension of that content. In addition to their use of strategies and comprehension of the content of the text, the students' conceptions about reading were also available for assessment in collaborative problem solving through the discussions about strategy uses.

Explicit explanation provides opportunities for assessment of the reasoning students use in employing strategies. The lack of structure for group discussions may present difficulties in assessing individual students. Whole language provides opportunities for assessment of students' notions about the reading process as well as their understanding of content. Because there is not as much explicit discussion of strategic reading behaviors, there is less opportunity to assess understanding of these behaviors than in the other approaches. However, assessment of reasoning and strategy use is possible. The use of individual conferences with the teacher about reading and writing, part of the program in many classes utilizing whole language, enables individual assessment.

The above assessment issues must be considered in determining the way in which instruction for self-regulation can and should be conducted, especially as teachers are called on to teach increasingly heterogenous groups of students. The final implementation issue to be discussed is the way in which heterogeneity can be accommodated by different approaches to instruction for self-regulation.

Heterogeneity

In Reciprocal Teaching and collaborative problem solving, incorporation of students of varying abilities was accomplished through the instructional format. Students who more quickly became competent in strategy use were able to use the strategies independently while those who needed more teacher assistance could receive it. The higher achieving students were afforded opportunities to elaborate and justify their statements while the lower achieving students were provided opportunities to observe and benefit from others doing so. The structure of Direct Instruction was not as adaptable to heterogenous groups of students. There were no provisions for students who mastered components of the strategies to proceed before the majority of the group members reached criterion.

Explicit explanation is more adaptable than Direct Instruction to heterogenous groups of students; teachers can individualize their responses to students' use of strategies during guided practice yet they are not constrained to focus the group on one step of a strategy until mastery is used. The whole language approach, with the emphasis on individuals pursuing their reading and writing interests, can be well suited to classrooms of students with a wide range of abilities, provided the teacher is able provide the necessary guidance for all of the students in reflecting on their reading and writing.

The student outcomes and implementation issues raised in the Palincsar et al. study (1989, 1990, 1991, in press) provide frames from which to consider which teacher activities, or instructional approach, may be most facilitative of the development of self-regulation with particular groups of students. One further way in which we can think about differences among these approaches, and the others considered in this chapter, is in terms of the role of student peers in facilitating the development of knowledge and beliefs of self-regulated readers. This issue is in keeping with current interest in conceptualizing classrooms as communities of inquiry.

The peer group had little if any role in Direct Instruction. The flow of talk was between individual students and the teacher, with minimal opportunity for students to interact with each other or to reflect on each other's contributions. As there were external, unambiguous standards for correct and incorrect application of strategies, discussions about personalized approaches to strategy use did not occur. The peer group had a much more dominant role in Reciprocal Teaching as the students responded to and commented on each other's interpretation of the text in the structured dialogues, working as a group to understand the text. Transcripts of Reciprocal Teaching over time have shown diminished teacher talk and increased peer dialogues as students become more able and confident in using the strategies to discuss and reflect on the texts. Collaborative problem solving, by its nature, involved peers working together in partners or in the whole group to identify strategies, employ them with text, and evaluate their usefulness.

Peer interaction is an important component of whole language. Students share their reactions to what they read as well as their writing with their classmates through such activities as author's chair, letters to each other about what they are reading (Atwell, 1987), or simply talking to each other about their literary pursuits (Klein, 1989). These activities are a product of and foster students' willingness to take risks, a characteristic of students who believe in their reading and writing abilities. Our survey of the approaches to reading instruction provide a range of activities teachers and students can be involved in as they work towards students achieving the goals of self-regulated reading. The approaches embody differing conceptions of teaching and learning, as well as of what students need to know to reach the goals of strategic reading. More investigations into both implementation and student outcomes of differing instructional approaches, both those discussed in this section as well as others, will help us make decisions about tasks, degree of explicitness about strategies, and student and teacher roles that will be most facilitative of meeting our goals.

A final consideration for how we instruct reading pertains to working with students of differing reading achievement levels. Should lower achieving readers be instructed differently than those who are not experiencing reading difficulties? Attention to strategies may interfere with proficient readers' automatized use of them, slowing down and confusing these students' comprehension and learning. It is likely these students may not need the degree of attention to strategic knowledge and behaviors that other students do although their knowledge can be solidified through providing explanation and justifications to their peers (Webb, 1989).

As we need to ensure that we are providing instruction that challenges proficient readers, we also need to ensure that we are not denying access to instruction towards our reading goals with low achieving students through differential instruction, an instructional concern to which we now turn.

Differential Instruction

The work of Allington and others (Allington, 1980; Allington & McGill Franzen, 1989; Collins, 1981; McGill-Franzen & Allington, 1991) has raised concern about the lack of focus in instruction for low achieving readers on the knowledge and skills needed for self-regulation. In addition, these studies have raised concern about the limited exposure to connected text in comparison with instruction provided to better readers. There is less of a focus on instruction for comprehension and more of one on decoding and isolated skills. Allington (1980), in reviewing many of the studies in this area, pointed to observed differences in the amount of engaged time students spent reading, time spent in oral versus silent reading, lesson emphases, and patterns of teacher interruptions.

Allington (1980) found differences in teacher interruption behaviors in high and low reading groups. Twenty 1st- and 2nd-grade teachers were observed teaching the two groups of students designated their best and worst readers. Students' oral reading errors as well as the teachers' responses to them were recorded. The teachers interrupted the poor readers when they made errors significantly more often than they interrupted good readers. Even if the errors were semantically appropriate, the poor readers were interrupted more often. The teachers' remarks were more likely to be directed at graphophonemic cues for the poor readers, whereas they emphasized semantics and syntactic cues for the good readers.

Collins (1982) analyzed the discourse style and interactional patterns in first- and third-grade reading groups. In the first-grade study, he found that decoding was emphasized in the low group, whereas comprehension was focused on in the higher group. He observed that the discussions in the third-grade classes studied were less collaborative in the low reading groups than in the high groups. Teachers incorporated fewer of the low group students' responses into subsequent questions, thus reducing the chances for dialogue to ensue. There was also less discussion of vocabulary and more disruptive overlapping of questions and answers (resulting in answers not always being acknowledged) in the low group. Both in the first and third grades, students in the low groups were receiving instruction that was not conducive to the development of reading as problem solving; similarly, their instruction did not teach or encourage these students to become actively involved in the reading process.

Reading instruction for students in special education and remedial reading classes has also been found to generally be lacking focus on strategic reading but rather to involve isolated drill, typically through seatwork activities (e.g., Allington, & McGill Franzen, 1989; Haynes & Jenkins, 1986; Ysseldyke, Thurlow, O'Sullivan, & Christensen, 1989). It appears that, too often, students who most need instruction in and exposure to the active, constructive nature of reading for understanding and learning are those who receive it least.

In response to the findings of Allington (1980) we suggest that, to meet the reading goals defined in this chapter, we need to insure that our instruction for all readers focuses on the development of strategic knowledge and behavior. This may be even more critical for lower ability readers, those students who are often found to lack the knowledge and beliefs that drive self-regulation. We are not necessarily advocating one approach to instruction over another. However, we do argue that it is imperative to look at instruction in terms of the level at which it provides opportunities for: (a) students to engage in strategic activities, (b) discussions that promote independent monitoring and regulation of reading, and (c) students to develop confidence in their reading abilities.

In addition, we need to provide all readers plentiful opportunity to read connected text. Stanovich (1986) has documented the Mathew effect in reading in
which good readers (the rich) are given more opportunities to read (to get richer)
and continue to become better readers whereas poor readers are prevented from
doing so, in part by not being given opportunities to read. Research (e.g., Taylor,
Frye, & Maruyama, 1990) points to the positive effects of time spent reading
connected text. Our concern is that we do not create Mathew effects in our reading
instruction.

References

Allington, R.L. (1980). Teacher interruption behaviors during primary grade oral
    reading. *Journal of Educational Psychology, 72*, 371-377.

Allington, R.L., & McGill-Franzen, A. (1989). School response to reading failure:
    Instruction for Chapter I and special education students in grades two, four, and
    eight. *Elementary School Journal, 89*, 529-542

Anderson, R.C., & Pearson, P.D. (1984). A schema-theoretic view of basic proc-
    esses in reading comprehension. In P.D. Pearson, R. Barr, M.L. Kamil, & P.
    Mosenthal (Eds.), *Handbook of reading research* (Vol. 1, pp. 255-291). White
    Plains, NY: Longman.

Anderson, R.C., Reynolds, R.E., Schallert, D.L., & Goetz, E.T. (1977). Frame-
    works for comprehending discourse. *American Educational Research Journal,
    14*, 367-382.

Atwell, N. (1987). *In the middle: Reading, writing, and learning with adolescents.*
    Portsmouth, NH: Heinemann.

August, D.L., Flavell, J.H., & Clift, R. (1984). Comparison of comprehension
    monitoring of skilled and less skilled readers. *Reading Research Quarterly, 20*,
    39-53.

Baker, L., & Brown, A.L. (1984). Metacognitive skills and reading. In P.D. Pearson
    (Ed.), *Handbook of reading research* (pp. 353-394). New York: Longman.

Baumann, J.F. (1984). The effectiveness of a direct instruction paradigm for
    teaching main idea comprehension. *Reading Research Quarterly, 20*, 93-115.

Baumann, J.F. (1988). Direct instruction reconsidered. *Journal of Reading Behav-
    ior, 31*, 712-718.

Bereiter, C., & Scardamalia, M. (1987). An attainable version of high literacy:
    Approaches to teaching higher order skills in reading and writing. *Curriculum
    Inquiry, 17*, 19-30.

Brown, A.L., Bransford, J.D., Ferrrara, R.A., & Campione, J.C. (1983). Learning,
    remembering, and understanding. In J.H. Flavell & E.M. Markman (Eds),
    Handbook of child psychology: Cognitive development (Vol. 3, pp. 77-166).
    New York: Wiley.

Brown, A.L., & Palincsar, A.S. (1985). *Reciprocal teaching of comprehension: A natural history of a program for enhancing learning* (Tech. Rep. No. 334). University of Illinois, Center for the Study of Reading: Champaign-Urbana.

Brown, A.L., & Palincsar, A.S. (1989). Guided cooperative learning and individual knowledge acquisition. In L. Resnick (Ed.), *Knowing, learning, and instruction: Essays in honor of Robert Glaser* (pp. 393-451). Hillsdale, NJ: Erlbaum.

Butkowsky, I.S., & Willows, D.M. (1980). Cognitive-motivational characteristics of children varying in reading ability: Evidence for learned helplessness in poor readers. *Journal of Educational Psychology, 72,* 408-422.

Carver, R.P. (1987). Should reading comprehension skills be taught? In J.E. Readence & R.S. Baldwin (Eds.), *Research in literacy: Merging perspectives: Thirty-Sixth yearbook of the National Reading Conference* (pp.115-126). Rochester, NY: National Reading Conference.

Collins, J. (1981). Discourse style, classroom interaction, and differential treatment. *Journal of Reading Behavior, 14,* 429-437.

Collins, A., Brown, J.S., & Newman, S.E. (1989). Cognitive apprenticeship: Teaching the craft of reading, writing, and mathematics. In L.B.Resnick (Ed.), *Knowing, learning, and instruction: Essays in honor of Robert Glaser.* Hillsdale, NJ: Lawrence Erlbaum.

Darch, C., & Kameenui, E.J. (1987). Teaching LD students critical reading skills: A systematic replication. *Learning Disability Quarterly, 10,* 82-91.

Delpit, L. (1988). The silenced dialogue: Power and pedagogy in educating other people's children. *Harvard Educational Review, 38,* 280-298.

Dole, J.A., Duffy, G.G., Roehler, L.R., & Pearson, P.D. (1991). Moving from the old to the new: Research on reading comprehension instruction. *Review of Educational Research, 61,* 239-264.

Duffy, G.G., & Roehler, L.R. (1987). The tension between information giving and mediation: Perspectives on instructional explanation and teacher change. In J.E. Brophy (Ed.), *Advances in research on teaching* (Vol. 1, pp. 1-33). Greenwich, CT: JAI.

Duffy, G.G., Roehler, L.R., Meloth, M.S., Vavrus, L.G., Book, C., Putnam, J., & Wesselman, R. (1986). The relationship between explicit verbal explanations during reading skill instruction and student awareness and achievement: A study of reading teacher effects. *Reading Research Quarterly, 21,* 237-252.

Duffy, G.G., Roehler, L.R., Sivan, E., Rackliffe, G., Book, C., Meloth, M., Vavrus, L.G., Wesselman, R., Putnam, J., & Bassiri, D. (1987). Effects of explaining the reasoning associated with using reading strategies. *Reading Research Quarterly, 22,* 347-368.

Durkin, D. (1978-1979). What classroom observations reveal about reading comprehension instruction. *Reading Research Quarterly, 15,* 481-533.

Forrest, D.L., & Waller, T.G. (1980, April). *What do children know about their reading and study skills?* Paper presented at the annual meeting of the American Educational Research Association. Boston.

Garner, R. (1980). Monitoring of understanding: An investigation of good and poor readers' awareness of induced miscomprehensions of text. *Journal of Reading Behavior, 12*, 55-63.

Garner, R. (1987). *Metacognition and reading comprehension.* New York: Ablex.

Garner, R., Wagoner, S., & Smith, T. (1983). Externalizing question-answering strategies of good and poor comprehenders. *Reading Research Quarterly, 18*, 439-447.

Gersten, R., Woodward, J., & Darch, C. (1986). Direct instruction: A research-based approach to curriculum design and teaching. *Exceptional Children, 53*, 71-31.

Goodman, K. (1986). *What's whole in whole language?* Portsmouth, NH: Heinemann.

Goodman, Y. (1989). Roots of the whole language movement. *Elementary School Journal, 90*, 113-127.

Graves, D. (1983). *Writing: Teachers and children at work.* Portsmouth, NH: Heinemann.

Haynes, M., & Jenkins, J.R. (1986). Reading instruction in special education resource rooms. *American Educational Research Journal, 23*, 161-190.

Johnson, P., & Winograd, P. (1985). Passive failure in reading. *Journal of Reading Behavior, 17*, 279-301.

Kierstead, J. (1985). Direct instruction and experiential approaches: Are they really mutually exclusive? *Educational Leadership, 42*(8), 25-30.

Klein, A.M. (1989). Meaningful reading and writing in a first grade classroom. *Elementary School Journal, 90*, 185-192.

McGill-Franzen, A., & Allington, R.L. (1991). The gridlock of low reading achievement: Perspectives on practice and policy. *Remedial and Special Education, 12*, 20-30.

McWhirter, A.M. (1990). Whole language in the middle school. *Reading Teacher, 43*, 562-565.

Meyers, M., & Paris, S.G. (1978). Children's metacognitive knowledge about reading. *Journal of Educational Psychology, 70*, 680-690.

Newman, J.M. (1986). *Whole language–Theory in use.* Portsmouth, NH: Heinemann.

Newman, J.M., & Church, S.M. (1990). Myths of whole language. *The Reading Teacher, 44*, 20-26.

Palincsar, A.S. (1985, April). *The un-packing of a multi-component multiple training package.* Paper presented at the annual conference of the American Educational Research Association, Chicago.

Palincsar, A.S. (1987, April). *Collaborating for collaborative learning of text comprehension.* Paper presented at the annual meeting of the American Educational Research Association, Washington, DC.

Palincsar, A.S. (1988). From the mystery spot to the thoughtful spot: The instruction of metacognitive strateiges. *Reading Teacher, 41*, 784-789.

Palincsar, A.S., & Brown, A.L.(1984). Reciprocal teaching of comprehension-fostering and comprehension-monitoring activities. *Cognition and Instruction, 1,* 117-175.

Palincsar, A.S., & Brown, A.L.(1989a). Classroom dialogues to promote self-regulated comprehension. In J.E. Brophy (Ed.), *Advances in research in teaching: Teaching for meaningful learning and self-regulation* (Vol. 1, pp. 35-71). Greenwich, CT: JAI.

Palincsar, A.S.& Brown, A.L. (1989b). Instruction for self-regulated reading. In L.B.Resnick & L.B.Klopfer (Eds.), *Towards the thinking curriculum: Current cognitive research.* Arlington, VA: Association of Supervision and Curriculum Development.

Palincsar, A.S., David, Y.M., Winn, J.A., Snyder, B.S., & Stevens, D.D. (1989, November). *The differential effects of reading procedures for teaching strategic reading.* Paper presented at the annual meeting of the National Reading Conference, Austin.

Palincsar, A.S., David, Y., Winn, J., & Stevens, D. (1990, March). *Examining the differential effects of teacher- versus student-controlled activity in comprehension instruction.* Paper presented at the annual meeting of the American Educational Research Association, Boston.

Palincsar, A.S., David, Y., Winn, J., & Stevens, D. (1991). Examining the context of strategy instruction. *Remedial and Special Education, 12,* 42-53.

Palincsar, A.S., Jones, B.F., Ogle, D.S., & Carr, E.G. (1986). *Teaching reading as thinking.* Alexandria, VA: The Association for Supervision and Curriculum Development.

Palincsar, A.S., Winn, J.A., David, Y.M., & Stevens, D.D. (in press). Approaches to strategy instruction reflecting different conceptions of teaching and learning. In L. Meltzer (Ed.), *Cognitive, linguistic, and developmental perspectives on learning disabilities.* Boston: College-Hill Press.

Paris, S.G., Lipson, M.Y., & Wixon, K.K. (1983). Becoming a strategic reader. *Contemporary Educational Psychology, 8,* 293-316.

Paris, S.G., & Oka, E.R. (1986). Self-regulated learning among exceptional children. *Exceptional Children, 53,* 103-108.

Paris, S.G., & Winograd, P. (1991). Promoting metacognition and motivation in exceptional children. *Remedial and Special Education, 11,* 7-15.

Paris, S.G., Wixon, K.K., & Palincsar, A.S. (1986). Instructional approaches to reading comprehension. In E.Z. Rothkopf (Ed.), *Review of research in education* (pp. 91-128). Washington, DC: American Educational Research Association.

Patching, W., Kameenui, E., Carnine, D., Gersten, R., & Colvin, G. (1983). Direct instruction in critical reading skills. *Reading Research Quarterly, 18,* 406-418.

Pearson, P.D. (1989). Commentary: Reading the whole language movement. Elementary School Journal, *90,* 231-241.

Pearson, P.D., & Dole, J.A. (1987). Explicit comprehension instrution: A review of the research and a new conceptualization of instruction. *The Elementary School Journal, 88,* 153-167.

Pearson, P.D., & Raphael, T.E. (1990). Reading comprehension as a dimension of thinking. In L. Idol (Ed.), *Dimensions of thinking and cognitive instruction* (pp. 209-240). Hillsdale, NJ: Erlbaum.

Pressley, M., Borkowski, J.G., & Schneider, W. (1987). Cognitive strategies: Good strategy users coordinate metacognition and knowledge. In R. Vasta & G. Whitehurst (Eds.), *Annals of child development* (Vol. 5, pp. 89-129). Greenwich, CT: JAI Press.

Pressley, M., Johnson, C.J., Symons, S., McGoldrick, J.A., & Kurita, J.A. (1989). Strategies that improve children's memory and comprehension of text. *Elementary School Journal, 90,* 3-32.

Roehler, L.R., & Duffy, G.G. (1986). Studying qualitative dimensions in educational effectiveness. In J.V. Hoffman (Ed.), *Effective teaching of reading.* Newark, DE: International Reading Association.

Rosenshine, B. (1979). Content, time and direct instruction. In P. Peterson & H. Walberg (Eds.), *Research on teaching: Concepts, findings, and implications* (pp. 28-56). Berkeley, CA: McCutchan.

Slaughter, H. (1988). Indirect and direct teaching in a whole language classroom. *Reading Teacher, 42,* 30-34.

Smith, F.(1984). *Reading without nonsense.* New York: Teachers College Press.

Staab, C.F. (1990). Teacher mediation in one whole language classroom. *Reading Teacher, 43,* 548-552.

Stanovich, K.E. (1986). Mathew effects in reading: Some consequences of individual differences in the acquisition of literacy. *Reading Research Quarterly, 21,* 360-407.

Taylor, B.M., Fyre, B.J., Maruyama, G.M. (1990). Time spent reading and reading growth. *American Educational Research Journal, 27,* 351-362.

Tierney, R.J., & Cunningham, J.W. (1984). Research on teaching reading comprehension. In P.D. Pearson (Ed.), *Handbook of reading research* (pp. 609-655). NY: Longman.

Venezky, R.L. (1986). Steps toward a comprehensive history of American reading instruction. In E.Z. Rothkopf (Ed.), *Review of research in education* (Vol. 13). Washington, DC: American Educational Research Association.

Watson, D. (1989). Defining and describing whole language. *Elementary School Journal, 90,* 129-141.

Webb, N. (1989). Peer interaction and learning in small groups. In N. Webb (Ed.), Peer interaction, problem-solving, and cogntion in small groups [Special issue]. *International Journal of Research in Education, 14,* 21-39.

Wisconsin Department of Public Instruction. (1986). *A guide to curriculum planning* (Bulletin No. 6305). Madison, WI: Wisconsin Department of Public Instruction.

Wood, P., Bruner, J., & Ross, G. (1976). The role of tutoring in problem solving. *Journal of Child Psychology and Psychiatry, 17,* 89-100.

Ysseldyke, J.E., Thurlow, M.L., O'Sullivan, P., & Christensen, S.L. (1989). Teaching structures and tasks in reading instruction for students with mild handicaps. *Learning Disabilities Research, 4,* 78-86.

Part III:
Reading in Adulthood

8
Reading Comprehension and the Use of Text Structure Across the Adult Life Span

Bonnie J. F. Meyer, Carole J. Young, and Brendan J. Bartlett

This chapter briefly examines the research literature dealing with reading comprehension across the adult life span. Reviewed are both basic research studies in the area of prose learning and studies of reading training with adults. The final portion of the chapter briefly describes a study that taught young and old adults a reading strategy.

The study of reading comprehension has been an active area of research over the last 2 decades (e.g., Pearson, 1984). The interaction of the reader and the structure of texts has been a particularly productive area of research on reading comprehension during this time. Contributions to our understanding of texts and reading comprehension have come from the areas of linguistics (e.g., Beaugrande, 1980; Grimes, 1975; Halliday & Hasan, 1976), rhetoric (e.g., Aristotle, 1960; Christensen, 1967; D'Angelo, 1979), folklore and story grammar (e.g., Mandler, 1987; Propp, 1958; Rumelhart, 1975; Stein & Glenn, 1979), artificial intelligence (e.g., Lehnert, 1981; Schank, 1975), education (e.g., Niles, 1965), educational psychology (e.g., Meyer, 1975, 1985), and psychology (e.g., Britton, Van Dusen, Glynn, & Hemphill, 1990; Frederiksen, 1977; Graesser, 1981; Kieras, 1985; Kintsch, 1974).

This basic research on prose learning stimulated gerontologists to examine age-related changes in memory with more naturalistic materials (Hartley, Harker, & Walsh, 1980). Research dealing with reading comprehension and aging has increased substantially within the last decade. Although age-related deficits are well-documented with verbatim recall of lists of words, numbers and such (Burke & Light, 1981), deficits are not always found with substantive recall of texts. Some types of older adults under certain task conditions with particular types of text can remember as much information as younger adults (Hultsch & Dixon, 1984; Meyer & Rice, 1983a, 1989). However, under the majority of reader, task, and text conditions tested so far in the laboratory-age differences in prose processing have been found. A number of reviews have been written recently about this growing body of literature on prose processing and aging (Cohen, 1988; Hartley, 1988, 1989; Hartley, Harker, & Walsh, 1980; Hultsch & Dixon, 1984; Meyer, 1987; Meyer & Rice, 1983a, 1989; Meyer, Young, & Bartlett, 1989; Zelinski & Gilewski, 1988).

Age Differences in the Amount of Information Remembered

Most of the research has focused on whether or not older people remember as much information from their reading as younger adults. Little work has looked at what types of reading skills decline or improve with age. Conflicting findings have been found in simply trying to determine age differences in the amount of information recalled by young and old adults. Some of the differences among extant studies on reading comprehension and aging can be explained by differences in education and verbal ability of sample participants. Age differences in text recall have been reported to interact with level of verbal ability (Meyer & Rice, 1983a; Poon, Krauss, & Bowles, 1984; Taub, 1979; Zelinski & Gilewski, 1988). Individual differences approaches in cognitive psychology have indicated compatible findings related to the advantage for individuals with good verbal skills (e.g., Hunt, 1978; Perfetti, 1985).

Some incompatibility among the findings from studies on prose learning and aging can be explained by differences in education and verbal ability of samples. Age deficits in prose recall are regularly found for average and low verbal adults with mainly high school education (Cohen, 1979; Dixon & von Eye, 1984; Dixon, Hultsch, Simon, & von Eye, 1984; Dixon, Simon, Nowak & Hultsch, 1982; Glynn, Okun, Muth, & Britton, 1983; Meyer & Rice, 1983a, 1983b; Spilich, 1983; Spilich & Voss, 1982; Surber, Kowalski, & Pena-Paez, 1984; Taub, 1979; Zelinski, Light, & Gilewski, 1984). However, all of the discrepancy cannot be explained, because some studies with highly educated, high ability old adults report aging deficits (Cohen, 1979; Gordon & Clark, 1974; Light & Anderson, 1985; Meyer & Rice, 1983b; Zelinski, Light, & Gilewski, 1984), whereas others do not (Harker, Hartley, & Walsh, 1982; Mandler & Johnson, 1977; Meyer & Rice, 1981, 1983a; Young, 1983). In general, age differences appear to be attenuated when subjects possess superior levels of semantic abilities.

In an attempt to determine factors underlying verbal ability that affect reading comprehension, Rice and Meyer (1985) examined the reading behaviors of young and older adults of high and average verbal ability. Answers to questionnaires indicated that certain reading behaviors were related to success on prose learning tasks for both young and old adults, and old adults with average vocabulary scores reported the lowest incidence of these behaviors. High scorers on recall tasks were those who were highly practiced at reading and who took an analytical approach to reading of text. Specifically, older adults of high verbal ability reported more enjoyment of reading and spent more time reading than did older adults of average verbal ability. These data are compatible with a practice explanation; that is, older adults with high verbal skills perform as well as young adults on some prose recall task because they practice the necessary reading skills.

This practice explanation was further investigated with a diary study (Rice, 1986a, 1986b). Over the space of 5 weeks, 54 participants kept structured diaries in which they recorded how they spent their time, including what materials they read and the length of time spent reading each item. These data were used to determine if activities varied as a function of differences in the age and vocabulary skills of the participants. Of particular interest was whether older adults who were high in verbal ability did more reading than average ability ones, as would be predicted by the practice effect of the experiential model.

With respect to the effects of age and vocabulary level on the everyday activities of adults, the findings demonstrated that age and vocabulary were secondary to requirements of daily life (school, employment, retirement) in determining the patterning of daily activities. The daily requirements of schooling and career were of overriding importance in determining the types of activities engaged in by adults. Thus, it was not the case that older adults who were high in verbal ability showed markedly different patterns from average ability adults in their reading and other activities, as would be predicted by the practice effect. However, there were some significant differences between the older high vocabulary adults and the older average vocabulary adults in reading activities, but not other activities. Older average vocabulary adults read less, spent less time reading for interest, and spent less time reading materials other than the newspaper. Thus, the data provide some indirect support for the practice hypothesis of the experiential model in that older adults of high verbal ability did get more practice at reading than did older adults of average ability.

Although the questionnaire and diary data lent some support for the practice effect, an exploratory multivariate analysis (Rice & Meyer, 1986) did not give much support to the power of this practice effect in explaining prose recall performance. Four hundred twenty-two young, middle-aged, and old adults read and recalled two passages and answered questions about their background, reading habits, and recall strategies. Results indicated that a decrease in quantity of recall appeared with increasing age, though verbal ability was a better predictor of recall than was age. A recall strategy factor representing a paragraph-by-paragraph retrieval strategy produced the highest simple correlations with total recall. Reading habit factors appeared very seldom in the multiple regression analyses and produced only a few positive correlations in the simple regressions. This almost total absence of the reading habit factors from the multiple regression analyses would appear to provide little support for the practice effect explanation of age differences in recall performance.

Relating the diary data to recall data, Rice and Meyer (1986) showed that total time spent reading in everyday life correlated with recall performance in the laboratory $(r = .32, p < .05)$. *In a multiple regression analysis, four reading categories together accounted for 40% of the variance. They included technical journals, science books, textbooks, and religious materials (primarily the Bible) for 12%, 10%, 6% and 6%, respectively. These findings are in line with the questionnaire data reported in Rice and Meyer (1985) and the practice explanation for aging deficits.*

However, the study (Rice & Meyer, 1986) indicated that it is not only quantity of practice, but quality as well. Completely opposite relations between newspaper reading and prose recall performance were found for average and high verbal older adults. For older adults of average ability, time spent reading newspapers correlated negatively ($r = -.91$) with recall, whereas older adults of high verbal ability showed a strong positive correlation ($r = .89$). Total time spent reading all materials showed a similar pattern for the average verbal old adults; the primary material read by the average verbal old adult was the newspaper. There does not appear to be a simple linear relation between practice in reading and recall, but instead, a certain skill level may be necessary before practice is effective.

Age Differences in Speed

Some research relates to the reading skill of speed. Slowing in processing ability with age is evident with discourse. Six of the extant prose learning studies controlled presentation time. All but one of these studies (Mandel & Johnson, 1984) reported age deficits. The exceptional study had the slowest presentation time (102 words per minute); the rates of the other studies were 120 words per minute or faster. Across several studies (Cohen, 1979; Mandler & Johnson, 1977; Meyer & Rice, 1983b; Petros, Tabor, Cooney, & Chabot, 1983), texts were presented orally without visual exposure. Zelinski el al.(1984) had their subjects read the text while it was being read to them at a fast pace. Surber et al. allowed their subjects 11 minutes and 30 seconds to read a five and a half page text. Petros et al. expected an age by rate (120 wpm vs. 160 wpm) interaction, but did not find it. Rate impaired the recall performance to an equivalent degree for young and old subjects. The speed between 102 wpm and 120 wpm appears critical for exceeding an optimal level of processing by old adults. Meyer and Rice (1987) reported the reading time data from a study with 160 high and average verbal old and young adults; the average reading speed of old adults was 121 wpm, whereas it was 144 wpm for young adults. A pace of 120 wpm is too quick for about half of the old adults, whereas it is well within the optimal range for nearly all young adults. However, other researchers using shorter texts (Hartley, 1986; Light & Anderson, 1985) have reported nonsignificant differences in the reading times of young and old adults.

Hartley, Cassidy, and Lee (1986) reported slower reading times per proposition for older adults than younger adults. After determining each subject's normal reading rate, they presented texts to them at a fast or slow rate. Working under a model of reduced processing resources with aging, they expected speed to hurt the older adults more than the younger adults. However, they found age deficits and speed deficits, but age and speed did not interact.

The extant studies with long texts and a self-paced presentation have reported no age-related deficits (Harker et al., 1982; Meyer & Rice, 1981; Thompson & Diefenderfer, 1986). Surber et al. (1984) and Zelinski et al.(1984) also used long texts and found aging deficits, but they limited reading time to 136 wpm for Surber et al. (1984) and 155 wpm for Zelinski et al. Longer articles may call for reading skills more frequently used in the lives of older adults.

One explanation for greater age deficits for faster paced presentations than for slower or self-paced presentations focuses on slowing with aging (Birren, 1974). Older adults are thought to be disadvantaged primarily in terms of the speed with which they can carry out mental operations such as encoding, comparison, and response selection and execution (Birren, Woods, & Williams, 1980). Another explanation emphasizes a reduction in working memory capacity with increasing age (Cohen, 1979, 1988; Petros et al., 1983; Spilich, 1983). Self-paced conditions should help to reinstate information lost from working memory and serve as a memory aid to compensate for any lost capacity. Some sophistication in reading skills may be necessary before older adults can compensate through rereading and review.

Age Differences in Awareness and Use of Text Structure

An important reading skill is the ability to utilize the structure in text (e.g., Aulls, 1982; Chall, 1983; Herber, 1978; Meyer, 1975; Niles, 1965). The structure of text specifies the logical connections among ideas as well as subordination of some ideas to others. It is this structure that primarily differentiates text from simple lists of words or sentences.

The Levels Effects. Most studies examining age differences in sensitivity to text structure have examined the levels effect. The levels effect, in which information high in the hierarchical structure of a passage is better recalled than information low in the structure, is taken as evidence that the reader is sensitive to the relative importance of the ideas in a passage as it is organized by the author. Research has consistently shown the levels effect (e.g., Mandler & Johnson, 1977; Meyer, 1975).

Several explanations have been proposed to explain the levels effect in memory (Meyer, 1975). One explanation states that the influence of level on recall is due to selective attention; that is, readers recognize high level content as important and therefore devote extra effort to learning it. Support for this position comes from studies finding longer reading times for high level information (Cirilo & Foss, 1980; Dee-Lucas & Larkin, 1987). Other explanations do not predict a correlation between reading time and level. The model of comprehension proposed by Kintsch and van Dijk (1978) attributes the levels effect to repeated processing received by high level information as readers integrate low level ideas with high level information. Also, Britton (Britton, Meyer, Hodge, & Glynn, 1980; Britton, Meyer, Simpson, Holdredge, & Curry, 1979) and Yekovich and Thorndyke (1981) have proposed accounts of the levels effect that rely on retrieval mechanisms. Probably all of these phenomena—selective attention, extra rehearsal, and retrieval—are related to the levels effect (Meyer, 1984).

Numerous recent studies have looked for age differences in sensitivity to prose structure by examining the levels effect for each age group. These studies do not present consistent findings with respect to older adults' use of text structure; they will be reviewed in this section and an attempt will be made to understand the reasons for these inconsistent results.

Mandler and Johnson (1977) presented clearly organized stories auditorially at a slow pace to adults who were above average in verbal ability and education and found no deficits in total recall nor in the levels effect for older adults. Meyer and Rice (1981) had the same type of subjects read a lengthy expository text without many explicit organizational cues; they also found no deficits in total recall. However, the age by level interaction narrowly missed significance. Post-hoc multiple comparison tests showed that the young group's recall of high level information was significantly greater than their recall of medium and low level information, but the levels effect, although in the usual pattern, did not reach significance for middle-aged and old subjects. With respect to answers to questions, the old and middle groups were able to correctly answer significantly more detail questions than did the young group. There were no differences in questions about main ideas. All age groups remembered the main ideas equally well, but young adults recalled more of the logic and major details that supported these main ideas, whereas the older groups recalled more of the minor details at the lowest levels of the content structure.

In an experiment with 300 young, middle, and old adults with high or average verbal ability, subjects assigned to different conditions read different versions of two expository texts (Meyer & Rice, 1983a, 1989). In some conditions the top-level structure, hierarchical structure, and major logical relations were emphasized, whereas in other conditions the structure was de-emphasized and the details were emphasized. An interaction among the emphasis plans, level in the content structure, age, and verbal ability appeared over tasks and times. This interaction resulted from little or no levels effects for the average verbal young adults and the high verbal old adults under conditions that de-emphasized the structure and emphasized the details in comparison to the other groups where larger levels effects were found. In addition, the group of high verbal old adults showed the greatest changes in the type of information remembered in response to different emphasis conditions. For this group of subjects, a 19% difference was found in the recall of high and low level information with structure emphasized, whereas only a 1% difference was found between the two levels without emphasis on the structure. It is interesting to see in light of the results of Meyer and Rice (1981) that the only age comparison not showing age deficits for old adults was recall of details by high verbal adults under emphasis conditions focused on details and away from structure.

High verbal old adults can be highly sensitive to the levels in the organization of prose. However, their display of the levels effect is dependent on how clearly the structure of the text is emphasized and signaled. When this structure is not explicitly signaled and emphasis is placed on specific details, the older adults focus on these details and are either drawn away from the main ideas and logical relationships or are unable to identify these logical relationships without explicit cues (Cohen, 1979).

Further analyses (Meyer & Rice, 1989) showed that the high verbal old adults were the only group that improved their recall of details (9%) when details were emphasized in the text (e.g., "notable" year of 1840). Young and old adults of high verbal ability were equivalent in their recall of details when they were emphasized, but when they were not emphasized the old adults' recall of them fell, whereas the emphasis manipulation did not affect the young adults. The passage used by Meyer & Rice (1981) contains little signaling, many dates, names, and numbers, and is not highly organized; it is similar to the manipulations in the Meyer and Rice (1983b) study involving no signaling of structure and specific details. Thus, the findings of Meyer and Rice (1981) appear to be limited to high verbal old adults with passages that contain historical dates, names, and other details where the structure is not explicitly signaled.

The issue remains whether the minimal levels effect exhibited by high verbal older adults on passages without signaling and with emphasized details results from processing the details at the expense of the main ideas or simply from an inability to comprehend the logical relationships among the main ideas when they are not explicitly signaled. Research exists on both sides of the latter issue; some studies show age deficits in making inferences (Cohen, 1979; 1981), whereas others do not (Belmore, 1981). Light and Anderson (1985) found that old adults could make inferences to correctly match pronouns to their referent if they could remember the sentence with the referent. However, they had more trouble remembering these sentences than young adults as the distance between the pronoun and the referent sentence increased.

Meyer and Rice (1989) systematically manipulated signaling of logical structure, signaling of details, and the specificity of details in order to better understand this issue. The detail manipulation involved substituting general details, such as "early last century," for specific details, such as "1829." The magnitude of the levels effects was examined for high verbal old adults to see if they process details at the expense of logical relations and main ideas, thereby reducing the levels effect, or if instead they cannot figure out logical relations without signaling, thereby decreasing their recall of main ideas and the magnitude of the levels effect. The data supported the first explanation; the recall data for both free and particularly the cued conditions for logical relations indicated that high verbal older adults can identify and store these relationships when they are not explicitly signaled. When specific details are present and text structure is not emphasized, high verbal old adults appear to process details at the expense of logical relationships and main ideas. The greater effects of these emphasis conditions on high verbal old adults over high verbal young adults may result from reduced cognitive capacity with aging (Cohen, 1988; Light, Zelinski, & Moore, 1982) where the effort processing details reduces that available for main ideas.

The research reviewed above (Mandler & Johnson, 1977; Meyer & Rice, 1981, 1989) indicates that when text is clearly organized with emphasis on structure and main ideas, young, middle-aged, and old adults are sensitive to text structure. Disparate findings with respect to the levels effect for these three studies can be reconciled by examining the clarity of organization and emphasis of the prose and the verbal ability of the learners.

Hultsch and Dixon (1984) argue that their study (Dixon et al., 1984), as well as their literature, supports the claim that age differences in use of organization in text depends on the verbal ability of the subjects. Specifically, they state that high verbal college graduates show greater age deficits for details (low level information), whereas lower verbal high school graduates show greater deficits for main ideas. The Dixon et al. (1984) study asked 108 young (20 to 39), middle-aged (40 to 57), and old (60 to 84) adults to read six short (98 words) passages about health and nutrition at their own pace. Young and middle-aged adults recalled more information than old adults. They reported an age by verbal ability by level interaction. For high verbal adults, the three age groups did not differ in their recall of high level information, but the young recalled more than the middle-aged adults, and they both recalled more than the old on the lower level ideas. In contrast, all three of the lower verbal groups differed significantly on the high level ideas and showed clear age deficits; for the other levels, the young and middle-aged subjects did not differ but were superior to the old adults.

Dixon et al. (1984) suggest that the literature also supports this pattern; Cohen (1979) and Dixon et al. (1982) found greater age deficits on main ideas and are said to have tested low verbal adults. This is the case for the Dixon et al. study. However, Cohen (1979, 1981) reports deficits in gist or main idea recall for high verbal adults; recall of details was not reported. Dixon et al. (1984) explain that Byrd (1981), Labouvie-Vief, Schell, and Weaverdyck (cited in Dixon et al., 1984), Spilich (1983), and Zelinski, Gilewski, and Thompson (1980) found greater deficits in recall of details and tested high verbal college-educated adults. However, information on the types of subjects in terms of verbal ability and education is not available for Zelinski et al. (1980).

The only study that Hultsch and Dixon (1984) could not incorporate into their interpretation was the Meyer and Rice (1981) study, because in this study with high verbal college graduates, older adults recalled details as well (free recall) or better (questions) than young adults. However, the data from Meyer and Rice (1989) show that this discrepancy can be clarified by examining the organization and emphasis of the texts. For the texts with emphasized structure, the pattern found by Dixon et al. (1984) holds. In contrast, on the versions with de-emphasized structure and emphasized details, this pattern is reversed; for high verbal adults, the results are consistent with Meyer and Rice (1981), whereas for the lower verbal adults, there are greater age deficits on details than on main ideas.

Petros et al. (1983), Surber et al. (1984), and Zelinski et al. (1984) also have examined aging and the levels effect. Petros et al. asked adults with high and low education (no vocabulary data) to listen to two stories; they report no interaction between age, level, and education, and the scores are not available to examine the education groups with respect to age and level. However, collapsed over education a pattern similar to that for high verbal adults on well structured texts is found;

greater aging deficits are found on the lowest level details than on the most important ideas. The authors point out that both age groups are sensitive to text structure because a levels effect is found for both groups. Surber et al. asked above average verbal young and old adults to read and recall a 1,563 word passage on commercial fishing. Young adults recalled more information overall and more information at the three most important levels than old adults, but the two groups did not differ at the lowest level details. These results fit the pattern for text whose structure and main ideas are not clearly emphasized; perhaps this is the case for this lengthy article. The study by Zelinski et al. (1984) does not appear to fit neatly into the age by verbal ability by organization interaction outlined above.

Rating Importance of Ideas In addition to looking at the levels effect, another method for investigating age differences in sensitivity to the hierarchical structure of text has been to ask subjects to rate the information in text according to its importance. Using this method, Mandler and Johnson (1977) and Petros et al.(1983) had subjects judge the importance of ideas in stories. They found that young and old adults did not vary in rating the importance of information. Petros et al. also examined their data in terms of the education level of the adults (high = *M* of 18 years vs. low = 12 years); no differences were found in rating the importance of ideas in a Japanese folk tale from the fifth-grade level. These findings for the high and low education groups of old adults are contrary to findings reported by Meyer (1984). Adults higher in education (*M* = 17 years) judged information high in the structure of an expository text from the high school level as more important than did adults with less education (*M* = 12 years).

Meyer, Young, and Bartlett (1989) asked young and old adults to underline the 10 most important ideas from texts before and after instruction in using text structure. There were no significant age effects, but instruction interacted with pretest versus posttest performance. Adults who received instruction about text structure increased their underlining of high level information, whereas those without this instruction decreased in underlining these main ideas.

Use of the Text's Top-Level Structure In a study (Meyer, 1983) with average verbal old adults (48th percentile) the best predictor of their recall from texts was whether or not they used the text's top-level structure to organize their recall protocols. These findings indicate that the ability to identify and utilize the author's top-level organization is a crucial skill in reading comprehension for older adults. Another interesting finding was an age and structure interaction when high school educated old adults were compared to ninth graders of average vocabulary performance. For both groups, use of the top-level structure greatly facilitated recall. However, ability to utilize the author's top-level structure was even more crucial to recall for the older group (34% recall when the structure was used and 13.5% when not used, vs. 28% recall when the structure was used and 15 % when it was not used for the ninth graders). For both the older subjects and the ninth graders when the text's structure was not used, the subjects tended to simply list sentences they remembered from the passage with no attempt to interrelate the sentences.

In contrast with the finding with average verbal adults, a study with higher verbal ASU alumni from young, middle, and old age groups found no age-related differences in use of top-level structure; nearly all of the adults from each age group used the same top-level structure as that used in the text to organize their recall (Meyer, Rice, Knight, & Jessen, 1979). Other studies (Meyer & Rice, 1989; Rice & Meyer, 1985) looked at age and verbal ability and found that high verbal adults from all age groups used the text's top-level structure more often than average verbal adults. More significantly, age interacted with verbal ability. Old and young high verbal adults did not differ in their use of the text's top-level structure, but average verbal young adults used the text's top-level structure more than average verbal old adults.

Another way to study text structure has been to see if one discourse type is more memorable than another. Meyer and Rice (1983b) looked to see if older adults perform better after listening to passages organized with a comparison top-level structure than with a collection of descriptions. Meyer and Freedle (1984) found that graduate students remember more facts about such topics as dehydration if two views about the topic are compared rather than simply describing three paragraphs of attributes about the topic. This finding has been replicated by Carrell (1984). In the Meyer and Rice (1983b) study young, middle-aged, and old adults with above average scores on the WAIS vocabulary test listened to passages of two topics organized either as a comparison or as a collection of descriptions. Main effects of discourse type and age were statistically significant. The comparative structure yielded superior performance on recall of the identical information for all three age groups. In contrast, adults with average scores on the Vocabulary subtest of the WAIS do not show facilitation in recall from the comparative structure (Vincent, 1985). This lack of effect from discourse type held for young, middle-aged, and old adults with these lower scores on the WAIS. Thus, lack of facilitation by the comparison structure was related to verbal ability, but not to age.

The latter portion of this chapter returns to this issue of top-level structure by looking at some of the research from our laboratory. An intervention study (Meyer, Young, & Bartlett, 1989) is described that taught young and old adults how to use the top-level structure in texts to improve reading comprehension and memory.

Summary of the Research on Age Differences and Prose Learning

Many of the discrepancies in the literature with regard to the magnitude of age deficits in prose learning can be explained by examining reader, task, and text variables. A number of factors are associated with a reduction of age deficits in reading comprehension; greater prose recall in older adults is related to higher levels of education and higher scores on vocabulary, verbal productive thinking, and associative memory tests. Also, better memory from text by older adults is associated with more time spent reading in everyday life (particularly for adults with effective reading comprehension strategies), more prior knowledge on a topic, and greater familiarity with the reading and recall task. Better performance is found for slower or self-paced presentation; a pace of 120 wpm or faster appears to adversely affect the recall of old adults more than young adults. The text variable of emphasis was shown to correlate with different findings reported by investigators. For texts with emphasis placed on well organized structures, young and old adults with high vocabulary scores are sensitive to text structure; they exhibit large levels effects, and greater age-related deficits are found in recall of details. On these same texts, old adults with average vocabulary scores show less sensitivity to text structure and exhibit greater deficits on main ideas. However, with text that de-emphasizes organization and emphasizes details, the opposite pattern is found. For the highly verbal adults, fewer age deficits are found for details than for main ideas. For average verbal adults, fewer age deficits are found for main ideas than for details. High verbal old adults appear to utilize text structure as well as young adults. They show facilitation in recall after listening to text structured with the more organized comparative structure than with the less organized descriptive structure. They are very sensitive to the emphasis plans of an author. When specific details are emphasized over structure, old adults appear to use their resources to process details at the expense of fully processing main ideas and logical relationships. These findings suggest that when writing for these older adults, care should be given to explicitly signal the major logical relationships, if examples with specific facts are given in the text. If dates, names, and numbers are not critical to the message, they should be deleted.

The greater effects of emphasis conditions for high verbal old adults than for high verbal young adults may result from reduced cognitive capacity with aging, where the effort required for processing details reduces that available for figuring out implicit logical relationships among major propositions in text. It has been shown moreover that text without signaling requires more cognitive capacity than the same text with signaling (Britton, Glynn, Meyer, & Penland, 1982). The performance of young adults with average vocabulary scores on these same texts mirrors the pattern for old high verbal adults. It could be argued that these manipulations have similar effects on these two groups and not on high verbal young adults because high verbal young adults have more cognitive capacity than average verbal young adults who were less endowed and high verbal old adults who have experienced declines in capacity with increasing age. Alternatively, use of the structure in text may be more automatic, requiring less conscious capacity in the high verbal young adults. These text manipulations have no effect on average verbal older adults who perform quite poorly under all text conditions; this could reflect their initial limited capacity that was further reduced by aging. However, performance of old adults with average vocabulary scores also could result from changes in educational practice over the generations. Signaling words and text structures may have been taught to the young adults but not to the old adults.

Reading and Comprehension Training

Research in training the elderly to improve their reading comprehension is severely limited. A review paper by Glynn and Muth (1979) summarizes documentation of the deficits of the elderly in text-learning capabilities and attributes the deficits primarily to defective attentional and organizational processes. The authors advocate the use of instructional strategies to counteract these deficits, and they provide evidence that such strategies do benefit elderly learners. They describe priming strategies, such as instructional objectives, conceptual prequestions, and advance organizers, and processing strategies, such as mediational devices (verbal and imaginal), typographical-curing systems (underlining and boldface), and note-taking techniques. They recommend the use of these strategies, because they help students to focus on key concepts, better organize ideas for storage and retrieval, or integrate new ideas with related prior knowledge. However, notice how all of these strategies fall to the instructor to implement them or to instruct learners to use them. None have been treated as a comprehension strategy that learners, especially the elderly, need to be trained to use.

To find training studies of comprehension and reading skills, we have to turn to research with younger adults, and we find that the bulk of the published literature describes college or university remedial reading programs. A typical program was described by Burgess, Cranney, and Larsen (1976), as a laboratory-type class. Practice materials were available and progress folders maintained under minimal supervision. All participants in the program were volunteers and, in the assessment of program effectiveness, those who chose not to participate served as controls. After conclusion of the program, those who had participated had a significantly higher grade point average than those who had not, but clearly there was a motivational factor involved that could not be ruled out as an explanation for the findings.

In a review of college reading programs (Heerman, 1983), it is evident that much of the evaluative research in this area suffers from lack of adequate control groups. Nonetheless, the research shows distinct advantages in reading skill (rate, vocabulary, and comprehension) for experimental groups that receive reading instruction. Furthermore, the gains appear to last a substantial amount of time: 60 weeks in one study, 3 and 6 months in another, and 5 semesters in another. Other studies show positive effects of reading instruction on grades, as well as other measures of academic success, such as course hours completed. The instructional methods used in these studies varied from straightforward reading instruction, to general study skills, to tutoring in reading specific types of course material.

Reading instruction that is geared toward a specific type of material has met with success in various areas. Pachtman (1977) designed a training program for first-year law students that contained three components: comprehension, study skills, and analytical thinking. Those students who received training in these three areas subsequently scored higher than control subjects on a measure of critical thinking and reading ability, and on a measure of reading comprehension. Trained students also had higher first-term grades than control students.

Research with Air Force personnel has shown that specific training about how to extract the vital information from a passage of text resulted in personnel who were better able to locate and remember information pertinent to their particular jobs (Huff, 1977).

Pertaining to reading programs for older adults, some excellent reviews of Adult Basic Education (ABE) are published, as well as some individual studies. The highlights of these will be presented here.

Gold and Horn (1982) evaluated a tutorial program for adult illiterates in the Baltimore City area. Seventy-six adults aged 16 to 60 years, all reading below fifth-grade level, were assigned to experimental and control groups and were pre- and posttested on verbal language development, word recognition, locus of control, listening comprehension, and reading skills. Between the testing, the experimental group was tutored by trained volunteers for an average of 3 hours a week for 12 to 15 weeks. Analysis of gain scores showed that the tutored group made significantly more progress than the control group on word recognition and a variety of reading skills.

A computer-assisted literacy program for adults was offered at Pennsylvania State University (Golub, 1980). This particular program used as its reading materials passages pertaining to an assortment of careers, so that adults were acquiring specific job-related content while improving their general reading skills. Pre- and posttests showed that students made significant improvement on phonics, vocabulary, comprehension, reading level, and reading rate. Unfortunately, there was no control group for comparison purposes.

The Army has also had considerable success in teaching illiterate soldiers how to read (Otto, 1970). The materials were especially developed, the pupil-instructor ratio was 15:1, and regularly scheduled appraisals of the training were conducted. Sixty-two % of the participants initially reading at the first-grade level were taught to read at the fourth-grade level after 12 to 16 weeks of instruction. The most progress was made by soldiers who initially tested at higher reading levels.

Otto (1970) has reviewed the early published reports on several ABE literacy programs throughout the United States. These programs had a wide age range of clientele, all of whom were at such a low reading level as to be classified as functionally illiterate. The progress of students in the programs was regularly evaluated by means of standardized reading tests. Among the conclusions, he notes are: (a) Several different methods of teaching reading are effective, but which is most effective is related to the initial reading level of the student; (b) age, IQ, and beginning reading level did not affect a student's rate of progress in the program; (c) highly trained teachers are not necessary for a successful program—even high school graduates can be effective reading teachers; and (d) despite efforts to compact the education into a short period of time, it is still a quite lengthy process to bring adults' reading skill up to an acceptable level, and the actual amount of time it may take is highly individual.

Cook (1977) has recorded the history of adult literacy education. She notes that, although programs were started as early as 1900, no serious attempts to evaluate their success were made until the 1960s. Then, research began to appear that compared the numerous teaching methods in use to try to identify the most effective ones. Although no one or two methods ever consistently outperformed the others, the surge of research served to launch a healthy phase of curriculum development and expansion. The decade of the 1970s saw literacy research expand to include topics of motivation, materials, and measurement criteria.

Clearly, there is much to offer to adults with poor reading skills to help them gain competence and complete their basic education but what of training for older adults who have good reading ability, but want to improve their more advanced skills? There is very little research available in this area.

Shearin (1976) evaluated a program for teaching critical reading skills to adults. He used volunteers aged 20 to 59 and trained them over a period of 8 weeks to develop a questioning attitude, determine reliability of information, and detect propaganda material. He then compared them to a control group on a measure of critical thinking and a measure of reading comprehension skills. On the measure of critical thinking trained subjects improved from pre- to posttest significantly more than did untrained subjects but not on the measure of reading comprehension. Also, this improvement was not related to the age, education level, nor initial reading skill level of the individuals.

Glover and his colleagues (Glover, Zimmer, Filbeck, & Plake, 1980) found that college students could be taught to identify the semantic base of a passage of text simply by having the students practice with feedback. Students were told to identify the minimum number of words that expressed the meaning of each five-line unit of a text. Periods of feedback were alternated with base line periods for three groups of subjects, with the clear result that while feedback was available, subjects improved markedly in their identification of key words, and their incorrect identifications decreased accordingly. Also of interest is the finding that general reading comprehension (measured by the Nelson-Denny Reading Test) improved significantly from pre- to posttest. Apparently this process of semantic base identification is closely related to reading comprehension as measured by this test, so that training in one transfers to the second.

A number of studies involving young adults focus more directly on the structure of texts. The first (Geva, 1983) provided community college students with extensive training (20 hours over 5 weeks) on searching out expository formats of causation and process. The students used a flowcharting procedure to draw out ideas from a text or their related prior knowledge as nodes with specified relationships among them. On a posttest, the students showed significant improvement in representing text structure and content. They outperformed controls who had received training in speed reading, text skimming, and searching out key words and conjunctions. Geva (1983) reported similar significant gains in reading scores on the Nelson-Denny Reading Test (Nelson, & Denny, 1973) for both the experimental and control groups. When the same types of subjects were separated into less skilled and moderately skilled subgroups, a significant ability effect was apparent. Less skilled readers seemed to have profited more from the instruction as ascertained by gain scores on the standardized reading test. For this less skilled group particularly, learning to recognize and use these types of text structures resulted in more effective reading of expository text.

Closely related to Gena's (1983) work is that of Dansereau and his colleagues (e.g., Dansereau, Brooks, Holley, & Collins, 1983; Diekhoff, Brown, & Dansereau,

1982; Holley, Dansereau, McDonald, Garland, & Collins, 1979; Lambiotte, Dansereau, Cross, & Reynolds, 1989). They have found networking or mapping strategies to facilitate learning from text by college students. For example, Holley et al. (1979) trained college students to convert prose into hierarchically organized node-link diagrams, called networks, using a set of six experimenter-provided links (part of link, type of link, leads to link, analogy link, characteristic link, and evidence link). After training, the students used the networking strategy in studying a 3000-word passage taken from a geology textbook. Five days later they completed four types of tests about this passage: multiple choice, short answer, essay, and a summary-oriented concept cloze. Compared to a control that received no treatment, the trained group showed superior performance, primarily on the cloze and essay tests. Also, like Geva (1983) they reported greater improvement for lower ability students, measured by Holley et al. (1979) via grade point averages.

Three studies exposing college students to indirect instruction or minimal amounts of training point to some facilitation of memory from identifying the structure of text. Thorndyke (1977) had one group of subjects read a story organized in the same way as a target narrative passage with different content. A second group read a story with the same content as the target passage but organized differently. A third group had different content and different organization. He observed greater adherence to the organization of the target passage and better recall from the first group. Meyer, Rice, Bartlett, and Woods (1979) conducted a similar study with expository text and added another group that simply received a description of the structure for the target passage prior to reading it. There was a trend for information about the structure given implicitly or explicitly to facilitate recall and speed of reading, but the differences narrowly missed statistical significance. However, Barnett (1984) gave college students a brief description of the appropriate text structure before reading a research report or a journal article and found facilitation of memory. Subjects recalled significantly more information after 2 days than either subject who received the description about text structure after reading or who received no description of text structure.

A more extensive training program with adults (Carrell, 1985) modified Bartlett's (1978) program for ninth-grade students in order to teach students who have English as a second language (ESL) about the structure or plan strategy. The results showed that the training significantly increased the amount of information that intermediate level ESL students could recall. Similar types of training procedures were used by Cook (1982) to help college students identify the structures found in science textbooks. A 10-hour training program taught students to recognize the major prose structures (generalization, enumeration, sequence, classification, compare/contrast) and to outline passages from their own chemistry textbooks. Trained subjects showed substantial pretest to posttest gains in recall of main ideas and in problem solving as compared to a control group.

The study described below is the only research available that systematically teaches old and young adults how to utilize the structure of texts. The training approach comes from work with children and text structure (Bartlett, 1978). There is a substantial body of literature on teaching text structure to children (see Armbruster, Anderson, & Ostertag, 1987 or Meyer et al., 1989 for reviews).

A Study to Improve Reading Comprehension in Old and Young Adults

A recent study (Meyer et al., 1989) examined the effectiveness of a reading strategy for improving the reading comprehension and memory of young and old adults. The reading strategy examined was called the plan strategy and taught readers to utilize the writing plans or top-level structures in texts to facilitate encoding and retrieval. This strategy was identified by examining what over 1000 adults wrote down when they read and recalled short magazine articles. Successful readers at all ages appear to search out and follow the text's superordinate relational structure and focus on the text's message and how it relates to supporting major details. They approach text with knowledge about how texts are conventionally organized and a strategy to seek and use the top-level structure in a particular text as an organizational framework to facilitate encoding and retrieval.

This research posed the question: Can instruction aimed at teaching the plan strategy improve the reading comprehension of high school educated older adults with average to high average vocabulary scores? Adults with these characteristics have been shown to exhibit large age deficits in using the top-level structure of texts and signals in text that cue readers to this organization (e.g., "in contrast," "as a result"). The intervention program directly taught these skills in which these older adults are deficient.

We screened out adults who were using the strategy on the pretest. Thus, the instruction was aimed at adults who were not using the reading strategy and as a result could most benefit from the instruction. Eliminated from the sample were 12% of the older adults and 33% of the younger adults who exhibited consistent use of the strategy on four recalls written prior to instruction.

Young and old adults were stratified on vocabulary scores and then randomly assigned to three groups. One group learned about five basic top-level structures or writing plans used by authors to organize their ideas. They learned to recognize these structures in everyday reading materials and use these structures to systematically search their memory for what they learned from an article. Another group simply practiced reading and remembering information from their reading. They started with short materials and worked up to longer ones. They read the same materials as the people in the strategy group. Both the strategy and practice groups met for one and a half hours a day for 5 days spread over 2 weeks. The final group received no instruction. All participants were tested a day prior to instruction, 2 days after the completion of the instruction, and 2 weeks after the instruction. During the testing sessions the subjects read and recalled four passages; recalled one of these passages again after a delay; took a standardized reading comprehension test; underlined the most important ideas in passages; answered main idea,

Table 8.1
Five Basic Writing Plans and Signals
that Cue Readers to these Plans

Writing Plan and Definition	Signals
Description	
Descriptive ideas that give attributes, specifics, or setting information about a topic. The main idea is that attributes of a topic are discussed. E.g., newspaper article describing who, where, when, and how.	for example, which was one, this particular, for instance, specifically, such as, attributes of, that is, namely, properties of, characteristics are, qualities are, marks of, in describing, _____
Sequence	
Ideas grouped on the basis of order or time. The main idea is the procedure or history related. E.g., recipe procedures, history of Civil War battles, growth from birth to 12 months.	afterwards, later, finally, last, early, following, to begin with, to start with, then, as time passed, continuing on, to end, years ago, in the first place, before, after, soon, more recently, _____
Causation	
Presents causal or cause and effect-like relations between ideas. The main idea is organized into cause and effect parts. E.g., directions: if you want to take good pictures, then you must ....; explanations: the idea explained is the effect and the explanation is its cause.	as a result, because, since, for the purpose of, caused, led to, consequence, thus, in order to, this is why, if/then, the reason, so, in explanation, therefore, _____
Problem/Solution	
The main ideas are organized into two parts: a *problem* part and a *solution* part that responds to the problem by trying to eliminate it, or a *question* part and an *answer* part that responds to the question by trying to answer it. E.g., scientific articles often first raise a question or problem and then seek to give an answer or solution.	problem: problem, question, puzzle, perplexity, enigma, riddle, issue, query, need to prevent, the trouble, _____ solution: solution, answer, response, reply, rejoinder, return, comeback, to satisfy the problem, to set the issue at rest, to solve these problems, _____

Writing Plan & Definition	Signals
Comparison Relates ideas on the basis of differences and similarities. The main idea is organized in parts that provide a comparison, contrast, or alternative perspective on a topic. E.g., political speeches, particularly where one view is clearly favored over the other.	not everyone, but, in contrast, all but, instead, act like, however, in comparison, on the other hand, whereas, in opposition, unlike, alike, have in common, share, resemble, the same as, different, difference, differentiate, compared to, while, although, _____ _____ _____ _____
Listing Can occur with any of the five writing plans. Listing simply groups ideas together. Passages are often organized as a listing of descriptions about a topic. A sequence always contains a listing of ideas, but the idea are ordered sequentially. A listing can occur when groups of courses are presented, groups of effects are listed, groups of solutions are posited, groups of ideas are contrasted to another idea, and so forth.	and, in addition, also, include, moreover, besides, first, second, third, etc., subsequent, furthermore, at the same time, another, _____ _____ _____ _____

detail, and problem-solving questions about texts; and filled out questionnaires about reading strategies and attitudes.

The remainder of this chapter will describe briefly the training materials and basic findings from their evaluation. A complete copy of the training materials and a detailed account of their evaluation can be found in Meyer et al., (1989).

Training Materials Instruction with the plan strategy taught the learners to employ a deliberate plan or strategy for remembering what they read. In reading, they were taught to choose the organizational plan used by the writer to organize his or her ideas. In remembering, they were taught to use the same organizational plan.

On the first day, the rationale, power, and limitations of the strategy were discussed. They learned about five basic plans for organizing expository text. These plans were description, sequence, causation, problem solution, and comparison.

In the training program, each plan was discussed in detail, and examples were given using the main captions of advertisements found in magazines. Advertisements were used the first day because they are familiar, fun to use, and often clearly depict these writing plans.

The participants were told that many texts will reflect more than one of these five basic plans. Examples from television programs, newspapers, and stories were used to point out to the students that the strategy involves finding the overall plan used in the text rather than plans used to organize details in a text. The concept of signaling words was introduced and then the students worked in pairs of partners for the remainder of Session 1. First, they examined five advertisements to determine the overall plans. Next the partners wrote advertisements in two specified plans to sell their new invention, the safety pin. Finally, they wrote a vivid picture of a tiger devouring his trainer with the other plans. Feedback was given for their performance on these tasks.

Session 2 focused on teaching other signaling words for each plan and the idea that listing can occur with any of the five plans. The students carefully read and quizzed their partner about Table 8.1. This table was used at all subsequent training sessions and in their home reading; additional signaling words discovered were added to the table. In this session, they identified the plan and signaling for short magazine entries. After discussing their answers with their partners, the class discussed them with diagrams of the overall plan and its major structures. The remainder of the session was spent reading and sorting 17 passages into the five plans and reading and recalling 2 passages.

In Session 3, the rationale for using the plans in text to increase memory was emphasized. They were told to ask two questions before reading a passage: What is the plan for this passage? What is the main idea that fits this plan? In addition, specific steps for recall were given, and a young and old adult modeled reading and recall texts from each of the five basic organizational types.

Next, the students read and recalled two passages, getting feedback on their progress in using the strategy after each passage was recalled. A key phrase in the program was "choose it, use it, or lose it."

In Session 4, students received a detailed report of their strengths and areas to work on to master the strategy. For this session and the final session, partners were assigned by pairing a proficient student with a less proficient student. In addition, instruction and practice were given in applying the strategy to longer passages and muddled passages.

In the fifth session, another detailed report of their progress was given to the students. The session was spent eliminating any difficulties and giving the students practice in using the strategy. In Sessions 3, 4, and 5, the mnemonic aspects of each particular plan were stressed. For example, for the comparison plan, it was repeatedly pointed out that opposing views often are compared on many of the same issues such as, one political candidate's views on abortion, taxes, government spending, and defense and then the other candidates views on these same issues. Students discovered that their memory was improved if they remembered that a comparison plan was used and the number and name of the issues compared. For example, one should remember that the candidates were compared on four issues: abortion, taxes, government spending, and defense. In recalling a passage, they were instructed to check to see if they had mentioned each issue from the two perspectives.

Remembering one issue for one compared view can often jog their memory for the opposite position's view of the issue.

Did Training Increase Use of the Plan Strategy? Instruction with the plan strategy did significantly and dramatically increase use of this strategy by both young and old adults deficient in the use of the strategy prior to instruction. For example, on the first posttest most (93%) of the old and young adults in the strategy group used the problem solution structure to organize their recalls, whereas most of the old and young adults in the other groups did not. This superiority in use of the top-level structure was maintained by both the old and young adults in the strategy group when these passages were recalled 2 weeks later. Also, on the passages read 2 weeks after instruction 87% of the adults in the strategy group used the problem solution structure, whereas 83% of the adults in the other two groups did not. Consistent findings also were found for other structures and on other tasks, such as sorting passages and asking questions about the organization of texts and changes in each reader's strategies. Old adults appeared to be able to acquire this skill after five lessons as well as the young adults on all tasks, but the sorting task, where young adults in the strategy group could correctly sort more passages (82%) than the old adults in this group (71%).

Did Training Increase Information Remembered? The recall data showed that the three groups significantly improved their performance on recall tests over the duration of the instruction. Thus, practice alone on the tasks improved performance. However, young and old adults in the strategy group improved significantly more than those in the other groups on free recall of information in texts. These findings also held on performance answering main idea questions. Questionnaire data and other tasks indicated that training with the strategy focused the learner's attention away from details and toward the main ideas in texts.

Did Training Effect Other Measures of Reading Competency or Enjoyment? Although we expected the training to influence use of the strategy and free recall, we also administered measures to test for unexpected outcomes of the training. These measures included performance on a standardized reading comprehension test, parts of another reading test, recognition of topics read, ability to answer thought questions, and a questionnaire about interest and enjoyment of reading. The only measures showing statistically significant gains for the strategy group were the measures of interest and enjoyment of reading.

In summary, young and old adults in the strategy group increased their ability to use the strategy, to recall text, and to correctly answer main idea questions. They shifted in the types of information considered important and claimed improved reading strategies, superior memory for their reading in the laboratory and everyday life, and increased interest in and enjoyment of reading. Old and young adults improved equivalently from this instruction and maintained their improvement over time.

This study investigated a reading strategy that is not fully developed by a large portion of adults after leaving high school. However, it was easily acquired with training and could be included in adult literacy programs.

References

Aristotle (1960). *The rhetoric of Aristotle.* (L. Cooper, Trans.). New York: Appleton-Century-Crofts.

Armbruster, B.B., Anderson, T.H., & Ostertag, J. (1987). Does text structure/summarization instruction facilitate learning from expository text? *Reading Research Quarterly, 22,* 331-346.

Aulls, M.W. (1982). *Developing readers in today's elementary school.* Boston, MA: Allyn and Bacon.

Barnett, J.E. (1984). Facilitating retention through instruction about text structure. *Journal of Reading Behavior, 16,* 1-13.

Bartlett, B.J. (1978). *Top-level structure as an organizational strategy for recall of classroom text.* Unpublished doctoral dissertation, Arizona State University, Tempe, AZ.

Beaugrande, R. de (1980). *Text, discourse, and process.* Norwood, New Jersey: Ablex.

Belmore, S.M. (1981). Age-related changes in processing explicit and implicit language. *Journal of Gerontology, 36,* 316-322.

Birren, J.E. (1974). Translations in gerontology—from lab to life: Psychophysiology and speed of response. *American Psychologist, 29,* 808-815.

Birren, J.E., Woods, A.M., & Williams, M.V. (1980). Behavioral slowing with aging: Causes, organization, and consequences. In L.W. Poon (Ed.), *Aging in the 1980s: Psychological issues* (pp. 293-308). Washington, DC: American Psychological Association.

Britton, B.K., Glynn, S., Meyer, B.J.F., & Penland, M. (1982). Use of cognitive capacity in reading text. *Journal of Educational Psychology, 73,* 51-61.

Britton, B.K., Meyer, B.J.F., Hodge, M.H., & Glynn, S. (1980). Effect of the organization of text on memory: Tests of retrieval and response criterion hypotheses. *Journal of Experimental Psychology: Human Learning and Memory, 6,* 620-629.

Britton, B.K., Meyer, B.J.F., Simpson, R., Holdredge, T.S., & Curry, C. (1979). Effects of the organization of text on memory: Tests of two implications of a selective attention hypothesis. *Journal of Experimental Psychology: Human Learning and Memory, 5,* 496-506.

Britton, B.K., Van Dusen, L., Glynn, S. M., & Hemphill, D. (1990). The impact of inferences on instructional text. In A. C. Graesser & G. H. Bower (Ed.), *The psychology of learning and motivation* (Vol. 25, pp. 53-69). San Diego, CA: Academic Press.

Burgess, B.A., Cranney, A.G., & Larsen, J.J. (1976). Effect on academic achievement of a voluntary university reading program. *Journal of Reading, 19,* 644-646.

Burke, D.M., & Light, L.L. (1981). Memory and aging: The role of retrieval process. *Psychological Bulletin, 90,* 513-546.

Byrd, M. (1981). *Age differences in memory for prose passages.* Unpublished doctoral dissertation, University of Toronto, Toronto, Canada.

Carrell, P.L. (1984). The effects of rhetorical organization on ESL readers. *TESOL Quarterly, 17,* 441-469.

Carrell, P.L. (1985). Facilitating ESL reading by teaching text structure. *TESOL Quarterly, 19,* 727-752.

Chall, J.S. (1983). *Stages of reading development.* New York: McGraw-Hill.

Christensen, F. (1967). A generative rhetoric of the paragraph. In M. Steinmann (Ed.), *New rhetorics* (pp. 108-133). New York: Scribner's.

Cirilo, R. & Foss, D. (1980). Text structure and reading time sentences. *Journal of Verbal Learning and Verbal Behavior, 19,* 96-109.

Cohen, G. (1979). Language comprehension in old age. *Cognitive Psychology, 11,* 412-429.

Cohen, G. (1981). Inferential reasoning in old age. *Cognition, 9,* 59-72.

Cohen, G. (1988). Age differences in memory for texts: Production deficiency or processing limitations? In L.L. Light & D.M. Burke (Eds.), *Language, memory and aging* (pp. 171-190). New York: Academic Press.

Cook, L.K. (1982). *The effects of text structure on the comprehension of scientific prose.* Unpublished doctoral dissertation, University of California, Santa Barbara, CA.

Cook, W.D. (1977). *Adult literacy education in the United States.* Newark, DE: International Reading Association.

D'Angelo, F.J. (1979). Paradigms as structural counterparts of topoi. In D. McQuade (Ed.), *Linguistics, stylistics, and the teaching of composition* (pp. 41-51). Akron, OH: University of Akron Press.

Dansereau, D.F., Brooks, L.W., Holley, C.D., & Collins, K.W. (1983). Learning strategies training: Effect of sequencing. *Journal of Experimental Education, 51,* 102-108.

Dee-Lucas, D., & Larkin, J.H. (1987). *Attentional strategies for studying scientific texts.* Pittsburgh, PA: Carnegie-Mellon University.

Diekhoff, G.M., Brown, P.J., & Dansereau, D.F. (1982). A prose learning strategy training program based on network and depth-of-processing models. *Journal of Experimental Education, 50,* 180-184.

Dixon, R.A., Hultsch, D.F., Simon, E.W., & von Eye, A. (1984). Verbal ability and text structure effects on adult age differences in text recall. *Journal of Verbal Learning Behavior, 23,* 569-578.

Dixon, R.A., Simon, E.W., Nowak, C.A., & Hultsch, D.F. (1982). Text recall in adulthood as a function of level of information, input modality, and delay interval. *Journal of Gerontology, 37,* 358-364.

Dixon, R.A., & von Eye, A. (1984). Depth of processing and text recall in adulthood. *Journal of Reading Behavior, 26,* 109-117.

Frederiksen, C.H. (1977). Structure and process in discourse production and comprehension. In M.A. Just & P. Carpenter (Eds.), *Cognitive processes in comprehension* (pp. 313-322). Hillsdale, NJ: Lawrence Erlbaum.

Geva, E. (1983). Facilitating reading through flowcharting. *Reading Research Quarterly, 18*, 384-405.

Glover, J.A., Zimmer, J.W., Filbeck, R.W., & Plake, B.S. (1980). Effects of training students to identify the semantic base of prose materials. *Journal of Applied Behavior Analysis, 13*, 655-667.

Glynn, S.M., & Muth, K.D. (1979). Text-learning capabilities of older adults. *Educational Gerontology, 4*, 253-269.

Glynn, S.M., Okun, M.A., Muth, K.D., & Britton, B.K. (1983). Adults' text recall: An examination of the age-deficit hypothesis. *Journal of Reading Behavior, 15*, 31-45.

Gold, P.C., & Horn, P.L. (1982). Achievement in reading, verbal language, listening comprehension and locus of control of adult illiterates in a volunteer tutorial project. *Perceptual and Motor Skills, 54*, 1243-1250.

Golub, L.S. (1980). A computer assisted literacy development program. In L.S. Johnson (Ed.), *Reading and the adult learner* (pp. 47-54). Newark, DE: International Reading Association.

Gordon, S.K., & Clark, W.C. (1974). Application of signal detection theory to prose recall and recognition in elderly and young adults. *Journal of Gerontology, 29*, 64-72.

Graesser, A.C. (1981). *Prose comprehension beyond the word.* New York: Springer-Verlag.

Grimes, J.E. (1975). *The thread of discourse.* The Hague: Mouton.

Halliday, M.A.K., & Hasan, R. (1976). *Cohesion in English.* New York: Longman.

Harker, J.O., Hartley, J.T., & Walsh, D.A. (1982). Understanding discourse—a life-span approach. In B.A. Hutson (Ed.), *Advances in reading/language research* (Vol. 1, pp. 155-202). Greenwich, CT: JAI Press.

Hartley, J.T. (1986). Reader and text variables as determinants of discourse memory in adulthood. *Psychology and Aging, 1*, 150-158.

Hartley, J.T. (1988). Individual differences in memory for written discourse. In L.L. Light & D.M. Burke (Eds.), *Language, memory, and aging.* New York: Academic Press.

Hartley, J.T. (1989). Memory for prose: Perspectives on the reader. In L.W. Poon, D.C. Rubin, & B.A. Wilson (Eds.), *Everyday cognition in adulthood and late life* (pp. 135-156). New York, NY: Cambridge University Press.

Hartley, J.T., Cassidy, J.J., & Lee, D.W. (1986, August). *Prior knowledge, processing load, and age in memory for prose.* Paper presented at the annual meeting of the American Psychological Association, Washington, DC.

Hartley, J.T., Harker, J.O., & Walsh, D.A. (1980). Contemporary issues and new directions in adult development of learning and memory. In L.W. Poon (Ed.), *Aging in the 1980's* (pp. 239-252). Washington, DC: American Psychological Association.

Heerman, C.E. (1983). Research on college reading programs and student retention efforts. *Reading World, 22*, 203-212.

Herber, H.L. (1978). *Teaching reading in content areas* (2nd ed.). Englewood Cliffs, NJ: Prentice-Hall.

Holley, C.D., Dansereau, D.F., McDonald, B.A., Garland, J.C., & Collins, K.W. (1979). Evaluation of a hierarchical mapping technique as an aid to prose processing. *Contemporary Educational Psychology, 4*, 227-237.

Huff, K.H. (1977). *A job oriented reading program for the Air Force: Development of field evaluation.* (US AFHRL Tech. Rep. No. 77-34).

Hultsch, D.F., & Dixon, R.A. (1984). Memory for text materials in adulthood. In P.B. Baltes & O.G. Brim, Jr. (Eds.), *Life-span development and behavior* (Vol. 6, pp. 77-108). New York: Academic Press.

Hunt, E. (1978). Mechanics of verbal ability. *Psychological Review, 85*, 109-130.

Kieras, D.E. (1985). Thematic processes in the comprehension of technical prose. In B.K. Britton & J. Black (Eds.), *Understanding expository text* (pp. 89-107). Hillsdale, NJ: Lawrence Erlbaum.

Kintsch, W. (1974). *The representation of meaning in memory.* Hillsdale, NJ: Lawrence Erlbaum .

Kintsch, W., & van Dijk, T.A. (1978). Toward a model of text comprehension and production. *Psychological Review, 85*, 363-394.

Lambiotte, J.G., Dansereau, D.F., Cross, D.R., & Reynolds, S.B. (1989). Multi-relational semantic maps. *Educational Psychology Review, 1*(4), 331-367.

Lehnert, W.G. (1981). Plot units and narrative summarization. *Cognitive Science, 5*, 293-331.

Light, L.L., & Anderson, P.A. (1985). Working-memory capacity, age, and memory for discourse. *Journal of Gerontology, 45*, 737-747.

Light, L.L., Zelinski, E.M., & Moore, M. (1982). Adult age differences in reasoning from new information. *Journal of Experimental Psychology: Learning, Memory, and Cognition, 8*, 435-447.

Mandel, R.G., & Johnson, N.S. (1984). A developmental analysis of story recall and comprehension in adulthood. *Journal of Verbal Learning and Verbal Behavior, 23*, 643-659.

Mandler, J.M. (1987). On the psychological reality of story structure. *Discourse Processes, 10*, 1-29.

Mandler, J.M., & Johnson, N.S. (1977). Remembrance of things parsed: Story structure and recall. *Cognitive Psychology, 9*, 111-151.

Meyer, B.J.F. (1975). *The organization of prose and its effects on memory.* Amsterdam: North Holland.

Meyer, B.J.F. (1983). Text structure and its use in studying comprehension across the adult life span. In B.A. Hutson (Ed.), *Advances in reading/language research* (Vol. 2, pp. 9-54). Greenwich, CT: JAI Press.

Meyer, B.J.F. (1984). Text dimensions and cognitive processing. In H. Mandl, N. Stein, & T. Trabasso (Eds.), *Learning from texts* (pp. 3-52). Hillsdale, NJ: Lawrence Erlbaum.

Meyer, B.J.F. (1985). Prose analysis: Procedures, purposes, and problems. In B.K. Britton, & J. Black (Eds.), *Understanding expository text* (pp. 11-64; 269-304). Hillsdale, NJ: Lawrence Erlbaum.

Meyer, B.J.F. (1987). Reading comprehension and aging. In K.W. Schaie (Ed.), *Annual review of gerontology and geriatrics* (Vol. 7, pp. 93-115). New York: Springer.

Meyer, B.J.F., & Freedle, R.O. (1984). The effects of different discourse types on recall. *American Educational Research Journal, 21,* 121-143.

Meyer, B.J.F., & Rice, G.E. (1981). Information recalled from prose by young, middle, and old adults. *Experimental Aging Research, 7,* 253-268.

Meyer, B.J.F., & Rice, G.E. (1983a). Learning and memory from text across the adult life span. In J. Fine & R.O. Freedle (Eds.), *Developmental studies in discourse* (pp. 291-306). Norwood, NJ: Ablex.

Meyer, B.J.F., & Rice, G.E. (1983b, December). *Effects of discourse type on recall by young, middle, and old adults with high and average vocabulary scores.* Paper presented at the National Reading Conference, Austin, TX.

Meyer, B.J.F., & Rice, G.E. (1989). Prose processing in adulthood: The text, the reader and the task. In L.W. Poon, D.C. Rubin, & B.A. Wilson (Eds.), *Everyday cognition in adult and later life* (pp. 157-194). New York, NY: Cambridge University Press.

Meyer, B.J.F., Rice, G.E., Bartlett, B.J., & Woods, V. (1979). *Facilitative effects of passages with the same structure and different content on prose recall.* Unpublished manuscript, Arizona State University.

Meyer, B.J.F., Rice, G.E., Knight, C.C., & Jessen, J.L. (1979). *Effects of comparative and descriptive discourse types on the reading performance of young, middle, and old adults* (Prose Learning Series No. 7). Tempe, AZ: Arizona State University, Tempe, AR.

Meyer, B.J.F., Young, C.J., & Bartlett, B.J. (1989). *Memory improved: Reading and memory enhancement across the life span through strategic text structures.* Hillsdale, NJ: Lawrence Erlbaum.

Nelson, N.J., & Denny, E.C. (1973). *Nelson Denny Reading Test.* Boston: Houghton Mifflin.

Niles, O.S. (1965). Organization perceived. In H.H. Herber (Ed.), *Perspective in reading: Developing study skills in secondary schools.* Newark, DE: International Reading Association.

Otto, W. (1970). Reading and ABE: What we know, what we need to know. In W.S. Griffith & A.P. Hayes (Eds.), *Adult basic education: The state of the art* (pp. 110-128). Washington, DC: United States Government Printing Office.

Pachtman, A.B. (1977). The effects of a reading and language arts program on the critical thinking and critical reading of the first-year law student. *Dissertation Abstracts International, 38A,* 2431A-2432A.

Pearson, P.D. (Ed.). (1984). *Handbook of research in reading.* New York: Longman.

Perfetti, C.A. (1985). *Reading ability.* New York: Oxford University Press.

Petros, T., Tabor, L., Cooney, T., & Chabot, R.J. (1983). Adult age differences in sensitivity to semantic structure of prose. *Developmental Psychology, 19*, 907-914.

Poon, L.N., Krauss, I.K., & Bowles, N.L. (1984). On subject selection in cognitive aging research. *Experimental Aging Research, 10*, 43-49.

Propp, V. (1958). *Morphology of the folktale* (L. Scott, Trans.). Bloomington: Indiana University, Research Center in Anthropology, Folklore, and Linguistics.

Rice, G.E. (1986a). The everyday activities of adults: Implications for prose recall: Part I. *Educational Gerontology, 12*, 173-186.

Rice, G.E. (1986b). The everyday activities of adults: Implication for prose recall: Part II. *Educational Gerontology, 12*, 187-198.

Rice, G.E., & Meyer, B.J.F. (1985). Reading behavior and prose recall performance of young and older adults with high and average verbal ability. *Educational Gerontology, 11*, 57-72.

Rice, G.E., & Meyer, B.J.F. (1986, April). *The relation of everyday activities of adults to their prose recall.* Paper presented at the meeting of the American Educational Research Association, San Francisco, CA.

Rumelhart, D.E. (1975). Notes on a schema for stories. In D.G. Bobrow & A.M. Collins (Eds.), *Representation and understanding: Studies in cognitive science* (pp. 211-236). New York: Academic Press.

Schank, R.C. (1975). *Conceptual information processing.* Amsterdam: North Holland.

Shearin, C.W. (1976). An evaluation of a program to teach critical reading skills to adult volunteers. *Dissertation Abstracts International, 37A*, 1355A.

Spilich, G.J. (1983). Life-span components of text processing: structural and procedural differences. *Journal of Verbal Learning and Verbal Behavior, 22*, 231-244.

Spilich, G.J., & Voss, J.F. (1982). Contextual effects upon text memory for young, aged-normal, and aged memory-impaired individuals. *Experimental Aging Research, 8*, 45-49.

Stein, N.L., & Glenn, C.G. (1979). An analysis of story. In Freedle (Ed.), *Discourse processing: Multidisciplinary perspectives* (pp. 53-120). Norwood, NJ: Ablex.

Surber, J.R., Kowalski, A.H., & Pena-Paez, A. (1984). *Effects of aging on recall of extended expository prose. Experimental Aging Research, 10*, 25-28.

Taub, H.A. (1979). Comprehension and memory of prose materials by young and old adults. *Experimental Aging Research, 5*, 3-13.

Thompson, D.N., & Diefenderfer, K. (1986, April). *The use of advance organizers with older adults of limited verbal ability.* Paper presented at the meeting of the American Educational Research Association. San Francisco, CA.

Thorndyke, P.W. (1977). Cognitive structures in comprehension and memory of narrative events. *Journal of Memory and Language, 24*, 612-630.

Vincent, J.P. (1985). *Effects of discourse types on memory of prose by young, middle-age, and old adults with average vocabularies.* Unpublished doctoral dissertation, Arizona State University. Tempe, AR.

Yekovich, F.R., & Thorndyke, P.W. (1981). An evaluation of alternative functional models of narrative schemata. *Journal of Verbal Learning and Verbal Behavior, 20,* 454-469.

Young, C.J. (1983). *Integration of facts across textual distances by young and old adults.* Unpublished masters thesis, Arizona State University. Tempe, AR.

Zelinski, E.M., & Gilewski, M.J. (1988). Memory for prose and aging: A meta-analysis. In M.L. Howe & C. Brainerd (Eds.), *Cognitive development in adulthood.* New York: Springer-Verlag.

Zelinski, E.M., Gilewski, M.J., & Thompson, L.W. (1980). Do laboratory tests relate to self-assessment of memory ability in the young and old? In L.W. Poon, J.L. Fozard, L.S. Cermak, D. Arenberg, & L.W. Thompson (Eds.), *New directions in memory and aging: Proceedings of the George Talland Memorial Conference* (pp. 519-544). Hillsdale, NJ: Lawrence Erlbaum.

Zelinski, E.M., Light, L.L., & Gilewski, M.J. (1984). Adult age differences in memory for prose: The question of sensitivity to passage structure. *Developmental Psychology, 20,* 1181-1192.

9
Reading and Memory for Prose in Adulthood: Issues of Expertise and Compensation

Roger A. Dixon and Lars Bäckman

Do the many processes or aspects of cognition "age" alike or differently? How similar is cognitive aging within or across age cohorts? Do reading skills decline inevitably with advancing age? Is there less evidence for age-related decrements in memory for such ecologically relevant materials as prose passages than for lists of words or nonsense syllables? What are the conditions under which adults might develop or maintain highly skilled levels of reading and memory for prose performance? Given that reading and memory skills are complex and multi determined, is it possible to suffer age-related decline in one or more components and still maintain successful performance levels into old age?

These are some of the questions that concern us in our research. We acknowledge, however, that we will not attempt to answer definitively all of these questions in this chapter. They operate at quite different levels of analysis. Some focus on general issues with which all researchers in the cognitive psychology of adulthood must be concerned, whereas others are derivative and more specifically related to the present chapter. Nevertheless, we will endeavor to convey both our reasons for posing them and for attempting to address them conceptually and empirically.

An initial goal of this chapter is to describe briefly recent conceptions and methods of research in the cognitive psychology of expertise and compensation. More specifically, we explore in some detail the application of these conceptions and methods to the topic of reading and memory for prose in adulthood. In pursuing this goal we divide our discussion into three major parts. First, we summarize some trends in the cognitive psychology of adult development and aging. We focus, in particular, on extant research elucidative of some aspects of skilled prose reading or recall. Second, we elaborate our view that an interesting avenue for programmatic research is one that addresses the relationship between expertise and compensation. In the context of reading and memory for prose in adulthood, expertise is defined broadly as well practiced and maintained high levels of reading or memory performance skills. In this context, compensation is defined as the use of substitutable components of reading or memory for prose skills such that the aging individual maintains relatively high performance levels despite suffering decrements in other components. In this way, it is conceivable that some maintenance of high performance levels throughout adulthood may be achieved through continual exercise of the same components of skilled reading and memory (expertise) or through substitution of alternative components (compensation). To illustrate this view, we summarize, in the third section, our own initial efforts to investigate this relationship. In particular, we are interested in whether an hypothesized naturally occurring expertise of late adulthood (metaphoric interpretive skill) can compensate for naturally occurring decline in the molecular components of prose reading and recall (for metaphoric vs. nonmetaphoric passages).

One Perspective on Cognitive Aging

Several observers have identified a discrepancy between the apparent everyday competency of normal older adults and their relatively low observed performance on numerous laboratory tasks measuring cognitive abilities (Baltes, Dittmann-Kohli, & Dixon, 1984; Salthouse, 1987a, 1990). In everyday life many older adults perform numerous cognitively demanding tasks at a competent (if not, in some cases and in some domains, expert) level. In some situations this performance is equivalent or superior to that of younger adults. In the laboratory, however, older adults perform a wide range of tasks at a level considerably inferior to that of their younger counterparts. Several interpretations of this "lab-life" discrepancy have been proffered (Salthouse, 1987a). These include focusing on the joint but separate processes of growth and decline in cognitive aging (e.g., Baltes, 1987) and focusing on the role of practice and experience in cognitive aging (e.g., Salthouse, 1987a, 1987b).

Our perspective owes much to both of these interpretations. It is grounded in the observation that there is indisputable evidence for decline in psychometric test performance or episodic memory performance (Craik, 1977) and concomitant suggestive evidence regarding personal perceptions and stereotypes of decline, especially in late adulthood. Nevertheless, it has been suggested—and some historical work indicates that this is not an isolated or recent phenomenon (Dixon & Baltes, 1986)—that there are aspects of cognition that exhibit stabilization or perhaps even progression, given a variety of "appropriate" testing methods or supportive (task) performance conditions (e.g., Bäckman, 1985, 1989; Baltes et al., 1984; Charness, 1989; Denney, 1982; Dixon & Baltes, 1986; Labouvie-Vief, 1982, 1985).

Quite often, the argument goes, these aspects of cognition are associated with (a) the practical, cognitively demanding situations of daily, leisure, and professional life, (b) the natural course of cultural experience and knowledge accumulation, (c) select domains of specialization or expertise, or (d) such hypostatized domains of cognition as advice giving or wisdom. From some quarters has come the suggestion that, because the less pragmatic dimensions of cognitive functioning are overrepresented in, for example, standard psychometric tests and typical laboratory cognitive tasks, the typical finding of age-related performance decrements may not be a valid indicator of the overall cognitive readiness, adaptiveness, or everyday performance of older adults (Baltes & Willis, 1979; Berg & Sternberg, 1985; Labouvie-Vief, 1982, 1985). In particular, it may underrepresent that quite functional mental activity that occurs in daily life and the reserve capacity of older adults that, given proper training and practice, can be tapped as a source of further advancement or as a resource for compensation for other declining functions. However, it is also apparent that not all recent efforts to develop measures of "practical cognition," "practical problemsolving," or even wisdom have resulted in robust positive age differences (i.e., older adults performing better than younger adults; for reviews and examples see Baltes & Smith, 1990; Denney, 1989; A. Hartley, 1989; Labouvie-Vief, 1990; Salthouse, 1982).

This perspective appears to rest on three main related principles of cognitive development throughout adulthood (Dixon & Baltes, 1986): (a) There is an age-related decline in many basic components of cognitive functioning, especially in the very late years, but there may be some stabilization in some contextually supported, well practiced, skilled, ecologically relevant, and practical domains; (b) under normal (and, especially, optimal) conditions there is also sufficient reserve capacity so as to nurture an (at least temporary) increase in performance, especially if appreciable interest, effort, training, motivation, or social support are present; and (c) there seems to be a concomitant adaptive compensatory feature of mental functioning that allows for the inevitable decrements in late adulthood to be less debilitating, less generalized (i.e., more localized) and, less transferred to selected other skilled or everyday features than might be otherwise expected.

These principles have led to the generation of a number of general research questions. Indeed, these principles underlie the questions posed at the outset of this chapter. In the remainder of this chapter we concentrate on a subset of these questions. In particular, we identify selected conditions under which skilled performance in prose reading and recall is displayed by older adults. Furthermore, we examine some ways in which maintenance of such skills may support inferences regarding cognitive compensation.

In sum, there are some conditions in which the typical age differences (in which young adults perform at a superior level to older adults) may be attenuated. In some cases, these situations are related to the experience or expertise of older adults. We are interested in the effects of experience or expertise on the attenuation of age differences in measures of prose reading and recall. For example, there have been numerous hypotheses that age differences may be attenuated when (a) the language or verbal experience of older adults is invoked or maximized, (b) older adults have pertinent prior knowledge or schemata available, or (c) older adults process selected prose passages "thematically," "metaphorically," "integratively," or in terms of social meaning or life morals. The testable implication is that older adults who are experts or skilled in one of these areas may be able to compensate for general decline in the components of reading fluency and prose recall (e.g., lexical decision, working memory span) and maintain performance (for selected texts) at relatively high levels.

Skilled Prose Reading and Recall

With respect to discourse processing and prose recall, the evidence regarding expert performance is not as complete or empirically sound as for such domains as physics, bridge, or chess (see Charness, 1987, 1989; Hoyer, 1985). However, there are some legendary exceptional performances in remembering prose (e.g., historical poems and stories) stemming from the oral tradition of former times, the oral tradition in contemporary preliterate societies, and even theater, where some actors have claimed to be "fast studies" with respect to learning texts of plays (e.g., Yates, 1966).

In Table 9.1 some examples of studies on expertise, broadly defined, in prose reading and recall in adulthood are presented. Although none of this work is developmental, these studies are illustrative in at least two ways. First, this work has demonstrated that the notion of highly skilled cognitive performance is in a global way applicable to prose reading and recall. Unusual and exceptional performances have been documented. Second, in some of the cases middle-aged and older adults have been found to be able to perform at such highly skilled levels (although the age documentation has not been carefully done).

In the few studies examining prose processing skill and adult age, expertise has been conceived of within a normal range of functioning and usually as a variable with which to compare and differentiate within and across adult age groups. For example, old and young adult age groups might be divided into roughly equivalent high and low skill subgroups and compared on selected measures of reading or recall of stories. Among the typical categories of skills related to text recall and aging are the following:

(a)   language experience and verbal skill, both of which may be positively correlated with adult age;

(b)   the availability of pertinent prior knowledge or schemata; and

(c)   the hypothesized age-related tendency for older adults to process some language materials metaphorically, thematically, wisely, or in terms of morals or social meaning.

All these skills could conceivably act as cognitive support systems (Bäckman, 1985, 1989) for reading and prose memory in older adults. We will discuss them in turn.

Table 9.1.
Some Examples of Studies on Expertise in
Prose Processing in Adulthood

Study	Domain or Test	Subject Characteristics
Carver (1985)	Speed Reading Test	Adults: 1. Speed Readers 2. Professionals 3. College Students 4. Exceptional Comprehenders
Hunt & Love (1982/1982)	Bartlett's Indian Folk Tale	V.P., Middle-aged Latvian Mnemonist
Intons-Peterson & Smyth (1987)	Verbatim Memory of Prose	Expert (Quick Studies) and Novice Students
Rubin (1977)	Long-TermVerbatim Memory for Prose and Verse	Undergraduates
Stratton (1917/1982)	Literal Knowledge of the Talmud	Hebrew Scholars: "Shass Pollak"
Wilding & Valentine (1985)	Dubes African Story (Immediate, 8-Day)	T.E., Adult Mnemonist

Verbal Skills

The literature addressing the interaction of verbal skills and adult age is somewhat sparse. With respect to language and verbal skills, the predominant (usually single) indicator has been vocabulary score. Nevertheless, some results are supportive of the general direction of the hypothesized relationship. For example, Meyer and Rice (1983) compared four subsamples of young and old adults in text recall. For the subsample comparison of high verbal old adults with normal verbal young adults, no age differences were observed, even though there was an overall main effect for age (in favor of young adults) in the study. In a second example, a median split procedure was used to generate two verbal ability groups, high verbal (HV) and low verbal (LV), in each of three age groups (Dixon, Hultsch, Simon, & von Eye, 1984). For free recall of information from a series of short expository texts, there were main effects for age (in favor of young adults), verbal ability (in favor of HV), and level of information (where main ideas [or Level 1] were recalled better than subordinate ideas [Level 2], and these were recalled better than details of the text [Levels 3 and 4]). The most relevant finding, however, was a three-way interaction among age, verbal ability, and level of information. For LV subjects, at the level of main idea recall, young adults performed better than middle-aged adults, who performed better than old adults. For HV subjects, there were no age differences in recall of the main ideas of the texts, but there were age differences at the level of text details.

The literature pertaining to this issue is still growing. For example, in a study of two large samples of adults, Dixon, Hultsch, Hertzog, and Comish (1986) used procedures similar to those of Dixon et al. (1984). The stories the subjects were asked to read, however, were quite different; they were long personal narratives varying in their degree of structural coherence. The results in both samples were similar. For the relatively well structured narrative the results were similar to those described above. However, for the less well structured story only the standard levels effect was apparent (i.e., all three age groups recalled main ideas better than details, and HV adults did better than LV adults, but verbal ability showed no tendency to interact with age and levels of information). For the least well structured story the effect was dramatically different. Although there were age effects and verbal ability effects, there was no levels effect (i.e., separate horizontal lines across levels of information were observed).

There are a number of provisos and qualifications attendant to these three selected studies. Among the prominant ones are: (a) the limits inherent in the use of single vocabulary measures as indicators of verbal or language skill, (b) methodological limitations of comparisons based on categorical variables and the median split procedure, and (c) the verbal skill variable was assessed within the normal range of healthy adults, that is, no true "language experts" were tested. Research pursued along the avenues implied in these qualifications would be useful (see J. Hartley, 1986; Hultsch, Hertzog, & Dixon, 1984). Given the current literature, however, a tentative conclusion may be offered. For some prose passages, age differences in the discovery and utilization of the hierarchical organization of texts may be related to, among other things, the verbal skills of the reader.

Prior Knowledge

A second category of skills relevant to reading and prose memory is that of prior knowledge or schemata, the presence of which could make the reader analogous to the expert in other domains of memory (Ericsson, 1985). In one study on memory for scripts and aging, Light and Anderson (1983) found some evidence for equivalence in young and old adults in recognizing typical and atypical script actions. This suggested that both young and old adults can benefit from generic knowledge (i.e., they can integrate it with new information).

In another published study in this area, Hultsch and Dixon (1983) reasoned that, because age and cohort groups have experienced relatively unique cultural and historical events, they may differ in terms of prior knowledge or schemata (read: expertise) regarding some historically relevant topics. On the basis of a pilot study, which examined the amount of knowledge of young, middle-aged, and old adults about 28 entertainment figures taken from varying cohorts, a set of 4 figures was selected: Steve Martin (young story type), Susan Hayward (middle-aged story type), Mary Pickford (old story type), and Bob Hope (general across-age story type). Each figure was better known by subjects within the corresponding age groups than by subjects in the other two age groups, except for Bob Hope, who was known equally well by all three age groups.

One short (115 words) biographical sketch of each of these figures was developed and presented to young, middle-aged, and old subjects. Subjects were asked to read and remember each of the stories individually. The comparison of young and old subjects across these four story types is revealing. Although there was an overall main effect for age (in favor of young adults), the old adults performed as well as the young adults in remembering what they had read of the stories about Mary Pickford (old story type) and Bob Hope (general story type). Thus, the suggestion was that age differences in prose recall performance may be present or absent depending on the level of expertise or prior knowledge regarding the to-be-remembered material possessed by the various age groups.

Processing Style

A third category of skills that may be related to prose reading, recall, and aging is the hypothesized tendency for older adults to process prose materials differently than they did as younger adults. Specifically, whereas younger adults process language materials for relatively verbatim meaning, older adults process such materials thematically or metaphorically. This hypothesis has both a modest and a bold version. The modest version is so-named because it suggests that this functional tendency occurs for selected older adults only. The bold version, on the other hand, is based on conceptions of aging that suggest that successful functioning may be associated with a more global, naturally occurring development of an experience-based emphasis on thematic, integrative, or metaphoric processing (e.g., Adams, Labouvie-Vief, Hobart, & Dorosz, 1990; Labouvie-Vief, 1990; Labouvie-Vief & Schell, 1982).

If either version of the hypothesis is to be tested, then merely counting the number of propositions recalled, or even the number of higher order propositions in some systems of text representation that follow the surface structure of the passage closely (e.g., Kintsch, 1974), may not reveal the influence of this expertise. In prose recall and aging work, the topic of sensitivity to passage structure (identification and recall of main ideas vs. details) is seemingly relevant. However, conflicting results have emerged (e.g., Dixon, Simon, Nowak, & Hultsch, 1982; Petros, Tabor, Cooney, & Chabor, 1983; Zelinski, Light, & Gilewski, 1984). The results pertaining to main idea recall by older adults often depend on such factors as: (a) the number of levels of information; (b) the propositional analysis (if any) used; (c) the kind of scoring done, that is, whether gist or verbatim as well as the hierarchy of scoring decisions made by experimenters; (d) the structure and content of the stories; and (e) individual differences in reading and memory skills (see Hultsch & Dixon, 1984; Zelinski & Gilewski, 1988).

The bold version of the hypothesis has only recently begun to receive empirical attention (Adams et al. 1990; Adams, Dorosz, Holmes, Bass, Gossiaux, & Labouvie-Vief, 1985; Adams & Labouvie-Vief, 1986; Dixon & Bäckman, 1988; Labouvie-Vief, 1990). The issue to which this hypothesis is directed may be summarized as follows: In reading some texts, do most normal older adults transform the verbatim meaning into gist or interpretive units of meaning? Do they, as a function of a life course of rich experience with their culture, process appropriate language materials more thematically, more wisely, or more in terms of social meaning than they did as younger adults? Do they thereby produce a qualitatively different form of "recall" from that produced by younger adults? A subsequent question is whether these qualitatively different forms of recall are functional or serve compensatory purposes. In any event, this different form of processing and performance might be overlooked with irrelevant stimulus materials (e.g., passages of inappropriate content or structure) or insensitive scoring procedures (Labouvie-Vief & Schell, 1982). Again, this hypothesis is considered bold for it operates at a more universal level than the modest version.

Prior to the work of Labouvie-Vief and colleagues (1982) little research on the bold version of the hypothesis had been conducted. In our own work on reading and prose recall (see Hultsch & Dixon, 1984, 1990) we looked for evidence of a "different" form of processing in the protocols of numerous samples of older adults. These samples had read prose passages ranging from brief expository texts about recent news items and health-related topics to long personal narratives about individuals or families experiencing a typical life crisis. Given these passages and instructions emphasizing gist recall, it was not unusual to observe that older adults produced more elaborations in their protocols (i.e., statements that are consistent with the story or real world knowledge about the topic of the story, but which were not actually contained in the story) than younger adults. However, the number of these elaborations was small compared to the number of accurate recall propositions they produced, even when they performed badly compared to younger adults. These studies were not designed to encourage elaborations or interpretations, and thus it is certainly not definitive that no evidence for a distinctively different processing and commenting style by older adults was observed.

Two recent studies have reported results pertaining to a version of this hypothesis. Indirect, but nevertheless relevant, evidence was found by Gould, Trevithick, and Dixon (1991) in a study of collaborative prose recall in young and old individuals, dyads, and tetrads (groups of four). A qualitative analysis of the elaborations revealed that young and old adults produced an equivalent number of elaborations closely linked to the story or theme (*denotative elaborations*). In contrast, older adults produced more interpretive, evaluative, and personal comments about the story (which were called *annotative elaborations*). One possible (and positive) interpretation of the pattern of results is that older adults made their retelling of the stories more interesting with a few personal comments, even though they were briefer (less verbatim) than the those of the younger adults.

For several reasons, the Gould et al. (1991) data are only indirectly relevant to the hypothesis under consideration. First, the task was not one of reading a passage, but rather listening to one. Second, the annotative elaborations may not be similar to the Adams et al. (1990) category of interpretations, although they occasionally did address issues of interpretation and integration. Adams et al. presented their young and old adults with either fables or nonfables and requested either verbatim recall, gist recall, gist recall plus moral, or a summary from them. They found that instructions at recall were related to the predominant form of the protocol; for example, asking adults to produce gist recall plus the moral of the story was related to the presence of interpretive statements. They also found a tendency for older adults to produce integrative or interpretive styles of protocols for the nonfable passages. Although this study offers data that are closest to being consistent with the bold hypothesis, the results are also not definitively supportive.

In the next section of this chapter we turn to other recent efforts to systematically explore this hypothesis. Specifically, in this study we were interested in testing whether a clear, generalized, naturally occurring shift in style of processing, interpretation, or recall in adulthood could be observed using an explicit set of theory-based predictions.

Compensation in Prose Reading and Recall

Our efforts to investigate the relationship between adult cognitive development and the potentially functional role that compensation may play began with a review, a working definition, and a model of compensation (Bäckman & Dixon, 1986, in press). Although the literature on compensation is vast, there were relatively few efforts to elaborate the concept. Thus, in our review we focused our attention on such relevant but diverse research areas as:

(a)   sensory handicaps, where the hypothesis is that a loss in one sensory system (e.g., visual, auditory) may be balanced by an increased sensitivity in another;

(b)   brain injury, where both the brain, under some conditions, is physiologically capable of restoration of function through the substitution of neuronal structures and pathways, and brain-injured patients evince compensatory behaviors (e.g., ideographic reading and affective-prosodic processing strategies in aphasic patients);

(c)   social interaction, where physical or social adjustments may be made to compensate for losses or deprivations in social roles (e.g., unemployment, retirement) or companionship (e.g., widowhood); and

(d)   cognitive deficits, where a number of compensatory behaviors, such as context utilization in reading difficulties (Stanovich, 1984) and anticipation of impending characters by older skilled typists (Salthouse, 1984), help overcome deficits.

Based on a review of research in these and other literatures, as well as on an examination of the few conceptual treatments of compensation (e.g., Bäckman, 1985; Baltes, 1987; Rohwer, 1976; Salthouse, 1987a), we identified several underlying issues and themes (see Bäckman & Dixon, in press). To some extent, the literature we reviewed was typified by some attention to one or more of the following issues: (a) the origins of compensation, (b) the mechanisms of compensation, (c) the forms of compensation, and (d) the consequences of compensation. We discuss these briefly, after presenting a working definition, in the following subsection.

Definition and Some Issues of Compensation

In general, compensation can be inferred when an objective or perceived mismatch between accessible skills and environmental demands is counterbalanced (either automatically or deliberately) by investment of more time or effort (drawing on normal skills), utilization of latent (but normally inactive) skills, acquisition of new skills or, such that a change in the behavioral profile occurs, either in the direction of (a) adaptive attainment, maintenance, or surpassing of "normal" levels of proficiency or (b) maladaptive outcome behaviors or consequences. This working definition is deliberately general and complex; it covers considerably more specific cases and issues than we discuss in this chapter. For present purposes, it is sufficient to note that, in the typical case, compensation can be inferred when an objective or perceived deficit in a given skill is counterbalanced by an increase in a substitutable skill such that task performance is normalized or maximized.

Issues

In the typical case, compensation *originates* in a mismatch between available skills and environmental demands, and usually (but not always) when there is a deficit in the former and the latter is relatively unchanged. The typical *mechanism* of compensation is as follows: A match is achieved or approached between the skill (or component thereof) and environmental demands usually through a counterbalancing increase in a skill or component. Alternative mechanisms, such as changes in expectations or goals, are possible. Compensatory behaviors may be located at different points along two major dimensions. First, they may occur with relatively more or less awareness (deliberate vs. automatic). Second, they may differ more or less qualitatively from normal behaviors that accomplish the same goals. The latter variation in form is especially relevant to compensation in reading and memory for prose in adulthood. As we see below, such compensation may take at least the following forms: (a) investment of more effort, (b) utilization of latent but inactive skills, and (c) acquisition of new skills. With respect to *consequences*, compensation usually involves gains substituting for losses and is therefore generally positive or adaptive. There are, however, several examples of compensation that are, at one level of analysis or another, maladaptive. Indeed, we should note that, as is indicated by the generality and complexity of the working definition, there are numerous important qualifications for each of these issues. A more detailed discussion of the definition, the issues and qualifications, and the literatures from which they were derived, may be found elsewhere (Bäckman & Dixon, in press). Our present goal is to describe how we have applied this model to the cognitive psychology of adulthood and, especially, prose reading and recall.

Application to Prose Reading and Recall

The issue with which we are concerned is the conditions under which normal adults might maintain reading and memory for prose skills into old age. Our specific research question is: Can older adults compensate for decrements in the molecular components of prose reading and recall through the utilization of a maintained skill, thus performing at a level equivalent to that of younger adults in the free recall (and other performance measures) of selected texts? We began by focusing on the four major issues of compensation as they applied to the present topic. For example, if compensation were to occur, it would probably originate in an adult age-related deficit in some primary components of reading or memory skill that is apparent given the reading demands of the laboratory. That is, older adults would suffer deficits in indicators of molar reading or memory skills because of aging-related decrements in molecular components of those skills. One probable mechanism of compensation in this scenario would be a counterbalancing age-related increase in an alternative molecular component of skilled reading or memory. The consequence of compensation in this case would be adaptive insofar as it promoted successful reading and comprehending of materials encountered in the everyday ecology of older adults. Such compensatory behavior could be arguably maladaptive if it promoted successful reading exclusively for materials not encountered in everyday life or if success in reading and remembering one variety of materials resulted in a regressive trend for many other varieties. As alluded to above, there are at least three possible forms in which such compensation might occur. For the most part the forms illustrated in Figure 9.1 are hypothetical; there are virtually no specific data related unambiguously to any complete sequence in the three forms of compensation. Nevertheless, each sequence in each of the forms is based on either extensions of extant data or on active, testable hypotheses. The number *1* in a given rectangle represents a well functioning component of a human reading "system". Two or three *1s* in a rectangle are meant to represent a successfully functioning reader. For example, in the first sequence (compensation via investment of more effort) for a reader with well functioning components of (what we will call for the sake of simplicity) general literacy (L), working memory capacity (WMC), and utilization of context (UC), it may be inferred that the molar system is working well. One way to impair WMC is through alcohol intoxication. If a reader suffers a deficit in WMC for this reason, the molar skill may be affected. However, there is some evidence for recognition memory that, even if WMC is impaired because of alcohol intoxication, through sheer effort the overall system may continue to function at a normal level. This is illustrative of what is meant by compensation via the investment of more effort. It is conceivable that, with aging,

1. Compensation via Effort (Without Substitution)

2. Compensation via Activation of a Latent Skill or Component

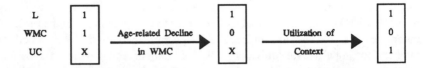

3. Compensation via Acquisition of a New Skill or Component

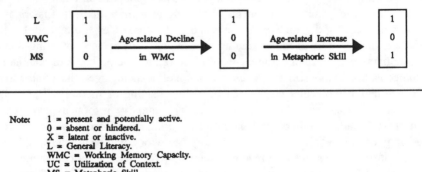

Note: 1 = present and potentially active.
         0 = absent or hindered.
         X = latent or inactive.
         L = General Literacy.
         WMC = Working Memory Capacity.
         UC = Utilization of Context.
         MS = Metaphoric Skill.

Figure 9.1. Three hypothesized forms of compensation in reading and memory for prose.

some maintenance of molar reading and memory performance levels might occur through simply concentrating or trying harder (see Jennings, Nebes, & Yovetich, 1990). The second form of compensation (via activation of a latent skill or component) is based in part on the work of Stanovich (e.g., 1980, 1984; Stanovich & West, 1983). There is some evidence that WMC may decline with advancing age (e.g., Hultsch & Dixon, 1990). More importantly, as described in the first section of this chapter, there is considerable evidence that numerous molecular components of molar reading and memory skills decline with age (i.e., WMC is used illustratively here). If WMC declines, then the overall molar reading skill for an affected individual may be impaired. Stanovich (e.g., 1980, 1984) has demonstrated how the utilization of context may serve a compensatory purpose for inferior readers. Whether activation of the UC component may substitute for a declining WMC (or other) component is unclear, but it is a tantalizing possibility deserving of further research.

Finally, the third hypothetical form (compensation via acquisition of a new skill or component) is distinguished from the second in that it involves the emergence of a new skill not previously a part of successful reading. Our view is that it is this form that is represented in some theories of successful aging such as that of Labouvie-Vief (1982; Labouvie-Vief, Schell, & Weaverdyck, 1980). In addition, our own efforts to investigate compensation in reading and memory for prose concentrated on this form. If there is an age-related decline in the molecular components of reading and memory (e.g., in WMC) and at the same time an age-related increase in a potentially substitutable component (e.g., metaphor intrepretive skill), then it may be possible to observe evidence for compensation. The important remaining questions are: (a) whether such compensation would occur for most normal adults (the aforementioned bold hypothesis) or only for highly selected adults (the modest hypothesis), (b) what mechanism might be operating that would relate metaphoric skill to reading and prose recall, and (c) how to set up an experiment the logic of which would compel an inference either for or against such compensation. It is to this topic, and a brief summary of our recent empirical effort, that we now turn.

Considering a Bold Hypothesis

The hypothesis we chose to test was not as bold as it could have been. We were concerned with whether unselected older adults could compensate for decrements in the molecular components of prose reading and recall through a generalized age-related increase in skill at interpreting metaphors. We chose metaphor interpretation for several reasons. First, although it is rarely mentioned as a molecular component of reading, we were selective (or modest) in certain aspects of our hypothesis. We predicted that, if compensation would occur, it would probably not occur for all possible texts, but selectively for metaphoric texts. Second, there is evidence that there may be an age-related increase in metaphor interpretation skill (e.g., Boswell, 1979). Third, we speculated that the mechanism of the relationship between metaphoric skill and metaphoric text reading and recall might be as follows:

(a)   Older adults seem to interpret metaphors more synthetically than younger adults, who are more literal (Boswell, 1979);

(b)   Synthetic interpretation may require a "deeper" semantic analysis of the materials than does a literal interpretation (i.e., it may require more elaboration and more inferential activity); and

(c)   all of these cognitive operations might support a higher level of reading and recall performance for relevant texts.

Thus, we did not test the boldest possible hypothesis; that would have involved a prediction that such compensation would occur naturally (and universally) in adulthood and be applicable to a wide variety of prose passages. In the following paragraphs we summarize this study; for more details see Dixon and Bäckman (1991).

A logical pattern of age-related results is required before an initial inference of compensation can be proffered. A summary of the critical logical steps (and associated predictions) is presented in Table 9.2. A basic feature of this pattern is that an age-related deficit in the components of reading fluency (e.g., WMC, lexical decision) and an indicator of the molar skill (e.g., free recall of nonmetaphoric texts) is counterbalanced by age-related equivalence or reverse superiority on a substitutable component (e.g., metaphor interpretation) such that age-equivalent performance on a similar molar skill is observed (e.g., free recall of metaphoric texts). Materials pertaining to each of the logical steps and associated predictions were collected and administered to groups of young (*M* age = 25.6 years) and old (*M* age = 68.8 years) normal, community-dwelling volunteer adults.

Four stories were developed, each with an equivalent number of words (range = 111 to 116), sentences (nine), and propositions (range = 56 to 60, using the system of Kintsch, 1974). The passages were designed to vary along two dimensions: (a) metaphoric versus nonmetaphoric and (b) high versus low propositional density. Only the former variation is relevant for present purposes. Thus, there were two typical passages (nonmetaphoric expository texts on the topics of nature and nations) and two metaphoric passages (on the topics of slavery and a call). Participants were asked to read each passage, rate each on a series of dimensions, and then retell (in writing) the passages in their own words. Such protocols may be scored for multiple response measures: gist recall (number of propositions correctly recalled using a relaxed, gist criterion), elaborations (statements consistent with the topic of the text but not actually contained in it), metaphorical statements (metaphors produced by the participant that were not a part of the reading materials), macrostatements (statements of a general, thematic, summary nature), metastatements (statements about the process of thinking about and remembering the passages), and intrusion errors (within-story errors in accuracy). The hypothesized compensatory mechanism—metaphor interpretation— was measured via the task described in Boswell (1979). Participants were given six metaphors (sentences that were meaningful but not literally true, and that contained a topic and a vehicle) and asked to interpret them. Again, in the original study, older adults performed better than younger adults in this task.

The pattern of results matched very closely the predicted pattern. With regard to Prediction 1a (Table 9.2), there were significant reading component and reading comprehension and text recall correlations (range = .1 to .8). This finding replicated and extended the results of Baddeley, Logie, Nimmo-Smith, and Brereton (1985). With regard to Prediction 1b, young adults performed reliably better than old adults on the four component tasks. Prediction 2, that old adults would perform better than young adults on the metaphor interpretation task, was also confirmed. As rated by an independent group of expert judges, both older males and older females interpreted metaphors significantly more synthetically than their younger counterparts. On Prediction 3, as expected, young adults performed significantly better than old adults on the gist free recall of propositions from typical (nonmetaphoric) passages. Thus, with respect to free recall, the stage was set for the evaluation of Prediction 4: Is there indeed evidence in an unselected sample of adults for this

Table 9.2

Logical and Empirical Steps Leading to an Inference of
Compensation in Prose Reading and Recall

1. Molecular component and molar task performance: (a) For both young and old adults, significant correlations between components (e.g., working memory span, lexical decision) and molar task (e.g., reading comprehension, prose recall). (b) Significant age difference (young > old adults) on all molecular tasks.
2. Hypothesized compensatory mechanism: (a) Significant correlations (for old adults) between metaphor interpretation and recall of metaphoric texts. (b) Signifcant age difference (old > young adults) on metaphor interpretation.
3. Molar age-related deficit (young > old adults) on prose recall (for typical or nonmetaphoric passages).
4. Compensation-related Predictions (a) Bold prediction: old>/+ young adults on prose recall (for metaphoric passages). (b) Modest prediction: expert old >/= young adults on other response measures (e.g., elaborations, interpretations, metaphor production).
5. Conclusion: If this pattern is observed, there is some evidence that old adults may compensate for deficits in the molecular components of prose reading and recall by using metaphoric skill in processing suitable texts.

form of compensation in prose reading and recall? For the gist free recall of
metaphoric passages, young adults still performed better than old adults. For this
response measure, then, the pattern of results was very close to, but missing a
critical element of, that required to support an inference of compensation.

Not indicated in the preceding brief summary, however, are the results for the
other response measures. For three of these (viz., elaborations, metaphor production, and metastatements), it was found that young and old adults performed at
equivalent levels. These findings would encourage the bold hypothesis, except for
the fact that the frequency of all three of these categories was quite small. Hence,
a floor effect is a competing explanation. Overall, then, despite the observation of
numerous logical and empirical preconditions, the bold hypothesis of a generalized,
age-related compensation for specific deficits in reading fluency through the
utilization of metaphoric skill, did not receive support in this study. It is uncertain
whether this result is due to the bold hypothesis being too bold (i.e., it may work,
but only for more selected samples) or to materials or instructions that are still too
lab-like rather than life-like (Labouvie-Vief, in press). An additional issue concerns
the nature of the hypothesized compensatory mechanism in the present study.
Specifically, it is possible that metaphoric skill is not a unitary construct. Metaphor
interpretation may draw on a different aspect of metaphoric skill than does metaphor memory. Whereas metaphor interpretation may not require any new learning

(drawing primarily on semantic knowledge), metaphor recall might draw primarily on typical encoding and retrieval processes.

Conclusion

One issue with which we are concerned is the conditions under which normal older adults might maintain skills in reading and memory for prose. We suggested that there are individual differences in (a) the level attained in such demanding cognitive activities, (b) whether the skill is maintained, and (c) the cognitive profile of (or reasons for the) maintenance. We speculated that such maintenance might occur under several interrelated conditions:

(1)   Older adults who have had a life history of experience in reading or remembering prose (either as a profession or as a leisure activity) might maintain a high level of performance on related performance tasks primarily as a function of continued practice and training and continued adequate support from the same molecular components of the molar skill (expertise);

(2)   Older adults who have experience or expertise in reading or memory for prose might maintain high levels of functioning through compensatory mechanisms continuous with the molar skill, such as investment of more effort or utilization of a latent contributory component, both of which may be accomplished either deliberately or automatically; or

(3)   Older adults may perform at normal (as compared to the performance of younger adults) or high levels by compensating (either deliberately or automatically) via substitution of alternative, age-related, cognitively supportive skills (or components thereof).

It appeared to us that hypotheses derived from the third situation might have both bold and modest versions. The bolder version, suggesting that such compensation might occur as a natural function of adaptive, successful aging, was the object of considerable conceptual and empirical interest in this chapter. We reported the logic, design, and results of one study designed to test this hypothesis for one sample of unselected (normal) adults using selected materials and tasks. These data do not support the presence of a generalized, age-related compensation for deficits in molecular components of reading and memory for prose through the utilization of metaphoric skill, even for metaphoric prose passages. This conclusion is drawn despite the observation in this study of all (but one) of the predicted relationships among the components and the molar tasks; the missing one, level of performance for metaphoric prose passages, was critical. The more general conclusion, however, is that efforts to investigate such questions can benefit from explicit operational definitions, predictions, criteria, and theoretical models.

Although the results summarized in this chapter do not speak to the modest, or expertise, version of the hypothesis, the experimental procedures (including explicit predicitons of relations among constructs) are applicable. In our present research we are investigating several variants of this hypothesis. Employing similar logic and designs, it is possible to test highly selected older adults (language experts) to examine the developing dynamic between expertise and compensation. For example, we have recently examined the performance of selected metaphoric experts on the tasks described above (Dixon & Bäckman, 1991). For these experts—but not for normal controls—a performance profile more consistent with an inference of compensation was observed. Thus, our present conclusion is that, at the very least, the modest hypothesis deserves further investigation. Although this hypothesis does not imply as optimistic a picture of general aging as the bold hypothesis, it is not a pessimistic one. Furthermore, it is an hypothesis that is easily linked theoretically and empirically to a growing body of research on expertise, compensation, and aging.

References

Adams, C., Dorosz, M., Holmes, C., Bass, S., Gossiaux, D., & Labouvie-Vief, G. (1985, November). *Qualitative age differences in story recall*. Paper presented at the annual meeting of the Gerontological Society of America, New Orleans.

Adams, C., & Labouvie-Vief, G. (1986, November). *Modes of knowing and language processing*. Paper presented at the annual meeting of the Gerontological Society of America, Chicago.

Adams, C., Labouvie-Vief, G., Hobart, C.J., & Dorosz, M. (1990). Adult age group differences in story recall style. *Journal of Gerontology: Psychological Sciences, 45,* 17-27.

Bäckman, L. (1985). Compensation and recoding: A framework for aging and memory research. *Scandinavian Journal of Psychology, 26,* 193-207.

Bäckman, L. (1989). Varieties of memory compensation of older adults in episodic remembering. In L.W. Poon, D.C. Rubin, & B.A. Wilson (Eds.), *Everyday cognition in adulthood and late life.* New York: Cambridge University Press.

Bäckman, L., & Dixon, R.A. (1986, September). Compensation and adaptive cognitive functioning in adulthood. In M.M. Baltes & D.L. Featherman (Chairs), *Optimal living for aging.* Symposium conducted at the European Conference on Developmental Psychology, Rome.

Bäckman, L., & Dixon, R.A. (in press). Psychological compensation: A theoretical framework. *Psychological Bulletin.*

Baddeley, A., Logie, R., Nimmo-Smith, I., & Brereton, N. (1985). Components of fluent reading. *Journal of Memory and Language, 24,* 119-131.

Baltes, P.B. (1987). Theoretical propositions of life-span developmental psychology: On the dynamics between growth and decline. *Developmental Psychology, 23,* 611-626.

Baltes, P.B., Dittmann-Kohli, F., & Dixon, R.A. (1984). New perspectives on the development of intelligence in adulthood: Toward a dual-process conception and a model of selective optimization with compensation. In P.B. Baltes & O.G. Brim, Jr. (Eds.), *Life-span development and behavior* (Vol. 6). New York: Academic Press.

Baltes, P.B., & Smith, J. (1990). Toward a psychology of wisdom and its ontogenesis. In R.J. Sternberg (Ed.), *Wisdom: Its nature, origins, and development.* Cambridge: Cambridge University Press.

Baltes, P.B., & Willis, S.L. (1979). The critical importance of appropriate methodology in the study of aging: The sample case of psychometric intelligence. In F. Hoffmeister & C. Miller (Eds.), *Brain function in old age.* Heidelberg: Springer-Verlag.

Berg, C.A., & Sternberg, R.J. (1985). A triarchic theory of intellectual development during adulthood. *Developmental Review, 5,* 334-370.

Boswell, D.A. (1979). Metaphoric processing in the mature years. *Human Development, 22,* 373-384.

Carver, R.P. (1985). How good are some of the world's best readers? *Reading Research Quarterly, 20,* 389-419.

Charness, N. (1987). Component processes in bridge bidding and novel problem-solving tasks. *Canadian Journal of Psychology, 41,* 223-243.

Charness, N. (1989). Age and expertise: Responding to Talland's challenge. In L.W. Poon, D.C. Rubin, & B.A. Wilson (Eds.), *Everyday cognition in adulthood and late life.* New York: Cambridge University Press.

Craik, F.I.M. (1977). Age differences in human memory. In J.E. Birren & K.W. Schaie (Eds.), *Handbook of the psychology of aging.* Princeton, NJ: Van Nostrand Reinhold.

Denney, N.W. (1982). Aging and cognitive changes. In B.B. Wolman (Ed.), *Handbook of developmental psychology.* Englewood Cliffs, NJ: Prentice-Hall.

Denney, N.W. (1989). Problem-solving in adulthood. In L.W. Poon, D.C. Rubin, & B.A. Wilson (Eds.), *Everyday cognition in adulthood and late life.* New York: Cambridge University Press.

Dixon, R.A., & Bäckman, L. (1988). Text recall and aging: Toward research on expertise and compensation. In M. Gruneberg, P. Morris, & R. Sykes (Eds.), *Practical aspects of memory.* Chichester: John Wiley.

Dixon, R.A., & Bäckman, L. (1991). *Prose processing and recall in adulthood: A test of a general model.* Unpublished manuscript, University of Victoria, Victoria, British Columbia, Canada.

Dixon, R.A., & Baltes, P.B. (1986). Toward life-span research on the functions and pragmatics of intelligence. In R.J. Sternberg & R.K. Wagner (Eds.), *Practical intelligence: Nature and origins of competence in the everyday world.* New York: Cambridge University Press.

Dixon, R.A., Hultsch, D.F., Hertzog, C., & Comish, S.E. (1986, May). *More on verbal ability and text structure effects on text recall in adulthood.* Paper presented at the First Cognitive Aging Conference, Atlanta, GA.

Dixon, R.A., Hultsch, D.F., Simon, E.W., & von Eye, A. (1984). Verbal ability and text structure effects on adult age differences in text recall. *Journal of Verbal Learning and Verbal Behavior, 23,* 569-578.

Dixon, R.A., Simon, E.W., Nowak, C.A., & Hultsch, D.F. (1982). Text recall in adulthood as a function of level of information, input modality, and delay interval. *Journal of Gerontology, 37*, 358-364.

Ericsson, K.A. (1985). Memory skill. *Canadian Journal of Psychology, 39*, 188-231.

Gould, O.N., Trevithick, L., & Dixon, R.A. (1991). Adult age differences in elaborations produced during prose recall. *Psychology and Aging, 6*, 93-99.

Hartley, A.A. (1989). The cognitive ecology of problem solving. In L.W. Poon, D.C. Rubin, & B.A. Wilson (Eds.), *Everyday cognition in adulthood and late life*. New York: Cambridge University Press.

Hartley, J.T. (1986). Reader and text variables as determinants of discourse memory in adulthood. *Psychology and Aging, 1*, 150-158.

Hoyer, W.J. (1985). Aging and the development of expert cognition. In T.M. Schlecter & M.P. Toglia (Eds.), *New directions in cognitive science*. Norwood, NJ: Ablex.

Hultsch, D.F., & Dixon, R.A. (1983). The role of pre-experimental knowledge in text processing in adulthood. *Experimental Aging Research, 9*, 17-22.

Hultsch, D.F., & Dixon, R.A. (1984). Memory for text materials in adulthood. In P.B. Baltes & O.G. Brim, Jr. (Eds.), *Life-span developmental psychology* (Vol. 6). New York: Academic Press.

Hultsch, D.F., & Dixon, R.A. (1990). Learning and memory in aging. In J.E. Birren & K.W. Schaie (Eds.), *Handbook of the psychology of aging* (3rd ed.). San Diego: Academic Press.

Hultsch, D.F., Hertzog, C., & Dixon, R.A. (1984). Text recall in adulthood: The role of intellectual abilities. *Developmental Psychology, 20*, 1193-1209.

Hunt, E., & Love, T. (1982). The second mnemonist. In U. Neisser (Ed.), *Memory observed: Remembering in natural contexts*. San Francisco: W.H. Freeman.

Intons-Peterson, M.J., & Smyth, M.M. (1987). The anatomy of repertory memory. *Journal of Experimental Psychology: Learning, Memory, and Cognition, 13*, 450-500.

Jennings, J.R., Nebes, R.D., & Yovetich, N.A. (1990). Aging increases the energetic demands of episodic memory: A cardiovascular analysis. *Journal of Experimental Psychology: General, 119*, 77-91.

Kintsch, W. (1974). *The representation of meaning in memory*. Hillsdale, NJ: Erlbaum.

Labouvie-Vief, G. (1982). Dynamic development and mature autonomy: A theoretical prologue. *Human Development, 25*, 161-191.

Labouvie-Vief, G. (1985). Intelligence and cognition. In J.E. Birren & K.W. Schaie (Eds.), *Handbook of the psychology of aging* (2nd ed.). New York: Van Nostrand Reinhold.

Labouvie-Vief, G. (1990). Wisdom as integrated thought: Historical and developmental perspectives. In R.J. Sternberg (Ed.), *Wisdom: Its nature, origins, and development*. Cambridge: Cambridge University Press.

Labouvie-Vief, G. (in press). Modes of knowledge and the organization of development. In M.L. Commons, C. Armon, F.A. Richards, & J. Sinnott (Eds.), *Beyond formal operations: 2. The development of adolescent and adult thinking and perception.* New York: Praeger.

Labouvie-Vief, G., & Schell, D.A. (1982). Learning and memory in later life. In B.B. Wolman (Ed.), *Handbook of developmental psychology.* Englewood Cliffs, NJ: Prentice-Hall.

Labouvie-Vief, G., Schell, D.A., & Weaverdyck, S.E. (1980, November). *Recall deficit in the aged: A fable recalled.* Paper presented at the annual meeting of the Gerontological Society of America, San Diego, CA.

Light, L.L., & Anderson, P.A. (1983). Memory for scripts in young and older adults. *Memory & Cognition, 11,* 435-444.

Meyer, B.J.F., & Rice, G.E. (1983). Learning and memory from text across the adult life span. In J. Fine & R.O. Freedle (Eds.), *Developmental studies in discourse.* Norwood, NJ: Ablex.

Petros, T.V., Tabor, L., Cooney, T., & Chabor, R.J. (1983). Adult age differences in sensitivity to semantic structure of prose. *Developmental Psychology, 19,* 907-914.

Rohwer, W.D., Jr., (1976). An introduction to research on individual and developmental differences in learning. In W.K. Estes (Ed.), *Handbook of learning and cognitive processes* (Vol. 3). Hillsdale, NJ: Erlbaum.

Rubin, D.C. (1977). Very long-term memory for prose and verse. *Journal of Verbal Learning and Verbal Behavior, 16,* 611-621.

Salthouse, T.A. (1982). *Adult cognition: An experimental psychology of human aging.* New York: Springer-Verlag.

Salthouse, T.A. (1984). Effects of age and skill in typing. *Journal of Experimental Psychology: General, 113,* 345-371.

Salthouse, T.A. (1987a). Age, experience, and compensation. In C. Schooler & K.W. Schaie (Eds.), *Cognitive functioning and social structure over the life course.* Norwood, NJ: Ablex.

Salthouse, T.A. (1987b). The role of experience in cognitive aging. In K.W. Schaie (Ed.), *Annual review of gerontology and geriatrics* (Vol. 7). New York: Springer.

Salthouse, T.A. (1990). Cognitive competence and expertise in aging. In J.E. Birren & K.W. Schaie (Eds.), *Handbook of the psychology of aging* (3rd ed.). San Diego: Academic Press.

Stanovich, K.E. (1980). Toward an interactive-compensatory model of individual differences in the development of reading fluency. *Reading Research Quarterly, 16,* 32-71.

Stanovich, K.E. (1984). The interactive-compensatory model of reading: A confluence of developmental, experimental, and educational psychology. *Remedial and Special Education, 5,* 11-19.

Stanovich, K.E., & West, R.F. (1983). On priming by sentence context. *Journal of Experimental Psychology: General, 112,* 1-36.

Stratton, G.M. (1982). The mnemonic feat of the "Shass Pollak." In U. Neisser (Ed.), *Memory observed: Remembering in natural contexts.* San Francisco: W.H. Freeman.

Wilding, J., & Valentine, E. (1985). One man's memory for prose, faces and names. *British Journal of Psychology, 76,* 215-219.

Yates, F.A. (1966). *The art of memory.* London: Routledge & Kegan Paul.

Zelinski, E.M., & Gilewski, M.J. (1988). Memory for prose and aging: A meta-analysis. In M.L. Howe & C.J. Brainerd (Eds.), *Cognitive development in adulthood: Progress in cognitive development research.* New York: Springer-Verlag.

Zelinski, E.M., Light, L.L., & Gilewski, M.J. (1984). Adult age differences in memory for prose: The question of sensitivity to passage structure. *Developmental Psychology, 20,* 1181-1192.

10
"Seductive Details" and Adults' Learning from Text

Ruth Garner

Imagine that you have been asked to read a three-paragraph text on the topic of differences among insects. The information in this text has already been rated by another group of adult readers for importance and interest. Raters have reported that generalizations about insect differences are very important, but not at all interesting. On the other hand, they have reported that novel, active, concrete, personally involving details about such things as clicking beetles and buzzing flies are very interesting, but not at all important. Given that importance and interest appear to diverge, what information are you likely to recall?

Our initial study of what we have come to call "seductive details" (Garner, Gillingham, & White, 1989) was designed to answer that question. In this chapter, I present that study and subsequent work on adults' interest and learning from text.

Clicking Beetles, Buzzing Flies, and Mangled Arms

As I have said, in an initial experiment on seductive details, we asked adults to read a three-paragraph text about differences among insects (Garner et al., 1989). One of the paragraphs follows:

> Some insects live alone, and some live in large families. Wasps that live alone are called solitary wasps. A Mud Dauber Wasp is a solitary wasp. Click Beetles live alone. When a Click Beetle is on its back, it flips itself into the air and lands right side up while it makes a clicking noise. Ants live in large families.

It is fairly obvious why raters found the first sentence to be important, but uninteresting, and why they found the flipping and clicking sentence (a seductive detail) to be just the opposite: interesting, but unimportant. Note that the flipping and clicking information is actually irrelevant in a paragraph about insects' living patterns.

Half of the adults in our sample read the entire text with seductive details; half read it without. Recall of important information differed dramatically by condition. Whereas adults who read the text without seductive details recalled an average of 93% of the important generalizations about insect differences, adults who read the text with seductive details recalled an average of only 43%. In this latter group, readers recalled a combination of important and interesting information, and in no case did a reader recall all important generalizations, though this occurred frequently in the no-detail group.

The finding that adult readers' attention is apparently diverted from important generalizations to seductive details is reliable. Wade and Adams (1990) asked different readers to read a different text with much the same result.

In Wade and Adams' (1990) study, nonparticipant adults once again rated a text for importance and interest, this time a biography about Horatio Nelson's naval career. Again, those ratings diverged. A sentence such as, "Nelson first distinguished himself by blockading Toulon, a port city on the coast of France, and capturing Corsica" was rated as high importance/low interest. On the other hand, sentences such as "During the battle, Nelson's right arm was badly mangled up to the elbow" and "She fell in love with the battered, one-eyed, one-armed naval hero and became his mistress" were rated as high interest/low importance. Note that Nelson's victories are relevant in a text about his naval career, but mangled arm and love affair information is not. However, these latter topics are examples of what—with death, sex, danger, and destruction—have been called "absolutely interesting things" (Schank, 1979, p. 280).

A second group of adults, assessed to be reading at two ability levels, then read the Nelson text. Interest was a much better predictor than importance of what information would be recalled. In fact, the category of information best recalled was high interest/low importance (i.e., seductive details). All students, regardless of ability, remembered more interesting than uninteresting information.

Astrophysics, Terminal Illness, and a Wager

After we had determined that interest is powerfully associated with learning from text, we wanted to refine our understanding of the seductive detail phenomenon. We set out to examine effects of general interestingness of text and placement of seductive details (Garner, Alexander, Gillingham, Kulikowich, & Brown, 1991).

We speculated that highly interesting detail may be interesting simply by virtue of its "standing out" in generally uninteresting text. Earlier work done by Hidi and her colleagues (e.g., Hidi, Baird, & Hildyard, 1982) had suggested to us that whereas narratives in school textbooks were usually rated as having a number of interesting ideas, expositions in school textbooks (similar to the science texts we were using) were usually rated as having very few interesting ideas. We wanted to investigate the seductive detail effect for texts at different levels of general interest.

We also thought that readers might be less vulnerable to the seductive detail effect (i.e., they might actually recall a number of important generalizations) for texts that isolated interesting details as informational asides, rather than presenting them embedded in paragraphs containing the important generalizations. The use of asides might signal a distinction in importance of information (Hare, Rabinowitz, & Schieble, 1989; van Dijk & Kintsch, 1983). Signaling has come to be considered essential for readers who encounter difficulty in constructing generalized meaning from generalizations, relevant detail, and irrelevant detail in text (E. Kintsch, 1990).

We wrote a new text, a longer one, on the topic of Stephen Hawking, the noted physicist, and his scientific work. The text was based on an article that had appeared in *Newsweek* (Adler, Lubenow, & Malone, 1988). We prepared four versions, employing a full factorial design to test for separate and combined effects of general interestingness and placement of seductive details.

To manipulate general interestingness for this text, we began two versions of the Hawking piece with a paragraph intended to be personally involving on a universally interesting theme (death at an early age),and we deleted this introductory paragraph from the other two versions. The introductory paragraph was as follows:

> Stephen Hawking is a theoretical physicist who holds Newton's chair at Cambridge University. Though it is difficult to assess the career of a still young and still active scientist, Hawking is widely regarded as the most brilliant theoretical physicist since Einstein. Stephen Hawking is dying. Unable to speak, he is paralyzed by a progressive, incurable disease, amyotrophic lateral sclerosis, better known as Lou Gehrig's Disease. It is not clear whether or not, within the time left to him, Hawking will be able to unlock the essential secrets of the universe. He works from morning to night on Grand Unification Theory.

The content for most of the rest of the text was Hawking's scientific work, which raters assessed as high importance/low interest: his attempts to link theories of relativity and quantum mechanics, his ideas about black holes, his Oxford paper on grand unification theory. We speculated that presenting information about the scientist before information about his science might make the text more interesting overall (and, thus, might make seductive details less prominent). Raters confirmed that this first paragraph was personally involving; they described it as "fascinating," "intriguing," and "sad."

To manipulate placement of seductive details, we presented irrelevant information rated as high interest/low importance (a wager Hawking has with Kip Thorne at Cal Tech, involving the possibility of winning a subscription to *Private Eye*) in a separate midtext paragraph in two versions, and we embedded the same information in a paragraph about black holes in the other two versions. As I have said, we speculated that seductive details presented as asides might divert less attention from scientific generalizations than the same details combined with generalizations.

Once again, across conditions, interest predicted what information would be recalled. Despite only "really important information" being elicited in unstructured recall, adult readers recalled an average of only 44% of the generalizations rated important, whereas they recalled nearly as much (an average of 35%) of the unimportant, unelicited, but highly interesting wager information. In structured recall, all adults answered a question about the wager correctly; however, the adults provided an average of only 52% correct responses to three questions eliciting information rated important. Placement of seductive details made no difference whatsoever, but general interestingness of text did produce one effect: Students who read generally interesting text were more successful than students who did not in providing important generalizations in unstructured recall.

Do Importance and Interest Ever Converge?

To this point in the chapter, I have presented recall patterns for both boring, important generalizations and extremely interesting, irrelevant details. The patterns are clear: Even when only the former are elicited, it is the latter that are recalled. What about information that is both important and interesting, or at least somewhat so?

The study just discussed (Garner et al., 1991) provides some insight here. As I mentioned, raters in the study had rated generalizations about Hawking's scientific work as high importance/low interest. Specifically, they had identified the following ideas as fitting this description: (a) Grand Unification Theory links theories of relativity and quantum mechanics, (b) Stephen Hawking is working on Grand Unification Theory, and (c) the goal of Grand Unification Theory is to explain the origins of the universe. As I also mentioned, they had rated irrelevant details about the wager Hawking has with Thorne as high interest/low importance.

What I have not mentioned so far is that raters created an additional category for the Hawking text: moderate importance/moderate interest. Rated as fitting this description was information about black holes. This information could then be characterized as somewhat interesting detail, though not as seductive detail (i.e., it supported important scientific generalizations and was not irrelevant to the rest of the text).

Recall of this information was very high. In 96% of the adult readers' unstructured recall protocols, this information appeared. Furthermore, 100% of the adults answered a question about black holes correctly. That is, recall of black hole information, for both unstructured and structured measures, exceeded recall of generalizations rated important (44% and 52%, for unstructured and structured recall, respectively).

We interpret these results—that ideas rated as high interest/low importance (the wager) and as moderate interest/moderate importance (black holes) were frequently recalled, whereas ideas rated as low interest/high importance (scientific generalizations about Grand Unification Theory) were less frequently recalled—to mean that interest is a better predictor of recall than importance, and that this pattern holds whether or not interesting ideas support important ideas in text.

The association between interesting detail and recall seems especially powerful when one remembers that it holds wherever interesting details are placed, for short texts and for long, for science expositions and for biography, across reader ability groups, and with a variety of recall measures. Interest is a critical variable in adults' learning from text, and, as Wade and Adams (1990) pointed out, it can no longer be neglected in research on learning from text. It has been our contention recently that reader interest and reader beliefs may be as important to our understanding of text comprehension as the more extensively investigated factors of reader knowledge and reader strategies (Garner & Alexander, 1991).

I am also persuaded by Wade and Adams' (1990) argument that the seductive detail effect probably holds for media other than text. In a very informal assessment of a few lectures delivered in university classrooms, I have been surprised by the high proportion of irrelevant detail to relevant detail and important generalizations. Perhaps this imbalance accounts in part for the complaint often voiced by students: "But, I didn't know that was important to learn!" Perhaps teacher talk at elementary, secondary, and college level, should be examined for important information versus seductive detail. Low knowledge students, for whom few concepts and few associations on a topic exist (Anderson, 1984; Voss, 1984), may be particularly vulnerable to ineffective sorting out of important and unimportant information in classrooms where seductive details are presented.

What About Reader Knowledge and Interest?

In an important paper published in 1980, W. Kintsch argued that, everything else being equal, interest in any given text is determined by how much a reader knows about the topic of the text. Kintsch suggested that interest is low with little knowledge, higher with more knowledge, and low again when the reader's knowledge reaches a point where little new information can be acquired from the text.

Think about the Hawking text that we have been discussing. If Kintsch (1980) is correct, adults who have never studied atoms, gravity, or the cosmos would have no way to relate text information to existing knowledge structures and would be mostly uninterested in the text. Adults with some knowledge of the origins of the universe and of Hawking's work would be interested in reading the piece. However, experts in astrophysics who have read Hawking's book, *A Brief History of Time* (1988), would be mostly uninterested, for there would be little they could learn from reading the text.

In our most recent investigation of interest and recall in adult readers (Garner & Gillingham, 1991), we set out to investigate Kintsch's (1980) claim. We wanted to know more about associations among knowledge, interest, and recall in adult readers.

We shortened our Hawking text slightly and partitioned the information in such a way that, though repeated references to Hawking and his scientific work helped the text "hang together" (Halliday & Hasan, 1976), only paragraph 1 presented information about Hawking's struggle with Lou Gehrig's Disease, only paragraph 2 presented information about the specifics of Grand Unification Theory, only paragraph 3 discussed black holes, and only paragraph 5 discussed current theories about origins of the universe.

Paragraph 4 appeared in half of the texts presented to adult readers; for the other half, this paragraph was deleted. This paragraph presented the seductive detail information about Hawking's wager with Thorne. Though our primary focus in this study was association among knowledge, interest, and recall in adult readers, we decided to include a seductive detail manipulation one more time.

Knowledge was assessed in advance of reading, interest was assessed during reading, and recall was assessed after reading. One week before reading of the text, we administered a pretest of five questions, each one probing knowledge of a specific paragraph subtopic. Interest was determined by asking readers to rate the information in each paragraph as high, moderate, or low interest just after completing the paragraph. Recall, just as in the previous study, was elicited in an unstructured measure ("recall just the really important information that you read about Stephen Hawking") and a structured measure (short answer responses to five questions, each eliciting information from a separate paragraph of text).

One of the most intriguing findings in this study was that the seductive detail effect was muted. Recall was quite high for unstructured recall (72%) and higher still for structured recall (82%). However, there was—for the first time in this line of inquiry—no difference in recall of information rated important by condition (i.e., reading seductive details vs. not reading them). It seems that attention was not diverted from important generalizations to seductive details. For whatever reason, there was an absence of high interest among these adult readers in information about Hawking's wager with Thorne.

Another intriguing finding was high association among four of five sets of variables: knowledge and interest, knowledge and unstructured recall, interest and unstructured recall, and interest and structured recall. Though we were a bit surprised to find a lack of association between knowledge and structured recall, we attributed this result to high overall structured recall performance and the resulting restriction of range.

Our interest in the association between knowledge and interest was, of course, what had prompted design of the study; we examined that association a bit more. The data provided compelling support for Kintsch's (1980) position. We found that 60% of the low knowledge readers rated paragraph information as low interest, whereas 40% of them rated it as high interest. In stark contrast, only 5% of the moderate knowledge readers rated paragraph information as low interest, whereas 95% of them rated it as high interest. Finally, 60% of the high knowledge readers rated paragraph information as low interest, whereas 40% of them rated it as high interest. Just as Kintsch (1980) had suggested, readers knowing *almost nothing* or *almost everything* were more uninterested than interested in the Hawking text; however, readers knowing *something* were more interested than uninterested.

This result, pending replication, seems to have educational significance (i.e., it seems to offer information about when readers are most likely to learn from text). I turn now to this and other implications arising from this line of inquiry.

"Good" Interesting Text and Background Knowledge

I am compelled by the data emerging from a number of studies discussed here to suggest that "good" interesting (and informative) text engages readers, but does not distract them. It provokes momentary pleasure and heightened attention without providing irrelevant information that diverts attention from the main topic of the text. It is interesting without being seductive.

It was both encouraging and discouraging to examine how adult readers responded to black hole information in the early Hawking study (Garner et al., 1991). It was encouraging to see that scientific information was perceived by readers as at least moderately interesting (and then was recalled with high frequency). It was discouraging to note that provision of this supporting material was insufficient to cause readers to recall the generalizations that the black hole information supported (i.e., the apparently boring generalizations about Grand Unification Theory).

Hidi and Baird (1988) found much the same result for children. Salient descriptions of individual inventors provided in their experimental text were well recalled, but important generalizations about general characteristics of inventors and scientific aspects of inventions were not. A good example of differential recall is the following: Whereas a description of Spenser, who invented the thermostat, working in a lumber camp and opening a furnace door to see if a fire needed more wood was recalled by 100% of a sixth-grade sample in immediate recall and by 71% of the sixth graders a week later, the generalization that the function of a thermostat is to measure temperature in houses was recalled by only 24% of the sixth graders on both occasions.

It seems that counting on interesting supporting detail to direct interest (and thus recall) to important, but less interesting, generalizations is unwise. Instead, writers need to make the generalizations themselves more interesting. Graves et al. (1991) suggested that information in text can be interesting without being irrelevant (and, therefore, seductive). Absolutely interesting topics, such as those identified by Schank (1979) are one possible component of this sort of interest. Other components of interesting text identified by Graves and his colleagues (1991) were: dramatic verbs, character identification, and concrete detail (all presenting or supporting important ideas in the text).

What we discovered about reader knowledge in the later Hawking study (Garner & Gillingham, 1991) may also, as I suggested earlier, be significant in this discussion of good interesting text. Surely it is the case that low knowledge readers approaching informative texts—which are full of important generalizations to be read, stored, and retrieved—are likely to be uninterested. A more effective learning situation would ensure that these readers would receive some background information from instructors or textbook authors prior to reading. Then, newly transformed from low knowledge to moderate knowledge readers, they might be more interested in important information encountered in text. Being more interested, they might recall more information. This scenario, potentially important for learning from text in both children and adults, merits empirical scrutiny.

References

Adler, J., Lubenow, G.C., & Malone, M. (1988, June). Reading God's mind. *Newsweek*, pp. 56-59.

Anderson, R.C. (1984). Some reflections on the acquisition of knowledge. *Educational Researcher, 13*, 5-10.

Garner, R., & Alexander, P.A. (1991, April). *Skill, will, and thrill: Factors in adults' text comprehension.* Paper presented at the meeting of the American Educational Research Association, Chicago, IL.

Garner, R., Alexander, P.A., Gillingham, M.G., Kulikowich, J.M., & Brown, R. (1991). Interest and learning from text. *American Educational Research Journal, 28*, 643-659.

Garner, R., & Gillingham, M.G. (1991). Topic knowledge, cognitive interest, and text recall: A microanalysis. *Journal of Experimental Education, 59*, 310-319.

Garner, R., Gillingham, M.G., & White, C.S. (1989). Effects of "seductive details" on macroprocessing and microprocessing in adults and children. *Cognition and Instruction, 6*, 41-57.

Graves, M.F., Prenn, M.C., Earle, J., Thompson, M., Johnson, V., & Slater, W.H. (1991). Improving instructional text: Some lessons learned. *Reading Research Quarterly, 26*, 110-122.

Halliday, M.A.K., & Hasan, R. (1976). *Cohesion in English.* New York: Longman.

Hare, V.C., Rabinowitz, M., & Schieble, K.M. (1989). Text effects on main idea comprehension. *Reading Research Quarterly, 24*, 72-88.

Hawking, S.W. (1988). *A brief history of time.* Toronto: Bantam.

Hidi, S., & Baird, W. (1988). Strategies for increasing text-based interest and students' recall of expository texts. *Reading Research Quarterly, 23*, 465-483.

Hidi, S., Baird, W., & Hildyard, A. (1982). That's important but is it interesting? Two factors in text processing. In A. Flammer & W. Kintsch (Eds.), *Discourse processing* (pp. 63-75). Amsterdam: North Holland.

Kintsch, E. (1990). Macroprocesses and microprocesses in the development of summarization skill. *Cognition and Instruction, 7*, 161-195.

Kintsch, W. (1980). Learning from text, levels of comprehension, or: Why anyone would read a story anyway. *Poetics, 9*, 87-98.

Schank, R.C. (1979). Interestingness: Controlling inferences. *Artificial Intelligence, 12*, 273-297.

van Dijk, T.A., & Kintsch, W. (1983). *Strategies of discourse comprehension.* New York: Academic.

Voss, J.F. (1984). On learning and learning from text. In H. Mandl, N.L. Stein, & T. Trabasso (Eds.), *Learning and comprehension of text* (pp. 193-212). Hillsdale, NJ: Erlbaum.

Wade, S.E., & Adams, R.B. (1990). Effects of importance and interest on recall of biographical text. *Journal of Reading Behavior, 22*, 331-353.

11
Instruction and Remediation in Reading Among Adult Illiterates

Richard D. Robinson

The establishment of a literate society is one that has been a dominant concern of not only educators but also politicians from the earliest days of our country. Thomas Jefferson, writing in a letter to James Madison in 1787, noted,

> Above all things, I hope the education of the common people will be attended to; convinced that on their good senses we may rely with the most security for the preservation of a due degree of liberty.

This emphasis on the importance of universal literacy has continued through our history to the present day. President Reagan, speaking on International Literacy Day (September 7, 1983), underscored the scope of the problem when he said,

> ...it will take a unified effort by all our people to achieve our goal: the elimination of adult functional illiteracy in the United States.

Numerous accounts in the popular press and trade books such as Jonathan Kozol's recent book, *Illiterate America* (1986), and First Lady Barbara Bush's personal literacy advocacy campaign, have only underscored this continuing concern about the problem of adult illiteracy.

Not only is there an awareness of the problem of adult illiteracy, there is also a growing concern about whether there are the resources and a true national incentive to correct the present situation. Despite the fact that this country has had a long tradition of compulsory education, with school attendance being one of the highest in the world, there still remains the seemingly persistent problem of the illiterate adult in our society. This problem remains in the face of numerous program efforts to eradicate illiteracy with major commitments of financial resources at both the national and local levels.

At the center of this problem has been the fact that a comprehensive definition of what is meant by the term illiteracy has proven to be an illusive and almost undefinable concept. Because there has been virtually no consensus on what the term literacy means, programs designed to meet the needs of the adult illiterate have tended to be fragmented and with little purpose or content. In addition, because of this uncertainty as to what constitutes illiteracy, student placement was often arbitrarily based on inappropriate or limited assessment information. Thus, students who have participated in many literacy programs find they have had different reasons for their involvement from those goals and objectives originally established for the programs.

In this chapter a definition of literacy will be discussed as well as the development of programs to meet the needs of the adult illiterate. Additional material will be presented on assessing adults with language disabilities and what is currently known and what is being done about illiteracy in this country.

Definition of Literacy

Even the most cursory review of the myriad writings in the field of literacy reveals the problems associated with an adequate definition. Vagueness and ambiguity prevail, which makes comparison between the results of studies and reports virtually meaningless. Where at one time the literate person was described in the most narrow of terms, such as grade level completed or the ability to sign one's name, this is no longer the case. The literate person is not simply the one who has attained a certain level of proficiency in language ability but is also able to effectively be a participant in the social environment in which they live.

Langer (1986 a, 1986b) notes that literacy needs to be thought of in a broader context than simply the ability to read and write. For a definition of literacy to be meaningful, it must be in relation to the unique requirements of a specific society. What would be considered adequate language proficiency in one cultural setting may, in another, be less than what is needed to be successful. Thus, one definition of literacy would be the ability to think and reason in a particular society in relation to the individual requirements of that society.

In 1985 the National Assessment of Educational Progress (NAEP) completed a landmark study of illiteracy among America's young people. This critical study of approximately 3600 adults between the ages of 21 and 25 covered a wide range of literacy tasks typically found at work, at school, and at home. The NAEP based their definition of literacy on the work of a number of experts in the field and represents probably the most current thinking in the area. Their discussion led to this definition of literacy:

> Using printed and written information to function in society, to achieve one's goals, and to develop one's knowledge and potential (Kirsch, 1986, xiii).

This is an important definition of literacy in several respects. It first moves beyond the identification of a specific set of standards as a measure of literacy success. Rather than being able to sign one's name, or having passed a given grade level, this definition places the emphasis on performance in relation to the requirements of the society in which it occurs. Second, it reflects the current thinking of reading and language researchers who consider meaningful literacy activities as those directly related to a personal understanding of what is encountered on the printed page. Beginning with the work of Gray (1969) and extending through four national assessments in reading (e.g., *Becoming a Nation of Readers*, 1985; *The Reading Report Card*, 1985), the concept of literacy, as reflected in this definition, is now most heavily weighted according to the individual's performance in relation to one's need to use literacy skills in a particular society (Duffy & Roehler, 1986; Mason & Au, 1986; Robinson & Good, 1987).

Recent discussion concerning a definition of literacy has expanded into other areas including science (Shipman, 1986), media technology and reading (Asheim, 1987), and cultural literacy (Edwards, 1984; Ransom, 1987; Shanker, 1987). Of particular note in defining cultural literacy has been the work of Kirsch (1984, 1985, 1986). His recent book, *Cultural Literacy: What Every American Needs to Know* (1987), has directed national attention to determining what degree of knowledge constitutes the literate person in our society. According to Kirsch (1984), the person who is culturally literate is the individual who has acquired extensive knowledge about the literature and history of Western civilization. He further argues that this information is critical because writers, speakers, and teachers assume their audiences all have this background knowledge. Although many would agree that cultural literacy is an important part of a person's background knowledge, some do disagree with the idea that simply learning isolated facts constitutes a literate individual (O'Hanian, 1987; Warnock, 1985, 1986).

With these varying definitions of literacy, there is little certainty about establishing the full extent of illiteracy in this country. Figures range from less than a million to over 100 million persons who would be considered illiterate. Probably the most accurate figures that are currently available are those from the NAEP study (Kirsch, 1986), which indicate that approximately "one-third of all Americans over age 18 lack the reading, writing, comprehension, and math skills necessary to function effectively in our society" (*Project Literacy Newsletter*, 1987).

The NAEP study used three distinct literacy skills in their measurement of literacy. They included:

1. *prose literacy*—the knowledge and skills needed to understand and use information from texts that include editorials, news stories, poems, and the like. Three qualitatively different aspects of reading comprehension were identified as important for successful performance on the prose scale— matching information from a question to identical or corresponding information in text, producing or interpreting text information, and generating a theme or organizing principle from text. Each of these aspects contributes to a broad range of difficulty, with significant overlap in difficulty among the three.

2. *document literacy*—the knowledge and skills required to locate and use information contained in job applications or payroll forms, bus schedules, maps, tables, indexes, and so forth. Difficulty of the tasks on the document scale was associated with increases in the number of features or categories

of information the reader has to locate and the number of categories of information in the document that can serve as distractors (or plausible right answers), as the information needed to answer a question has less obvious identity with the information stated in the document.

3. *quantitative literacy*—the knowledge and skills needed to apply arithmetic operations, either singly or sequentially, that are embedded in printed materials, such as in balancing a checkbook, figuring out a tip, completing an order form, or determining the amount of interest from a loan advertisement. Task difficulty is associated with the particular operation required (addition, subtraction, multiplication, and division), the number of operations needed, and the extent to which the numerical information is embedded in print (Kirsch & Jungeblat, 1986, p. 4).

The findings of this study represent the most current information available on the literacy skills of America's youth, and because of their importance, they are quoted below:

Findings

1. The literacy problem identified for the nation's young adults can be characterized in two ways: Although the overwhelming majority of young adults adequately perform tasks at the lower levels on each of the three scales, sizable numbers appear unable to do well on tasks of moderate complexity. Only a relatively small percentage of this group is estimated to perform at levels typified by the more complex and challenging tasks.

2. Inevitably, smaller percentages of young adults are found to perform at increasing levels of proficiency on each of the scales. The fact that fewer and fewer individuals attain these moderate and high levels of proficiency is most pronounced for young adults who terminate their education early and for minority group members.

3. Black young adults, on average, perform significantly below white young adults—by almost a full standard deviation. Hispanic young adults, on average, perform about midway between their black and white peers. These differences appear at each level of education reported.

4. Home support variables (such as parents' education and access to literacy materials) were found to be significantly related to the type and amount of education and to the literacy practices reported by young adults. These, in turn, help to explain differences in literacy skill levels.

5. On average, young adults perform significantly better on the NAEP reading scale than do in-school 17-year-olds. This finding suggests that further education and participation in society contribute to the improvement of reading skills represented by that scale.

6. Only about 2% of this young adult population were estimated to have such limited literacy skills that it was judged that the simulation tasks would unduly frustrate or embarrass them. Roughly 1%, or about half, of this group reported being unable to speak English.

7. The non-English-speaking one percent, instead of attempting the simulation tasks, responded to a set of oral-language tasks. The comparatively low performance indicates that this group (about 225,000 people) may have a language problem that extends beyond processing printed information (Kirsch & Jungeblat, 1986, p. 4).

These conclusions of the NAEP study have important implications for future research, program planning, and policy decisions in adult literacy and will be discussed in more depth in the final section of this paper on the current status of adult literacy in this country.

Adult Literacy Programs

Historically, the programs designed to teach the adult illiterate have been considered adjunct activities for the public school system. The general consensus has always been that the nation's schools were in the primary business of training children and youth and that instruction for any other population, such as the adult illiterate, was only tangentially related to their primary purpose for existence. The result of this emphasis has been the placing of adult instruction, particularly that dealing with the adult illiterate in the least desirable category in a school's priorities. Harman (1984) summarized this attitude by stating:

> Overwhelmingly, educational energies have been devoted to the construction, development, and enhancement of primary, secondary, and tertiary institutions, not to building frameworks for adult education outside the normative school system. The types of programs which are necessary for dealing with adult functional literacy fall, then, within the least developed realm of educational practice. Practically, this situation is manifest in restricted and restrictive budgets, lack of adequate infrastructure, an insufficient properly trained and organized instructional corps, a deep chasm in academic attention both in instruction and research, and in a lamentable lack of professionalism. Despite numerous starts and a wide range of activity, the field of adult education is in many ways still in an embryonic stage. (p. 26)

Throughout the history of adult literacy programs, a number of assessment procedures have been developed to measure the degree of success of these efforts. These have ranged from the simple totaling of the numbers of participants in a program through the use of well developed guidelines for internal evaluation. It is the latter procedure that has seemed to have the most effective results particularly in relation to the meaningful evaluation of an adult literacy program.

Evaluation of the Adult Illiterate

In many adult literacy programs, testing procedures are a significant aspect of the total curriculum. Students are screened at the beginning of their instruction using a wide array of both formal and informal tests. As they progress through their

educational programs, other measures of academic achievement are then administered at various times. Curriculum decisions related to teaching procedures, materials to be used, and student advancement are frequently made strictly on the basis
of these test results.

Farr and Carey (1986) note that a model of assessment, as described previously,
has major limitations. To simply use tests to describe how well a student may be
doing or how far they have progressed since the last test, removed from the social
context of the reasons for the assessment, is a serious misuse of testing. This
situation is particularly true for those who work with the adult illiterate.

Although test results can and do indicate academic achievement over a span of
time they do not tell how this progress relates to the reasons an adult may be in a
particular program. Is the student in class only to be able to read the most elementary
of material such as a cookbook or a telephone directory, or are they there to
complete a high school diploma or finish a computer course? Relevant answers to
these and other questions about each student's purpose for their education are not
answered by the use of assessment instruments.

Three criteria are suggested by Farr and Carey (1986) in determining whether a
particular test should be used for gathering information. They include the following:

1. Will this test provide the information that is really needed? That is, does
    the test sample from the domain of behaviors of pertinent interest, and does
    the test provide a realistic context?
2. Does the test provide a convenient and nonthreatening means of collecting
    the needed information?
3. Does the sample of behaviors included on the test cover enough different
    situations to insure that the results will be both valid and reliable? (p. 3).

Each of these points has importance for those who plan and administer evaluation procedures with the adult illiterate. Far too often tests are given that have very
little relevance for the adult who has problems with language, particularly reading.
Difficulties include reading tests that were designed and written for children and
contain illustrations and content that are clearly inappropriate for the adult learner
(Bowern & Zintz, 1977; Newman, 1980; Otto & Ford, 1967). Other tests by their
very nature may prove to be threatening to adults who are self-conscious about their
current literacy abilities. Tests that require students to continue until they reach the
failure level or tests that are based on verbal responses in a group situation are
typical examples of this problem.

In attempting to deal with the many inherent difficulties in adult assessment,
there has been increased use of various forms of informal tests with the adult
illiterate. The word *informal* means without prescribed rules and regulations. In
contrast to standardized tests, informal approaches to measuring reading ability
adhere less strictly to rigid testing procedures. For informal testing to be successful,
however, teachers must have the right attitudes towards their students, as well as
appropriate beliefs about their roles as instructional leaders.

Consider the following questions carefully:

Am I willing to listen to my adult students and respect their feelings and attitudes about past reading experiences?

Does my relationship with adult students allow them to be open and candid about their ideas related to reading?

Does my conception of my role as a reading instructor include the belief that adult students and teachers can work together cooperatively?

Do I provide students with opportunities for as wide a use of literacy as possible and am I aware of how each individual is progressing in the various uses of reading? (Robinson & Good, 1987, p. 187)

These are important questions that instructors working at all levels must ask themselves when working with students who are developing their literacy skills.

Recent work in the area of miscue analysis, particularly related to the observation of readers, has importance for the teaching of reading to the adult illiterate. Note the following factors that instructors need to be aware of when observing or evaluating a reader:

Concepts About Print and Print Settings
1. To what extent does the adult reader attend to print? For example, does the reader focus on the print as someone else is reading?
2. Does the reader expect the print to make sense and have personal meaning? For example, does the student seek out materials that will satisfy his or her need for information about completing tax forms?
3. How does the reader use information from the print setting (i.e., where the print is found, its format, who asked that it be read, why it is being read)?

Use of Background Knowledge
1. How does the adult reader bring background knowledge and linguistic information to the reading situation?
2. How does the adult reader approach text? Is there an effort made to appreciate and live the written experiences by relating the text to his or her own life?
3. How does the adult reader use memory as a reading aid? For example, when asked to read a familiar or self-authored story, does the reader use memory (i.e., familiarity with the material) as a basis for predicting and making inferences?

Use of Strategies
1. How does the adult reader handle the information-giving systems of language? Does the reader use a flexible strategy that encompasses all language cues (e.g., semantic, grammatical, sound/symbol) to construct meaning or does the reader rely on a single cueing system (e.g., symbol/sound)?

2. Does the adult reader proficiently sample, predict, and construct meaning from text?
3. Does the reader monitor his or her reading by asking, "Am I making sense of what I am reading"?
4. Does the reader self-correct when the flow of language and meaning is interrupted?
5. Is there a dialect or first-language influence on the adult student's reading, and how does the reader handle this influence?
6. What strategies does the adult reader use to approach suitable but unfamiliar text?

View of Self as Reader
1. What does the adult student think of himself or herself as a reader?
2. In what circumstances and how often does the adult student make the decision to read?
3. What risks are taken by the adult student as he or she reads?
4. How realistic is the adult student's judgment of his or her knowledge of concepts and discourse forms needed to read various texts (e.g., science of history materials, poems, or drama)?

Other informal measures include interest inventories and incomplete sentences. The following are typical of questions asked from each type:

INTEREST INVENTORY
Name _____ Age _____

1. What do you like to do after work?
2. What do you like to do in the evenings, after dinner?
3. Are you a member of any club?
4. What are your favorite sports?
5. Do you play any sports on an organized team?
6. Do you take any additional lessons (karate, music, dancing)?
7. What is your favorite television show?
8. What is your favorite movie?
9. What books and magazines do you have at home?
10. How often do you visit the library?
11. What is your favorite book?
12. What is your favorite magazine?
13. What famous person do you admire the most?

Following any program of assessment there needs to be careful attention given to organizing an effective program of remediation for the adult illiterate. The following questions should be considered:

1. What is the adult student's reading problem? Could I write a description of the difficulty, noting important aspects of the problem?
2. What kinds of tests and interviews were given to the adult student? Do I understand the content and purposes of the assessment procedures? What do the results of the tests mean, particularly in relation to the current reading program?
3. Who should work with the adult student to correct the reading problem?
4. What other information do I need to know?
   a. How long will the reading remediation take?
   b. Is further assessment needed? (Robinson & Good, 1987, p.198)

INCOMPLETE SENTENCES

Directions: Complete the following sentences to express how you really feel. There are no right answers or wrong answers. Put down what first comes into your mind. Work as quickly as you can.

1. Today I feel _____
2. When I have to read, I _____
3. I get angry when _____
4. My idea of a good time _____
5. I can't understand why _____
6. I feel bad when _____
7. To me, books _____
8. People think I _____
9. I like to read about _____
10. On weekends, I _____
11. I don't know how _____
12. I hope I'll never _____
13. I wish people wouldn't _____
14. I'm afraid _____
15. I am at my best when _____
16. I'd rather read than _____
17. When I read math _____
18. The future looks _____
19. I feel proud when _____
20. I like to read when _____
21. I would like to be _____
22. For me, studying _____
23. I often worry about _____
24. I wish I could _____
25. Reading science _____
26. I look forward to _____
27. I wish someone would help me _____

28.   I'd read more if _____
29.   Special help in reading _____
30.   Every single word is _____
31.   My eyes _____
32.   The last book I read _____
33.   I read better than _____
34.   I would like to read better than _____

(Robinson & Good, 1987, pp. 196, 197)

Effective remediation of a reading problem, whether it be a child's or adult's, is based on well organized instruction (Harris & Sipay, 1985; McCormick, 1987). The following issues need to be considered when planning reading instruction for the adult illiterate:

1.   *Use a variety of materials.* Instructors commonly make the mistake of using a single textbook for remedial work, often the very material a student has previously had difficulty reading. Students need to read a variety of new books, magazines, etcetera that are selected according to reading level and interest.

2.   *Use materials appropriate to an adult student's reading level.* Instructors should select reading material that is appropriately matched to adult students' reading levels. If in doubt, however, it is always better to begin with material that is too easy and use more challenging material later. Introducing material that is too difficult at the beginning of remediation will likely cause students to fail, thus discouraging them from further reading.

3.   *Use interesting materials.* Nothing discourages students, both children and adults who are having difficulty reading, more than material that they find boring. Even before remedial work begins, the instructor needs to find out as much as possible about an adult's experiences and interests and to select relevant reading materials (see interest inventory).

4.   *Improve adult students' self-concepts.* Many adults who have reading problems also have low self-concepts in regards to schooling and academic work, having experienced much failure in school. Self-worth and school performance may be related so closely in students' minds that both must be altered if successful remediation is to occur. The instructor must be able to show the adult student in a realistic manner exactly what the reading problem is and the procedures that will be used to correct it. More importantly, the instructor and student should discuss the student's reading successes and strengths as well. Slow readers need to be shown that even though they may have problems, they are not failures as readers or as persons. One of the best ways to correct low student self-esteem is to make certain that students enjoy high rates of success on remedial work. Adults, too, need to experience success.

5.   *Inform adult students of their progress.* Typically the progress of adults with reading problems may be slow and not always evident to them.

Teachers must make students aware of even small amounts of progress. Keeping previous lessons and comparing them with current work illustrates success to students. Adults who clearly see that they are becoming better readers will be motivated to continue.

6. *Adult students should find in their remediation instruction a desire to continue to improve in reading.* All reading remediation should encourage students to continue to read and to enjoy reading. Anything less indicates a fundamental problem in the reading instruction that needs to be corrected. (Robinson & Good, 1987, p. 199)

Despite the fact that informal assessment has been shown to be a far more effective approach to the testing of the adult illiterate, standardized reading tests will be an important part of adult education programs. The results of these tests will unfortunately be used to make fundamental curriculum decisions for many adults. Guthrie and Lissitz (1985) note the inherent problems with the use of standardized tests in this manner:

Decisions about what to teach, how long to spend on a topic, and whether it has been learned to a level adequate for independent performance by the student are indispensable to a teacher and are probably impossible information to obtain from a standardized test. Consequently, using formal standardized tests as a basis for instructional decisions raises the hazard of ignoring the causes of successful learning, which is the only basis for enhancing it. (p. 28)

Current Status of Adult Literacy in This Country

The problem of adult illiteracy and attempts to eradicate it have been a national concern for many years. A large measure of this situation has simply been the need to identify and describe the current situation as it relates to the adult illiterate. The six major findings of the NAEP study (Kirsch & Jungeblat, 1986) represent the most current and detailed information that is available on the status of adult illiteracy in this country. It is for this reason that the conclusions of this study will be briefly discussed.

1. The findings of this 1985 study clearly indicate that "illiteracy" is not a *major* problem for the population of 21-25-year olds. It is also clear, however, that "literacy" *is* a major problem. (p. xvi)

Obviously this finding is based on the definition of illiteracy that is used. The NAEP study indicated that virtually all of the subjects could sign their names and read material appropriate for a fourth grader—this at one time being the standard for literacy in the military almost half a century ago.

Additional information indicated that the young adults were successful at the skills and strategies that fell at the lower end of the prose, document, and quantitative scales. For example 95% of the subjects were able to succeed at "writing a brief description about a job, locating a fact in a sports article, matching grocery store coupons to a shopping list, entering personal information on a job application, and filling in information on a phone message" (Kirsch, 1985, p. xvii).

The general conclusion that young adults are illiterate, particularly in relation to school-based reading tasks and those associated with reading activities in nonschool contexts, is not supported by the data. More advanced levels of language processing posed increased difficulties for this group (see Number 3 in this discussion).

2. Unless appropriate intervention strategies are developed and implemented to meet the diverse needs of these current young adults as well as to promote higher literacy proficiencies among the younger, school-age populations, there will be a less literate pool of young adults in the next decade from which colleges, universities, industry, and the military will be able to draw to meet their human resource needs. (Kirsch & Jungeblat, 1986)

The results of this study clearly show that, although young adults are able to read successfully using simpler reading tasks, more advanced language processing skills were difficult if not impossible. The pool of young adults is projected to decline in the next decade from 21 million to roughly 17 million. Because of this shrinking labor pool, the problem of illiteracy among these persons will have an increasingly more dramatic effect on the country in terms of economic productivity at the very least.

3. Analyses suggest that, in many instances, literacy tasks require individuals to apply complex information-processing skills and strategies. Some tasks, for example, require the reader to identify needed information, locate that information in complex displays of print, remember it, combine it with additional information, and transfer it onto a form or separate document. It is the difficulties associated with employing these skills that characterize the literacy problem for sizable numbers of the young adult population. Very few young adults are estimated to be "illiterate" in the sense that they are unable to decode print or comprehend simple textual materials. (Kirsch & Jungeblat, 1986)

The results of this study clearly indicate that it is at the higher levels of information-processing that many of the subjects began to have difficulty. Tasks such as summarizing written material, forming a personal opinion about a prose selection, and organizing factual material all proved to be difficult for these young adults. Thus for jobs that require the use of advanced reading skills, many of these subjects would have increasing difficulty in successful job performance. They could be identified as illiterate in these situations.

4. To the extent that the skills identified in this literacy study are important for full participation in our society, the results from this assessment raise questions about whether we should seek better ways to teach the current curriculum or whether we need to reconsider both what is taught and how we teach it. (Kirsch & Jungeblat, 1986)

As noted earlier, many current adult education programs are based on programs and materials developed for elementary students. The concept that the adult illiterate is really only "a tall child" and can benefit from learning experiences more appropriately used for children is obviously false. Although the adult learner may need the most basic instructional materials, such materials must be cast in a form so as to capitalize on the older individual's wide background and personal need for literacy. Such materials must be cast in a form or presented in a way to capitalize on the adult learner's strengths and present capabilities.

> 5. This study reveals that the small percentage of young adults who are among the least literate in America also tend to be lower in performance on oral-language tasks, suggesting a more general problem than simply an inability to use printed information. (Kirsch & Jungeblat, 1986)

Approximately 1% of this sample were unable to respond to even the simplest of the reading tasks. For these subjects, oral-language tasks were substituted for the reading activities. It was found that almost half of this group also had severe problems with the oral-language tasks as well. The results suggest that for a small percentage of the young adult population there is a general overall problem with language, no matter its form or format. Adult educators need to be aware of this type of student and make appropriate modifications in program content to meet these rather unique learning problems.

> 6. Becoming fully literate in a technologically advanced society is a lifelong pursuit, as is sustaining health. Both are complex and depend upon a number of factors. So, just as there is no single action or step that, if taken, will insure the physical health of every individual, there is no single action that, if taken, will insure that every individual will become fully literate. (Kirsch & Jungeblat, 1986)

The ultimate goal of all literacy training is to develop readers who are able to use this skill in a manner that will enhance their lives. No matter the type of reading or the proficiency required, each citizen of our society has the right to be literate to a degree that is acceptable for their individual life styles and goals.

Although the literacy problem is one that has been and is a continuing concern, it must be put in perspective. As noted in the NAEP report (Kirsch & Jungeblat, 1986) in summarizing their findings:

> The above discussion helps to specify the extent of the literacy problem and it becomes apparent that characterizing America as an 'illiterate nation' is a little like characterizing America as a 'diseased nation.' Although millions of our citizens suffer each year from debilitating illnesses, as a nation we are living longer and healthier lives than ever before. Similarly, although some of our citizens reach adulthood unable to read and write, as we have seen, illiteracy is not a major problem for young adults. Nevertheless, the results of this assessment do indicate that literacy *is* a problem for young adults and we turn now to an examination of the nature of that problem. (p. xx)

References

Asheim, L. (1987). *The reader-viewer-listener.* Washington: Library of Congress.

Becoming a nation of readers (1983). Report prepared by R.C. Anderson, E.H. Hiebert, J.A. Scott & I.A.G. Wilkinson. U.S. Department of Education, Washington DC: The National Institute of Education.

Bowren, F.R., & Zintz, M.V. (1977). *Teaching reading in adult basic education.* Dubuque, IA: William C. Brown.

Duffy, G., & Roehler, L.R. (1986). *Improving classroom reading instruction.* New York: Random House.

Edwards, A.T. (1984). Cultural literacy: What are our goals? *English Journal, 73,* 71-72.

Farr, R., & Carey, R.F. (1986). *Reading: What can be measured?* Newark, DE: International Reading Association.

Gray, W.S. (1969). *The teaching of reading and writing, an international survey.* Paris: UNESCO.

Guthrie, J.T., & Lissitz, R.W. (1985). A framework for assessment-based decision-making in reading education. *Educational measurement: Issues and practices.* New York: Houghton Mifflin.

Harman, D. (1984). *Functional illiteracy in the United States: Issues, experiences, and dilemmas.* San Francisco: Far West Lab for Educational Research and Development.

Harris, A. & Sipay, E. (1985). *How to increase reading ability.* New York: Longman.

Hirsch, E.D. (1984, January). *Cultural literacy.* Paper presented at the National Adult Literacy Conference, Washington, DC.

Hirsch, E.D. (1985). Cultural literacy doesn't mean core curriculum. *English Journal, 74,* 47-49.

Hirsch, E.D. (1986). Cultural literacy does not mean a list of works. *ADE Bulletin, 84,* 1-3.

Hirsch, E.D. (1987). *Cultural literacy: What every American needs to know.* Boston: Houghton Mifflin.

Kirsch, I.S., & Jungeblat, A. (1986). *Literacy: Profiles of America's young adults.* Princeton, NJ: National Assessment of Educational Progress. (ERIC Document Reproduction Service No. ED 275 701)

Kozol, J. (1986). *Illiterate America.* New York: Doubleday.

Langer, J.A. (1986a). *A sociocognitive perspective on literacy.* (ERIC Document Reproduction Service No. ED 274 988)

Langer, J.A. (1986b). *Literate communication and literacy instruction.* (ERIC Document Reproduction Service No. ED 276 020)

Mason, J.M., & Au, K.H. (1986). *Reading instruction for today.* Glenview, IL: Scott Foresman.

Mayer, S.E. (1984). *Guidelines for effective adult literacy programs.* Minneapolis: Rainbow Research.

McCormick, S. (1987). *Remedial and clinical reading instruction.* Columbus, OH: Merrill.

Newman, A.P. (1980). *Adult basic education reading.* Boston: Allyn and Bacon.

O'Hanian, S. (1987, May 21). Finding a loony list while searching for literacy. *Education Week, 7.*

Otto, W., & Ford, D. (1967). *Teaching adults to read.* Boston: Houghton Mifflin. *Project Literacy Newsletter.* (1987). New York: CI Stems.

Ransom, B. (1987, April 21). Questioning the meaning of literacy. *Education Week, 7.*

The reading report card. (1985). Princeton, NJ: National Assessment of Educational Progress.

Robinson, R.D., & Good, T. (1987). *Becoming an effective reading teacher.* New York: Harper and Row.

Shanker, A. (1987, July 19). Literacy goes beyond reading. *New York Times.*

Shipman, P. (1986, October 1). A culture divided by science. *Education Week, 6, 4.*

Warnock, J. (1985). Cultural literacy : A worm in the bud? *ADE Bulletin, 82,* 1-7.

Warnock, J. (1987). Reply to Hirsch's comment on "Cultural Literacy: A worm in the bud." *ADE Bulletin, 84,* 4-5.

Part IV:
Reading Across
the Lifespan

12
Studying Across the Life Span

John W. Thomas and William D. Rohwer, Jr.

Studying can be defined as self-directed learning undertaken in anticipation of a future performance event. Although tests are the performance events most often associated with studying in academic contexts, in other contexts individuals commonly study in preparation for other kinds of performances as well. Job seekers study the firms of prospective employers in preparation for interviews. Lawyers study rulings in prior cases to prepare written and oral arguments. Advertising agents study market surveys to prepare publicity campaigns. Consumers study product review periodicals in preparation for major purchases. Prospective tourists study tour guides to enhance their travel experiences.

It appears reasonable to suppose that studying becomes an increasingly central form of learning with increases in age. In the early grades of schooling, learning occurs primarily in the classroom under the direction and supervision of the teacher. By the time students reach college age, however, they are called upon to read and integrate large amounts of information on their own. This trend continues beyond the years of formal schooling, for on those occasions when adults engage in studying, they do so largely at their own instigation and for their own performance purposes (Tough, 1977).

From middle childhood through adulthood, reading is a major component of studying. Much of the information learned through studying is initially gained by reading. Moreover, reading also plays a prominent role when learners subject information to additional processing. For example, reading is involved when notes are reorganized, summarized, or merely reviewed.

The focus of the present chapter is on such reading and reading-related components of studying. As is the case for other components of studying, these reading components can vary widely in effectiveness. Thus, the aim of the chapter is to develop further a set of hypotheses (Rohwer, 1984; Rohwer & Thomas, 1987; Thomas & Rohwer, 1986) intended to account for variations in study effectiveness as a function of environmental features. The chapter begins with a preliminary characterization of effective studying. Presented next are data about variations in the study activities of adolescents and relationships between these variations and corresponding ones in the demand and support features of the courses in which these adolescents were enrolled. These data and extrapolations from them are then examined to determine how environmental demands and supports may shape study activities throughout the life span. This perspective leads to speculation regarding apparent continuities and discontinuities in environmental demands and supports throughout the life span, as well as about the potential implications of such continuities and discontinuities for study effectiveness.

Characteristics of Effective Studying

Study events can range in duration and complexity from relatively brief and simple ones, such as reading a short text passage in advance of a quiz, to demanding self-instructional ones carried out over protracted periods of time, such as preparing for a professional licensing examination. Adults who decide at some point in their lives that they would like to learn a new body of knowledge, often carry out a complete course of instruction on their own. Studying in this more elaborate sense can involve planning a curriculum, finding resources, establishing performance criteria and subgoals, managing time on tasks, and evaluating the degree of one's learning throughout the study episode.

Studying, in all but its most primitive forms, combines both self-teaching and self-regulated learning. That is, it requires both the application of principles of effective instruction and the exercise of habits and dispositions necessary to sustain study effort over time. Good studiers would seem to be individuals who can arrange a suitable learning environment, select and use appropriate methods for processing information, and manage their behavior to ensure that a desired outcome is achieved.

Much has been written recently concerning the essential features of a mature, proficient, self-regulated, metacognitive learner. Corno (1986), for example, describes six distinct types of volitional control processes associated with proficient self-directed learning. Pressley, Borkowski, and O'Sullivan (1985), among others, stress that cognitive competence at studying requires not just a repertoire of appropriate strategies but also general and specific strategy knowledge necessary to direct strategy use, as well as procedures for acquiring new strategies. Good studiers have been described as mature, detective-like, problem solvers who develop and carry out, often in environments that offer limited guidance, sophisticated strategic plans of action focused on self-defined goals (Bransford, Nitsch, & Franks, 1977).

The evident importance and complexity of studying have instigated efforts to construct descriptive and explanatory accounts of how study proficiency develops. Despite these efforts, however, we have achieved only a preliminary understanding of the psychology of studying or of how its constituent phenomena change and develop across the life span (Rohwer, 1984). Our state of knowledge about the development of study proficiency can be likened to an unassembled jigsaw puzzle.

In the case of academic studying, we know, for instance, that students themselves are primarily responsible for constructing and instigating their study procedures, but that they deploy them largely in response to course demands (reading assignments, texts, tests, grading practices). We also know that there is at least one juncture in the life span, college entrance, about which many persons voice the judgment that students' study procedures are inadequate for subsequent course demands (Roueche, Baker, & Roueche, 1984).

This specificity of study activities to the demands of the environment may be one key to a fuller understanding of studying phenomena: what prompts students to study and to study in different ways, what discourages studying, and what promotes the development of productive study procedures and practices. Our understanding of studying to date comes from research grounded primarily in the traditions of differential and personality psychology, and secondarily in those of developmental and experimental psychology. Still needed in order to construct a theory of studying is a coherent selection from these traditions, one that can encompass the interrelationships among student characteristics, environmental features, study activities, and outcome factors (Brown, Bransford, Ferrara, & Campione, 1983; Rohwer, 1984; Rohwer & Thomas, 1987). Such a theory of studying, however, must not only account for variance in study practices between study environments and between students in particular environments, but also for the development of study proficiencies and deficiencies across age and grade levels. Although existing theoretical propositions as well as pertinent available research provide useful pointers toward such a theory, additional steps are necessary. One of these steps is that of building a base of descriptive data that is sufficiently analytical and comprehensive to expose the nature of the studying phenomena to be explained.

A Developmental Investigation of Studying

Recently, we conducted an investigation intended to contribute to such a data base. The investigation involved a survey of students' study practices at three grade levels: junior high school, senior high school, and college. We collected self-report data on students' routine and test preparation study activities, as well as on the courses within which these students studied at two universities, four high schools, whose graduates tend to enroll in these universities, and three junior high schools, which serve populations comparable to those served by the high schools. The courses sampled were all American history or government courses with the exception of one course at the college level, which was a European history course.

Information on course characteristics was derived from analyses of course documents. These analyses yielded scores for each course on 28 course features, 17 of which are relevant to the present chapter because of their potential effects on students' reading activities.

Our hypothesis was that these course features would have one of three kinds of effects on reading-related study activities. Some course features were expected to increase the importance of a particular study activity. These features we called *demands*. For example, texts that are filled with abstract, unfamiliar words should present a greater challenge to students than texts filled with concrete, familiar words. In the former case, some students might be prompted to engage in more frequent comprehension-enhancing activities while reading than in the latter case. Thus, we predicted that the more difficult the assigned readings, the greater the importance, in terms of academic achievement, of engaging in comprehension-enhancing activities such as asking questions, making notes of difficult words, looking back, etcetera In short, demands are course features that put a premium on particular kinds of study practices.

Course features of a second kind were expected to increase the engagement of most students in relevant study activities. We refer to these kinds of course features as *supports*. For example, texts that contain chapter previews or other devices to signal gradations of importance across the information presented were expected to encourage or support selective processing during reading.

A third kind of course feature, *compensations*, can reduce the effective demands made by a course. For example, by providing a list of the questions to appear on a forthcoming test, an instructor would abrogate the need for students to engage in selective processing on their own. Such features act to compensate for engagement in relevant study activities. Thus, we hypothesized that the presence of compensatory supports would reduce engagement in particular study activities.

Course features that might affect reading and reading-related study activities can be divided into two main categories: source materials, and criterion performances. The category of source materials includes all of the documents that a student might use in reading or reviewing information for a course. These sources might include a textbook, an original source assigned for the course, a reference source, and any auxiliary visual material, such as handouts, provided by the instructor. For the purposes of our investigation, data were collected on 11 features of source materials, including 4 demand features, 6 support features, and 1 compensation feature. The demand features consisted of (a) selection, indexed by information load (the number of words assigned per day); (b) comprehension, indexed by the difficulty of the assigned readings (ratings of paragraph comprehensibility, noun and meaning-unit concreteness, and word frequency counts); and (c) memory, indexed by the number of details in the reading assignments. The support features indexed the extent to which the assigned readings incorporated aids for selection, previewing, comprehension, and memory (including mnemonic aids). The compensation feature pertained to integration, and was indexed by ratings of the extent to which assigned readings presented information in an integrated form.

The second category of course features hypothesized to affect reading-related study activities is the nature of the criterion performances. In our investigation, the focus in this category was on the nature of the examinations given. Five demand features, along with one support and one compensation feature of these tests were appraised. The demand features included (a) the retention interval, that is the length of the interval between test events, (b) transformational demands, the extent to which the wording and substance of the test items departed from the wording and substance of information presented in the assigned reading (e.g., low demand items were those rated as calling for reproduction or recognition of text information, whereas high demand items called for interpretation or inference based on the information given), and the relative importance, for successful test performance, of three kinds of knowledge products that could be obtained from processing the readings, (c) verbatim production, (d) comprehension, and (e) integration. The selection support feature consisted of the extent to which test items were derived in a principled, predictable way from the assigned reading. The compensation feature was indexed by ratings of the extent of congruence between the test items and the wording and substance of information in instructor-provided handouts. High scores on this last feature, then, would constitute course-specific compensation for all forms of reading-related information processing, except verbatim memory processes, which would otherwise have been demanded by questions on the examination.

Standardized mean scores for each course were derived for each of the preceding 17 features. These scores were subjected to unweighted means analyses of variance, in which courses were treated as the sampling unit, to estimate the proportions of variance associated with linear and quadratic grade level trends. The results are shown in Table 12.1.

Across the educational levels stretching from junior high school through senior high school to college, the analyses of features of source materials revealed the four kinds of trends shown in Figure 12.1: (Panel A), a positive linear trend in selection demands (amount of reading assigned), coupled with a negative linear trend in selection support; (Panel B), a linear increase (although not significant) in the comprehension demands imposed by the character of the reading assigned, and a nonsignificant decrease in the amount of comprehension support provided; (Panel C) a significant increase between the secondary and college levels in integration demands (number of independent sources assigned) offset, presumably, by a roughly corresponding increase in integration compensation; (Panel D) a U-shaped change in memory demands (amount of detail in sources with a signficant linear decrease in support for mnemonic use. Thus, only in the case of integration is there evidence that increases in demands across grade levels are matched by increasing compensation for the kind of processing required. In contrast, it appears that in the absence of increasing supports, students themselves must autonomously meet the increasing demands on selection and comprehension.

Table 12.1 also contains the results associated with features of examinations. Three aspects of these results are noteworthy. One is the increase between the secondary and college levels in memory demands as indexed by the length of the retention interval, especially in view of the previously reported lack of increasing memory support across these levels. Similarly, the second aspect of the results, namely, the lack of increases with level in the principled selection of test items, takes on significance in connection with the previously reported increase in selection demands made by assigned readings. The remaining aspects of the results are displayed in Figure 12.2. Shown in this figure are (a) a decrease between the secondary and college levels in the importance of verbatim information as indexed

Table 12.1

Grade-level Means and Analysis of Variance
Results for Document Course Features

Course Features	Means			F-ratios		
	JHS	SHS	College	Linear	Quadratic	Error MS
Source Features						
Demands						
Selection	-0.732	0.178	2.314	73.58**	3.97	0.269
Comprehension	-0.534	0.318	0.651	3.46	0.22	0.867
Integration	-0.253	-0.253	2.532	45.67**	15.22**	0.363
Memory	-0.482	0.526	-0.725	0.16	4.66**	0.780
Supports						
Selection	0.459	-0.114	-1.440	9.88**	0.52	0.780
Previewing	0.083	-0.012	-0.306	-.30	0.03	1.092
Comprehension	0.010	0.159	-0.923	1.86	1.08	1.001
Memory	-0.090	0.074	0.000	0.02	0.04	1.098
Mnemonics	0.654	-0.285	-1.377	13.42**	0.03	0.656
Compensations						
Integrated Presentation	-0.201	-0.150	1.730	10.50**	3.14	0.758
Examinations						
Demands						
Retention	0.441	-0.643	1.546	5.02*	14.65**	0.521
Interval	0.175	0.225	-2.028	16.52**	6.02*	0.628
Verbatim	-0.227	0.338	-0.838	0.85	2.30	0.941
Comprehension	-0.174	-0.284	2.341	28.89**	11.39**	0.468
Integration Transformational	0.057	-0.334	1.583	6.42*	4.90*	0.775
Supports						
Principled Selection	-0.014	-0.123	0.737	1.16	0.64	1.039
Compensations						
Test-handout congruence	0.427	-0.077	-1.494	10.10**	0.76	0.781

*p < .05
**p < .01

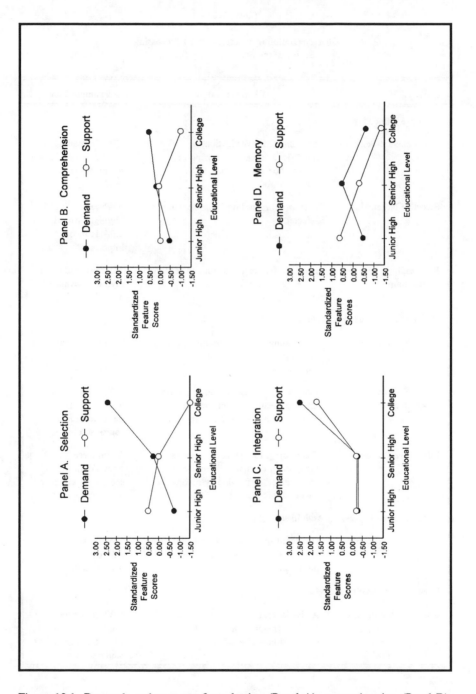

Figure 12.1. Demands and supports for selection (Panel A), comprehension (Panel B), interation (Panel C), and memory (Panel D) as a function of grade level.

Table 12.2

Characterization of Reading-related Processing
Scales of the Study Activity Survey

Scale	Characterization	Example Items
Selective Allocation Activities		
Test Relevant Selection	Self-initiated investigation, identification, and processing of information that is likely to be important for a test.	"(While reading) I identify points that might be on the test."
Selective Notetaking	Purposeful recording of information selected.	"(While reading) I highlight what I think is most important."
Pre-Reading Preparation	Planning for selection prior to reading.	"(Before reading) I review relevant notes."
Generative Processing Activities		
Verbatim Processing	Elaborating or transforming mental modality of target information to enhance memorability.	"(While studying for the test) I made up a rhyme."
Comprehension Processing	Explicating, investigating, or inquiring into the meaning of information to enhance comprehension or memory.	"(While studying) I tried to explain important ideas to someone else."
Integrative Processing	Elaborating, reorganizing, contrasting, integrating, or summarizing newly encountered or previously recorded or encoded information.	"(While reading) I write down the specific similarities between topics."
Nongenerative Processing Activities		
Duplicative Processing	Unaltered re-encoding or mental recycling of previously encountered information.	"(While studying) I read over my reading notes."
Executive Monitoring Activities		
Cognitive Monitoring	Active checking of one's own state of comprehension or memory for information.	"(While reading) I can tell how hard it will be to remember major points.

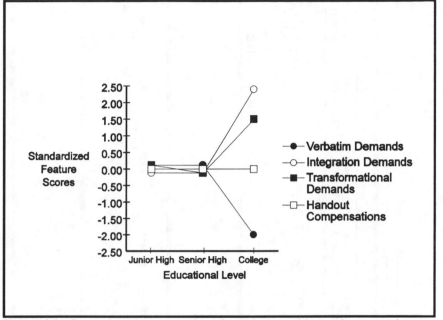

Figure 12.2. Demands and compensations for verbatim and integrative processing as a function of grade level.

by the proportion of such items on these tests, (b) an increase between these levels in the importance of integrated information, (c) an increase across levels, consistent with the preceding trends, in transformational requirements, coupled with (d) corresponding decreases in the compensation provided by instructors' handouts, that is, decreases in the congruence of test items with the wording and substance of information presented in these handouts. At the secondary levels, it appears, instructors tailor their examination questions to the verbatim characteristics of the information presented in text assignments and provide support for verbatim processing in the handouts they furnish students. At the college level, in contrast, examination questions depart substantially from the wording of information as presented in reading assignments, and little direct aid is provided for dealing with these transformational requirements.

These results for examination features imply that with increases in educational level, students are increasingly called upon to engage independently in the selection and integration of information presented in reading assignments in order to cope with the demands of criterion tests, and to retain this integrated information over longer periods of time. The increases in examination demands for integrated information may be offset somewhat by the corresponding increases in integrative text presentations noted previously. Nevertheless, according to the results for examination features, college level tests call for additional integrative processing not specifically provided in either assigned texts or instructor handouts.

Table 12.3

Grade Level Means and Summary of Unweighted Means Analyses
of Variance in Study Activity Engagement

Source	df	SASR Scale							
		Test Focus	Selective Notetaking	Prereading Preparation	Duplicative Processing	Verbatim Processing	Comprehensive Processing	Integrative Processing	Cognitive Monitoring
F-Ratios									
Linear	1	39.58**	4.32*	12.90**	130.79**	NA	3.70	20.88**	0.12
Quadratic	1	1.50	13.40**	2.17	0.12	NA	0.00	3.93*	5.77*
Error MS		0.37	0.54	0.83	0.47	NA	0.43	0.42	0.43
Error df		1208	1194	1192	1206	NA	1187	1185	1212
Means									
Junior High		3.15	2.56	2.60	3.18	NA	2.66	2.53	3.05
Senior High		3.25	2.44	2.39	2.88	NA	2.61	2.55	3.14
College		3.43	2.67	2.36	2.61	NA	2.57	2.74	3.04
F-Ratios									
Linear	1	35.97**	69.75**	NA	37.75**	19.24**	4.85*	1.43	6.04*
Quadratic	1	7.76**	5.06*	NA	0.13	0.02	0.00	18.95**	0.05
Error MS		0.42	0.83	NA	0.50	0.52	0.39	0.42	0.60
Error df		1043	1044	NA	1028	1016	1031	1037	1046
Means									
Junior High		3.26	2.81	NA	2.58	1.77	2.47	2.22	3.18
Senior High		3.55	3.27	NA	2.39	1.63	2.42	2.05	3.25
College		3.59	3.43	NA	2.23	1.51	2.36	2.28	3.34

*p < .01   **p < .05

Given these grade level differences in demand and support features of assigned readings and tests, do students engage more frequently in corresponding reading activities than in those that are less important and less supported? As part of our investigation of studying, we collected data on the kinds of study activities engaged in by students at the three grade levels. A locally developed self-report instrument, the Study Activity Survey, was administered to all participants in order to assess their frequency of engagement in different kinds of study activities. This inventory is divided into two forms, Form R, which assesses students' routine study activities, and Form T, which surveys the activities students engage in while preparing for a test. In the case of both forms, students were instructed to respond with reference to the particular course in which the survey was administered.

The survey was designed to assess both in-class study activities and out-of-class activities and to measure both cognitive and self-management practices. The items asked students to indicate the frequency with which they engaged in an activity by responding on a five-point scale ranging from *never* to *always*. A large proportion of items on both forms have to do with reading and reading-related activities. In fact, 8 of the 15 scales that make up the Study Activity Survey bear directly on reading. Descriptions and an illustrative item for each of these 8 scales are shown in Table 12.2. Three of these scales (test-relevant selection, selective notetaking, and prereading preparation) are regarded as reflections of selective allocation activities because they assess the extent to which students differentially attend to information of perceived criterion relevance or inherent importance. Also included in the Study Activity Survey is 1 nongenerative processing scale, duplicative processing. Three of the remaining scales we refer to as generative processing scales because their constituent items all involve the investment of strategic effort in processing: verbatim processing, comprehension processing, and integrative processing. The final scale, cognitive monitoring, is made up of items that reflect the frequency of self-assessments of the status of comprehension and memory.

To assess differences across educational levels in the frequency of study activity engagement, scale means were computed for each of the two forms of the survey and were subjected to univariate, unweighted-means analyses of variance. A summary of the results of these analyses, along with scale means as a function of levels, is shown in Table 12.3.

The results indicate the following trends: (a) an increase across levels of engagement in selective allocation activities, except for that of prereading preparation, (b) a similar increase in integrative processing activities, at least for routine studying, (c) a linear decline across levels in verbatim and comprehension processing activities during test preparation, (c) a strong linear decline in engagement in duplicative processing activities, and (d) an increase in engagement in cognitive monitoring activities during test preparation.

These results for periods of routine studying provide support for the contention that variations across levels in the character of reading-related study activities engaged in are associated with the differences in the patterns of reading demands and support characteristics of the courses students take. Figures 12.3, 12.4, and 12.5 illustrate graphically the several patterns of association obtained. In Figure 12.3,

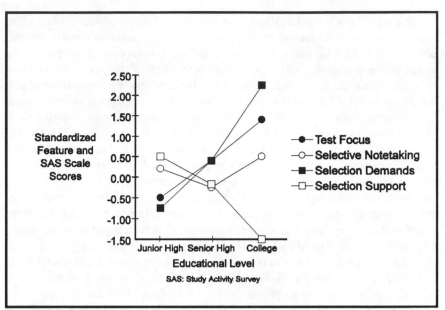

Figure 12.3. Selective allocation study activities and demands and supports for selection as a function of grade level.

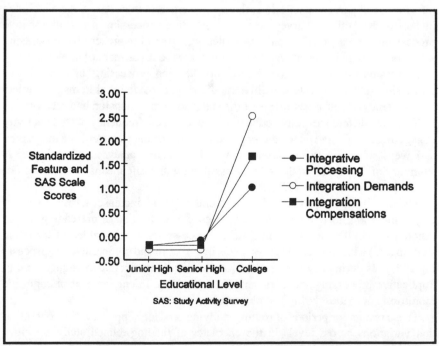

Figure 12.4. Integrative processing activities and demands and compensations for integration as a function of grade level.

Table 12.4

Hypothesized Shifts in Environmental Features that Affect Selective Allocation and Generative Processing Activities across the Life Span

Environmental Features		Educational Levels					
		elementary	junior high	high school	college	graduate school	adult life
Selective Allocation Activities							
Demands	Information load	low	low	low	moder. high	high	moder. to high
	Number of Sources	one	one	one to few	few to many	many	many
	Criterion requirements	low	low	low	high	high	various
Supports	Text	many	many	some	few	few to none	none
	Instructor	many	many	some	few to none	few to none	none
Compensations	Instructor	many	many	some	few to none	none	none
Generative Processing (Integration) Activities							
Demands	Information load	low	low	low	med. to high	high	med. to high
	Difficulty of sources	low	low	moderate	high	high	high
	Number of sources	one	one	one to few	few to many	many	many
	Retention interval	short	short	short	moder. long	moder. long	various
	Criterion requirement for integration	none	none	low	high	high	high
Supports	Text	few	few	some	few	few	few
	Instructor	few	few	some	many	few	none
Compensations	Integrated presentations	few	few	some	many	some	none
	Source-Criterion overlap	identical	identical	substantial	partial	minimal	none

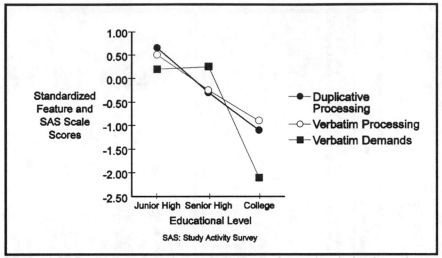

Figure 12.5. Duplicative processing, verbatim processing, and verbatim demands as a function of grade level.

the trend for engagement in selective allocation activities during routine studying is displayed against the trend for selection demands (information load) and selection supports. With increases in grade level, the demand for selection increases as does student engagement in the selective allocation activities of selective notetaking and focus on test relevance, even though selection support decreases. In Figure 12.4, engagement in integrative processing during routine studying, along with text-based demands and compensations for such processing, are plotted as a function of grade level. As predicted, increases in the incidence of such processing are almost parallel with increases in demands for it. Contrary to our initial hypothesis, however, the incidence of engagement also parallels the relevant compensation feature.

The outcomes for periods of test preparation, however, do not provide equally strong support for our hypotheses. For example, consider the trends associated with examination course features and generative versus nongenerative test preparation study activities. Consistent with the hypotheses, as shown in Figure 12.5, the demand for verbatim information decreases across levels as does engagement in duplicative and verbatim processing. Engagement in integrative processing, however, does not increase as would be expected given the increase in demand for integrated information (see Figure 12.6). Note also that compensation for such processing, as indexed by test-handout congruence declines significantly across levels. One conjecture about this unexpected result involves a reconceptualization of compensation features. If such features function as supports rather than compensations for corresponding kinds of processing during reading and reading-related activities, the increase across levels in integration support during routine studying and the decline in such support during test preparation would account for the observed trends in integrative processing. An alternative conjecture arises from a

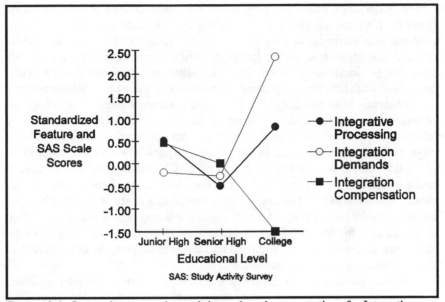

Figure 12.6. Integrative processing and demands and compensations for Integration as a function of grade level.

comparison of the mean engagement scores for periods of routine and test preparation studying. Apparently, engagement in all forms of processing activity is less frequent during test preparation, whereas engagement in selective allocation activities and cognitive monitoring increase. Thus, it may be that by the onset of a test preparation period, students have completed much of their reading-related processing activity and engage mainly in selective review and cognitive self-assessment activities.

Viewed as a whole, the results from this investigation indicate that demand and support features of the academic courses sampled change measurably across the period of adolescence. Moreover, they also suggest that in many cases the reading-related study activities students engage in shift in ways that correspond with these changes. One interpretation of these associations is that instructors may invest their courses with features that correspond with the kinds of reading-related study activities that are within the developmental capabilities of their students. Whereas this interpretation is quite credible, it appears to be incomplete. During periods of routine studying, for example, engagement in integrative reading processes is no more frequent at the senior high school than at the junior high school level even though the developmental capabilities of the older students are presumably more advanced than those of the younger. The stability of such engagement across these levels, coupled with its increasing frequency at the college level, parallel the observed changes in demands and supports for integrative processing. Thus, to a significant extent, shifts across levels in the character of reading-related study activities appear to stem from changes in course features.

This proposition raises the question of how level-to-level changes in course features affect the development of reading-related study proficiencies. If the proposition is generalized, it raises the broader question of how environmental demands and supports affect the development of such proficiencies across the life span, that is, across the earlier years of schooling and beyond the school years throughout adult life. Two conjectural steps can be taken to address these questions.

First, continuities and discontinuities in the patterns of demands and supports between adjacent educational levels can be described with the purpose of making inferences about conditions under which the development of study proficiency might be facilitated or impeded. In some cases, changes between levels in the kinds of reading-related study activities demanded may be manageable in the sense of being within the developing capabilities of students. In such cases, the changes should be associated with increases in study proficiency as students are called upon to assume more responsibility for self-directed learning and as they expand their repertoire of information- processing strategies. However, when changes in demands are abrupt and not accompanied by sufficient support, the development of study proficiency should be retarded.

A second speculative step that can be taken is to extrapolate from the preceding results about course demands and reading-related study activities to educational levels prior to adolescence and to ages beyond the adolescent period. The questions to be addressed in such extrapolations include: How continuous are the changes in demands across the K-12 and postsecondary ranges? What might be the discontinuities between adjacent levels of schooling and how might these discontinuities account for patterns of study activities that might be observed at these levels? To what extent do the demands at educational levels that represent the highest grade reached for portions of the population prepare individuals to engage autonomously in reading-related study activities in adult life?

Lifespan Continuities and Discontinuities in Environmental Features

Specified in Table 12.4 are continuities and discontinuities in demands, supports, and compensations presumed to influence students' engagement in two classes of reading-related study activities: selective allocation activities and generative processing activities. The magnitude and the nature of these demands and supports are characterized for the three educational levels investigated in our research. In addition, hypothetical characterizations are provided for three additional periods: elementary school, graduate school, and postschool life.

Selective Allocation Activities

Selective allocation activities during reading are those that serve to focus study efforts. Elsewhere (Thomas & Rohwer, 1986), we have divided this class of activities into two subclasses: (a) differentiating among and within sources of information in accord with considerations of importance and criterion relevance and (b) identifying and eliciting cues regarding criterion relevant information. Selective allocation activities also include those that serve to allocate study time or intensity of study effort differentially within or between source materials.

Selective allocation activities have been singled out as important for a variety of school-like reading tasks. Ninth-grade students who are able to identify the author's top-level structure in texts are superior to their peers in comprehension in terms of both immediate and delayed recall performance (Meyer, Brandt, & Bluth, 1980). Depending, of course, on the nature of the criterion test, the ability to select and record the most important idea units from a text passage has been found to be the hallmark of the proficient student at the elementary school (Brown & Smiley, 1978), high school (Peper & Mayer, 1986; Shimmerlik & Nolan, 1976), and college (Kiewra & Fletcher, 1984) levels.

The extent to which students engage in selective allocation activities is presumed to depend on at least three kinds of demands, two kinds of supports, and one kind of compensation. The necessity to make judgments about what is most important prior to and during reading should increase with the amount of information to be covered, the number of sources, and the extent to which the material selected by the instructor for inclusion on examinations is selected in some principled fashion ("top-level structure" in Meyer et al.'s (1980) terms). In addition, the tendency of students to be selective in their study activities should also depend on the support provided in the source materials and by the instructor. This support includes highlights, outlines, and other signals in the sources and in handouts supplied by the instructor. Compensation consists of explicit instructor-provided designation of the importance or criterion relevance of information. Under conditions of low demand and support or under conditions of high compensation, the probability that students themselves will be selective while reading should be less than under conditions of high demand or support, coupled with low compensation.

Consider the selection demands that occur in the elementary and secondary grades. Throughout these grades, information load is relatively low. Students are given reading assignments, but the assignments are usually the kind that can be completed in less than an hour. Moreover, students are often given time during the school day to complete these assignments. Throughout this period, assignments typically cover a single source. When more than one book is used, these books tend to be introduced at different times in a year and do not usually overlap within a marking period. Finally, the demand on selection associated with unit tests tends to be fairly low. Most of the tests administered during this period tend to call for the reproduction of information (Fleming & Chambers, 1983). In our experience with teacher-developed American history tests, the items that make up these tests were not often drawn from the main ideas of a chapter. Instead, they were usually selected from the factual statements in the chapter, with one such factual statement being no more likely to appear on the test than another. Under such conditions, it may be counterproductive to be selective in one's reading.

Supports for selection provided routinely at the elementary and secondary levels are primarily of two kinds: supports that appear within the text or within supplementary material and supports generated by the teacher. Texts typically contain supports in the form of self-help questions that can prompt students to allocate their attention selectively across the information presented. Text-based supports also include the workbooks and exercises that are common at the elementary school level. Teacher handouts are another form of selection support. In our observations of classrooms at the junior high and high school levels, teacher handouts were almost universal. These handouts consist of lists, outlines, practice questions, or a combination of such devices that can prompt student engagement in selective reading. Thus, according to our hypothesis, the liberal provision of supports in texts and by instructors should heighten selective allocation activities.

This tendency, however, is overridden by the even more liberal provision of compensations at the elementary and secondary levels. Texts include, invariably, not only selection supports, but also aids such as lists, outlines, and highlighted words and phrases. These aids serve, in effect, to do students' selection for them. Moreover, instructors' handouts not only provide students with cues about what might be on the test, they often provide, in advance, the very questions and sometimes even the answers that will make up the examination. As the grade-level means for the feature, test-handout congruence (shown in Table 12.1), indicate, such compensation decreases very gradually, even across the secondary school years.

Across the elementary and secondary years, then, the effective demands for selective allocation appear to increase in a slow, continuous way. Whereas a rationale might be given, in terms of structural theories of development, for the low levels of selection demands at the primary and elementary school levels, such a rationale would lack credibility in the case of senior high school courses. In any event, apparent continuity in effective demands for selective allocation across the elementary and secondary levels may account for some commonly reported observations.

First, the combination of low demands and high compensations for selective allocation may explain why students at the secondary level have often failed to demonstrate proficiency at selective reading tasks in laboratory studies. Brown, Smiley, & Lawton (1978) investigated the abilities of college students and students in Grades 5 through 12 to select retrieval cues for remembering the main ideas from text passages. Although they found the ability to differentiate between more important and less important material from a passage to increase somewhat with grade level, they found a dramatic shift between 12th-grade and college students' tendencies to select material in a way that matched task demands. Students were given multiple trials until they could demonstrate the ability to recall all of the ideas presented in a passage. During test trials, students were allowed to retain a limited list of idea units from the passage to serve as retrieval cues. Students in Grades 5 through 12 tended to select the most important units as retrieval cues even after they had demonstrated their ability to recall this information without aid and their inability to recall information of lesser importance. Over trials, college students, on the other hand, adopted the strategy of selecting, as retrieval cues, elements of intermediate importance and those elements that caused them recall difficulties in previous trials. In this study and in an earlier study (Brown & Smiley, 1977), there were no significant differences between college and high school students in their ability to differentiate important from less important ideas in text passages. The major difference between these two age groups, as demonstrated in the Brown et al. (1978) study, was in their relative appreciation of the value of selection in light of the demands of the task.

According to the present analysis, such sensitivity to the value of selection comes from experience. High school students have not experienced the kinds of task or test demands that makes selective processing necessary. College students, who are more apt to experience both reading assignments and test demands that put a premium on selection, are more apt to develop and practice selection strategies when reading and studying and are more sensitive to the situations that call for the application of these strategies.

This lack of experience in selective reading may explain why high school graduates are often identified as being unprepared for studying at the college level. The onset of college represents a significant discontinuity in the demands that courses make on students' selective allocation activities. At the college level, the information load increases dramatically. Reading assignments often involve texts without imbedded aids and are usually unaccompanied by teacher-developed handouts. This shift in demands and compensations, as well as in supports, may contribute to the study difficulties experienced by many entering freshmen. There are now special remedial programs or courses in almost every college and university across the country (Roueche, et al., 1984). The salience of these difficulties is supported by the experience at the University of California, an institution known for selecting only the most well prepared high school graduates. At this university, *elective* courses offered at a special student learning center are taken by more than one third of lower division students.

This shift at the college level in the importance of selective allocation activities may also explain the emergence and apparent importance, at this level, of selection activities referred to as cue-conscious and cue-seeking behavior. According to some survey and qualitative research on these phenomena, students who are successful in college courses tend to be those who are sensitive to the demands of the course, especially the criterion requirements. This sensitivity is embodied in the ability to decipher cues implicit in instructors' lectures or comments and the disposition to seek out information about criteria for assessing course grades by asking questions of the instructor or others (Entwistle, Hanley, & Hounsell, 1979; Miller & Parlett, 1974). The inference, though untested, is that such cue-conscious and cue-seeking behavior is less apparent and important at the secondary level because direct compensations for these cues are typically provided in the form of handouts and test preparation reviews.

There may be other changes in the demand for selective allocation activities across the life span. At the graduate level, there is often a shift toward the exclusive use of original sources, and it is common for students to have to deal with a relatively large number of sources. Although there are also changes in the nature of the criterion tasks at the graduate level, the requirement to "wade through" a large amount of fairly difficult material is one of the hallmarks of graduate work. Graduate students are routinely judged on their ability to produce written or oral products that are based on selective readings, listening, and library research. In addition, in graduate school, lectures rarely overlap with the reading, readings typically consist of original sources rather than textbooks, and handouts that support or compensate for selection activities are rare, as are instructor-led, examination review sessions. It could be argued that to the extent to which postschool life is characterized by the need to selectively hunt through multiple, original sources, graduate school represents better preparation for these tasks than either college or high school.

With respect to postschool studying, the demands on selection will vary with the learning objective and the criterion task. The study activities of postschool adults invariably involve learning a skill or learning to perform some task and, also, limitations in the time available for reading and studying (Tough, 1968). Under these conditions, the absence or low degree of instructor or text-based supports for selection is presumed to heighten the effective demands on selective allocation activities such as finding the best source, asking selective questions, allocating time in a sensible fashion, and identifying and recording central information.

Generative Processing Activities

Generative processing activities include a number of strategies that serve to increase the comprehensibility of material to be learned, to construct relationships among ideas within the material to ideas in other sources, or to make the material more memorable through the use of mnemonic devices. According to the generativity principle (Thomas & Rohwer, 1986), the more a study activity involves the reformulation of given information or the generation of information beyond that which is explicitly given, the more effective it will be in enhancing certain kinds of criterion performance.

The importance of generative processing activities has been demonstrated in a number of research investigations. Prompting students to integrate new material with prior learning has been shown to facilitate both retention and transfer performance (Meyer, 1987). Likewise, inducing students to generate connections among ideas to be learned has been shown to facilitate reading comprehension performance (Anderson, 1979; Davey & McBride, 1986). The value of generative processing activities is presumed to lie in revealing gaps in one's comprehension of the ideas inherent in the material (Bransford, Stein, Shelton, & Owings, 1981), or in enhancing the meaning of to-be-learned material either through connections with material in long-term memory or through interconnections among ideas in the material to be learned (Meyer, 1987). Generative processing is "deep" processing in the Craik and Lockhart (1972) sense and "distinctive encoding" in the Glover, Plake, & Zimmer (1982) sense.

The demand in study situations for students to engage in generative processing activities is hypothesized to vary with relevant demands, supports, and compensations. In academic contexts, demands that affect engagement in generative processing should include the amount of information to be processed, the difficulty of sources, the number of sources, the length of the retention interval, and the explicit requirement for generative processing associated with the structure of the text and the nature of the criterion items. Supports that should increase engagement in generative processing include such devices as text- or instructor-provided questions that require the construction of relationships. Compensations that should serve to reduce the effect of generative processing demands include the presentation, in source materials themselves or by the instructor, of explicitly stated relationships matched to the demands of the test. The compensations listed in Table 12.4 are based on the demand for one class of generative processing activities, integrative processing. These compensations include the explicit presentation of integrated propositions in source materials or in lectures and the presence of high degrees of overlap between the products required on the criterion measure and these explicit statements. Such overlap has two dimensions in typical academic contexts: (a) the wording of the items in the test is the same or similar to the way that material was covered in the readings, lectures, or handouts or (b) the knowledge product required by the items in the test is the same or similar to the way the required item of knowledge was presented in the course. A test that contains items that do not overlap with the information presented in the course could be composed of questions calling for familiar responses where the questions have never been introduced before or of questions calling for responses that require transformations of or going beyond the information given in the course.

We hypothesize that students should be prompted to engage in generative integrative processing when the material to be studied is moderately difficult, when they know that they will have to retain the information for some time, when there is a relatively large amount of information to be learned, when there are clear indications that the course requires integration, and when the course provides support for such processing. We also hypothesize that the extent to which they engage in integrative activities will be reduced by courses that provide pre-integrated material and by indications that autonomous integration is not necessary for successful performance in the course. Such indications can come from the kinds of questions introduced in class, the kinds of questions asked on tests, or the kind of coaching provided for those tests.

Throughout the elementary and secondary school years, the amount of information that must be processed in a given assignment or for a particular unit is relatively small. This combined with the relatively short retention intervals and low to moderate difficulty of source materials, creates a situation where there is no particular felt need on the part of students to process information in a generative fashion. More important perhaps, there is not, at least in our experience, much external press to integrate information. Instructions given by the instructor, in-class activities, including discussions and exercises to be completed in class or for homework, and test items primarily stress knowledge of independent items of information, sometimes stress knowledge of concepts and principles, and rarely stress interpretation or the construction of relations.

A similar pattern is described by Fleming and Chambers (1983) in their analysis of the teacher-developed tests administered in Cleveland Public Schools. The authors reviewed over 300 tests and 8,800 items from kindergarten through the twelfth grade in all the core subject matter areas. Items were classified into one of six categories: three knowledge categories and three application or skill categories. They found that the percentage of items classified as knowledge items (knowledge of terms, knowledge of facts, or knowledge of principles) accounted for 69%, 94%, and 69% of the all of the items at the elementary school, junior high school, and high school levels respectively. For science and social studies courses alone, where reading and studying in preparation for tests is perhaps most typical, the percentage of factual items on the teacher-made tests was found to be 94%, 92%, and 89% for the three levels. No matter what the nominal demands for comprehension, integration of ideas, or critical thinking in these courses, the result of experience with these tests in all likelihood changes the effective demand, for most students, to that of verbatim reproduction of information and the dominant study activity to that of rote or duplicative processing.

At the college level, the nominal demand for integrative processing increases to a significant degree. Although some college courses are similar in demand structure to high school courses, many others pose new and different demands on students. These demands include relatively long reading assignments; the use of original sources in addition to or instead of textbooks, sources that are structured to present ideas rather than events or items of information; class discussions that emphasize understanding of concepts and principles rather than knowledge of facts; multiple rather than single sources; and long rather than short intervals between test events. Such demands not only characterize college courses, but those of graduate school and study activities commonly engaged in throughout much of adult life as well.

The implication of these demands is that students are expected to engage in activities that they have not engaged in before and, in some instances, activities that involve skills they may not have acquired. For example, in reading original sources, students are more apt to come across words or ideas that are incomprehensible than is the case with textbooks. In many of these courses, it is implicitly expected that students will engage in adjunct activities under their own direction in order to resolve comprehension problems while reading. Students are also expected to decide, on their own, how to pace the completion of their reading assignments. Instead of 1-day assignments to be completed in class, in study hall, or at home, students are given several days, sometimes several weeks, to complete their assignments and are almost always expected to complete their reading outside of class time. This latter kind of assignment combined with long intervals between test events give reading a new significance at the college level. For many students, this translates into the felt need to establish a study schedule, to develop a system for taking and reviewing notes, and to engage in some activity while reading and reviewing that preserves selected information and ensures retention of important ideas over long periods of time. Finally, students at the college level are expected to be facile at locating and integrating the central ideas within and between reading sources. This expectation is manifested not only in the structure of the sources assigned at this level, but also in demands associated with other aspects of the course including class discussions, assigned papers, and test items.

These demands pose a potentially disruptive situation for entering college students that is often mitigated, at least in our observations, by instructor-provided supports for integration. These supports include lectures that present, in integrated fashion, the central ideas from the readings, and the moderate use, compared to secondary schools, of teacher-developed handouts. The focus of these handouts at the college level is on relationships between ideas rather than facts or events as was the case in secondary school courses. Moreover, they act as supports for generative processing rather than as compensations for it. Thus, the effective demands for generative processing are significantly higher at the college level than at the elementary and secondary levels.

Effective demands for generative processing are presumed to increase to even greater levels at the graduate school level where supports for integration are few and compensatory presentations and examination practices are rare. Likewise, study tasks associated with postschool life are presumed to involve moderate to high demands on integration activities. In addition, postschool study tasks are especially demanding of the generative processing activities of comprehension and integration because of the absence of supports and compensations accompanying such tasks. That this absence of aids enhances demands on comprehension and integration is quite apparent to anyone who has tried to learn a skill such as computer programming or a body of knowledge such as the rules governing professional football by means of reading and studying.

This combination of high demand and support for integration characteristic of college versus secondary level courses may explain some anomalies in the literature. First, there appears to be a contradiction between findings that associate college achievement with engagement in generative processing activities (e.g., deep processing versus shallow processing; Goldman & Warren, 1973; Schmeck & Grove, 1979; Svensson, 1977; Thomas & Bain, 1982) and findings that show relatively low levels of engagement in generative processing activities in college courses (Brennan, Winograd, Bridge, & Hiebert, 1986; Christopoulos, Rohwer, & Thomas, 1987).

In our research for example, we examined differences across educational levels in the effectiveness of a class of generative test preparation study activities, comprehension processing, and a class of nongenerative activities, duplicative processing. Within each course at each level, the effectiveness of these activities was indexed by first classifying students into upper, middle, and lower thirds, or tertiles, in terms of their self-reported frequency of engaging in each of these classes of reading-related study activity. Next, this classification was treated as a factor in an unweighted means analysis of variance in achievement. Achievement was indexed in terms of standard scores of the grades students received on the tests administered in the sampled courses. Thus, the larger the positive difference in achievement between high and low tertile groups, the more effective a given study activity, and the larger the negative difference, the more ineffective the activity.

Across levels, the effectiveness of duplicative processing during test preparation did not vary significantly, nor was it significantly effective at any level. In contrast, the effectiveness of comprehension processing increased from a mean tertile difference (in standard score units) of - 0.466 at the junior high school level to a difference of +0.862 at the college level.

Given such an increase in the effectiveness of this form of generative processing, one might expect a similar trend across levels in engagement, especially in comparison with the ineffective activities reflected by the duplicative processing scale. To the contrary, however, as shown in Table 12.3, engagement in comprehension processing declined significantly across educational levels. Moreover, even though self-reported engagement in duplicative processing also declined significantly across levels, engagement in these activities at the college level remained nearly as high as engagement in the more effective generative activities. Apparently, many college students don't know want's good for them.

Another inference from our survey is that engagement in generative processing, although beneficial, may not be crucial at the college level. Students who are duplicative processors, who study by reading and rereading, by copying notes, and by repeating material to themselves, are able to get by in college. Whether or not these students are able to maintain what they have learned over time or apply their learning in subsequent situations remains to be assessed. The evidence from laboratory studies is that the use of rote, duplicative strategies in studying meaningful text is a handicap in situations where long-term retention or transfer is important (Meyer, 1987).

A second common anomaly concerning college level studying is the absence of a strong relationship between time spent studying and academic achievement (Jensen Delucchi, Rohwer, & Thomas, 1985; Schuman, Walsh, Olson, & Etheridge, 1985). Schuman et al., for example, found that time spent studying, no matter how the study time period was measured, showed only a low positive relationship with GPA or with course grades. At least two inferences from such findings are possible. First, at the college level, it may not matter how much or how often one studies, but it does make a difference how one spends the time. Time spent engaging in test-relevant, generative processing may be more highly related to course achievement than overall time spent studying (cf. Jensen Delucchi et al., 1985; Svennson, 1977). A second inference is that time spent studying is only minimally related to achievement because the importance of studying is overshadowed by the importance of attending to integrative lectures and other aids provided in class. Some support for this inference is provided in the Schuman et al. study. They found the correlation between class attendance and GPA to be more than two and one half times greater than that between time spent studying and GPA ($r=.28$ versus $r=.11$).

A third anomaly that has been observed in research with college students is that these students are commonly able to deploy mature processing strategies when requested, yet are not disposed to do so spontaneously when working on their own. For example, Baker (1979) reported low levels of comprehension monitoring on the part of college students. In this study, students were asked to read passages that contained one of three kinds of confusion: inconsistencies, unclear references, and inappropriate connectives. Only 38% of the embedded intrusions were detected and less than one third of the students detected the inconsistencies and inappropriate connectives while reading under uninstructed conditions. The confusions introduced in the text passages by Baker (1979), and especially the ones that were least detected, were all violations of logical relationships between ideas introduced in separate sentences. To detect these confusion, it is necessary to consider some statement in comparison with a previous statement in the text. To detect an inconsistency, for example, the student would need to notice that a statement of evidence violates a prior claim. A similar finding is reported by Baker & Anderson (1982) who found almost half of the sample of college students failed to report one or both of the inconsistencies that were embedded in the text passages they received. It would seem from the results of these studies that a substantial number of college students are insensitive to logical violations in the relationships between ideas in the passages they read. Although most of them appreciate the logical inconsistencies between statements when they are asked specifically about them (Baker & Anderson, 1982), their typical approach to reading does not seem to include the recognition and interpretation of relationships between ideas.

According to the present analysis, the inference is that such absence of cognitive monitoring may be tied to the fact that reading for meaning is a relatively new activity for college freshman. They have no experience with the requirement to think about what they are reading while they are doing so. For them, reading has typically and consistently been a way to learn facts. The requirement to read idea laden sources and then to describe, without aids, the relationships between these ideas in class or on a performance measure is, for the most part, an alien experience. As a consequence, they are not particularly competent at the requisite skills involved in reading for meaning and, if they possess them, they are not inclined to recognize when these skills should be deployed while reading.

Conclusion

So far we have argued that the progression of demands that courses place on students' reading-related study activities throughout the elementary and secondary school years falls short of fostering proficiency at self-directed learning. The lack of demands for selective and generative processing and the presence of processing compensations and tests that require reproduction and recognition of facts combine to impede the development of capabilities that are useful, sometimes necessary, for successful performance on postsecondary study tasks. We have also speculated that the continuities in demands that seem to exist within the elementary and secondary levels and the discontinuity associated with the transition to postsecondary education may produce a large number of students who have difficulty adapting to new and more rigorous demands in selective and generative processing imposed at the college level.

This analysis has focused thus far on two classes of study activities for which data are available: selective and generative processing activities. Future analyses of the development of study proficiency across the life span might focus on additional skills and dispositions that are associated with expert studying in different demand settings, and also examine the extent to which environmental features throughout the life span serve to promote or impede the development of these attributes. Two such attributes that might be the focus for such research and analysis are the characteristics of executive monitoring and self-efficacy. In academic contexts, two course characteristics that may be associated with the development of proficiency at these student characteristics are supports in the form of providing feedback to students on their study activities and the demand for self-initiated studying.

First, consider the incidence of these two course characteristics. Although the survey data necessary to verify these claims are not available, it seems reasonable to assert that throughout the elementary school, secondary school, and college years, students are rarely given the opportunity, through informative feedback, to discover the adequacy and effectiveness of their study methods. On the contrary, students are given minimal information about their performance and about the adequacy of their study methods. They are almost never given information about the link between the two. That is, students are given reading assignments and lectures that they are expected to process, more or less on their own, in preparation for tests covering the material. These tests are usually returned, sometimes with comments, more often with a letter or numerical grade. Although teachers may expect that this kind of information about test performance will affect the quality and quantity of students' reading and test preparation activities, the evidence is that students at the secondary level of schooling do not change their study activities as a result of such general information about test performance. Students at this level need practice in matching study strategies to particular kinds of performance outcomes and then evaluating the results of their use (Ghatala, 1986). Even college level students are sometimes not able to alter their study strategies effectively as a result of experience with tests unless they are given specific item-level information about their performance (Pressley, Snyder, Levin, Murray, & Ghatala, 1987).

During this period, it is also rare for schools to administer diagnostic measures focused on students' reading-related study methods. Students are sometimes given surveys of study methods. However, these surveys tend to be general measures of attitudes or knowledge unrelated to study methods. More importantly, they are almost never administered in ways or with content that takes into account the specificity of study methods to the demands of courses and study tasks (Rohwer, 1984).

The evidence available currently on how students' study activities can be changed and improved provides indirect evidence for the importance of informative feedback. Studies that have successfully improved students' study proficiency typically employ some procedure for appraising students of the connection between the quality and quantity of their study activities and their subsequent performance as well as the necessity to match study activities to the demands of the task (Brown, et al., 1983; Pressley, Snyder, & Cariglia-Bull, 1986). Some of these studies have produced dramatic improvements in students' comprehension-fostering activities as well as generalization to private study behavior (Brown, Palincsar, & Armbruster, 1984; Day, 1986). Yet, in common practice, at no point in students' education does this kind of feedback occur, with the possible exception of instruction in decoding during the elementary years.

Next, consider the demand on self-initiated study. Again, although there are no data to substantiate the claim, it seems that, compared to the academic context, many more of the reading and study episodes that occur during adult life are self-initiated. Many of these study episodes may be prompted by external demands such as those from the job or from maintenance requirements in the home, but it is rare for adults to have reading or studying requirements defined for them by others. Most study events engaged in by adults are self-defined, self-initiated, and self-regulated. There are no reading lists, no assignments, and no due dates. There are few external rewards available except those associated with the final product that results from studying. Moreover, adults typically have a clear purpose in mind when they undertake study; that is, they have a definite and specific conception of the performance they intend their studying to make possible.

Contrast this situation to the way courses are structured throughout the formal educational years. Reading and studying are invariably explicit or implicit requirements of courses. In most instances, source books are provided or named, pages of reading are assigned, a time period within which the reading is to be completed is set by the instructor, and a certain amount of support is often provided to help students initiate, manage, and complete the study effort. Reading and studying are guided activities throughout formal schooling. More importantly, these activities are rarely engaged in on the students' initiative alone. With the possible exception of the graduate school level and occasional student-initiated independent study courses at other levels, it is unusual for students to define and carry out reading or studying tasks of an academic nature on their own, nor do they have a clear conception in advance of the specific performance criteria they will be required to meet. Even in the best cases, they typically acquire such a conception only after they have attempted to meet the criteria—when their papers or tests are returned by the instructor.

These two course features, the absence of feedback supports and the absence of demands on self-initiated reading and studying, are hypothesized to have particular consequences in the development of the habits, dispositions, and competencies that define proficiency at studying, academic and otherwise. First, the absence of feedback at any stage of the development of study strategies is hypothesized to impede the acquisition of executive monitoring capabilities and to limit the number and quality of study methods in students' repertoires. Students who are not accustomed to evaluate the effectiveness of what they do when they read or study and who are not aware of the value of altering their activities to match the demands of the task may not acquire, or may not acquire as readily, the kinds of selective and generative processing methods that will be beneficial in later life.

Second, the absence of demands of self-initiated study, or more accurately, the continual presence of courses that place decisions regarding the content and purposes of studying in the hands of the instructor, may prepare adults inadequately for assuming the responsibility for learning in later grades and post-school life. The continuity of external supervision and direction characteristic of formal schooling may be dysfunctional with respect to the demands of adult life. Adults, having been conditioned to read and study in preparation for a test, may, in the absence of such test events, regard reading and studying as an unnecessary part of their lives. Such freedom from reading and studying may, in fact, be one of the highlights of adult life for these former students. However, it is tempting to believe that the situation could be different. It is possible that a progression of courses that somehow prompt students to read and study on their own for reasons of self-enhancement rather than test preparation might succeed in producing adults who are not only able, but willing, to be lifelong learners.

Third, variance in both feedback and the opportunity to engage in self-initiated and self-directed learning may affect yet another characteristic associated with proficient studying: self-efficacy. Self-efficacy, in the context of academic study-ing, is the self-assessment of one's academic capabilities, usually relative to others, and the belief that one can affect academic outcomes through effort. Positive feelings of self-efficacy have been linked with the use of selective and generative study activities (Thomas, Iventosch, & Rohwer, 1987; Kurtz & Borkowski, 1984), with the disposition to expend effort intensely and persistently on learning tasks (Bandura, 1982; Butkowsky & Willows, 1980), and with the tendency to engage in task-appropriate self-monitoring and self-talk during learning (Ames, 1984; Kuhl, 1985).

The influence of course features on students' evaluations of personal efficacy is apparently quite substantial, although much of the existing research concerns the effect of so-called ego-threatening conditions such as goal structure, type of reward, and workload (Ames & Archer, 1987; Ames & Felker, 1979; Bandura & Schunk, 1981; Bates, 1979; Frieze, 1980; Mayer, 1983). Evidence concerning the relation-ship between the presence of feedback and self-efficacy and between opportunities for self-initiation or self-regulation and self-efficacy are somewhat more indirect and in need of further examination (Corno, 1987; Corno & Rohrkemper, 1985; Covington & Beery, 1976; Thomas, 1980). Such research should focus on the effect of innovative instructional environments on students' engagement in different kinds of study activities and on the mediating role of self-efficacy in promoting proficiency at academic studying.

References

Ames, C. (1984). Competitive, cooperative, and individualistic goal structures: A cognitive motivational analysis. In R.E. Ames & C. Ames (Eds.), *Research on motivation in education* (Vol. 1, pp. 177-208). New York: Academic Press.

Ames, C., & Archer, J. (1987). *Achievement goals in the classroom: Student learning strategies and motivation processes.* Paper presented at the annual meeting of the American Educational Research Association, Washington, DC.

Ames, C., & Felker, D. (1979). An examination of children's attribution and achievement-related evaluation in competitive, cooperative, and individualistic goal structures. *Journal of Educational Psychology, 71,* 413-420.

Anderson, T.H. (1979). Study skills and learning strategies. In H.F. O'Neil, Jr. & C.D. Spielberger (Eds.), *Cognitive and affective learning strategies* (pp. 77-79). New York: Academic Press.

Baker, L. (1979). Comprehension monitoring: Identifying and coping with text confusions. *Journal of Reading Behavior, 11,* 365-374.

Baker, L., & Anderson, R.I. (1982). Effects of inconsistency of information on text processing: Evidence for comprehension monitoring. *Reading Research Quarterly, 17,* 281-294.

Bandura, A. (1982). Self-efficacy mechanism in human agency. *American Psychologist, 37*(2), 122-147.

Bandura, A., & Schunk, D.H. (1981). Cultivating competence, self-efficacy, and intrinsic interest through proximal self-motivation. *Journal of Personality and Social Psychology, 41,* 586-598.

Bates, J.A. (1979). Extrinsic reward and intrinsic motivation: A review with implications for the classroom. *Review of Educational Research, 49,* 557-576.

Bransford, J.D., Nitsch, K.E., & Franks, J.J. (1977). Schooling and the facilitation of knowing. In R.C. Anderson, R.J. Spiro, & W.E. Montague (Eds.), *Schooling and the acquisition of knowledge* (pp. 31-56). Hillsdale, NJ: Erlbaum.

Bransford, J.D., Stein, B.S., Shelton, T.S., & Owings, R.A. (1981). Cognition and adaptation: The importance of learning to learn. In J.H. Harvey (Ed.), *Cognition, social behavior and the environment* (pp. 93-110). Hillsdale, NJ: Erlbaum.

Brennan, S., Winograd, P.N., Bridge, C.A., & Hiebert, E.H. (1986). A comparison of observer reports and self-reports of study practices used by college students. *Solving problems in literacy: Thirty-fifth yearbook of the National Reading Conference.*

Brown, A.L., Bransford, J.D., Ferrara, R.A., & Campione, J.C. (1983). Learning, remembering, and understanding. In J.H. Flavell & E.H. Markman (Eds.), *Handbook of child psychology: Cognitive development* (Vol.3, pp. 77-106). New York: Wiley.

Brown, A.L., Palincsar, A.S., & Armbruster, B.B. (1984). Instructing comprehension-fostering activities in interactive learning situations. In H. Mandl, N.L. Stein, & T. Trabasso (Eds.), *Learning and comprehension of text* (pp. 255-286). Hillsdale, NJ: Erlbaum.

Brown, A.L., & Smiley, S.S. (1977). Rating the importance of structural units of prose passages: A problem of metacognitive development. *Child Development, 48,* 1-8.

Brown, A.L., & Smiley, S.S. (1978). The development of strategies for studying texts. *Child Development, 49,* 1076-1088.

Brown, A.L., Smiley, S.S., & Lawton, S.W.C. (1978). The effects of experience on the selection of suitable retrieval cues for studying texts. *Child Development, 49,* 829-835.

Butkowski, I.S., & Willows, D.M. (1980). Cognitive-motivational characteristics of children varying in reading ability: Evidence for learned helplessness in poor readers. *Journal of Educational Psychology, 72,* 408-422.

Christopoulos, J.P., Rohwer, W.D., Jr., & Thomas, J.W. (1987). Grade-level differences in students' study activities as a function of course characteristics. *Contemporary Educational Psychology, 12,* 303-323.

Corno, L. (1986). The metacognitive control components of self-regulated learning. *Contemporary Educational Psychology, 11,* 333-346.

Corno, L. (1987). Teaching and self-regulated learning. In D.C. Berliner & B. Rosenshine (Eds.), *Talks to teachers* (pp. 249-266). New York: Random House.

Corno, L., & Rohrkemper, M. (1985). The intrinsic motivation to learn in classrooms. In C. Ames & R. Ames (Eds.), *Research on motivation in education* (Vol. 2, pp. 53-92). New York: Academic Press.

Covington, M.V., & Beery, R.G. (1976). *Self-worth and school learning.* New York: Holt, Rinehart & Winston.

Craik, F.I.M., & Lockhart, R.S. (1972). Levels of processing: A framework for memory research. *Journal of Verbal Learning and Verbal Behavior, 11,* 671-684.

Davey, B., & McBride, S. (1986). Effects of question-generation training on reading comprehension. *Journal of Educational Psychology, 78,* 256-262.

Day, J.D. (1986). Teaching summarization skills: Influences of student ability and strategy difficulty. *Cognition and Instruction, 3,* 193-210.

Entwistle, N.J., Hanley, M., & Hounsell, D.J. (1979). Identifying distinctive approaches to studying. *Higher Education, 8,* 365-380.

Fleming, M., & Chambers, B. (1983). Teacher-made tests: Windows on the classroom. In W.R. Hathaway (Ed.), *Testing in the schools.* San Francisco: Jossey-Bass.

Frieze, I.H. (1980). Beliefs about success and failure in the classroom. In J.H. McMillan (Ed.), *The social psychology of school learning* (pp. 39-78). New York: Academic Press.

Ghatala, E.H. (1986). Strategy monitoring training enables young learners to select effective strategies. *Educational Psychologist, 21,* 43-54.

Glover, J.A., Plake, B.S., & Zimmer, J.W. (1982). Distinctiveness of encoding and memory for learning tasks. *Journal of Educational Psychology, 74,* 189-198.

Goldman, R., & Warren, R. (1973). Discriminant analysis of study strategies connected with college grade success in different major fields. *Journal of Educational Measures, 10*, 39-47.

Jensen Delucchi, J., Rohwer, W.D., Jr., & Thomas, J.W. (1985). Study time allocation as a function of grade level and course characteristics. *Contemporary Educational Psychology, 12*, 365-380.

Kiewra, K.S., & Fletcher, H.J. (1984). The relationship between levels of notetaking and achievement. *Human Learning, 3*, 273-280.

Kuhl, J. (1985). Volitional mediators of cognition-behavior consistency: Self-regulatory processes and action versus state orientation. In J.Kuhl & J.Beckman (Eds.), *Action control* (pp. 101-128). New York: Springer-Verlag.

Kurtz, B.E. & Borkowski, J.G. (1984). Children's metacognition: Exploring relations among knowledge, process, and motivational variables. *Journal of Experimental Child Psychology, 37*, 335-354.

Mayer, M.L (1983). On doing well in science: why Johnny no longer excells; Why Sarah never did. In S.G. Paris, G.M. Olson, & H.W. Stevenson (Eds.), *Learning and motivation in the classroom*. Hillsdale, NJ: Erlbaum.

Meyer, B.J.F., Brandt, D.N., & Bluth, G.J. (1980). Use of top-level structure in text: Key for reading comprehension of ninth-grade students. *Reading Research Quarterly, 16*, 72-103.

Meyer, R.E. (1987). Instructional variables that influence cognitive processes during reading. In B.Britton & S.Glynn (Eds.), *Executive control processes in reading* (pp. 201-216). Hillsdale, NJ: Erlbaum.

Miller, C.M.L., & Parlett, M.R. (1974). *Up to the mark: A study of the examination game*. London: Society for Research into Higher Education.

Peper, R.J., & Mayer, R.E. (1986). Generative effects of notetaking during science lectures. *Journal of Educational Psychology, 78*, 34-38.

Pressley, M., Borkowski, J.G., & O'Sullivan, J.T. (1985). Metamemory and the teaching of strategies. In D.L. Forrest-Pressley, G.E. MacKinnon, & T.G. Waller (Eds.), *Metacognition, cognition, and human performance* (pp. 111-153). New York: Academic Press.

Pressley, M., Snyder, B.L., & Cariglia-Bull,T. (1986). How can good strategy use be taught to children?: Evaluation of six alternative approaches. In S. Cormier & J. Hagman (Eds.), *Transfer of learning: Contemporary research and applications*. Orlando, FL: Academic Press.

Pressley, M., Snyder, B.L., Levin, J.R., Murray, H.G., & Ghatala, E.S. (1987). Perceived readiness for examination performance (PREP) produced by initial reading of text and text containing adjunct questions. *Reading Research Quarterly, 22*, 219-236.

Roueche, J.E., Baker, G.A., & Roueche, S.D. (1984). *College responses to low-achieving students: A national study*. Orlando, FL: HBJ Media Systems.

Rohwer, W.D., Jr. (1984). An invitation to a developmental psychology of studying. In F.J. Morrison, C.A. Lord, & D.P. Keating (Eds.), *Advances in applied developmental psychology* (Vol 1, pp. 1-57). New York: Academic Press.

Rohwer, W.D., Jr, & Thomas, J.W. (1987). The role of mnemonic strategies in study effectiveness. In M.A. McDaniel, & M. Pressley (Eds.), *Imagery and related mnemonic processes: Theories, individual differences, and applications* (pp. 428-450). New York: Springer-Verlag.

Schmeck, R.R. (1983). Learning styles of college students. In R.F. Dillon, & R.R. Schmeck (Eds.), *Individual differences in cognition* (Vol 1, pp. 233-280). New York: Academic Press.

Schmeck, R.R., & Grove, E. (1979). Academic achievement and individual differences in learning processes. *Applied Psychological Measurement, 3*, 43-49.

Schuman, H., Walsh, E., Olson, C. & Etheridge, B. (1985). Effort and reward: The assumption that college grades are affected by the quantity of study. *Social Forces, 63*, 945-966.

Shimmerlik, S.M., & Nolan, J.D. (1976). Reorganization and the recall of prose. *Journal of Educational Psychology, 68*, 779-786.

Svensson, L. (1977). On qualitative differences in learning: III. Study skills and learning. *British Journal of Educational Psychology, 47*, 233-243.

Thomas, J.W. (1980). Agency and achievement: Self-management and self-regard. *Review of Educational Research, 50*, 213-240.

Thomas, J.W., Iventosch, L., & Rohwer, W.D., Jr. (1987). Relationships among students characteristics, study activities, and achievement as a function of grade level and course characteristics. *Contemporary Educational Psychology, 12*, 334-364.

Thomas, J.W., & Rohwer, W.D., Jr. (1986). Academic studying: The role of learning strategies. *Educational Psychologist, 21*, 19-41.

Thomas, P.R., & Bain, J.D. (1982). Consistency in learning strategies. *Higher Education, 11*, 249-252.

Tough, A. (1968). Why adults learn: A study of the major reasons for beginning and continuing a learning project. *Monographs in Adult Education, 3*.

Tough, A. (1977). Major learning efforts: Recent research and future directions. *Adult Education, 28*, 250-263.

13
Change in Reading Ability and Attitudes from Childhood to Adulthood: A Life Span Perspective

M Cecil Smith

Introduction

Research on the development of reading abilities has often failed to view the discontinuous nature of how reading skills are used in different reading contexts throughout the life span. Reading skills and abilities will vary in forms, contents, and purposes at different times, depending upon both environmental and intrapersonal factors. Reading for a job-related task relies upon much different skills than reading a child's bedtime story, for example. There is also evidence that reading in high school does not prepare the individual for the often specialized forms of reading found in the adult world of work (Mikulecky, 1982). There may be as much skill development in reading-to-learn in adulthood as there is when learning-to-read in childhood. A life span examination of reading can inform both researchers and practitioners about: (a) how the process of learning-to-read enhances reading-to-learn and (b) how reading-to-learn enhances cognitive development.

The research reported in this chapter was undertaken to examine the development of reading skills from a life span developmental perspective. A sample of adults who were tracked through their school years in a longitudinal study were the subjects of this study. All were assessed on several standardized and experimental reading measures in a follow-up study approximately 20 years after graduating from high school.

A life span examination of reading skills is important for several reasons. First, reading skills are used throughout most of any literate person's lifetime. Second, there are important shifts in the purposes for reading at different points across the life span. Third, studying the acquisition of reading skills in early childhood in isolation from how such skills are used throughout the later school years and in adulthood limits our understanding of intellectual development via reading. Fourth, the research methodologies present for studying reading skill at one age may or may not be appropriate for studying reading at any other age, given that reading occurs for different reasons and in different contexts throughout life. Fifth, given the controversies extant in the literature on cognitive declines with age (e.g., Baltes & Schaie, 1976; Horn & Donaldson, 1976), it is necessary to examine how particular cognitive abilities are used in specific contexts over time. Reading provides such a context.

Life span developmental psychology has greatly influenced the philosophies and methodologies of experimental psychologists during the past decade (Baltes, 1987; Rebok, 1987). Reading is amenable to examination from a life span perspective, because it is a cognitive skill that is used, and that undergoes various changes, throughout the course of the individual reader's life span. Reading comprehension skills develop in the years in which reading is taught at school. Once the child has mastered the basics of reading (e.g., letter-sound correspondence, word recognition) and becomes a proficient reader, further developments occur in knowledge acquisition through reading and by other means. One of the most cherished goals of American education is the development among students of a lifelong interest in reading (Gentile, Haas, & Robinson, 1985). School reading curricula are created with the implicit intention of encouraging students to make reading an important daily ritual. Much classroom activity in the primary grades is directed toward reading instruction, and children are encouraged to practice reading outside of the classroom (Anderson, Wilson, & Fielding,, 1988; Taylor, Frye, & Maruyama, 1990).

Reading comprehension skills continue to develop well beyond the years when the child is learning to read. Developments in areas such as cognitive monitoring and vocabulary acquisition, for example, enable the growth of more mature comprehension skills, which are put to use across a range of reading contexts. The subsequent school years provide opportunities for—in fact require—reading as a way of learning about the world.

Adults read to learn about the world when engaged in leisure reading or other kinds of reading activities–either purposefully or unintentionally. The knowledge gained from reading a variety of text sources allows the individual to improve the quality of his or her life. Until quite recently, little attention has been focused on examining the skills of literate adults. This lack of attention may be due, in part, to the assumption that if an individual is literate, reading problems do not exist for that person because he or she possesses at least the minimum competencies for reading to "survive" in society. Recent research has shown, however, that many literate adults need to improve their literacy skills. A National Assessment of Educational Progress study of American adults aged 21 to 25 (Kirsch & Jungeblut, 1986) found that although illiteracy is not a problem for these persons, *literacy* is. That is, sizeable numbers of these individuals have difficulty with literacy tasks of moderate complexity, such as interpreting the instructions for an appliance warranty.

Another factor resulting in a lack of attention to the skills of literate adults has to do with the allocation of scarce resources. Much energy and research funding is directed toward understanding how children learn to read and how to instruct them in reading. Less attention is paid to understanding what kinds of reading behaviors these persons engage in when they grow to adulthood. This is reflected in reading research—there is only one published study that examines "literacy performance" across the life span (Northcutt, 1975).

Although adults are rarely required to study and remember text information in the same manner as school-age children, there are many instances in which adults do study texts for a variety of purposes. Adults read all kinds of job-related materials, for example, and these contain information that they must know expertly (Kirsch & Guthrie, 1984). There are many events in everyday life in which adults may be formally tested over information that they have read (e.g., employment examinations or the written portion of a driver's license test). There is also the growing trend of adults returning to formal educational settings in adult basic education classes, vocational retraining workshops, and university courses to retool their skills in order to remain abreast of changes in the workplace. How effective, then, are the reading comprehension skills that typical adults possess for the reading tasks encountered in their lives? The study described in this chapter attempts to answer this question. The cognitive variables of interest in this study are briefly reviewed in the next section.

Comprehension and Memory

Good comprehension and memory abilities are important for reading at any age. The competent reader understands and is able to remember important information in text. Reading involves an active search for meaning. Readers construct meaning from text through the trial-and-error processes of formulating, testing, and accepting or rejecting hypotheses about the text information (Mason & Au, 1986). This means that the reader must make connections between his or her knowledge of the world and knowledge of the text in order to comprehend. Comprehension occurs when the reader establishes logical connections between ideas in a text and his or her prior knowledge (Johnston, 1983). Many research studies have examined the development of these skills among children who are learning to read (for a review, see Pearson & Gallagher, 1985). There is also much interest in discovering the most effective ways to teach comprehension in reading classrooms (Dole, Duffy, Roehler, & Pearson, 1991; Winn & Palincsar, this volume).

A long tradition in psychology has explored the development of memory abilities related to reading (e.g., Barlett, 1932; Huey, 1908; Mandler & Johnson, 1977; Meyer & Rice, 1983; Meyer, Young, & Bartlett, this volume; Paris, 1975; Paris & Lindauer, 1977; Perfetti & Goldman, 1976). Utilizing the information in a text requires readers to process the text to the extent that they can retrieve the information from memory when needed. Many experimental memory tasks have been used to examine adults' abilities to recall text information (e.g., Dixon & Bäckman, this volume; Hultsch, Hertzog, & Dixon, 1984; Meyer & Rice, 1983).

Generally, the initial research in this area, which compared younger and older adults, demonstrated age-related declines in memory abilities. Often, however, what appears to be deficits in older adults' memory for text information is actually due to differences between age groups in verbal ability, educational attainment, and prior knowledge (Meyer, 1987). Also, task demands and text characteristics play a role in how well information is recalled, and these factors may have different effects on persons of varying ages. This caveat does not diminish the fact that some adults do suffer some decrements in their memory skills with age (Craik, 1977). However, such decline is not the general rule.

The cognitive skills required for comprehending and remembering text information are not static. The skills acquired in childhood develop and change with age (DiVesta, Hayward, & Orlando, 1979; Paris, 1975; Paris & Lindauer, 1977). It is reasonable to assume that, with experience, these cognitive skills will be more highly developed in adulthood (Pressley, Beard, & Brown, 1991). Losses in certain cognitive skills due to aging may be compensated for by gains due to experience with a variety of reading forms and tasks. The cumulative influences of educational attainment and occupational pursuits and achievements can influence the development of reading skills (Fisher, 1978; Gray & Rogers, 1956; Mikulecky, 1982) as well as the particular types of skills that develop.

Reading also appears to have an impact on reflective thought (Francis, 1987). Readers must consciously consider the thoughts of authors as well as their own thoughts about what they are reading. The ways in which written language must be considered as it is being read makes reading a powerful tool for the development of metacognitive processes (Garner, 1987).

Metacognition and Reading

Metacognition refers to a person's knowledge of his or her own cognitive abilities, and the strategies that allow readers to control and regulate their reading behavior, such as knowing how much effort to expend in order to remember a piece of information (Flavell, 1984). An individual might choose from a variety of strategies that are helpful in reducing the mental effort needed for such a task. Thus, metacognition can be said to consist of two components that overlap to varying degrees depending upon the cognitive task. These are: (a) knowledge about cognition and (b) regulation of cognition (Baker & Brown, 1984a).

The second category consists of the self-regulatory behaviors used by readers to fix up reading problems (Baker & Brown, 1984a). These actions include looking back in a text to retrieve information, skimming over unimportant details, and utilizing textual cues (e.g., pictures) to aid one's understanding. Because reading is an important way of acquiring information and knowledge, the development and use of these strategic behaviors is crucial to proficient reading.

A reader who can monitor his or her own comprehension and memory efforts has a better basis for choosing appropriate reading strategies when problems are encountered (Winograd & Johnston, 1982). Comprehension monitoring involves the evaluation and regulation of one's own comprehension processes (Baker, 1979). When comprehension fails, monitoring allows the reader to draw upon his or her repertoire of strategies in order to repair the problem. Good readers recognize when comprehension and memory strategies are needed to aid in the understanding and remembering of text information (Baker & Brown, 1984a). Brown and De-Loache (1978) claim that comprehension monitoring strategies do not automatically develop with age, but are dependent on the reader's prior knowledge and expertise.

Because metacognitive strategies are crucial to being a good reader, it is important to examine how these strategies develop and are related to comprehension and memory skills. Several questions regarding metacognitive abilities for reading were addressed in the research described in this chapter. These are: (a) What is the relationship between adults' reading comprehension skills and comprehension and memory monitoring? (b) Is it possible to predict how well adults can monitor their comprehension and memory of text from childhood measures of reading comprehension?

Development of Reading Attitudes

Attitudes are also assumed to be an important factor in the development of reading skills (Alexander & Filler, 1976). People possess particular attitudes about reading: as a way of acquiring knowledge, as a leisure activity, or even as an unpleasant task to be avoided. It is likely that the attitudes that people possess concerning reading are a result of their early experiences with reading—both at home and in school. Frankly, we know very little about how reading attitudes develop, how they may be influenced by instruction or modeling, and how they change over time. No longitudinal research to date has examined how early reading abilities and activities may shape adults' reading attitudes.

The reading attitudes of the adults in the study reported here were examined in relationship to occupation and educational attainment. The relationship between reading attitude and reading performance was also examined.

Much can be learned about how people approach reading tasks by examining their reading attitudes. The attitude an individual has about reading as an intellectual activity will affect the person's motivations for reading, reading ability, and reading habits. Although there is some evidence that reading attitudes are amenable to change over time in childhood (Healy, 1963, 1965; Parker & Paradis, 1986), there is no direct evidence that adults' reading attitudes result from childhood attitudes about reading. There is some evidence that occupational reading demands in adulthood influence adults' reading attitudes (Kirsch & Guthrie, 1984). Adults' reading attitudes are often pragmatic: When reading has a rewarding outcome (e.g., job advancement, relaxation), it is more highly valued (Harvey & Sullivan, 1978).

It is reasonable to assume that attitudes about the importance of reading as a necessary life skill are created *before* children begin to read. Literate parents are likely to model for their children appropriate reading behaviors and attitudes (Hanson, 1969; Hiebert, 1979). Entry into school and the subsequent, formalized approach to reading instruction may serve either to heighten or diminish the child's enthusiasm for reading. These attitudes will indirectly influence: (a) a person's choices of favorite subjects in school, (b) career choice, and (c) entry into an occupation.

No reading research to date has focused on a group of individuals and tracked the development of their reading skills throughout childhood and then directly compared childhood ability to adult reading comprehension skills, while taking into account the influences of educational and occupational achievements. Such an effort was the focus of the research reported in this chapter. This research project was also concerned with assessing the development of metacognitive reading skills and reading attitude from childhood to adulthood.

Method

The purpose of this study was to determine if adults' (a) reading comprehension ability, (b) metacognitive reading skills, and (c) attitudes about reading could be predicted from childhood measures of reading achievement and intelligence.

Sample

Adults who had participated as children in two longitudinal investigations of the effects of school reorganization on academic achievement in Wisconsin (Kreitlow, 1962, 1966) were recruited as subjects for this study. Four-hundred and nine adults from the population of 1,599 in both the original (1949 to 1961) and replication (1954 to 1966) studies were contacted by mail and asked to participate in a study of adults' reading skills. Eighty-four people participated. Fifty-six of these individuals were given standardized measures of reading comprehension and vocabulary and experimental measures of reading comprehension and memory for text. The experimental measures also included assessments of comprehension- and memory-monitoring abilities. These persons and the remaining 28 people completed detailed questionnaires, which asked for information about their daily reading habits and attitudes toward reading.

The measures of interest from the original Kreitlow studies (1962, 1966) included: (a) the metropolitan reading achievement subtest administered to students in 1st, 6th, and 9th grades, (b) the California reading achievement subtest was administered to 12th-grade subjects in lieu of the metropolitan, and (c) The

Kuhlman-Anderson Group Intelligence Test administered in 1st, 6th, 9th, and 12th grades.

The measures of interest for the adult study included: (a) An abbreviated version of the Nelson-Denny Reading Test (NDRT) was given, which contained a 50-item vocabulary and a 24-item comprehension subtest, (b) an experimental task was developed that required subjects to read a lengthy text passage and complete two 10-item tests, and, (c) a questionnaire was given that assessed adults' reading attitudes. Additional questionnaires on reading habits, work-related reading demands, and perceptions of changes in one's own reading skills over time were administered and are reported by Smith (1988a).

Experiment Subjects read one of two texts: (a) an easy passage (reading level equal to Grade 5) or (b) a difficult passage (reading level equal to college junior). Subjects in both conditions were instructed to read the passage in order to learn the information well enough to tell another person about the article. The topic was a binary star system and was taken from a weekly newsmagazine article. The original article was written at a 13th-grade reading level and was rewritten to obtain the two different reading levels required for the experiment. Both experimental versions contained five paragraphs and were of equal word length (520 words).

After reading, the passage was removed, and all subjects rated their understanding of the text information (how well they thought they could remember the information), their interest in the topic, and their prior knowledge of the topic. A 4-point rating scale was used (e.g., 4 = *understanding was very good*; 1 = *understanding was very poor*). These ratings were referred to as *passage-monitoring* indices.

Two 10-item tests were then administered. During the first test (memory test), subjects were not allowed to look at the text passage. Following the first test, subjects were given the text passage and told that they *should* refer to the text while answering questions for the second test (comprehension test). The rationale for the open book approach for the comprehension test was that it becomes a comprehension matter when the text is directly available for inspection, with memory demands diminished. In contrast, the closed book approach is a memory task, because the reader must retrieve information without access to the source (Levin, 1982).

Following each question on both tests, subjects rated how confident they were that they had correctly answered the question. These confidence ratings were considered to be indicators of comprehension- and memory-monitoring, and were referred to as *item-monitoring* indices. Both tests were timed, and everyone was given 10 minutes to complete each.

Results

Regression Analyses

The prediction of reading performance from childhood to adulthood was of interest in this study. Using multiple regression analyses, I attempted to determine how much variance on the adult performance measure (e.g., standardized and experimental measures of reading comprehension and memory) could be accounted for from childhood measures of reading achievement.

The measures of reading achievement and intelligence from the later school years (i.e., 9th and 12th grades) explained a larger proportion of the variance on the adult standardized and experimental tests than did the earlier childhood measures (i.e., 1st and 6th grades). These findings make sense intuitively, because as individuals progress through school, they encounter countless demands and opportunities for reading, thinking, and problem solving. For example, on the *NDRT*, the childhood reading achievement measures were regressed. The 9th- and 12th-grade measures were the best predictors of adult reading achievement; together, these accounted for 79% of the variance. The IQ measures were then regressed. The 1st-, 6th-, and 9th-grade IQ scores were significant predictors of adult reading achievement, with the respective correlations increasing at each grade level. These variables accounted for 58% of the variance. The 12th-grade IQ score was not significant, accounting for less than 1% of the variance.

Because reading achievement and intelligence are highly correlated, it was assumed that childhood IQ would be a better predictor of reading achievement in adulthood than would be the childhood measures of reading achievement. Obviously, intellectual skill underlies the ability to comprehend and remember. The reading achievement measures and the IQ scores were then regressed. This analysis revealed, however, that the 9th- and 12th-grade reading achievement scores were better predictors than the IQ scores, accounting for 79% of the variance.

There are at least two explanations for the finding that IQ is not the best predictor of reading comprehension ability. First, more intelligent persons are not always good readers (Jackson & Myers, 1982). They may be distracted by ideas unrelated to what they are reading, may only skim texts to get the gist, or may rely on their memory for or prior knowledge of, a topic rather than processing the text information fully. Second, as more difficult texts are encountered, comprehension depends on general language ability and prior knowledge (Resnick, 1984). Finally, the skills needed to perform well on IQ tests (e.g., logical and abstract reasoning, quantitative skills, sequencing ability) are not the same as those required for high performance on tests of reading comprehension (e.g., inferencing), although the skills certainly overlap.

This research suggests that there is both stability and change across several dimensions of reading from childhood to adulthood. Reading comprehension ability appears to remain fairly stable from early adolescence into middle adulthood. This finding lends support to other theoretical models suggesting a shift from learning-to-read in childhood to reading-to-learn in adolescence and adulthood (e.g., Chall, 1967). Other research has demonstrated that there are developmental changes in reading ability in areas such as prior knowledge, strategy use, and vocabulary acquisitions. The present study did not address these particular aspects of reading ability, however.

Cognitive monitoring. The relationships among childhood reading ability, adult monitoring skills, and adult reading attitudes were also examined using regression analysis. There were two assessments of memory monitoring: a rating of how well the text passage information could be remembered (passage-monitoring) and a confidence rating that memory test questions had been correctly answered (item-monitoring). There were also two comprehension monitoring measures: for comprehension of the passage information and for the comprehension test items. Regression analyses revealed that vocabulary and comprehension, and intelligence as assessed by the IQ tests, best fit the regression model for predicting item monitoring ability.

The passage memory monitoring measure was significantly correlated with the following variables: the passage comprehension monitoring measure ($r = .56$), the memory test ($r = .33$), and the item-monitoring measures for both the memory test ($r = -.28$) and the comprehension test ($r = .39$). The memory test item monitoring measure was significantly correlated with the 1st-grade IQ score ($r = -.37$). Memory monitoring and reading attitude were not correlated with one another.

These relationships suggest that individuals' monitoring of understanding and memory are less than optimum. Often, when a person believes that he or she has understood and can recall information from a text, subsequent test performance indicates an "illusion-of-knowing" (Glenberg & Epstein, 1985). This phenomenon occurs when the reader fails to correctly answer test questions while being confident that the text information has been understood (Schommer & Surber, 1986). The disparate correlations between passage memory-monitoring and the two tests' item-monitoring indices are likely due to the memory test being more difficult than the comprehension test for both text conditions. The subjects were less confident that they had answered the memory test questions correctly–even though their passage-monitoring ratings for memory were high following reading.

The regression analysis for the comprehension test item-monitoring measure revealed that reading comprehension and vocabulary test performance in 12th grade best fit the regression model, accounting for 41% of the variance. The comprehension test item-monitoring measure was significantly correlated with the comprehension ($r = .76$) and memory tests ($r = .45$). Comprehension monitoring appears to be necessary for *both* understanding and remembering test information. That is, understanding is a prerequisite for remembering.

The item-monitoring measure also correlated modestly with 9th- and 12th-grade reading comprehension ($r = .43$ for both) and 1st- and 9th-grade IQ scores ($r = .31$ and .46, respectively). Although these relationships are not very simple to interpret, it appears that the kinds of intellectual skills assessed by IQ tests and reading comprehension ability are crucial to the reader's ability to monitor how well text information is understood.

The passage comprehension-monitoring measure was significantly correlated with the Nelson-Denny comprehension subtest ($r = .27$), the memory and comprehension tests ($r = .43$ and $.40$, respectively), and the 12th-grade measure of reading comprehension ($r = .29$). These data suggest that those readers who accurately judge their understanding of text information are more likely to perform well on tests of comprehension and memory. Again, the ability to monitor understanding is crucial to comprehension and memory of text information. The correlation between comprehension test item-monitoring and reading attitudes was .26, suggesting that there is some interrelationship between reading comprehension, comprehension monitoring, and reading attitude.

Finally, a regression analysis also showed sex, age, and education to be predictive of reading attitudes, accounting for 36% of the variance on the reading attitude measure. The sex differences for reading attitudes are discussed in more detail later in this chapter. Education is a major mediator of reading attitudes: the more education a person attains, the more positive their attitudes toward reading.

Experiment results. Significant performance differences were found between the two conditions on the memory and comprehension tests, although the groups did not differ on their passage ratings of understanding, memory, prior knowledge, and topic interest. Given the same tasks, those who read the easy text outperformed those who read the difficult text–a finding that is not at all surprising.

Somewhat more surprising was that the experimental manipulation demonstrated that the adults who could be considered very good readers had problems understanding and remembering the text passages. Also, across both text conditions, subjects were better at monitoring their memory test performance than their comprehension test performance. That is, the subjects realized that they did not, or could not, recall the text information; they were more confident that they had understood the information–even when they did not. The results suggest that comprehension monitoring and memory monitoring are separable skills (see also Smith, 1988b). Monitoring ability interacts with text difficulty, however.

The adults who read the easy text were more accurate in monitoring their memory and understanding of the text information than were those who read the difficult text. The subjects who read the easy text were more accurate in monitoring their comprehension than their memory of the text information. Readers of the difficult text were better able to monitor their memory than their comprehension. That is, they recognized that they could not recall the very difficult text information accurately, even though they felt that they *had* understood the information. Those who read the easy text, on the other hand, appeared to have overestimated their ability to understand and remember the text information.

These findings suggest a subtle, yet salient, distinction between adults' memory-monitoring and comprehension-monitoring skills. Adults appear to be much more confident in their ability to understand information than to remember text information. Their confidence in understanding, however, tends to create a false sense of security that the information can indeed be recalled. When faced with the actual recall task, adults are much less confident that they have accurately remembered the information–particularly when the text is difficult.

The findings from the analyses of these metacognitive variables are not very "clean" and present some problems for explaining the differences on comprehension-monitoring and memory-monitoring ability. First of all, the passage-monitoring measure was not an "on-line" measure of monitoring: subjects rated their understanding and memory of the passage *after* reading, rather than while reading. This method may not be the most effective way to assess monitoring of understanding and memory (Baker & Brown, 1984b).

Reading attitude. Adults' reading attitudes were also examined, and reading attitude scores were correlated with their comprehension test scores to determine if there was any significant relationship. It was expected that those readers who scored high on the reading attitude measure (that is, those persons with a positive attitude toward reading) would have higher comprehension scores than those persons scoring low on the attitude measure (representing a negative attitude toward reading).

There was a modest ($r = .37$), but significant (p .01), relationship between scores on the comprehension test and the reading attitude measure. Generally, then, persons who scored high on the comprehension test also had high, or positive, attitudes toward reading. This is further supported by the finding that adults with a positive reading attitude are more likely to read more materials, read more frequently, and also evaluate their reading skills as being "better than average," as compared to low attitude readers. These results were obtained from the reading habits surveys completed by the adults. Having a good attitude about reading can have a positive effect on one's reading ability, as well as on one's reading behaviors.

I was also interested in determining if those individuals who were good readers in school had more positive reading attitudes as adults. Conversely, do those adults who were poor readers as children have negative reading attitudes as adults? The sample was divided into four groups: those persons who scored above the mean on the standardized reading achievement test at both 1st and 12th grades (*above average* group); those who scored below the mean on both tests (*below average* group); those who scored above the mean at 1st grade, but below the mean at 12th grade (*decline* group); and those who scored below the mean at first grade, but above the mean at 12th grade (*improve* group). There were 27, 11, 8, and 23 persons in each group, respectively. Fifteen persons had missing scores for one test or the other and were not included in this analysis.

The adult reading attitude scores for the persons in these four groups were then examined. A 4 X 3 (Group X Education level) analysis of variance revealed a significant difference between the four groups on the reading attitude score ($F = 3.07$, $df = 6, 57$, p .05), which favored the above average group. That is, those individuals who were above average performers on the reading comprehension tests in both 1st and 12th grades had the most positive reading attitudes as adults. The remaining three groups did not differ from one another on the reading attitude score. This analysis provides more evidence that reading attitude bears a positive relationship to reading ability and may in fact affect performance on reading tests.

The relationships among educational and occupational attainments and reading attitudes were then examined. Three levels of education were identified: high school degree or less; college experience (no degree) or technical school degree; and college degree or postgraduate experience. One-way analyses of variance were performed to determine if reading attitude scores varied by amount of education or level of occupation. Those individuals with more education (e.g., college graduate) had significantly higher reading attitude scores than those with less education (e.g., some college credit or technical school degree; high school degree). As expected, those persons with only a high school education had the poorest reading attitudes.

Significant differences were also apparent among the four occupational groups that were identified (professional, service, labor, homemaker). The professional group had the highest mean attitude score, followed by the service, homemaker, and labor groups, respectively. The labor group's mean attitude score was significantly lower than the other three groups. It is likely that individuals in the labor group have little time for reading and do not need to read for work. Also, reading is likely not reinforced as a useful activity in their personal lives. The analysis showed that most members of this occupational group spent less than 1 hour reading each day. These workers also had the least amount of education.

Sex differences were also found on the reading attitude measure. Females had more positive attitudes toward reading than did males, a finding that supports previous research (Mikulecky, Shanklin, & Caverly, 1979). The sex difference found consistently in childhood (Brown, 1979; Parker & Paradis, 1986; Wallbrown, Levine, & Engin, 1981) regarding reading attitude also holds for adults. There are several likely explanations to account for this sex difference in adulthood. For example, reading is often viewed as a passive activity and as being less masculine. Men are more likely to read to get things done, and women to read for leisure (Mikulecky et al., 1979). Women are more likely to be positively reinforced and have more motivations for reading than men (e.g., sharing information with friends and family).

Concluding Comments and Caveats

This longitudinal investigation of the development of reading comprehension skills, metacognitive abilities, and reading attitudes revealed several findings that will be of interest to those researchers who study changes in cognitive skills over large segments of the life span. The results of this study provide evidence that reading skills continue to develop into adulthood and are mediated by factors such as educational attainment, occupation, and attitudes about reading.

Adults who are good readers have positive attitudes about reading. Good readers are likely to spend more time reading, read a wider variety of different text sources, and read for a variety of different purposes such as for work or for leisure activities (Mikulecky et al., 1979). No direct evidence was obtained to demonstrate that adults with positive attitudes toward reading developed them in childhood. However, the good childhood readers were shown to have positive attitudes about reading as adults. Amount of education also affects reading attitudes. Individuals who continue their schooling are more likely to have favorable reading attitudes, because they recognize the intrinsic value of reading as a way of acquiring other skills, learning about the world, and as a source of pleasure.

Although reading attitudes probably develop early in life, these attitudes are amenable to change (Healy, 1963, 1965). Just how much change can be achieved and how this change affects reading development is a question for future research. Reading researchers who examine reading from a life span perspective should not ignore the effects of reading attitude on the development of adults' reading skills.

Implications for a Life Span Approach to Studying Reading

Reading ability is an important intellectual skill, which can be studied over most of the life span. Although our knowledge of the reading skills of children and young adults is extensive, we possess much less information about reading performance in middle and late adulthood. Most of the information, which we do have about the reading skills of adults, is derived from cross-sectional studies of text processing and memory for text information (e.g., Dixon & Hultsch, 1983; Glynn, Okun, Muth, & Britton, 1983; Meyer & Rice, 1983; Simon, Dixon, Nowak, & Hultsch, 1982; Spilich, 1983; Taub, 1979). Other researchers and educators have also been interested in determining what kinds of texts adults read (Gentile et al., 1985; Rice, 1986) and the literacy practices of adults (Guthrie & Greaney, 1991; Nell, 1988). This research has resulted in a broad picture of the reading interests of adults (e.g., Mikulecky et al., 1979).

Baltes (1987) has referred to gains and losses occurring in certain cognitive skills over the course of the life span. That is, developmental processes consist not only of growth and progression. Declines in certain abilities also occur (e.g., memory loss, decrease in processing speed, flexibility). Reading provides an avenue to explore gains and losses in cognitive skills throughout the life span. The study of the strategic behaviors that adults use to compensate for the loss of particular cognitive skills needed for reading is an area of interest to many. The gains that adults accrue regarding reading appear to be in such areas as "world knowledge," the ability to flexibly apply their knowledge in various contexts, developing understanding of how reading can enhance one's life, and the developing awareness of one's strengths and weaknesses when doing certain cognitive tasks (e.g., realizing that one can make better use of text information if notes are taken rather than depending upon an increasingly unreliable memory).

Metacognitive abilities are important for the development of good reading skills (Garner, 1987). Developments occur over time in a person's knowledge of his or her own cognitive processes and in the strategies for regulating cognitive efforts. The research presented in this chapter indicates that adults can, and do, monitor their cognitive efforts for reading but are better at monitoring understanding than at monitoring how well they can remember–regardless of text difficulty. Adults are more likely to say that they understand something than they are to say that they can recall the information. Monitoring of comprehension is important for successful understanding and recall, because understanding is a prerequisite for accurate recall. Other studies have suggested that comprehension-monitoring abilities continue to develop and improve with further education and more experience in reading across the life span (Zabrucky & Moore, 1991).

Adults tend to be more careful monitors when faced with difficult reading tasks. Adults judge their understanding and memory of highly technical or difficult texts to be poor but are somewhat better able to monitor their memory than comprehension. Good adult readers know that difficult texts require increased efforts for understanding and remembering. This knowledge alone does not necessarily help them understand and remember, however. Prior knowledge of the topic, adequate motivation for the task, and the ability to flexibly apply cognitive strategies are important performance dimensions as well.

There has been a burgeoning of interest in understanding and describing the course of cognitive growth and decline throughout adulthood (e.g., Baltes & Schaie, 1976; Horn & Donaldson, 1976). Related efforts have examined how these patterns of growth and decline affect skills in areas such as reading and problem solving (Hultsch, 1977; Robinson & Maring, 1976; Walmsley & Allington, 1980). Another trend likely to affect psychological research on adult populations is the growing number of aging adults. These persons will demand new and better services in health care and lifelong education, resulting in subsequent demands for more research funding. For example, researchers in diverse fields such as sociology, education, and urban studies are studying the recreational activities of adults (Freysinger, 1988). Reading is a predominant leisure activity for many adults (Guthrie & Greaney, 1991).

There continues to be much interest in understanding the abilities of young and old adults to recall information from text (Dixon & Bäckman, this volume). Other research has attempted to determine the maximum performance of adults (e.g., memorizing very long lists of words) and the concomitant skills needed for such performances under optimal conditions (Baltes & Baltes, 1980).

Reading research in adulthood lacks a clear theoretical model of how cognitive changes across the adult life span affect reading ability. There is a need for a descriptive model of particular gains and losses in reading skill and the compensatory mechanisms that develop concurrently with, or in reaction to, cognitive declines. These compensatory mechanisms or behaviors include the development of strategies, such as notetaking as a memory aid. Other behaviors include efforts at focusing attention or simply reading more often (i.e., practice). Certain skills may become more automatized and clearly offset cognitive deficits in memory, comprehension, cognitive monitoring, speed of processing, and so on. There is a growing interest in the reading skills of adults at all ages. Research has examined the literacy skills of adults at work (Sticht, 1982), when reading for leisure (Mikulecky et al., 1979) and for academic pursuits (Thomas & Rohwer, this volume). What is necessary now is a comprehensive model that attempts to describe developments in reading over the life span.

References

Alexander, J.E., & Filler, R.C. (1976). *Attitudes and reading*. Newark, DE: International Reading Association.

Anderson, R.C., Wilson, P.T., & Fielding, L.G. (1988). Growth in reading and how children spend their time outside of school. *Reading Research Quarterly, 23*, 285-303.

Baker, L. (1979). Comprehension monitoring: Identifying and coping with text confusions. *Journal of Reading Behavior, 11*, 363-374.

Baker, L., & Brown, A. (1984a). Metacognitive development in reading. In P.D. Pearson (Ed.), *Handbook of reading research* (Vol. 1, pp. 353-394). New York: Longman.

Baker, L., & Brown, A. (1984b). Cognitive monitoring in reading. In J. Flood (Ed.), *Understanding reading comprehension* (pp. 21-44). Newark, DE: International Reading Association.

Baltes, P.B. (1987). Theoretical propositions of life-span developmental psychology: On the dynamics between growth and decline. *Developmental Psychology, 23*, 611-626.

Baltes, P.B., & Baltes, M.M. (1980). Plasticity and variability in psychological aging: Methodological and theoretical issues. In G. Gurski (Ed.), *Determining the effects of aging on the central nervous system* (pp. 41-60). Berlin: Schering.

Baltes, P.B., & Schaie, K.W. (1976). On the plasticity of intelligence in adulthood and old age: Where Horn and Donaldson fail. *American Psychologist, 31*, 720-725.

Bartlett, F.C. (1932). *Remembering*. London: Cambridge University Press.

Brown, A.L., & DeLoache, J. (1978). Skills, plans, and self-regulation. In R. Siegler (Ed.), *Children's thinking: What develops?* (pp. 3-35). Hillsdale, NJ: Erlbaum.

Brown, M. (1979). Measuring attitudes to reading—more questions than answers. *Reading, 13*, 13-20.

Chall, J. (1967). *Learning to read: The great debate*. New York: McGraw-Hill.

Craik, F.I.M. (1977). Age differences in human memory. In J.E. Birren & K.W. Schaie (Eds.), *Handbook of the psychology of aging*. New York: Van Nostrand Reinhold.

DiVesta, F.J., Hayward, K.G., & Orlando, V.P. (1979). Developmental trends in monitoring text for comprehension. *Child Development, 50*, 97-105.

Dixon, R.A., & Bäckman, L. (in press). Reading and memory for prose in adulthood: Issues of expertise and compensation. In S.R. Yussen & M.C. Smith (Eds.), *Reading across the life span*. New York: Springer-Verlag.

Dixon, R.A., & Hultsch, D.F. (1983). Metamemory and memory for text relationships in adulthood: A cross-validation study. *Journal of Gerontology, 38*, 689-694.

Dole, J.A., Duffy, G.G., Roehler, L. R., & Pearson, P.D. (1991). Moving from the old to the new: Research on reading comprehension instruction. *Review of Educational Research, 61*, 239-264.

Fisher, D. (1978). *Functional literacy and the schools*. Washington, DC: National Institute of Education.

Flavell, J.H. (1984). *Cognitive development*. Englewood Cliffs, NJ: Prentice-Hall.

Francis, H. (1987). Cognitive implications of learning to read. *Interchange, 18*, 97-108.

Freysinger, V.J. (1988). *The experience of leisure in middle adulthood: Gender differences and changes since young adulthood*. Unpublished doctoral dissertation, University of Wisconsin, Madison.

Garner, R. (1987). *Metacognition and reading comprehension*. Norwoor, NJ: Ablex.

Gentile, L.M., Haas, A.M., & Robinson, R.D. (1985). The older adult as reader. In D.B. Lumsden (Ed.), *The older adult as learner: Aspects of educational gerontology*. New York: McGraw-Hill.

Glenberg, A.M., & Epstein, W. (1985). *Effects of goals on the self-assessment of comprehension of expository text*. Unpublished manuscript, University of Wisconsin, Department of Psychology, Madison, WI.

Glynn, S.M., Okun, M.A., Muth, K.D., & Britton, B.K. (1983). Adults' text recall: An examination of the age-deficit hypothesis. *Journal of Reading Behavior, 15*, 31-41.

Gray, W.S., & Rogers, B. (1956). *Maturity in reading: Its mature appraisal*. Chicago: University of Chicago Press.

Guthrie, J., & Greaney, V. (1991). Literacy acts. In R. Barr, M.L. Kamil, P. Mosenthal, & P.D. Pearson (Eds.). *Handbook of reading research, Vol. 2* (pp. 68-91). New York: Longman.

Hanson, H.S. (1969). The impact of the home literacy environment on reading attitudes. *Elementary English, 46*, 17-24.

Harvey, R.L., & Sullivan, L.G. (1978). What are the reading needs and interests of adults? *Adult Literacy and Basic Education, 1*, 29-32.

Healy, A.K. (1963). Changing children's attitudes toward reading. *Elementary English, 40*, 255-257, 279.

Healy, A.K. (1965). Effects of changing children's attitudes toward reading. *Elementary English, 42*, 269-272.

Hiebert, E. (1979). *The development of reading-related knowledge over the preschool years*. Unpublished doctoral dissertation. University of Wisconsin, Madison.

Horn, J.L., & Donaldson, G. (1976). On the myth of intellectual decline in adulthood. *American Psychologist, 31*, 701-719.

Huey, E.B. (1908). *The psychology and pedagogy of reading*. New York: Macmillan.

Hultsch, D.F. (1977). Learning to learn in adulthood. *Journal of Gerontology, 29*, 64-72.

Hultsch, D.F., Hertzog, C., & Dixon, R.A. (1984). Text recall in adulthood: The role of intellectual abilities. *Developmental Psychology, 20*, 1193-1209.

Jackson, N.E., & Myers, M.G. (1982). Letter naming time, digit span, and precocious reading achievement. *Intelligence, 6,* 311-329.

Johnston, P.H. (1983). *Reading comprehension assessment: A cognitive basis.* Newark, DE: International Reading Association.

Kirsch, I.S., & Guthrie, J.T. (1984). Adult reading practices for work and leisure. *Adult Education Quarterly, 34*(4), 213-232.

Kirsch, I.S., & Jungeblut, A. (1986). *Literacy: Profiles of America's young adults.* Princeton, NJ: Educational Testing Service.

Kreitlow, B.W. (1962). *Long-term study of educational effectiveness of newly-formed centralized school districts in rural areas.* (Cooperative Research Project No. 375). Madison, WI: University of Wisconsin, Department of Education.

Kreitlow, B.W. (1966). *Long-term study of educational effectiveness of newly-formed centralized school districts in rural areas, Part 2.* (Cooperative Research Project No. 1318). Madison, WI: University of Wisconsin, Department of Education.

Levin, J.R. (1982). Pictures as prose-learning devices. In A. Flammer & W. Kintsch (Eds.), *Discourse processing.* Amsterdam: North Holland.

Mandler, J.M., & Johnson, N.S. (1977). Remembrance of things parsed: Story structure and recall. *Cognitive Psychology, 9,* 111-151.

Mason, J.M., & Au, K.H. (1986). *Reading instruction for today.* London: Scott Foresman.

Meyer, B.J.F. (1987). Reading comprehension and aging. In K.W. Schaie (Ed.), *Annual review of gerontology and geriatrics, Vol. 7* (pp. 93-115). New York: Springer-Verlag.

Meyer, B.J.F., & Rice, G.E. (1983). Learning and memory from text across the adult life span. In J. Fine & R.O. Freedle (Eds.), *Developmental studies in discourse.* Norwood, NJ: Ablex.

Meyer, B.J.F., Young, C.J., & Bartlett, B.J. (in press). Reading comprehension and the use of text structure across the adult life span. In S.R. Yussen and M.C. Smith (Eds.), *Reading across the life span.* New York: Springer-Verlag.

Mikulecky, L. (1982). Job literacy: The relationship between school preparation and workplace actuality. *Reading Research Quarterly, 17,* 400-419.

Mikulecky, L., Shanklin, N.L., & Caverly, D.C. (1979). *Adult reading habits, attitudes, and motivations: A cross-sectional study.* (Monographs in Teaching and Learning, No. 2). Bloomington, IN: Indiana University, School of Education.

Nell, V. (1988). The psychology of reading for pleasure: Needs and gratifications. *Reading Research Quarterly, 23,* 6-50.

Northcutt, N. (1975). *Adult functional competency: A summary.* Austin: University of Texas, Industrial and Business Training Bureau.

Paris, S.G. (1975). Integration and inference in children's comprehension and memory. In F. Restle, R. Shiffrin, J. Castellan, H. Lindman, & D. Pisoni (Eds.), *Cognitive theory* (Vol. 1). Hillsdale, NJ: Erlbaum.

Paris, S.G., & Lindauer, K. (1977). Constructive processes in children's comprehension and memory. In R.V. Kail & J.S. Hagen (Eds.), *Perspectives on the development of memory and cognition*. Hillsdale, NJ: Erlbaum.

Parker, A., & Paradis, E. (1986). Attitude development toward reading in grades one through six. *Journal of Educational Research, 79*, 313-315.

Pearson, P.D., & Gallagher, M.C. (1985). The instruction of reading comprehension. *Contemporary Educational Psychology, 8*, 317-344.

Perfetti, C.A., & Goldman, S.R. (1976). Discourse memory and reading comprehension skill. *Journal of Verbal Learning and Verbal Behavior, 14*, 33-42.

Pressley, M., Beard, P., & Brown, R. (1991, April). *Is good reading comprehension possible?* Paper presented at the annual meeting of the American Educational Research Association, Chicago.

Rebok, G.W. (1987). *Life-span cognitive development*. New York: Holt, Rinehart & Winston.

Resnick, L.B. (1984). Comprehending and learning: Implications for a cognitive theory of instruction. In H. Mandl, N.L. Stein, & T. Trabasso (Eds.), *Learning and comprehension of text* (pp. 431- 444). Hillsdale, NJ: Erlbaum.

Rice, G.E. (1986). The everyday activities of adults: Implications for prose recall: Part I. *Educational Gerontology, 12*, 173-186.

Robinson, R.D., & Maring, G. (1976). The aging process and its relationship to reading: A review of literature for gerontology with implications for future research. In W.D. Miller & G.G. McNinch (Eds.), *Reflections and investigations on reading: Twenty-fifth yearbook of the National Reading Conference*. Clemson, SC: National Reading Conference.

Schommer, M., & Surber, J.R. (1986). Comprehension-monitoring failure in skilled adult readers. *Journal of Educational Psychology, 78*, 353-357.

Simon, E.W., Dixon, R.A., Nowak, C.A., & Hultsch, D.F. (1982). Orienting task effects on text recall in adulthood. *Journal of Gerontology, 31*, 575-580.

Smith, M.C. (1988a). *A longitudinal study of the development of reading comprehension skills, cognitive monitoring skills, and reading attitudes: Childhood to adulthood*. Unpublished doctoral dissertation, University of Wisconsin, Madison.

Smith, M.C. (1988b, April). *Comprehension-monitoring and memory-monitoring: Two sides of the same coin?* Paper presented at the American Educational Research Association annual meeting, New Orleans, LA.

Spilich, G.J. (1983). Life-span components of text processing: Structural and procedural changes. *Journal of Verbal Learning and Verbal Behavior, 22*, 231-244.

Sticht, T.G. (1982). Literacy at work. In B.A. Hutson (Ed.), *Advances in reading/language research* (Vol. 1). Greenwich, CT: JAI Press.

Taub, H. (1979). Comprehension and memory of prose materials by young and old adults. *Experimental Aging Research, 5*(1), 3-13.

Taylor, B.M., Frye, B.J., & Maruyama, G.M. (1990). Time spent reading and reading growth. *American Educational Research Journal, 27*, 351-362.

Thomas, J.W. & Rohwer, W.D. (in press). Studying across the life span. In S.R. Yussen & M.C. Smith (Eds.), *Reading across the life span.* New York: Springer-Verlag.

Wallbrown, F.H., Levine, M.A., & Engin, A. (1981). Sex differences in reading attitudes. *Reading Improvement, 18*(3), 226-234.

Walmsley, S.A., & Allington, R.L. (1980). Aging research in higher education: Research in the reading processes of the elderly. *Reading Psychology, 1,* 177-183.

Winn, J., & Palincsar, A.S. (in press). Reading instruction in childhood and adolescence. In S.R. Yussen & M.C. Smith (Eds.), *Reading across the life span.* New York: Springer-Verlag.

Winograd, P. & Johnston, P. (1982). Comprehension monitoring and the error detection paradigm. *Journal of Reading Behavior, 14,* 61-76.

Zabrucky, K., & Moore, D. (1991). Effects of skill on standards used by younger and older adults to evaluate understanding. *Reading Psychology, 12,* 147-158.

14
Remembering Stories: Studies of the Limits of Narrative Coherence on Recall

Steven R. Yussen and Randall L. Glysch

From early childhood to late adulthood, a common way people exchange information is through stories. Stories are used for entertainment, for inspiration, for dramatizing ethical and moral lessons, for sharing newsworthy happenings, and for explaining concepts in concrete and personal terms, to name just a few obvious purposes. It is no surprise, then, that there has been an explosion of interest and research by cognitive psychologists on how people remember and understand stories (Bower & Morrow, 1990; Mandler, 1987; Stein & Trabasso, 1982; Yussen, Mathews, Huang, & Evans, 1988). In this chapter we consider, in turn, (a) the nature of stories, (b) the major theoretical models used to describe stories and story comprehension, and, finally (c) recent findings obtained by the authors on the influence of coherence on people's memory for stories. We recognize that stories are consumed both by listening and reading. For convenience, we will refer to the story consumer primarily as a reader throughout the remainder of the chapter, confident that most (but not all) of what we have to say about reading and remembering stories can be generalized to listeners as well as to readers.

The Nature of Stories

Stories come in many forms. Some recount true events; others are fiction. Some are short and simple, as in the experimental narratives used by many cognitive psychologists (see the Appendix for examples); other stories are long and complex as in literary short stories or novels, with thousands of words, many events, and many levels of intended meaning and purpose. Some stories are designed to be told; they are part of an oral tradition. Other stories are meant to be read. Finally, some stories have a simple, linear structure, which is easily discerned. One or more characters engage in a series of actions that follow logically from one to the next, the characters' motivations are openly revealed in the text, and there is a logical conclusion to the problem(s) set for the characters. Other stories have a structure less readily discerned by the reader. The logic of characters' actions may be unclear, the motivations obscure, the connections among events confusing because key information is missing, the order of events is inverted, or the existance of many subplots to keep straight.

Given this diversity in narrative form, can we distill the essence of "story" or "narrative" for the purpose of scientific study? Cognitive psychologists believe we can, and they have proceeded accordingly. Their approach has been to identify a small set of defining elements to a story, to study these elements with simple narratives, and to examine a range of implications about how people of various ages remember, understand, and otherwise think with these narratives.

The following list is our own distillation of the defining elements of a story, as reflected in the recent work in reading and discourse analysis.

1. First, stories involve one or more characters who act for understandable reasons. Stories, then, have *characters*, *action*, and *character motivation*. One of the characters is usually central to the story; s/he is the protagonist. Action centers on this character, and the reader becomes preoccupied with tracking this character's fate—what s/he does and what happens as a consequence. The character may be real or fictional, and in the latter case when there are nonhuman characters (e.g., animals, trees, alien beings) or characters given capabilities beyond their means (e.g., babies with adultlike thought), their actions are understandable in terms of human motivation, perhaps with a special twist (e.g., Mr. Spock of "Star Trek" is a *logical* human; the baby in "Look Who's Talking" has adult-like perceptions but little ostensible experience yet with the world).

2. Implicit in a story is the notion that the character attempts *to solve a problem*; s/he wants to get somewhere, discover something, make something, or solve an existential crisis or dilemma, to list a few examples. The problem may be solved in a single effort; more likely the protagonist struggles over time and many separate attempts to reach his/her goal. The protagonist's attempts may be purely intrapsychic events—thoughts and feelings the character creates, for example; alternatively the attempt may be physical such as talking or physical movement. Similarly the outcome of the character's striving may be purely intrapsychic—again, thoughts or feelings that arise from the action.

3. Stories occur in a *physical world which can be imagined by the reader*. If the story in question is true, if it takes place more or less in our present time, and if it involves locations known to the reader, then representing this physical world is relatively straightforward for the reader. To the extent the story departs from these hypothetical features, and of course most stories do, its audience must work harder to create a representation of the story world and the characters acting in it. Our contemporary human experiences will dominate this representation, even as the story forces the reader to depart from these contemporary experiences and imagine the fictional world purposefully created in the story.

4. The story may be thought of as *an abstraction* that is constructed from the interplay of the written text of the author and the considerable knowledge (of language, of people, of the world, of stories and storytelling, etc.) brought to the text by the reader. It follows that there is no such thing as a single story, given a fixed text for a narrative; each reader constructs his/her own story. However idiosyncratic this representation may be for each reader, nonetheless, we should be able to divine some general features of the story, which each reader does or does not remember, understand, or otherwise process. The search for commonality, of course, is one task for science; it does not preclude the equally challenging task of discovering the unique story representations held by different people for the same text.

We turn next to a consideration of the major theoretical models used to describe stories and story understanding.

Theoretical Models of Story Memory and Understanding

Scripts

A considerable body of work has accumulated over the past 2 decades on how adults remember stories that they read or hear (e.g., Black & Bower, 1980; Kintsch, 1977; Mandler, 1987; Rumelhart, 1975; Schank & Abelson, 1977; Stein & Trabasso, 1982; Thorndyk, 1977; Trabasso & van den Broek, 1985; Yussen et al., 1988). One group of investigators (e.g., Bower, Black, & Turner, 1979; Nelson, 1978; Schank & Abelson, 1977) has amassed evidence to show that if a story conforms to a familiar *script*, subjects will recall it better than if the story is unscripted or contains improbable events. A script is the cognitive representation of a frequently occurring event in the culture, such as eating at a restaurant or visiting the doctor. Scripts contain events that unfold in a predictable, highly prescribed manner. For example, when we eat at a restaurant, we customarily enter, sit, eat, and leave, in that order. If any of these elements are left out or arranged in an unusual order when the story is presented, our memory for the story may be distorted as we actively attempt to fit it into a more predictable form.

Story Grammar

Another group of investigators (e.g., Mandler, 1987; Stein & Trabasso, 1982) have attempted to understand the internal *structure* of stories, using grammars and hierarchical tree structures. In this approach, a story is divided into contexts, events and sub-events (e.g., Mandler, 1987; Stein & Glenn, 1979), and the propositions that capture these elements are described with respect to the hierarchical "level" they occupy in a text hierarchy of propositions. The level of a proposition in a hierarchy and the number of other propositions to which it is directly linked in the hierarchy will predict the likelihood of remembering the proposition. Table 14.1 displays a simple story used by the first author and Stein and her colleagues (Stein & Trabasso, 1982) along with a description of the grammatical categories present in the single episode of the narrative. In a hierarchical sense, there are two or three levels in the story. The setting is at one level and governs the event that follows. Within the event, we can distinguish between the goal at a second level and the occurences that follow from the goal (describing these, perhaps at a third level). Consider, alternatively, the story "President" in the Appendix. It tells of someone who becomes interested in learning more about a famous political figure, next attempts to find a book about him, fails in their attempt to find such a book in a library, and finally succeeds in locating and purchasing a book in a local bookstore. This quick synopsis of our story "President" used in the studies reported later in the paper illustrates a longer story with more levels in an informational hierarchy. There are at least five recognizable levels: the setting (first level) dominates the initial motive to learn (second level) which in turn directs the first episode where the character goes to the library and fails to get a book (third level). The failure leads to a second goal attempt of searching in a bookstore (fourth level), which in turn leads to a successful outcome (fifth level). If a good hierachical arrangement is not present in the story or the arrangement is "camouflaged" (by, for example, scrambling the presented propositions), the story as a whole will prove more difficult to recall.

Table 14.1
Story Grammar Categories for a Simple One-Episode Narrative,
"Albert the Fish"

Setting	1	Once there was a big gray fish named Albert.
	2	He lived in a pond near the edge of a forest.
Initiating event	3	One day Albert was swimming around the pond.
	4	Then he spotted a big juicy worm on top of the water.
Internal	5	Albert knew how delicious worms tasted.
response	6	He wanted to eat that one for his dinner.
Attempt	7	So he swam very close to the worm.
	8	Then he bit into him.
Consequence	9	Suddenly, Albert was pulled through the water into a boat.
	10	He had been caught by a fisherman.
Reaction	11	Albert felt sad.
	12	He wished he had been more careful.

Causal Networks

Yet a third view of story form is based on a causal network model (e.g., Trabasso et al., 1984; van den Broek, 1988, 1989). In this view, particular propositions in a narrative are connected logically to other propositions in the narrative. Connections may vary both *qualitatively* and *quantitatively*. A character's motivation or overall goal may be linked to several subgoals that unfold until the final goal is accomplished. This produces a hierarchical quality to the story. An example is van den Broek's (1988) story about Jimmy, who sees a bike, wants one like it (overall goal), then attempts to save money (subgoal) and earn money (subgoal), until he finally has enough to buy it. A sequential version of the same story is created by rearranging the separate episodes so that the goals of working (Subgoal 1), earning money (Subgoal 2), and buying a bike (Subgoal 3) are not thematically connected. The hierarchical version of the story is qualitatively different from the sequential version, because it links the goals of the separate episodes whereas the sequential version does not create a goal linkage. The hierarchical version also differs quantitatively from the sequential version, because there are more links among the goal statements to one another and to the various action propositions in the story than are present in the sequential version. The goals and action propositions will, therefore, be remembered better in the hierarchical version than in the sequential version of the story.

Mental Models

A fourth and final view recently was offered by Bower and Morrow (1990). They suggest that to fully understand a story, the reader's principal task is to create a mental model for the story. The model includes a spatial representation of the people, places, and events described in the story. There is a kind of "scene" representation in working memory. As the story unfolds, the reader's working memory continually updates this scene, with the earlier scenes pushed into a longer term storage or forgotten. The scene representation is used to access necessary information and to draw appropriate inferences. For example, if a story mentions that two people stand facing each other on the porch of a large mansion, the reader can use this information to interpret a conversation between the characters and to understand that conversations held elsewhere in the house may not be heard. This spatial focus also means that the reader will be quicker to access information about these two characters or something about their immediate space, because this scene is at the moment "on-stage", that is, in working memory.

Recent Research on Story Coherence

What makes a narrative readily understandable and memorable? What increases the likelihood that a reader will remember most of the information contained in a story? No doubt, there are at least three important factors. One is the knowledge that the reader brings to bear on the story. If the story itself trades on events commonly known in the culture, for example, "scripted events" (e.g., Bower et al., 1979), or if the story deals with specific people, places, and events that are well known to the reader (e.g., Anderson & Pearson, 1984), the story is likely to be remembered and understood better than some story without these features.

A second quality is that the story generates engagement and interest in the reader, perhaps because one of the characters is valued and liked by the reader (Brewer & Lichtenstein, 1982), because particular details are regarded as novel and unusual (e.g., Garner, this volume), or because the topic of the story is one that has great appeal to the reader (e.g., Asher, 1980)

A third quality, and the one to receive the remainder of our attention in this chapter, is the structural adequacy of a story. For convenience, we refer to this quality as *story form*. We regard a story written with a high degree of structural adequacy as having good form; in contrast, a story written with a low degree of structural adequacy is regarded as having poor form. In principle, we should also be able to identify stories whose form is of some intermediate structural adequacy.

What do we mean, though, by structural adequacy or good form? If we restrict our attention to the four different models of text comprehension discussed earlier, there are four apparently different answers. (a) First, consider a script-based perspective. Given a story based on one or more scripted events, the story is well structured if elements of the script occur in their expected order and if there are no incongruous elements. By contrast, a story would be considered poorly structured if it contained scripted elements whose order is seriously violated and if it contained a number of incongruous elements. (b) Next, consider a story grammar description. Story grammars also contain particular categories of information ordered in particular ways (e.g., Setting + $Event_1$ + [$Event_2$] + ... + [$Event_n$]; Event = Initiating Event + Internal Response [Motive] + Attempt + Consequence + Reaction). Good form results from most or all of the categories of expected information occurring in their predicted order. However, if much of the expected information is missing or if the order of the expected information is seriously violated, great confusion can be the result. (c) Third, consider an answer based on the causal network theory. In this view, individual propositions in a story will be well understood and remembered if they have many causal links to other propositions in the story. Good story form results from many propositions in the story linked causally to many other propositions in the story. By contrast, poor story form results if most propositions in the story have infrequent or few causal links to other propositions in it. (d) Finally, consider an answer based on the mental model theory. In this view, a good story is one readily represented and with a succession of "represented scenes" easily linked to one another. Factors that interfere with the buildup of good mental representations and linkages among represented scenes contribute to poor story form.

Studies of the Good Form Effect on Memory for Stories

There is little doubt of the power of good story form to enhance both children's and adults' recall of narratives. With good form defined in a variety of ways consistent with the previously described models, many authors have demonstrated people's superior recall for stories presented in good form than in relatively poorer form (e.g., Mandler & Johnson, 1977; Stein & Nezworski, 1977; Yussen, Mathews, Buss, & Kane, 1980; Yussen et al., 1988). In a typical demonstration of this good form effect, subjects will read a narrative once or twice and then attempt to recall it. If versions of the narrative that are in good form produce better recall than other versions, the effect is verified. Not surprisingly, this is a common result, but what implications does the result have for the *real world* reading of narratives? One limitation of much of the research we cite is the difficulty of generalizing from results based on single readings of a text to be recalled. In the real world, we have the opportunity to reread information at will if it is confusing. Much of the discussion about the importance of good story form in the fields of cognitive psychology and discourse analysis then, may be *technically* correct but of limited *practical* importance, because if readers can readily overcome bad text structure "in their heads" with some rereading of the text, then how stories are written may not be as important as some believe. What is the *limit*, then, of the good story form effect? To answer this general question, we created a procedure that can be thought of as a "testing of the limits" of the good form effect. Using several complementary procedures across the studies to be reported shortly, subjects repeatedly read and recalled one of two stories, presented either with good text form or poor text form. Given the designs employed, it was possible to gauge the magnitude of the good form effect (i.e., the advantage to memory) after just 1 reading and recall trial and through as many as 12 readings and four separate recall trials.

There seems little doubt that good adult readers and older elementary school children reorganize confusing stories that they read or hear (e.g., Rahman & Bisantz, 1986; Stein & Nezworski, 1978; Yussen et al., 1988). Also when people are presented with a story in an unusual form (e.g., interleaved episodes, Johnson & Mandler, 1980), there is evidence that they can recall it in a more usual way (i.e., as noninterleaved episodes). However, such demonstrations of flexible recall often hinge on subjects being able to recall the story that was presented to them any way they choose, typically with different embellishments and (most importantly given the primary focus of the present experiments, here) outputting the propositions from the presented story in any order.

From our perspective, such demonstrations are important, but they overlook the issue of the power of good text form to enhance *verbatim* memory. If order and detail are important in stories (and they often are), we also need to assess how well good text form helps subjects to remember narratives "as they were." Conversely, the question becomes: How difficult is it for subjects to defeat poor text form in their story recollections, if they are required to remember stories verbatim? Good form might exert a more powerful effect on memory with the verbatim constraint. Subjects should find it relatively easy to preserve order and detail in recall with a good story schema, if it is well matched to the surface structure (order) of the story they read. By contrast, given a story whose surface order is confusing, it should be especially hard to remember it verbatim. The difficulty is that the subject is likely to use knowledge of good story form as a retrieval aid, which should directly interfere with recalling the propositions in their confusing order. If subjects perceive the difficulty after attempting retrieval, perhaps they will try to create a new idiosyncratic retrieval device to help make the required novel causal connections among adjacent propositions, but as will become clear later, even with short stories such as those we used in the studies to be reported, creating such an alternative representation does not work well as a scaffold for retrieval. The major focus in the experiments, then, is on the persistence of the good text form effect when subjects repeatedly attempt to recall stories verbatim.

A second question raised in the studies is the following: Does good text form produce parallel effects for both *learning* and *forgetting* of narratives? Most studies that have examined the effects of narrative memory tend to cloud the distinction between learning and forgetting effects, because subjects are not put through anything resembling an acquisition or learning phase. Given a text to remember, we can ask (a) how long (e.g., amount of time, number of study trials) it takes to reach some criterion of mastery and (b) how well the information is retained after some criterion level is reached. Research shows that forgetting of verbal information is not influenced by initial learning (e.g., Bogartz, 1990; Loftus, 1985). That is, given two or more different levels of learning some body of verbal information, there is considerable research to show that the rate at which the information is forgotten over time is often independent of the original levels of learning. This *independence* effect probably reflects that, however the information was originally learned, the nature of its storage and retrieval is similar for the different levels of original learning.

In the present research, we consider whether this independence generalization holds here, as well, or whether good story form also enhances retention over time, by slowing the rate at which information is forgotten. There are at least two major reasons why such a differential effect might be predicted for forgetting. One is that good narrative form might ensure that more of the initially remembered story information is being coded into permanent long-term storage as compared with poor narrative form. The second is that good narrative form can provide a better retrieval system for accessing information than an idiosyncratic form invented to circumvent bad form. We make no effort to verify either of these possibilities in the present studies or to clearly distinguish between them. Rather, we focus on the prior empirical question of whether good form does indeed influence the course of forgetting.

Overview of the Studies

Four experiments were completed with groups of adult volunteers. The first three experiments were with college students. The fourth experiment contrasted the recall of college students with that of highly verbal older adults. Although some research has identified qualitative changes in the way older adults tell and remember stories (e.g., Labouvie-Vief, 1980), the present work focused primarily on whether the pattern of facilitating effects of good story form were the same or different for young adults and for older adults. This, of course, could be determined independently of levels of recall, which we also reported for the younger and older adults. Simple age differences in level of recall were of little consequence for our purposes.

Experiments with Young Adults (1 to 3)

We used two narratives, one written by the first author, the other originally used by Omanson (1982) and later by Trabasso and his colleagues (e.g., 1985; see the Appendix). Both stories, in their standard version (good form), represent largely predictable human sequences of behavior and reactions (hence, good scripting), contain key elements of story grammar structures in each subevent (i.e., the initiating event, the attempt, and the consequence), and have many actions mentioned earlier in the story that are causally connected to many later actions and character states (hence, providing rich causal interconnectedness). By contrast, we created a scrambled version (poor form) of each story, by the careful permutation of individual propositions, which resulted in many script violations, incomplete subevent structures from a story grammar perspective, and thin causal interconnectedness (i.e., many propositions without later connections). In Experiment 2, we also created a partially scrambled version of each story by permutating the order of fewer propositions in each story so that the resulting script violations, incomplete subevent substructures, and causal interconnections, were not quite as extreme as in the completely scrambled stories.

The story "President" tells of a girl who becomes interested in the President one day, while watching him on television. It was written by the first author, Steven R. Yussen. She fails in an attempt to find a book about him in a library but later finds one in a bookstore. It has 22 propositions and is from 168 to 175 words long (depending on the version read). The story "Turtle" tells of two friends who spot a turtle in a pond while playing with a toy sailboat and the unsuccessful attempt by one of the friends to retrieve the creature to show to the second friend. It was written by Omanson (1982). It has 20 propositions and has 134 or 135 words (again, depending on the version). In the scrambled version, each sentence is intact, but the order of sentences is randomized across the narrative, with the constraint that no two adjacent sentences (from the standard version) are contiguous. For both

"President" and "Turtle", the alternative versions (i.e., standard, scrambled) are virtually identical in the wording of individual propositions. In the scrambled versions, minor changes were made in rhetorical connectives and pronoun references, however, so that understanding of scrambled versions would not be made worse by "local" semantic connections, which are patently misleading, so, in the scrambled version of each story, the comprehensibility of individual sentences is maintained, although the sense of the (standard) story as a whole is seriously violated, when analyzed by any of the text systems mentioned earlier (i.e., scripting, story grammar, or causal chains). Good form, then, was purposely defined in this overlapping way, so that any of the competing narrative analysis systems would yield the similar outcome of a very well organized versus a very poorly organized version for each story (and in Experiment 2, an intermediate case of organization). For convenience, each story was divided into propositions for presentation and later analysis of memory, utilizing the story grammar and causal framework.

These stories were difficult to memorize in just one or two readings, so there was considerable opportunity to improve with practice. Subjects read the stories, one proposition at a time (a single phrase or sentence was typed on a single strip of paper) and wrote out their recalls after each study trial. Given the design we employed, it was possible to gauge, precisely, the effect of good versus poor organization on subjects' recall in the face of opportunities to read through the entire story different numbers of times and to write out recalls different numbers of times.

Experiment 1

In the first experiment, the key questions of interest were these: Would the facilitating effect of good form (organization) persist across multiple opportunities to recall the story, and would the facilitating effect of good form (organization) be moderated by the number of opportunities subjects had to read the story in each study interval?

There were 64 student volunteers in the study. They were enrolled in educational psychology classes at a midwestern university, they were native English speakers, and most were women ($n = 55$), with an average age of 20.3 years.

Half of the students were randomly assigned to read stories that were standard (or well ordered); the other half read the same stories, with the order of propositions scrambled and a few minor wording changes. For each type of order, subjects were further divided randomly, so that half read through the story once before attempting each recall, whereas the other half read through the story three times before attempting each recall. Two stories were used, "President" and "Turtle". For each of the two orders (standard, scrambled) and reading repetition conditions (once, three times), half of the subjects were randomly assigned to read "President", and the other half read "Turtle". Each subject had three cycles of reading and recalling the story using booklets that printed each proposition on a separate page and instructions that asked them to read a single page at a time, without turning back (to control for reading repetitions). In conditions where subjects read a story three

Table 14.2 (Experiment 1)

Mean Percentage for Recall
Recall Trial and Reading Exposure

Story and Condition	Percentage of Propositions Recalled					
	Trial 1		Trial 2		Trial 3	
	1exp	3exp	1exp	3exp	1exp	3exp
Turtle story						
Standard mean	48	72	77	83	88	94
Scrambled mean	35	45	55	64	65	85
President story						
Standard mean	52	78	71	90	80	93
Scrambled mean	26	54	45	68	59	83
	Percentage of Propositions Disordered					
Turtle story						
Standard mean	2	4	9	3	4	2
Scrambled mean	11	17	11	20	16	20
President story						
Standard mean	4	0	4	1	4	0
Scrambled mean	12	21	17	24	26	24

times before each recall, they simply proceeded to read through the entire booklet and then returned to the beginning of the booklet to read it again for their next (second or third) reading. Testing was done in small groups of 5 to 10 and the procedure lasted 45 to 60 minutes. Recalls were written out on sheets of paper provided for each subject. Instructions emphasized verbatim recall of the story. There was no explicit feedback given after a recall trial.

Key results of the study are captured in Table 14.2, which reports the percentage of propositions recalled for both stories and the percentage of propositions that were recalled out of order in relation to the order in which they were actually read. Note the pattern of findings is the same for the two stories.

Considering the percentage of propositions recalled first, analyses showed that there was a significant effect for the number of times the students read the story (exposure); reading it three times promoted superior recall for all trials. There was also a significant effect of trials. Each succeeding recall trial yielded greater recall. Most importantly, however, notice the form (condition) effect, which was also highly significant. In each condition, recall was greater in the standard condition than in the scrambled condition. Importantly, this effect was still present after three trials and in the exposure condition (three Exp.), which had subjects reading the story a total of *nine* times by the last recall attempt.

The other measure concerned the percent of propositions recalled out of order, and it demonstrates primarily the effect of story form (condition). Those subjects trying to recall the scrambled story verbatim made more mistakes in preserving the order of the propositions as they were read, than did subjects recalling the standard (well ordered) story. Note again that this difficulty persisted across all three trials.

The major finding of Experiment 1 is that poorly ordered narrative information is difficult to memorize, even when subjects read the story repeatedly and have several opportunities to recall the story. The effect is robust, holding up for each of two different stories, as many as nine repeated readings of a story, and across three recall trials. The difficulty is further underscored by the outcome that when poorly arranged (scrambled) stories are recalled, subjects make more errors in preserving the order of the propositions as read than do subjects who have read well arranged (standard) stories. For the latter subjects, the proportion of errors approaches or is zero in some groups.

Experiments 2 and 3

Adopting the conventional distinction between learning and retention (or conversely, forgetting), we view this first experiment as dealing with learning. That is, subjects are given the task of memorizing a story to a perfect criterion, and each trial represents their progress enroute to that level of mastery. The trial-to-trial movement toward that goal represents increments in learning. The powerful effect of poor organization, then, is to interfere with learning, if we construe the standard organization condition as the comparison or natural reference point. Experiments 2 and 3 were designed to replicate and extend the findings about learning and to consider whether good organizational form might slow the rate of forgetting. They included a 24-hour retention test and a 1-week retention test (Experiment 3 only).

The impact of organization on forgetting. Assume that subjects, even with poor organization, eventually can overcome it and learn the information to perfect (or near perfect) criterion. After the criterion is reached, will the task of retaining the information be made easier because it was learned with the aid of good form, or are structural effects such as this one in prose learning just that, effects on learning rather than on retention? To address this question, Experiment 2 added an "unexpected" 24-hour retention test for each subject, to determine whether the condition of relatively good form would result in less relative forgetting than the conditions of relatively poorer form (i.e., the scrambled and partially scrambled conditions).

Additional questions about learning. It could be argued that the demonstration offered in Experiment 1 is a bit unfair when considered against the backdrop of real disorganization as we might find it in ordinary texts encountered in the everyday world. Real world texts, it might be argued, rarely are as confusing as the admittedly "confused" stories we set out to create in the scrambled conditions of our two stories, and in the real world, we can recall a story in a nonverbatim way, particularly to help us make more sense of it. It seems worthwhile, then, to consider whether milder forms of disorganization, likely to be encountered more frequently, and doing less violence to schematic expectations, also create extensive interference in learning. To this end, Experiment 2 included a condition in which our same two stories were each given a partially scrambled order. The partially scrambled order created an intermediate case of organization somewhere in between the extremes of Experiment 1, and Experiment 3 included a condition where subjects read a scrambled story, but were told to recall it so that it made a sensible story.

Details of Experiment 2

The subjects were a new group of 60 student volunteers selected as before. All were native English speakers, most were women ($n = 48$), and the average age, again, was 20.3 years. Students were tested in groups ranging from 10 to 18 at a time on the first day and in groups of 5 to 10 on the second day. The assignment of subjects to experimental condition was randomized within each group (using a procedure with prenumbered test packets similar to that of Experiment 1).

The design was as follows. One third of the subjects read standard narratives; another third read partially scrambled narratives; the remaining third of the subjects read *scrambled narratives*. Within each group, half of the subjects read the story "Turtle", the other half read the story "President". To simplify the design, all subjects read story booklets three times prior to each recall trial. On Day 1, there were four study and recall trials. The next day (Day 2), subjects returned and attempted to recall the same story (with the same order) without reading it again.

Details of Experiment 3

A new group of 48 students were recruited as before. All were native English speakers, most were women ($n = 37$), and the average age was 20.5. Students were tested in groups ranging from 5 to 10 on the first day, and slightly smaller groups in the 24-hour and 1-week retention intervals. Assignment to experimental condition was randomized within the groups (using prenumbered test packets as before).

One third of the subjects read a standard narrative; another third read a scrambled narrative; the remaining third read the scrambled narrative, with instructions to recall it so as to make a sensible story out of it. To simplify the design, the narrative used for all subjects was the story "Turtle". On Day 1, there were three study and recall trials. For each study trial, subjects read the story three times. On the next day (24-hour retention), subjects returned and attempted to recall the story (with the same retrieval instructions as on Day 1) without reading it again. The 24-hour retention procedure was repeated 1 week later (1-week retention).

Summary of Results from Experiments 2 and 3

The recall results for the first day are shown in Table 14.3 (for Experiment 2) and Table 14.4 (for Experiment 3). The mean percent of propositions recalled in the top half of each table displays level of recall. Appropriate statistical analyses revealed these common trends across the two experiments:

1.   There was a trials effect. Recall got better from trial to trial for each of the stories in each of the conditions.
2.   There was a powerful good form effect. Recall was better for the standard story presentation condition than for the scrambled story presentation condition. This held across all trials and both stories.
3.   The attempts to moderate the good form effect, by and large, *did not* work. Partial scrambling (Experiment 2) yielded results comparable to complete scrambling, and recalling scrambled stories so as to make sensible stories out of them (Experiment 3) produced recall similar to verbatim recall of the scrambled stories.

The mean percent of propositions recalled out of order (bottom half of table) displays the degree to which subjects had difficulty preserving the same order of propositions in recall as was encountered when reading the stories. The two tables again reflect powerful commonalities, backed up by appropriate statistical comparisons.

1.   Good form (standard condition) resulted in very few order violations; poorer form (scrambled condition) resulted in appreciably more order violations.
2.   The story form effect was robust with respect to story, trials, and degree of scrambling (partial, complete); that is, the effect varied very little as a result of these factors, within experiments, although absolute values of disordering varied somewhat across the two experiments.
3.   One experimental manipulation did moderate the influence of form. In Experiment 3, the make-a-story instruction significantly increased the amount of order violations compared to both of the other conditions. The explanation for this result is simple. These subjects had modest success in reordering the mixed-up stories as they recalled them.

To investigate forgetting, level of recall for the last trial of Day 1 was plotted against level of recall for the 24-hour delay and 1-week delay intervals. This is shown in Figure 14.1 (Experiment 2) and Figure 14.2 (Experiment 3). The key issue here is whether the degree of forgetting is the same across the three different presentation orders. One way to examine this issue (e.g., Loftus, 1985) is to measure the vertical gap between any pair of conditions at the two different time intervals and to determine if the gap is constant (essentially a main effect finding) or if the gap changes (essentially an interaction effect). A constant gap is consistent with a pattern where the groups who have attained different final levels of learning have similar rates of forgetting. A changing gap suggests a pattern where the groups who

Table 14.3 (Experiment 2)

Mean Percentage for Recall

Story and condition	Percentage of Propositions Recalled			
	Trial 1	Trial 2	Trial 3	Trial 4
Turtle story				
Standard mean	67	89	95	98
Partially scrambled mean	47	70	75	86
Scrambled mean	45	66	79	88
President story				
Standard mean	53	71	81	82
Partially scrambled mean	41	58	72	79
Scrambled mean	38	57	72	84
	Percentage of Propositions Disordered			
Turtle story				
Standard mean	4	2	2	0
Partially scrambled mean	10	10	15	5
Scrambled mean	11	14	11	8
President story				
Standard mean	1	1	1	0
Partially scrambled mean	9	10	10	12
Scrambled mean	26	41	35	37

have attained different final levels of learning display different patterns of forgetting.

A series of planned comparisons for each of the experiments tested for overall forgetting, forgetting over a day and over a week (Experiment 3 only), and for differential forgetting by condition. Although the forgetting curves are different for the two stories (in Experiment 2) and between the experiments, the statistical comparisons yielded parallel findings that were as follows:

1. Over the intervals in question (24 hours, 1 week), there was significant overall forgetting across the different conditions and the two stories.

2. Forgetting did not differ significantly by story or condition in either experiment. That is, despite the apparent differences in the appearances of the curves (in Experiment 2) and the different patterns between the experiments (2 and 3), none of the tests revealed significant departures of the

Table 14.4 (Experiment 3)

Mean Percentage for Recall

Presentation condition	Percentage of Propositions Recalled		
	Trial 1 M	Trial 2 M	Trial 3 M
Standard	61	82	91
Scrambled	47	64	78
Scrambled Make-a-story	41	58	71
	Percentage of Propositions Disordered		
Standard	5	3	3
Scrambled	23	22	21
Scrambled Make-a-story	51	57	59

curves (in a given set) from being parallel to one another. So, there was no evidence of differential forgetting.

Taken together, the findings of these two experiments corroborate and extend the results of Experiment 1. Even when subjects are given the opportunity to read a story 12 separate times (Experiment 2), when scrambling of the ideal presentation order is less severe (Experiment 2), and when subjects are free to retrieve the mixed-up story in a more ideal way (Experiment 3), the good form effect persists. It is clearly a *very* powerful phenomenon, but, two separate examinations of how adults forgot the stories over time, suggested that degree of good form had little differential effect on the rate of forgetting.

The Good Form Effect in Younger and Older Adults (Experiment 4)

We report one final study. In it, we sought to determine whether the main conclusions reached so far apply equally well to younger and older adults. Generalizing the findings across the adult life span is important, we thought, for several reasons. First, our intuition told us that our findings stem from a powerful organizing principle in memory for text; the results should not hinge on minor variables known to impact older adults' memory negatively, such as declines in memory span, slower processing of information, or loss of retention of detail-level information (e.g., Salthouse, 1982). Second, reading and telling stories is at least as salient for older adults as it is for young adults. In fact, some investigators have claimed that older adults are more prone to create narratives to help them remember and understand non-narrative information and events (e.g., Labouvie-Vief, 1980).

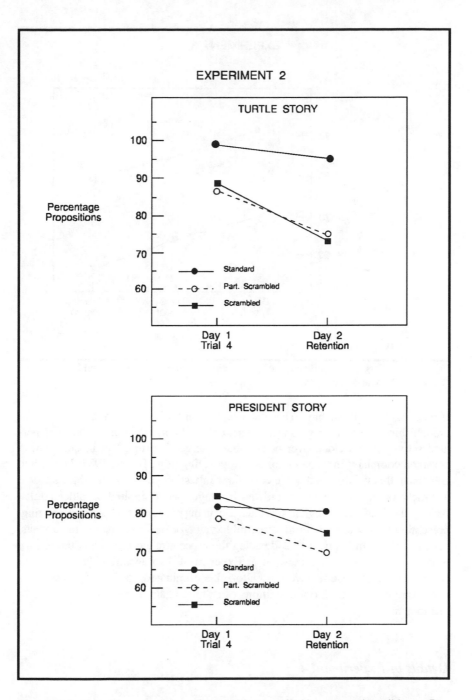

Figure 14.1. Forgetting: percentage of propositions recalled by story and condition on Day 1 and Day 2 (24 hour delay).

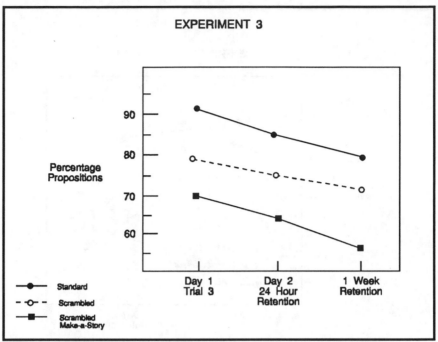

Figure 14.2. Forgetting: percentage of propositions recalled by condition on Day 1, Day 2 (24 hour delay), and 1 week (delay).

If older adults really do have a special predilection for inventing narratives and for embellishing information with their own narrative interpretations, such self-generated activity might cloud over or eliminate the good form effect in question. A common complaint in the study of cognitive aging (e.g., Baltes, 1987; Dixon and Bäckman, this volume) is that the conditions of testing young adult subjects create a variety of unfair and unnatural disadvantages when applied to older adults. Among the frequent ecological sins cited are: using materials that are uninteresting, presenting boring tasks with no discernible value or intrinsic interest to subjects, giving subjects little practice, and pacing the procedure too rapidly. Although we modified our procedure somewhat in Experiment 4 to accommodate our older subjects, most of these sins were not altogether eliminated, so, if the form effect is demonstrated in spite of our conditions of testing, again, it proves to be a robust phenomenon.

Details of Experiment 4

A total of 180 subjects were recruited; half were younger adult college students drawn from classes in educational psychology at the same university, the other half were older adults drawn from church groups and community centers in the same

Table 14.5

Means for Percent of Propositions Recalled for Different Presentation
Order and Recall Trial for Each Story by Age Group
(N = 90)

| | Younger Adults | | | | | | | |
| | Turtle Story | | | | Emma Story | | | |
Condition	T1[a]	T2[a]	T3[a]	T4[b]	T1[a]	T2[a]	T3[a]	T4[b]
Standard mean	763	927	970	860	533	783	830	707
Make-a-story mean	580	747	847	630	467	727	803	660
Random mean	530	707	840	580	303	503	617	450
	Older Adults							
	Turtle Story				Emma Story			
Condition	T1	T2	T3	T4	T1	T2	T3	T4
Standard mean	463	447	660	413	343	453	553	370
Make-a-story mean	343	453	523	337	243	360	477	260
Random mean	353	477	547	307	150	280	367	200

a = T1, T2, T3 are the three recall trials on Day One.
b = T4 is the recall following a One Week Delay.

city. The mean age of the young adults was 22.7 (range 18 to 32); the mean age of
the older adults was 73.3 (range 60 to 89). A 100-item vocabulary test, the Quick
Word Test (Borgatto & Corsini, 1960), yielded a mean of 71.4 (SD = 12.0) for the
younger adults and 83.2 (SD = 12.1) for the older adults. For some comparisons,
we also divided the older adults into an *old* and a *very old* group, using a median
split procedure. The old adults had a mean age of 69.0 and a mean vocabulary score
of 84.1 (SD = 11.04), and the very old adults had a mean age of 79.2 and a mean
vocabulary score of 82.0 (SD = 13.3). So, in contrast with the younger adults, the
old adults had significantly higher vocabulary knowledge, but there was little
difference in the vocabulary knowledge between the two subgroups of older adults.

Two narratives were used, the "Turtle" story (used as in Experiments 1 to 3),
and the "Emma" story, used previously in aging research (Spilich, 1983) and
thought to be particularly apt for elderly subjects given its theme of an elderly
woman celebrating a birthday and being surprised by a grandchild. Both stories
have 20 propositions, but the "Emma" story is wordier (and more natural), having
218 (standard) or 220 (scrambled) words compared to the shorter "Turtle" story

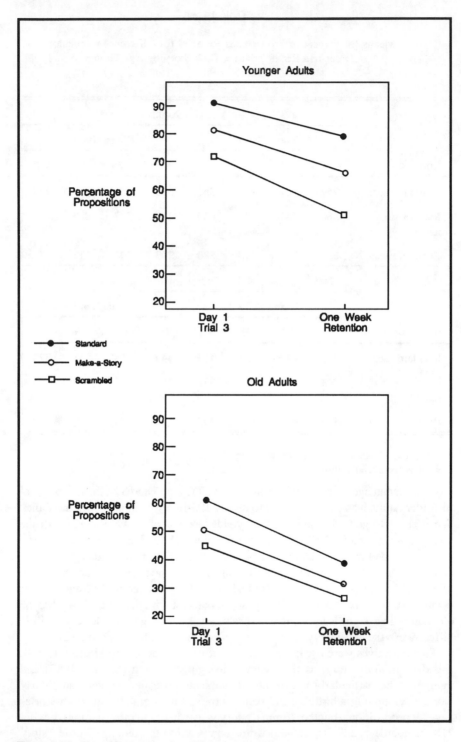

Figure 14.3. Forgetting curves for different age groups.

(134 to 135) words). As in the earlier experiments, we crafted a standard version of the "Emma" story and a scrambled version using the same rules as before.

The experimental design was as follows: At each age (younger adults, older adults), subjects were divided in half and assigned to learn either the "Turtle" story or the "Emma" story. For each age and story, subjects were further subdivided and randomly assigned to one of three conditions, replicating the standard, scrambled, and scrambled make-a-story design of Experiment 3.

The procedure paralleled those of Experiments 1 through 3. Subjects read the stories in booklets, with one proposition typed on each page. This time, subjects read through a booklet *three* times prior to each recall effort on Day 1, and there were a total of three recall trials. No looking back in booklets was permitted, and there was no feedback on performance following a recall attempt. One week later there was a surprise recall attempt, with no prior rereading of the story. To accommodate the older adults, the typefont used in the booklets was large, the procedure was paced more slowly, and smaller groups (one through three) were tested on each day.

The basic results for learning the story are shown in Table 14.5.

1. The "Emma" story proved more difficult for both younger and older adults than the "Turtle" story. On each recall trial and in each condition, a smaller percentage of propositions were recalled for the "Emma" story than for the "Turtle" story.
2. The younger adults recalled more than the older adults for both stories, across the various conditions and trials.
3. There was a trials effect. Subjects recalled increasingly more from trial to trial across the various conditions.
4. Finally, there was a significant condition effect. At both ages, subjects recalled more when presented the standard version of the stories than when presented with the scrambled version. This persisted across all three trials.
5. For the "Emma" story only, both the younger and the older subjects significantly benefitted from the instruction to recall the scrambled story so as to make a good story out of it. Their level of recall was higher in this condition than subjects who recalled the scrambled story verbatim.

Many aging researchers remind us that older adults are not homogeneous in their cognitive skills and performances. Other things being equal, it is common to find large differences in cognitive performance between younger old adults (say, in their 60s) and very old adults (say, in their late 70s and 80s). Since our sample of older adults included a broad age range, we subdivided them, by a median split procedure, to determine if the effects identified thus far accurately reflected the patterns of performance for both groups. Although the very old adults recalled less than the younger old adults in each condition, for each story, and for each trial (the effect varied from a 6 to 10 percentage point difference), all other patterns reported thus far held up for both groups — including, most importantly, the good form effect.

The basic results for forgetting are shown in Figure 14.3. The dominant parallelism of the curves for both the young adults and the old adults highlights what we found in our series of planned comparisons. There was no differential effect of forgetting by condition across the 1-week retention interval, at either age.

Conclusions

One sure conclusion from this series of experiments is that good story form creates a large and persistent advantage in memorizing narratives. Given virtually *identical* texts, but simply mixing around the order in which propositions were sequenced, subjects initially recalled anywhere from one-third to one-half more information in the standard versions than in versions with mixed-up propositions, and most importantly, this advantage persisted across many repeated efforts to read and recall the stories. Even after reading the story 9 to 12 separate times and benefitting from the feedback intrinsic to recall three times, subjects still remembered up to 15% less of the information in the mixed-up conditions.

Our attempts to moderate what might be perceived as extreme conditions of poor form and difficult constraints on retrieval did not alter this pattern of findings, except in one case. Even a moderate degree of disorganization in the stories produced lasting *interference* in subjects' repeated attempts to memorize them. And telling the subjects to recall a mixed-up story in a good form did not enhance their retrieval for two of the three stories. For the "Turtle" and "President" stories, the subjects were able to begin the process of unscrambling the mixed-up narrative at the outset of their retrieval efforts, but perhaps the stories were too complex to work out a complete unscrambling of them. Clearly, simply length was not the problem, because the "Emma" story, which was *longer*, proved more amenable to reorganization and better recall, given the instruction to recall it sensibly.

A second conclusion from the experiments is that although good story form enhances initial learning of narratives, there is not a differential advantage for retention of the narratives. The rate at which subjects forget information in stories is about the same regardless of whether subjects initially learned a story with good form or poor form and over intervals extending as long as 1 week. Of course, we cannot say for sure what the form of forgetting might look like over much more extended periods of time.

There is an alternative interpretation of these findings suggested by an anonymous colleague. The reviewer argues that by mixing around the order of propositions in our well ordered and scrambled texts, we actually produce two very different texts. This interpretation assumes that readers try to understand the writer's intention in the story, and the two orders create stories with different (hence, non-equivalent) author intentions or purposes. This interpretation may be correct, but we note that what makes the scrambled version difficult is the illusiveness of the intention. The variability present in how subjects recall the mixed-up stories suggests that they don't know just what that intention must be. This brings us full circle to the claim that the scrambled versions prove more difficult to remember, because the "surface information" contained in them is ordered so as to seriously violate narrative expectations.

Our old adults were, of course, quite bright and well educated, perhaps more so than the young adults in the final study. Hence, in the never ending task of trying to match adults across the life span adequately when conducting cross-sectional research, it's likely that we overmatched our young college students. However, the overmatching did not result in the old adults being better able to *recall* the narrative information than their young counterparts, so we should not easily dismiss the findings for the older adults as due to some especially outstanding recall skills.

These findings are important for scholars of prose learning and for educators concerned with the optimal presentation of textual information. The findings show that for stories, the good form effect is more than a short-lived consequence of one or two opportunities to read a story as occurs in many laboratory experiments. The effect is strong and persistent and needs to be taken seriously as a characteristic of text presentation that can have a large and lasting effect on students' learning. By utilizing three somewhat different narratives in these experiments and by testing adults across a broad age range, it was possible to show that the effects are generalizable and not idiosyncratic to specific texts.

References

Anderson, R.C., & Pearson, P.D. (1984). A schema-theoretic view of basic processes in reading. In P.D. Pearson (Ed.) *Handbook of reading research* (pp. 255-292). New York: Longman.

Asher, S.R. (1980). Topic interest and children's reading comprehension. In R.J. Spiro, B.C. Bruce, & W.F. Brewer (Eds.), *Theoretical issues in reading comprehension* (pp. 525-534). Hillsdale, NJ: L. Erlbaum.

Baltes, P.B. (1987). Theoretical propositions of life-span developmental psychology: On the dynamics between growth and decline. *Developmental Psychology, 23*, 611-626.

Black, J.B., & Bower, G.H. (1980). Story understanding as problem solving. *Poetics, 9*, 223-250.

Bogartz, R.S. (1990). Evaluating forgetting curves psychologically. *Journal of Experimental Psychology: Learning, Memory, and Cognition, 16*, 138-148.

Borgatta, E.F., & Corsini, R.J. (1960). The Quick Word Test. *Journal of Educational Research, 54*, 15-19.

Bower, G.H., Black, J.B., & Turner, T.J. (1979). Scripts in memory for text. *Cognitive Psychology, 11*, 177-220.

Bower, G.H., & Morrow, D.G. (1990). Mental models in narrative comprehension. *Science, 247*, 44-48.

Brewer, W.S., & Lichtenstein, E.H. (1982). Stories are to entertain: A structural-affect theory of stories. *Journal of Pragmatics, 6*, 473-486.

Dixon, R.A., & Bäckman, L. (in press). Reading and memory for prose in adulthood: Issues of expertise and compensation. In. S.R. Yussen & M.C. Smith (Eds.), *Reading across the life span*. New York: Springer-Verlag.

Garner, R. (in press). "Seductive details" and adults' learning from text. In S.R. Yussen & M.C. Smith (Eds.), *Reading across the life span.* New York: Springer-Verlag.

Johnson, N.S., & Mandler, J.M. (1980). A tale of two structures: Underlying and surface forms in stories. *Poetics, 9,* 51-86.

Kintsch, W. (1977). On comprehending stories. In M.A. Just & P.A. Carpenter (Eds.), *Cognitive processes in comprehension.* Hillsdale, NJ: Erlbaum.

Labouvie-Vief, G. (1980). Beyond formal operations: Uses and limits of pure logic in life-span development. *Human Development, 23,* 141-161.

Loftus, G.R. (1985). Evaluating forgetting curves. *Journal of Experimental Psychology: Learning, Memory, and Cognition, 11,* 396-405.

Mandler, J.M. (1987). On the psychological reality of story structure. *Discourse Processes, 10,* 1-29.

Mandler, J.M. & Johnson, N.S. (1977). Rememberance of things parsed: Story structure and recall. *Cognitive Psychology, 9,* 111-115.

Nelson, K.E. (1978). How children represent knowledge of their world in and out of language. In R.S. Siegler (Ed.), *Children's thinking: What develops?* Hillsdale, NJ: Lawrence Erlbaum.

Omanson, R.C. (1982). The relation between centrality and story category variation. *Journal of Verbal Learning and Verbal Behavior, 21,* 326-337.

Rahman, T., & Bisanz, G.L. (1986). Reading ability and use of a story schema in recalling and reconstructing information. *Journal of Educational Psychology, 78,* 323-333.

Rumelhart, D.E. (1975). Notes on a schema for stories. In D. G. Bobrow & A. Collins (Eds.), *Representation and understanding: Studies in cognitive science* (pp. 211-236). New York: Academic Press.

Salthouse, T.A. (1982). *Adult cognition.* New York: Springer.

Schank, R.C.E., & Abelson, R. (1977). *Scripts, plans, and goals.* Hillsdale, NJ: Lawrence Erlbaum.

Spilich, G.J. (1983). Life-span components of text processing: Structural procedural differences. *Journal of Verbal Learning and Verbal Behavior, 22,* 231-244.

Stein, N.L., & Glenn, C.G. (1979). An analysis of story comprehension in elementary school children. In R.O. Freedle (Ed.), *New directions in discourse processing.* Hillsdale, NJ: Lawrence Erlbaum.

Stein, N.L., & Nezworski, T. (1978). The effects of organization and instructional set on story memory. *Discourse Processes, 1,* 177-193.

Stein, N.L., & Trabasso, T. (1982). What's in a story: An approach to comprehension and instruction. In R. Glaser (Ed.), *Advances in instructional psychology* (Vol. 2, pp. 213-268). Hillsdale, NJ: Lawrence Erlbaum.

Thorndyke, P.W. (1977). Cognitive structures in comprehension and memory of narrative discourse. *Cognitive Psychology, 9,* 77-110.

Trabasso, T., Secco, T., & van den Broek, P. (1984). Causal cohesion and story coherence. In H. Mandl, N.L. Stein, & T. Trabasso (Eds.), *Learning and comprehension of text*. Hillsdale, NJ: Lawrence Erlbaum.

Trabasso, T., & van den Broek, P.W. (1985). Causal thinking and the representation of narrative events. *Journal of Memory and Language, 24*, 612-630.

van den Broek, P. (1988). The effects of causal relations and hierarchical position on the importance of story statements. *Journal of Memory and Language, 27*, 1-22.

van den Broek, P. (1989). Causal reasoning and inference making in judging the importance of story statements. *Child Development, 60*, 286-297.

Yussen, S.R., Mathews, S., Buss, R., & Kane, P. (1980). Developmental change in judging important and critical elements of stories. *Developmental Psychology, 16*, 213-219.

Yussen, S.R., Mathews, S., Huang, T., & Evans, R. (1988). The robustness and temporal course of the story schema's influence on recall. *Journal of Experimental Psychology: Learning, Memory and Cognition, 14*, 171-179.

Appendix

Standard and Scrambled Versions of Narratives

President (Standard Version)
1   Once there was a girl named Sue who lived in a city.
2   It was large and near a lake.
3   One day Sue saw the President speaking on TV.
4   He was talking about problems with energy.
5   She wanted to learn more about the President's background.
6   For example, she wanted to know where he grew up.
7   So Sue went to the library to find a book about him.
8   She went there one day after school.
9   But the library was closed that day.
10 Its front door was locked.
11 Sue was upset
12 and sat down on the steps to think.
13 Then she saw a bookstore next door
14 and there were people going into it.
15 She thought the store might help with her problem
16 because it looked very large and had many books.
17 So Sue searched carefully in the store
18 looking over all the shelves of books.
19 Finally, she found the right book.
20 It had the President's picture on it.
21 Sue was delighted at her fortune

22   and began to read the book immediately.

President (Scrambled Version)
 1   The bookstore looked very large and had many books.
 2   One day Sue saw the President speaking on TV.
 3   Sue saw a bookstore next door.
 4   The President was talking about problems with energy.
 5   Sue was delighted at her fortune.
 6   There were people going into the bookstore.
 7   Sue wanted to learn more about the President's background.
 8   She sat down on the library steps to think.
 9   She went to the library one day after school.
10   Once there was a girl named Sue who lived in a city.
11   She thought the store might help with her problem.
12   She looked over all the shelves of books.
13   The city was large and near a lake.
14   For example, Sue wanted to know where the President grew up.
15   Sue began to read the book immediately.
16   She searched carefully in the store.
17   The front door of the library was locked.
18   Sue went to the library to find a book about the President.
19   Sue found the right book.
20   She was upset.
21   The book had the President's picture on it.
22   The library was closed that day.

President (Partially Scrambled Version-Experiment 2 only)
 1   Once there was a girl named Sue who lived in a city.
 2   It was large and near a lake.
 3   Sue went to the library to find a book about the President.
 4   She went there one day after school.
 5   She wanted to learn more about the President's background.
 6   For example, she wanted to know where he grew up.
 7   One day Sue saw the President speaking on TV.
 8   He was talking about problems with energy.
 9   But the library was closed that day.
10   Its front door was locked.
11   Sue was upset
12   and sat down on the steps to think.
13   Finally, she found the right book.
14   It had the President's picture on it.
15   So Sue searched carefully in the store
16   looking over all the shelves of books.
17   She thought the store might help with her problem
18   because it looked very large and had many books.

19   Then she saw a bookstore next door
20   and there were people going into it.
21   Sue was delighted at her fortune
22   and began to read the book immediately.

Turtle (Standard Version)
1   One day Mark and Sally were sailing their toy sailboat in the pond.
2   Suddenly, the sailboat began to sink.
3   Mark was surprised.
4   He lifted the boat up with a stick
5   and found a turtle on top of it.
6   The turtle became frightened
7   and tried to crawl off the boat.
8   The turtle put Mark in a playful mood.
9   Mark thought the turtle was hurt.
10   Mark had always wanted Sally to see a turtle.
11   So he waded out to the turtle
12   and brought it back to her.
13   Sally thought Mark was going to hurt the turtle.
14   Sally felt sorry for Mark.
15   Sally tried to touch the turtle
16   but the turtle bit her.
17   Sally didn't like this
18   and threw the turtle into the pond.
19   The turtle crashed into the sailboat.
20   Sally knew she had made a mistake.

Turtle (Scrambled Version)
1   The turtle bit Sally.
2   Mark was surprised.
3   Sally thought Mark was going to hurt the turtle.
4   Mark lifted the boat up with a stick.
5   Sally felt sorry for Mark.
6   Mark found a turtle on top of the boat.
7   Mark brought the turtle back to Sally.
8   The turtle put Mark in a playful mood.
9   One day Mark and Sally were sailing their toy sailboat in the pond.
10   Sally tried to touch the turtle.
11   Sally threw the turtle into the pond.
12   Suddenly, the sailboat began to sink.
13   The turtle became frightened.
14   Sally didn't like this.
15   Mark had always wanted Sally to see a turtle.
16   The turtle tried to crawl off the boat.
17   The turtle crashed into the sailboat.

18   Mark waded out to the turtle.
19   Sally knew she had made a mistake.
20   Mark thought the turtle was hurt.

Turtle (Partially Scrambled Version-Experiment 2 only)
1   One day Mark and Sally were sailing their toy sailboat in the pond.
2   The turtle became frightened
3   and tried to crawl off the boat.
4   Mark lifted the boat up with a stick
5   and found a turtle on top of it.
6   Suddenly, the sailboat began to sink.
7   Mark was surprised.
8   The turtle put Mark in a playful mood.
9   Mark thought the turtle was hurt.
10   Mark had always wanted Sally to see a turtle.
11   Sally tried to touch the turtle
12   but the turtle bit her.
13   The turtle crashed into the sailboat.
14   So Mark waded out to the turtle
15   and brought it back to Sally.
16   Sally didn't like this
17   and threw the turtle into the pond.
18   Sally thought Mark was going to hurt the turtle.
19   She felt sorry for Mark.
20   Sally knew she had made a mistake.

Emma (Standard Version)
1   Emma awoke very early on the morning of her 85th birthday.
2   She quickly got dressed in her blue dress with the little flower on the waist.
3   She felt very excited about beginning the day.
4   She stopped for a minute to look out of her window.
5   The sun was slowly rising and the robins were singing.
6   On special days like this, friends and relatives would often stop by for a visit.
7   The person she most enjoyed seeing was her great-grandson, Michael.
8   Emma left her room and walked quickly and quietly down the long hall.
9   There were sounds of people stirring out of their beds.
10   She wanted to open the three birthday cards she received in the mail.
11   One card had a picture of Emma's sister and her children who lived in Miami.
12   She would write them as soon as she bought some new stationery.
13   After lunch, Emma settled into a nice comfortable chair.
14   She wanted to watch her favorite story on TV.
15   This was one soap opera she never missed.
16   Just as it was ending, she heard a child's voice.

17   The voice behind her said "Happy birthday, Grandma."
18   Turning around, she saw her great-grandson Michael.
19   And with a smile, Michael gave her a nice box of stationery.
20   Emma knew this was her best birthday she had ever known.

Emma (Scrambled Version)
 1   Just as the soap opera was ending, Emma heard a child's voice.
 2   Emma felt very excited about beginning the day.
 3   After lunch, Emma settled into a nice comfortable chair.
 4   Emma stopped for a minute to look out her window.
 5   Emma wanted to watch her favorite story on TV.
 6   The sun was slowly rising and the robins were singing.
 7   Emma would write them as soon as she bought some new stationery.
 8   Emma left her room and walked quickly and quietly down the long hall.
 9   Emma awoke very early on the morning of her 85th birthday.
10   This was one soap opera that Emma never missed.
11   Turning around, Emma saw her great-grandson Michael.
12   Emma quickly got dressed in her blue dress with the little flower on the waist.
13   On special days like this, friends and relatives would often stop by for a visit.
14   The voice behind Emma said "Happy birthday, Grandma."
15   Emma wanted to open three birthday cards she received in the mail.
16   The person Emma most enjoyed seeing was her great-grandson, Michael.
17   Emma knew this was her best birthday she had ever known.
18   And with a smile, Michael gave Emma a nice box of stationery.
19   One card had a picture of Emma's sister and her children who lived in Miami.
20   There were sounds of people stirring out of their beds.

The "President" story was used in Experiments 1 and 2; the "Turtle" story was used in all four experiments. The "Emma" story was used in Experiment 4 only.

Subject Index